MW01274879

About This Book

Why is this topic important?

The training and development industry covers a vast landscape of disciplines, practices, and opinions that only keeps growing larger. This book does hold a titillating collection of articles that cover a wide range of topics from a diverse number of perspectives. This book puts in one place more authoritative guidance and industry experience from some of the brightest folks in our field. These are just the folks who can offer you enough light to help you avoid the landmines of mistakes that litter the landscape.

What can you achieve with this book?

This all-in-one guide is perfect for anyone new to the field of training and development or for a veteran who is for quick, succinct practical nuggets that can be put to use right away. This book puts in one place valuable key lessons learned from years of professionals who have succeeded.

This book is your mentor. It will provide you with information, knowledge, experience, and encouragement. It is an atlas of learning maps to help you navigate the terrains of workplace learning and performance.

How is this book organized?

Information is presented in a collection of short articles that are well indexed for fast retrieval. The book is divided into five sections:

1. Designing Training
2. Delivering Training
3. Workforce Performance and Learning
4. Measurement and Evaluation
5. Professional Development

Each section has a collection of articles. There is an introduction and a conclusion to each section. The conclusions will continue the conversations you've had with authors while reading the articles. There will be challenging questions for you to consider, opportunities for self-reflection, and suggestions on how to learn more about each section's topic. The articles vary in length. Except for a small handful, almost all of them can be read in ten minutes or less. Each article begins with a passion statement. These passion statements constitute the heart and soul of the book. Through these passion statements, contributors share with us what they care about most and what they have discovered while working in the field.

About Pfeiffer

Pfeiffer serves the professional development and hands-on resource needs of training and human resource practitioners and gives them products to do their jobs better. We deliver proven ideas and solutions from experts in HR development and HR management, and we offer effective and customizable tools to improve workplace performance. From novice to seasoned professional, Pfeiffer is the source you can trust to make yourself and your organization more successful.

Essential Knowledge Pfeiffer produces insightful, practical, and comprehensive materials on topics that matter the most to training and HR professionals. Our Essential Knowledge resources translate the expertise of seasoned professionals into practical, how-to guidance on critical workplace issues and problems. These resources are supported by case studies, worksheets, and job aids and are frequently supplemented with CD-ROMs, websites, and other means of making the content easier to read, understand, and use.

Essential Tools Pfeiffer's Essential Tools resources save time and expense by offering proven, ready-to-use materials—including exercises, activities, games, instruments, and assessments—for use during a training or team-learning event. These resources are frequently offered in looseleaf or CD-ROM format to facilitate copying and customization of the material.

Pfeiffer also recognizes the remarkable power of new technologies in expanding the reach and effectiveness of training. While e-hype has often created whizbang solutions in search of a problem, we are dedicated to bringing convenience and enhancements to proven training solutions. All our e-tools comply with rigorous functionality standards. The most appropriate technology wrapped around essential content yields the perfect solution for today's on-the-go trainers and human resource professionals.

Essential resources for training and HR professionals

Our readers are invited to view and download supplementary
materials to this book including customizable forms and worksheets,
and bonus articles. Please see the Website Contents
for additional information. The materials are available
FREE with the purchase of this book at
www.pfeiffer.com/go/mentor

THE TRAINER'S PORTABLE MENTOR

EDITED BY

Terrence L. Gargiulo, Ajay M. Pangarkar, and Teresa Kirkwood

Pfeiffer
A Wiley Imprint
www.pfeiffer.com

Published by Pfeiffer
An Imprint of Wiley
989 Market Street, San Francisco, CA 94103-1741
www.pfeiffer.com

Library of Congress Cataloging-in-Publication Data

The trainer's portable mentor / edited by Terrence L. Gargiulo, Ajay M. Pangarkar, Teresa Kirkwood.
     p.   cm.
    Includes bibliographical references and index.
    ISBN 978-0-7879-9428-0 (paper/website)
       1. Employees—Training of.   2. Executives—Training of.   3. Organizational learning.
4. Employee training personnel.   I. Gargiulo, Terrence L., 1968–   II. Pangarkar, Ajay M.   III. Kirkwood, Teresa.
  HF5549.5.T7T66328   2008
  658.3'124—dc22

                                    2008002725

Acquiring Editor: Matthew Davis
Director of Development: Kathleen Dolan Davies
Production Editor: Dawn Kilgore

Editor: Rebecca Taff
Editorial Assistant: Lindsay Morton
Manufacturing Supervisor: Becky Morgan

Printed in the United States of America

Printing   10 9 8 7 6 5 4 3 2 1

Contents

Website Contents   xxi

Introduction   1

SECTION ONE: *Designing Training*

Introduction to Section One: Designing Training   7

Article 1:   **Avoiding Biased Questions for Training Needs Assessments, Grace Ann Rosile, Ph.D.**   13
Asking the right questions is much more important that having the right answers!

Article 2:   **Taxonomy of Learning Designs, David S. Weiss, Ph.D.**   21
Creative learning designs are the backbone of learning programs; give them the attention they deserve.

Article 3:   **Designing Instructional Strategies: A Cognitive Perspective, Kenneth H. Silber, Ph.D., and Wellesley R. Foshay, Ph.D., CPT**   29
Instructional designers should be using a wider range of more powerful instructional strategies, each suited to the types of knowledge needed for deep understanding and real expertise.

Article 4:   **Don't Be an Order Taker, Jane Bozarth, M.Ed.**   35
In our efforts to be responsive, collaborative, and supportive, and keep our bosses happy, trainers too often kowtow to the whims or mistakes of (probably) well-meaning managers.

Article 5:   **Never Lose Sight of Your Audience, Jean Marrapodi, Ph.D., CPLP**   39
Never lose sight of your audience or their goals. The rest almost takes care of itself.

Article 6:   **If You Don't Know Where You Are Going, You Will Probably End Up Somewhere Else, Toni Hodges DeTuncq**   45
If you don't know where you are going, you will end up some place you might not want to be. Instructional design is the art and science of building a roadmap that takes learners where they need to go.

Article 7:   **ISD—Faster/Better/Easier, Darryl L. Sink, Ed.D.**   53
The ISD process and training are means, not ends. Focusing on results, rather than focusing on providing training, causes decisions to be made in very different ways. The training development organization needs to be project-driven versus being process- and control-driven.

Article 8:   **Front-End Analysis, Implementation Planning, and Evaluation: Escaping the Pamela Syndrome, Harold D. Stolovitch, Ph.D.**   71
As learning and performance professionals, our mission is to produce results, not just interventions. When we don't analyze to determine whether what we do is necessary or sufficient, don't ensure proper implementation, and don't measure results credibly, we fail in that mission.

Article 9:   Creativity, Emergence, and the Design of Learning
               Experiences, Peter C. Honebein, Ph.D.   81
               "Wow!" That's what I say when my students,
               whether undergraduates or working professionals, do
               something in class that is truly revolutionary
               and inspiring. When it happens, I know that the
               learning experience was well designed.

Article 10:   Creating Sacred Space, Michael Milano   89
               I am more interested in the process of engaging
               learners than I am in the specific content of the
               learning event. I love finding ways to ask the
               right questions to open learners to something
               new; the right questions for them to apply what
               they already knew about the subject, about life,
               and about learning; the right questions to invite
               learners to determine the value of what has
               been learned.

Article 11:   e-Learning Content—Sorting Through the
               Tonnage: A Quick Anatomy Lesson for Those
               on the "Buy" Side, Steve D. Bordonaro, M.Ed.,
               and Frank P. Bordonaro, Ph.D.   97
               One key to successful talent development is to
               provide your people with the best learning assets
               you can find for the price. Your quest for quality
               is complicated by a need to master e- and blended
               learning solutions, where content proliferates and
               varies widely in quality.

Article 12:   Blended Learning Strategies for Knowledge
               Workers That Work, Deborah Stone, CPT,
               Steve Villachica, Ph.D., CPT, and John Endicott   107
               Making invisible problem-solving skills visible,
               through real-world practice, in authentic situations,
               modeled by living, breathing experts, is easier than
               you think.

Article 13: **Confessions of a Gamer: I See Games, Steve Sugar** 119

Have you ever seen a learning game that gets participants so energized, so involved, so committed to game play that they experience the topic from the inside? This is my payoff! This is what drives me to write the next game.

Conclusion to Section One 127

SECTION TWO: *Delivering Training*

Introduction to Section Two: Delivering Training 135

Article 14: **Make Adult Learning Come to Life, Jean Barbazette** 141

Make adult learning come alive!

Article 15: **Making Workshops Work: Lessons from an Old Pro, Hal Kane, Ph.D.** 151

Your first and foremost mission is to establish a strong connection with your audience. Tell them why you're leading from the front, show them why you need them to work collaboratively, and then never leave them behind.

Article 16: **Incredible Credibility, Terrence L. Gargiulo** 157

We already have the authority; standing in front of a group naturally grants us a certain position. Now our challenge lies in winning the trust and respect of others. We need to be accessible to our attendees, sensitive to their needs, and responsive to satisfying their learning objectives.

Article 17: **Enlarging the Pool of Participation at the Beginning of Any Training Session, Mel Silberman, Ph.D.** 161

Your training session will not spark active learning unless participants are eager to participate.

Article 18:   How Learners Are Motivated, Matthew
                  S. Richter   167

*Help participants to truly connect to the value
of what they are learning. Use activities to facilitate
higher levels of competence and engagement to
offer participants opportunities to discover their
own value.*

Article 19:   Applying Self-Determination to Training,
                  Matthew S. Richter   183

*Creating an intrinsically motivating environment
for a training situation requires a complete
understanding of multiple factors, such as the
goal of the training, how participants perceive the
training, the logistics of the training, learning styles,
trainer skills, and so forth. When you create
opportunities to expand participant autonomy
and engage them, phenomenal learning can occur.*

Article 20:   The Best Training I Never Did!, Glenn Smeaton   197

*Don't get me wrong, I have nothing against teachers
or trainers. I have seen some very effective trainers
and have admired their organizational and
presentational skills. Teaching and training are good
strategies to obtain specific results. Often, however,
the desired results are not achievable by formal
teaching or training. A glass of water, for instance,
can be lifesaving if the problem is thirst. It is not
much use, however, if the problem is drowning!*

Article 21:   Some Basics from a Couple of Training Pro's:
                  Training Is More Than What You Say, Terrence L.
                  Gargiulo and Robb Murray   203

*It's critical to honestly examine our basic assumptions
about how people learn. How much do people
learn through didactic explications? If people learn
more through making associations, then we must use
less "instruction," and more stimulation.*

Article 22: The Synergy of Co-Facilitation: Creating Powerful Learning Experiences, Dr. Vince Molinaro   209

Co-facilitation is a dynamic way to enhance the learning experience for participants. I am passionate about the "aha" moment—when learners gain new insights that open up creative opportunities for future growth and success.

Article 23: Learnertainment®, Lenn Millbower   217

Entertainment-based content relaxes the right hemisphere, in effect, baby-sitting it, keeping it busy with things it likes: cartoons, music, games, activities, visuals. Once the right hemisphere is playfully engaged, learning can commence without negative blocking emotions. Attention is riveted on the positive aspects of learning.

Article 24: Seven Strategies on How to Use Stories to Increase Learning and Facilitate Training, Terrence L. Gargiulo   227

Stories are fundamental to how we communicate, learn, and think. By staying tuned in to the group's ever-changing needs, you will be able to find the right stories to tell at the right time, elicit group members' stories, and increase learning.

Article 25: Dealing with Difficult Issues in Training, Terrence L. Gargiulo   235

Dealing with difficult issues in training is not easy stuff, nor can we follow any ready-made formula for how to deal with them, but responsibly leading a group through difficult issues is one of the most rewarding, humbling, and deepening experiences we can have as trainers.

Conclusion to Section Two   241

SECTION THREE: *Workplace Performance and Learning*

Introduction to Section Three: Workplace Performance
   and Learning   249

Article 26: Capturing Learning Opportunities Within Your
     Organization, Ajay M. Pangarkar, CTDP, and
     Teresa Kirkwood, CTDP   257
     How you use and develop employee knowledge will
     determine your level of success in a knowledge-based
     world.

Article 27: New Accountabilities: Non-Financial Measures
     of Performance, Ajay M. Pangarkar, CTDP, and
     Teresa Kirkwood, CTDP   265
     Where everything changes immediately, there is
     little time to wait to see what happened (financial
     outcomes). Decisions often need to be made at
     once to make things happen now—and the only
     way is through performance measures that provide
     a glimpse of future expectations and results.

Article 28: Discovery Learning: The Driving Force Behind
     Achieving Real Organizational Change,
     Catherine J. Rezak   277
     Today, the promise of sustainable change hinges on
     the human beings who comprise the organization;
     their knowledge, understanding, and learning are
     the organization's most sacred assets.

Article 29: The Integrated Approach to Leadership
     Development, Dr. Vince Molinaro and
     Dr. David S. Weiss   285
     Building leadership capacity is mission critical
     in organizations today. Many are experiencing a
     significant leadership gap. One of the ways to

*close the gap is to take a more integrated approach
to leadership development. We discuss why an
integrated approach is important and present the
eight steps to help you implement this kind of
approach in your organization.*

Article 30:   Independent Means: Taking Control of
              Internal Knowledge and Minimizing Dependency
              on External Expertise, Ajay M. Pangarkar, CTDP,
              and Teresa Kirkwood, CTDP   293
              *Take control of your organization's internal
              knowledge and you'll minimize your dependency
              on external expertise.*

Article 31:   Return on Intelligence: The New ROI,
              Ann Herrmann-Nehdi   299
              *Return on intelligence is your ultimate job, but
              in order to achieve it we must use all that we know
              about the brain.*

Article 32:   Turnover—Slaying the Monster One Touch
              at a Time, Dr. Frank P. Bordonaro   307
              *As a talent management executive, you are in a
              uniquely advantaged field position for defeating
              one of the great cost monsters in all of business:
              turnover. Because your role encompasses the whole
              range of talent touch points, you can use them all
              to surround and subdue the problem. Turnover is
              an opportunity for cost reduction and finding
              improved talent.*

Article 33:   Creating Credibility with Senior Management:
              A Simple Approach for Connecting Training to
              the Business, Timothy P. Mooney and Robert O.
              Brinkerhoff, Ed.D.   319
              *Most learning and development departments
              provide good training events that are well-intended,
              well-designed and well-liked. Yet, they fail to*

produce meaningful business impact for the
organization most of the time. The problem doesn't
lie in the training itself, but in how organizations
implement the training. The problem will only be
solved by educating the whole organization
(executives, managers, and employees) on how
to turn training into business results and then
building accountability for making this happen.

Article: 34:   Work Learning—Beyond the Classroom,
               Ajay M. Pangarkar, CTDP, and
               Teresa Kirkwood, CTDP   327
               How its learning environment empowers employees
               to develop imaginative strategies and innovative
               practices is the key to an organization's success in
               the marketplace.

Article 35:   A Business Approach to Learning: Increasing
               Profits Through Marketing Methodologies,
               Ajay M. Pangarkar, CTDP, and
               Teresa Kirkwood, CTDP   335
               Like every other investment a company makes,
               training must be "sold" to those unconvinced of
               its benefits. Proving the worth of training is essential
               for success.

Conclusion to Section Three   347

SECTION FOUR: *Measurement and Evaluation*

Introduction to Section Four: Measurement and Evaluation   353

Article 36:   Beyond ROI: To Boldly Go Where No Training
               Evaluation Has Gone Before, Ajay M. Pangarkar,
               CTDP, and Teresa Kirkwood, CTDP   361
               WLP professionals need to start thinking "outside of
               the course" and think in terms that connect with the
               business concerns and strategy objectives of the entity.

Article 37:   **Linking Learning Strategy to the Balanced Scorecard, Ajay M. Pangarkar, CTDP, and Teresa Kirkwood, CTDP**   371
This will facilitate the process of developing the right performance measures in a way that is inexpensive, relevant, and moves you beyond ROI.

Article 38:   **Taking a Strategic Approach to Evaluation: Proving and Improving the Value of Training, Timothy P. Mooney and Robert O. Brinkeroff, Ed.D.**   385
Asking the right evaluation questions will help the organization begin to determine not just what happened in the past, but how it can create positive results in the future.

Article 39:   **Measure and Optimize Training's Impact, W. Boyce Byerly, Ph.D.**   391
Go after the metrics that can show training's impact! A clear analysis shows impact and lets you pinpoint who benefits the most.

Article 40:   **Formative Evaluation: Getting It Right the First Time, Donald L. Kirkey and Gary A. DePaul, Ph.D.**   401
Our passion is for flawless and effective training delivery—the first time and every time.

Article 41:   **Measuring the Impact of Leadership: Fact or Fiction?, Ajay M. Pangarkar, CTDP, and Teresa Kirkwood, CTDP**   413
Leadership development and succession planning are at the top of the list of organizational concerns. With so many resources being devoted to leadership training, has anyone truly been able to measure the return it is promised to deliver? Is it possible to evaluate your investment against current evaluation techniques?

Article 42: Transition Planning Steps for Building and
Sustaining a Results-Based Learning Focus,
Holly Burkett   421
*Use an integrated change management approach
to build and sustain a results-based learning
and development focus. Proper prior transition
planning on the front end improves results on the
back end!*

Article 43: Demonstrating Your Worth to Management with
Credible, Business-Focused Results, Harold D.
Stolovitch and Paul Flynn   433
*To be a real player and have impact on an
organization, you have to show decision-makers
the money. No business critical results, no respect.*

Article 44: We Know We Got There, Toni Hodges DeTuncq   445
*It is essential to measure learning programs against
specific objectives. By closely aligning these objectives to
one another and giving participants an opportunity
to apply their new skills and knowledge, you help
achieve business or organizational goals and then your
program will be declared a success.*

Article 45: A Four-Part Strategy for Communicating
Business Value, Theresa L. Seagraves   455
*How you use metrics to communicate business
value is just as important as having the metrics
themselves.*

Article 46: Measuring Time to Proficiency, Steven C.
Rosenbaum   463
*Proficiency is a measure of being able to demonstrate
results at a desired level. Using proficiency as a
training measure dramatically changes the way
an organization approaches learning.*

Article 47:   Making "Cents" from Your Training ROI:
               How Organizations Can Make Training
               Accountable, Ajay M. Pangarkar, CTDP, and
               Teresa Kirkwood, CTDP   471
               Training is a significant investment for many
               organizations, and investors (shareholders and
               management) expect to see return on their investment.
               Certain methodologies can facilitate the process
               of showing training's ROI.

               Conclusion to Section Four   477

SECTION FIVE: *Professional Development*

               Introduction to Section Five: Professional Development   483

Article 48:   What Makes a Good Trainer and Facilitator,
               Tom Short   489
               If you talk to any adult educator about job satisfaction,
               they will probably recall numerous examples of
               watching their students conduct an effective
               training session for the very first time in front of
               a live peer group; in much the same way as a flying
               instructor observes a trainee pilots' first solo flight
               from the ground.

Article 49:   Lifelong Learning, Elaine Beich   503
               To be a true model of success and professionalism,
               WLP professionals need to model the importance
               of lifelong learning. They need to learn continuously
               in order to achieve all that they are capable of—and
               to astound themselves.

Article 50:   Learn to Communicate in Business-Speak, Ajay M.
               Pangarkar, CTDP, and Teresa Kirkwood, CTDP   511
               Leaders expect to hear results in terms they understand
               and find out how learning contributed to business

objectives. WLP professional must be able to translate their knowledge of training into business terms and speak in the language of business.

Article 51:   The Trainer as a CAPABLE Leader,
              Dr. Vince Molinaro and Dr. David S. Weiss   517
              Like most leaders today, trainers and OD practitioners need to attend to multiple priorities, make quick decisions, and implement initiatives at lightening speed. Operating continuously in this climate can be a personal leadership challenge.

Article 52:   Trusting Relationships in Learning,
              Dr. David S. Weiss   523
              Talented learning professionals know how to build trust. They excel at collaborating and influencing internal clients to embrace learning actively and willingly. But trust does not occur by accident. It results from delivering on assumptions and expectations.

Article 53:   The Need for Personal Vision, K. Jayshankar   529
              Vision is one of most important and fundamental concepts for building a great organization.

Article 54:   Ten Strategies for Building Successful Partnerships,
              Terrence L. Gargiulo   535
              Becoming adept at building partnerships is essential to your success and ongoing personal development.

Article 55:   Developmental Assignments, Cynthia D.
              McCauley   547
              Getting impatient waiting for the next great opportunity to build your leadership capacity? Look no further than your current job! It can offer you plenty of ways to stretch and grow.

Article 56:   **Don't Fight the Future, Jane Bozarth, Ed.D.**   555
Good trainers have nothing to fear from technology.

Article 57:   **Five Ideas on How to Take Charge of**
Your Recharging, Terrence L. Gargiulo   559
*As humans, we are bound to be tired and occasionally
feel burned out. Accept these passing phases with
grace. They are as real as the highs, and we can
bounce back with a little patience and effort.*

Conclusion to Section Five   563

Index   569
Who's Who in Training and Development   581

Website Contents

The following materials are available as supplementary free downloads at www.pfeiffer.com/go/mentor.

Section One: Designing Training

Articles

Locating "Project Management" Inside the Instructional Design Process by Charlene Muir Benjamin, M.S.

Talent Development Solutions: A Buyer's Checklist by Frank P. Bordonaro, Ph.D.

Section Two: Delivering Training

Forms and Worksheets

"Methods Variety Scale" from Article 14: Make Adult Learning Come to Life by Jean Barbazette

"Planning Sheet" from Article 17: Enlarging the Pool of Participants at the Beginning of Any Training Event by Mel Silberman

"Co-Facilitation Strategies Checklist" from Article 22: The Synergy of Co-Facilitation: Creating Powerful Learning Experiences by Dr. Vince Molinaro

Section Three: Workplace Performance and Learning

Articles

Where Passion Meets Mission: Keys to a Powerful Pairing by Frank P. Bordonaro, Ph.D., and Brian A. Schwartz, Ph.D.

Section Four: Measurement and Evaluation

Forms and Worksheets

"Checklist for Training Analysis," from Article 39: Measure and Optimize Training's Impact by W. Boyce Byerly

"High-Level Design Checklist," from Article 40: Formative Evaluation: Getting It Right the First Time by Donald L. Kirkey and Gary A. DePaul

"Pilot Group Feedback Form," from Article 40: Formative Evaluation: Getting It Right the First Time by Donald L. Kirkey and Gary A. DePaul

"The Object Map Template, " from Article 44: We Know We Got There by Toni Hodges DeTuncq

Section Five: Professional Development

Forms and Worksheets

"Adult Learning Principles," from Article 48: What Makes a Good Trainer and Facilitator by Tom Short

Learning Activity 48.1: Answers

"Adding Context to Training Sessions," from Article 48: What Makes a Good Trainer and Facilitator by Tom Short

"Using Leadership Models in Training," from Article 48: What Makes a Good Trainer and Facilitator by Tom Short

"Barriers to Learning," from Article 48: What Makes a Good Trainer and Facilitator by Tom Short

Learning Activity 48.4: Solutions

"Choice of Training Style," from Article 48: What Makes a Good Trainer and Facilitator by Tom Short

Articles

Great Leaders Don't Aspire to Be Great Managers by Ajay M. Pangarkar, CTDP, and Teresa Kirkwood, CTDP

Bonus Articles

Ready, Set, Lead! How to Jump-Start New Leaders by Jocelyn Berard

The Importance of Health and Wellness in Workplace Learning and Performance by Heather E. McKinney, Ph.D., Catherine Augustine, Ph.D., and William J. Rothwell, Ph.D., SPHR

To Solve Problems or Not: That Is the Question by Dr. David H. Jonassen

What Is Expertise? by Rob Foshay, Ph.D., CPT

Preparing for Unplanned Discussions by Val Carter

Training: Traditional, Online, or Blended? by Hafsa El Khettab, M.Ed., Ph.D., and Francois Ste-Marie, M.Sc.

Introduction

The Training and Development industry covers a vast landscape of disciplines, practices, and opinions that only keeps growing larger. We are passionate people. We love what we do. Everyone, even folks who are not as fortunate as we are to work in this industry, have experienced the thrill of watching someone learn. People get that special sparkle in their eyes. Then come those embarrassing audible ohs and ahs of wonder. If we're really lucky, we'll observe improvements in people's performance or behaviors that are linked to these epiphanies. This makes us tick. It's why I get up in the morning. My personal mission statement is: "I have a passion for inciting insight in others."

I learned long ago not to take my insights too seriously. However, I'm sure good at stirring the pot to guide myself and others to discover insights they want to make their own. That's what we're up to in this book. This book does not hold all of the information you need to know as a learning professional. That is neither realistic nor in keeping with the spirit and energy of this book. However, this book does hold a titillating collection of articles that cover a wide range of topics from a diverse number of perspectives. And this book puts in one place more authoritative guidance and industry experience from some of the brightest folks in our field that you can find.

So we have gifts and talents that enable us to conjure this magic of learning. Do you have a coach? Do you have a reliable map of the vast landscape we call Training and Development? Do you have a cheerleading squad? A little social facilitation never hurts. Do you have a mentor?

Pipe in the bright inspiring music here . . . give me a drum roll . . . play a trumpet fanfare. . . .

That's why you're holding this book and reading it. That's our job. We want to be a mentor to you, provide you encouragement on the difficult days, and give you a roadmap through the workplace learning and performance landscape.

Here's another scenario. . . .

Imagine that you are executive vice president of Training and Development (aka Workforce Learning and Performance) for a Fortune 100 company. It's your first month on the job, and two new managers join your team. Despite their experience, they walk into your office with a "deer in the headlights" look in their eyes. What do you say to them? Company politics and information aside, how do you get them revved up and confident to tackle their jobs?

This all-in-one guide is perfect for anyone new to the field of training and development or a veteran who is looking to be vitalized by quick, succinct practical nuggets that can be put to use right away. This book puts in one place valuable key lessons learned from years of supporting professionals to succeed. Information is presented in a collection of short articles that are well indexed for fast retrieval.

What this book is NOT: An exhaustive "how to" book. That would be impossible and an ingenious pursuit.

My co-editors Ajay Pangarkar, Teresa Kirkwood, and I have assembled an all-star cast of leading experts in our field. These are just the folks who can offer you enough light to help you avoid the landmines of mistakes that litter the landscape. We've all had our share of mistakes; I for one am grateful for each and every one of them. They have been my learning allies. And while I hope you have your own fair share of learning opportunities (aka mistakes), if we can help you avert a few of the ones we've already made, you will be freer to explore new terrain. This is how we will all continue to grow and prosper.

Structure of the Book

The book is divided into five sections:

1. Designing Training
2. Delivering Training
3. Workforce Performance and Learning
4. Measurement and Evaluation
5. Professional Development

Each section has a collection of articles. There is an intro and conclusion to each section. The conclusions will continue the conversations you've had with authors while reading the articles. There will be challenging questions for you to consider, opportunities for self-reflection, and suggestions on how to learn more about the section's topic. The articles vary in length. Except for a small handful, almost all of them can be read in ten minutes or less. Each article begins with a passion statement. These passion statements constitute the heart and soul of the book. Through these passion statements, contributors share with us what they care about most and what they have discovered. These are their pearls of wisdom. Stand on their shoulders and soar to new heights.

Some Ideas on How to Use the Book

There's no need to read this book in any order. In fact, it's probably best to wander through the pages picking and choosing articles that catch your attention. The Contents, the Introduction to each section, and the Index are some great places to help you decide where you want to start.

Let our contributors get your creative, analytical training and development juices going. Do not passively agree with everything you read. Challenge yourself to reflect and think about each article. In other words, read between the lines. Project your collection of unique experiences into the thinking space crafted by each article. Where are the correspondences? Where are the disconnects? What new insights do you discover along the way?

We see this book as a living and breathing entity. We want it to be an ongoing and evolving reflection of our industry. We invite you to interact with us. Between editions of the book we will post your thoughts, ideas, and new articles on the website for this book.

We hope you have as much fun reading the book as we did developing it. We learned so much about our field in the process. Now if I could only bring all of the contributors and you into my living room for an evening of conversation and discovery . . . maybe soon. In the meantime, let the journey begin!

SECTION ONE

Designing Training

Introduction to Section One

Fill a room full of Training and Development professionals, mention the word design, and expect a heated discussion with views all over the map. From hardcore Skinner behaviorists trying to condition every response to designers who advocate creating structured chaos—something akin to letting the inmates run the asylum. Very vogue these days but I'm not sure what it means. More on this later. So do you find the idea of architecting people's learning experiences an exciting prospect? If you do, then you are in the right place.

Designing training is riddled with pitfalls. These pitfalls are many, seductive, and very easy to fall into. I recall some of my early fumblings as an instructional designer. Imagine the following conversation in my well intentioned but naïve head:

> "Doesn't everyone learn the way I do? I'm the ideal learner—I'll
> just model the design on how I would want to learn the material.

I can forge a perfect path through these ideas, concepts, skills, information, and behaviors; it will be flawless. If the trainers just follow my blueprints, neither they nor the learners will ever go astray."

I relished the ideas of sitting in the director's learning chair calling out the intricate actions and gestures of each scene. Even a great movie director like Cecille de Mille would be jealous of my facility. I grin to myself while I relish my fantasy. Now fast forward the movie and what do we see. The next scene is a pile of evaluations from disgruntled learners and trainers and an endless stream of emails and unanswered voice mails. I'm drowning in shock. My dream is shattered, and I have to go back to the drawing board to figure out where I went wrong.

Designing training is fun and it's rewarding. Let's see whether we can remove some of the uncertainties and challenges and replace them with guidelines, best practices, and advice from some of the leading minds in our field.

Read these contributions with a pen and pad by your side. React, respond, and record your impressions. Compare your experiences with our contributors' experiences. The point is not to agree or disagree. Rather, I hope the thoughts of our esteemed colleagues will cause you to think. This is your path, and you can be as much of a pioneer as an advocate for tried-and-true practices. Learning is an endless field changing each moment as we adopt technologies, embrace generational differences, and challenge our notions of what constitutes learning.

Let's take a peak at what you'll find in this section. There are thirteen articles:

1. Avoiding Biased Questions for Training Needs Assessments
2. Taxonomy of Learning Designs
3. Designing Instructional Strategies: A Cognitive Perspective
4. Don't Be an Order Taker
5. Never Lose Sight of Your Audience

6. If You Don't Know Where You Are Going, You Will Probably End Up Somewhere Else
7. ISD—Faster/Better/Easier
8. Front-End Analysis, Implementation Planning, and Evaluation: Escaping the Pamela Syndrome
9. Creativity, Emergence, and Designing the Learning Experiences
10. Creating Sacred Space
11. e-Learning Content—Sorting Through the Tonnage: A Quick Anatomy Lesson for Those on the "Buy" Side
12. Blended Learning Strategies for Knowledge Workers That Work
13. Confessions of a Gamer: I See Games

Preview of the Articles

Professor Rosile kicks the section off. She delights and instructs us with a wonderful example of the central role that asking the right questions plays during the design process. As we spoke and she shared more about her work in narrative and HorseSense™—the ways in which we become sensitive to how we embody our stories—it became clearer to me why she is so finely tuned to the nuances of questions and listening. Here's how she summed it up for me: *"Asking the right questions is MUCH more important than having the right answers!"*

My conversation with David Weiss reminded me how easy it is to become disoriented by all of the instructional design models and technical jargon. However, in keeping with our earlier theme of seeing instructional design as a science and an art, David has discovered how to maintain his flare for creativity without sacrificing principles of good design, as you will see in his article.

Ken Silber and Rob Foshay bring the knowledge of cognitive learning theory to our field. They insist, *"Instructional designers should be using a wider range of more powerful instructional* strategies, each suited to the types of knowledge needed for deep understanding and real expertise." They explained to me how much things have evolved in the last forty years, and yet how we have not done as good a job as we could to apply these new insights. Ken and Rob helped me understand and delineate between different forms of knowledge and how these can and should drive our design process.

The next article, by Jane Bozarth, is a real wake-up call. She calls it a rant; however, I assured her I would hardly call her passion a rant. I even offered to join her campaign. Go to her website and order a campaign pin to wear at the next industry conference you attend. In her own words, here's what's on Jane's mind: *"In our efforts to be responsive, and collaborative, and supportive, and keep our bosses happy, trainers too often kowtow to the whims or mistakes of (probably) well-meaning managers."*

When I asked Jean Marrapodi what matters most to her in our industry, she was quick to say, "We've got to get the basics right." She captures this essence in her passion statement: *"Never lose sight of your audience or their goals. The rest almost takes care of itself."* Thanks, Jean! In the frenzy of juggling all the plates in our pantry of training, it's easy to lose sight of this deceptively simple truism.

Toni Hodges DeTuncq reminds us that as instructional designers we are neither artists nor scientists. We sit somewhere between. As Toni puts it, *"Instructional design is the art and science of building a roadmap that takes learners where they need to go."*

Darryl Sink and his associates have tackled some of the most challenging instructional design projects I have ever seen with amazing grace and ease. Maybe that's why they've won so many awards. They make instructional design look simple. Darryl's team ability to manage large scale projects made more sense to me when he explained one of his guiding principles to me in the following way: *"The instructional design process and training are means, not ends. Focusing on results, rather than focusing* on providing training, causes decisions to be made in very different ways. The training development organization needs to be project-driven versus being process and control-driven."

Our next contributor, Harold Stolovitch, needs no introduction. This is what was on Harold's mind: "*As learning and performance professionals, our mission is to produce results, not just interventions. When we don't analyze to determine whether what we do is necessary or sufficient, don't ensure proper implementation, and don't measure results credibly, we fail in that mission.*"

Peter Honebein brings a rich background in instructional system design and has been a part of many award-winning teams for his work. He's also on the leading edge of our industry. His recent work on co-creating with customers is worth checking out. When I asked Peter what good instructional design looks like in action, he said that it is the blending of the principles of learning experiences with good old systematic design—and he explains all this in his article.

Michael Milano is a man with a powerful vision. In our telephone conversations, he spoke in brave terms about the responsibility we have to make sure the learning spaces inhabited by our designs allow for people to reflect and grow in ways that go beyond learning objectives.

If you are in talent management or learning, you know that organizations everywhere are using smarter, more flexible learning management systems (LMSs) to deliver a growing share of their learning assets online. But progress on the content side also leads to profusion and confusion for decision makers. How can you choose the best content from this growing, and uneven, stock? Authors Bordonaro (Steve from the learning design side and Frank from the business side) draw on their work with designers, providers, and buyers. They offer some practical tips for efficiently screening, evaluating, and choosing e-learning content.

Our next contributor I met at an ISPI conference. It was one of those swift and furious meeting of minds. She and her team of instructional designers and consultants in Colorado are real dynamos. Deborah Stone and her team share how they work with subject-matter experts to create effective blended learning solutions. She and her colleagues have some great tips on how to "make invisible problem-solving skills visible."

A section on designing training would never be complete without taking a look at some of the alternative forms of deign and delivery. What struck me most about our next contributor is his humility. Steve Sugar is a guy who's written some of the most successful training games. You'll be hard-pressed to find a trainer who has not used one of his games at some point. Yet he works so hard to write games that add real value to the training process. And in this article you'll get to hear his story of how he started in his profession.

So don't wait any longer. Hurry up and turn to the article that caught your attention. Better yet, start from the beginning and read them all.

Article 1

Avoiding Biased Questions for Training Needs Assessments

Grace Ann Rosile, Ph.D.

Passion

Asking the right questions is MUCH more important than having the right answers!

How can you ask questions that help you to assess training needs when you don't know what you don't know, when you can not be sure what the problem is? The answer is to use diagnostic questions. These questions are different from interrogation or cross-examination questions which are designed to judge or assign blame. Diagnostic questions do not assume the nature of the problem is known, and they allow the people answering the questions to guide the inquiry in the early stages.

This sounds simple, and for some it is. For most of us though, it is difficult to ask questions that are not tainted with our own preconceptions about what the problem is and, also, what sort of solutions would be appropriate. Further, our perceptions of the problem are likely to be inaccurate due to the biases that affect how we attribute a cause of success or failure. Such "attributional biases" affect all of us, as explained below. In sum, the combination of jumping to a too-hasty diagnosis of the problem, along with the attributional biases always at work when we perceive causes of failure, can make performing an accurate needs assessments a tricky business.

The difficulty of composing diagnostic questions is demonstrated with the following brief case example. Students engaged in role playing this case example were instructed to generate diagnostic questions. Below you will see some of their results.

CASE EXAMPLE PART A

"The Forklifts" case example is based on a true incident: A company was experiencing problems because forklifts were breaking down much more often than expected. Executives had evidence that the forklift operators were not performing routine maintenance on the machines, maintenance that would have prevented many breakdowns. It was assumed the operators needed further training in maintenance procedures. The company called in some consultants.

The forklift case example was given to a group of junior and senior undergraduate students in my management development and training class. In teams, the students prepared questions to ask of other students who took the role of fork-lift operators. Those acting as operators were told the "whole" story (you will see this in Part B below), advised that they did not want to appear to be at fault in this, and told to otherwise play the role as they chose.

Following are some of the questions students asked in performing their diagnosis. After each question I have noted the unwarranted assumption embedded in the question. The questions are arranged in two groups. The first five questions are judging/blaming questions, ordered worst to least bad. Following those are six examples of better diagnostic questions, relatively free of judging and blaming.

Please note that during the in-class exercise, students were only able to come up with one exploratory diagnostic question (the last one listed, regarding improving working conditions). Fun exercises to improve ability to ask assumption-free questions are the old puzzlers like this one: "Dick and Jane lay dead on the floor. The curtain was flapping in the breeze. The door to the room was locked. How did Dick and Jane die?" Then allow questions to which the only answers can be either yes or no. (The answer to the riddle is at the end of this article.)

Judging and Blaming Questions

- Why do you think proper maintenance is not being done on forklifts? (Assumes improper maintenance is the problem)
- What can you tell me about the forklifts breaking down? (Assumes breakdowns are the problem)
- Why do you think the forklifts are breaking down? (Assumes these are breakdowns [not sabotage] AND that this person knows something about the breakdowns and sees the breakdowns as a problem)
- Do you think we have a problem with the forklifts? (Assumes the forklifts are the problem)
- Tell me about the problems you have at work. (Assumes there is awareness of a problem)

Now let's look at some questions that will allow the necessary information to emerge.

Exploratory Judgment-Free and Blame-Free Questions

- Tell me about your work.
- Tell me a story about your best day at work.
- Tell me about a worst day at work.
- What questions should I be asking about your work?
- What should I understand about your work?
- What are some suggestions you can make that might improve your working conditions?

Note: Since exploratory questions are so very open, they usually should be followed by questions like: Could you tell me more about that? Could you give me an example?

CASE EXAMPLE PART B

The consultants called in did not assume that the nature of the problem was known. Instead, they conducted a full-scale diagnosis of the problem. They engaged in face-to-face personal interviews with a horizontal as well as vertical cross-section of employees. They fed back their data in a "mirroring" phase. For example, if researchers found that one of the themes to emerge from the interviews was the lack of communication and participation in decision making, they would identify this theme and then cite several verbatim statements made by (unidentified, anonymous) employees. The "mirroring" session would provide these detailed, verbatim statements, such as the following: "I don't know why the bosses want us to unload those Wednesday trucks way back in the worst area of the parking lot. I think there are lots better places and times that would make my unloading job easier. But no one asked me about it, so I just do what I am told."

The consultants discovered that the combination of driving the forklifts on uneven ground outside the warehouse and uncomfortable seats without springs was causing physical distress to the operators. The operators began to hate the machines, and due to that hatred, they chose not to perform the prescribed maintenance. They knew how, they knew why, but they would not do it. This is a in which a cursory diagnosis might have led to futile training. Instead, the consultants uncovered the true problem, which did not require a training intervention.

Five Principles for Conducting Training Needs Assessments

Principle 1: Do Not Assume the Given or Apparent Problem Is the Problem

Move around the problem to ask questions from those above, below, in front, behind, and in the middle of the problem. Avoid questions that are problem-focused or solution-focused, because this often limits your inquiry into the nature of the problem.

Principle 2: Ask Exploratory Questions

Do ask people to describe, to explain, to tell you about their work.

Do use critical-incident-type questions through which they are asked to describe an especially good time at work, or an especially bad situation. Feed back your data to the people you interviewed to jointly interpret the findings.

Principle 3: Examine the Reward Systems Surrounding the Problem

Consider both the formal and informal reward systems in the organization. Here, the classic article "On the Folly of Rewarding A While Hoping for B" is perennially relevant. Are there any rewards for desired performance? Or are people either not rewarded, or perhaps even penalized, for performing as desired?

A former student told me the story of the military in his country being concerned about the high cost of weapon repairs. The country was not at war at the time, so they decided to penalize officers whose troops had high repair costs. The officers quickly discovered that the more the weapons were handled and used by the troops, the higher the repair costs. Their solution?

Lock away all weapons, to be taken out only when ordered. The troops rarely handled their weapons, and repair expenses dropped, but how well-prepared were these soldiers? It was a classic case of rewarding efficiency at the expense of effectiveness.

Bringing this back to our forklift case example, what happens when a forklift breaks down? Does this mean the operator has a break from work while a repair or replacement is completed? What behavior is rewarded?

Principle 4: Be Aware of Attributional Biases

Attribution theory tells us that we all have a tendency to protect our own egos when we fail at something, by attributing our failures to factors external to ourselves. Thus we fail to achieve our sales quota due to a slump in the economy, problems with the product, bad luck, etc. However, when we observe another person's failure, we tend to attribute it to factors internal to that person. So when our co-worker fails to achieve his or her sales quota, we tend to believe it is due to lack of ability or effort. This is why the workplace is full of so many stupid and lazy people. Of course, we ourselves are not like "them."

When I am observing others, I will tend to attribute failures to the lack of motivation or skill level of the people I am interviewing about the problem. Conversely, the people experiencing the problem will be affected by the self-serving bias that leads them to blame external factors for their problems, not seeing their own deficiencies in ability or effort. How can we avoid or correct for these attributional biases?

First, avoid the appearance of blaming. Often there is a tendency to point fingers and to focus on identifying the person or persons "causing" the problem. We assume that, if there is a problem, there must be someone causing it.

One helpful strategy to circumvent this cycle of blaming and denials is to conceptualize the problem as distinct from any person. Make this problem an actual character in your story. In the forklift case, we might have "The Breakdown Demon."

Principle 5: Allow for the Unexpected

Do ask people to suggest to you what else you should be asking about. Let the interviewees guide your inquiry in the early stages. Be open to people mentioning something totally unanticipated, and following up on it. Pay attention to non-verbals and supposedly irrelevant side comments, and use open follow-up questions to explore these leads.

Conclusion

The first step in training needs assessment is awareness of attributional biases that lead us to blame another's lack of ability or effort for failures. Armed with such awareness, we can better design relatively assumption-free questions. Asking true diagnostic questions that are exploratory rather than judgmental or blaming creates an adventure of discovery, and is the basis for an effective needs assessment.

So how did Dick and Jane die? The wind killed them. They were smothered to death in the air when the breeze blew their bowl off the windowsill. Dick and Jane were goldfish.

Article 2

Taxonomy of Learning Designs

David S. Weiss, Ph.D.

Passion

Creative learning designs are the backbone of learning programs—give it the attention it deserves.

A taxonomy learning design process is an innovative approach that balances the need for learning repetition (which is very important when introducing a mindset shift and behavioral changes) with the engaging process of using multiple approaches to learning. The outcome of a taxonomy design is a program that the participants experience as deepening, varied, compelling, and actionable.

Two key components of a taxonomy learning design process are (1) a careful review of the core objectives and (2) the identification of outcomes that need to be the focus of the learning experience. The core learning objectives are then balanced with multiple learning strategies. A taxonomy learning design maximizes the participants' ability to apply a focused set of skills and knowledge to the business realities following the learning experience.

The approach to taxonomy learning design for adult learners is taken from learning techniques used in special education for students who have learning difficulties. In special education, a deficiency in learning is not necessarily in the task or in the subject, but rather it is often in the presentation. Most learners with special needs would have greater potential to learn if they were presented with the task or subject in their optimal way of learning. The educator must be aware of all learning strategies when teaching learners with special needs.

The learning methodology assumes that each individual student has a unique learning style. The designer has to consider all the strategies of learning and apply the right strategy to each individual learning pathway. Educators who adopt this learning methodology have the following expectations:

- Learn all strategies so that they can teach according to the methods that maximize each student's learning.
- Only teach those who will learn by the method you know how to teach.
- Establish that learning has occurred when the student has successfully accomplished succeeding trials of the task or process.

So what does designing learning for special education students have to do with designing learning for adult learners?

Most adults without special needs have highly developed learning patterns. They may have succeeded in school, even though the learning strategies were limited to lecture, note-taking,

he over-stimulated work

ve learning patterns that

ning needs. Adult learn-

g experience bombarded

rupted with email mes-

m, distracted by many

In essence, they are so

strate behavior patterns

ning problems.

. They may sit pas-

els to keep themselves

w that captures their

this need for stimu-

s principle to learn-

their shows have to

ommercials to keep

s need to have the

y. The designer has

s times to make the

variety of strategies

ver-stimulated work

very difficult task

do so.

to their attention

arning, continuous

ractions.

learning are primarily because the learn-
ing designers and instructors do not use a suitable learning approach.
They have to access multiple learning strategies and teach participants in the learning styles that best suit their needs. It is essential
that the educator teaches to the learning styles of the participants.

The problem is exacerbated when you teach multiple people in one room who are all distracted and unable to focus their attention. Normal adult learning has similarities, so one approach can meet many needs. However, when adults learn in deviant ways due to their patterns of attention deficit, then you need multiple strategies to increase the possibility that you will meet the needs of participants with different learning styles.

Putting the Taxonomy Approach to Learning to Use

The "taxonomy" approach maximizes learning engagement and increases participants' ability to apply a focused set of skills and knowledge to their business realities. The balancing process of focusing on the learning content and applying innovative learning strategies will increase the participants' ability to apply learned skills and knowledge to their jobs after the program.

Here are three examples of courses and development sessions that used a taxonomy approach to learning design.

Example 1—Implementing Change

A large manufacturing company was in the process of major change in its industry. They decided to offer an "implementing change" course for their leaders. The executives knew their leaders were overwhelmed with the changes in the business, and they understood that they had to enhance the leaders' appreciation of how to implement the changes the company contemplated. One of the key tools their learning designers used to develop the course was a "taxonomy design table." The table is a document that summarizes the key content learning objectives (on the left) and the key learning strategies to be used (at the top).

The process helped designers identify how the same content could be taught several times by using multiple strategies of learning. For example, the participants took a pre-session, web-based assessment on their ability to implement change (Objective 1). They also heard an executive speak about implementing change, they participated in engaging interactive learning processes in the classroom, and they participated in an action learning process to put the implementing change ideas into action.

The multiple strategies of learning (see Figures 2.1 and 2.2) the five objectives for the session ensured that the participants would absorb the knowledge and know how to put it to use after the session.

Core Learning Objectives	Web-Based Multi-Rater	Executive Commitment and Ability	X-Dept Group Learning	Action Learning	Engaging Learning Techniques	One-to-One Feedback and Coaching	Follow-Up Community of Interest
Develop the leaders' ability to implement change as they define business problems and solutions.	X	X		X	X		
Develop capabilities as leaders (vs. managers), lead teams, coach others, and manage performance.	X		X		X	X	
Develop the leaders' capabilities as coaches and mentors of employees.					X	X	X
Integrate their multi-rater feedback and what they have learned into their development plans.	X					X	X
Build and strengthen the network of leaders within the organization.			X	X	X		X

Figure 2.1. Multiple Earning Strategies

Core Learning Objectives	Pre-Workshop Work and Team Assessment Survey	Case Study Analysis and Application	Executive Forum and Customer Panels	Multi-Media Computer Simulation	Breakthrough Action Planning	One-to-One Feedback and Coaching	Follow-Up Community of Interest
Increase the capability of leaders to operate interdependently in alignment with the company strategy.			X	X	X		X
Develop the leaders' systems awareness as they define business problems.	X	X		X			
Develop capabilities as leaders (vs. managers), lead teams, coach others, and manage performance.	X			X		X	
Integrate what they have learned into individual development plans.					X	X	
Build and strengthen the network of contacts among the management cadre in the company.			X				X

Figure 2.2. Multiple Earning Strategies

Example 2—Customer Focus Training

A technology organization had been very successful in the past. However, in the last year, new competitive forces started capturing their customer market by providing innovative customer segmentation, customizing services and offering multiple options to meet customer needs. The technology organization determined that it needed to develop a customer focus program that would give the sales and customer service leaders the tools and insights to enhance their customer focus and relationships. They also realized they needed to design the program quickly—and at the same time, make it effective. They used a taxonomy approach and designed a session that had specific content with multiple strategies of learning. Their leadership design was as shown in Table 2.1.

Table 2.1. Matching Content with Learning Strategies

Core Learning Objectives	Multiple Learning Strategies						
	Pre-Workshop Work and Team Assessment Survey	Case Study Analysis and Application	Executive Forum and Customer Panels	Multi-Media Computer Simulation	Breakthrough Action Planning	One-to-One Feedback and Coaching	Follow-Up Community of Interest
Increase the capability of leaders to operate interdependently in alignment with the company strategy.			X	X	X		X
Develop the leaders' systems awareness as they define business problems.	X	X		X			
Develop capabilities as leaders (vs. managers), lead teams, coach others and manage performance,	X			X		X	
Integrate what they have learned into individual development plans,					X	X	
Build and strengthen the network of contacts among the management cadre in the company.			X				X

The program included extensive pre- and post-session work that was integrated into the core learning content objectives. The session itself focused intensely on the learning objectives, but instructors kept the program interesting and varied by using the taxonomy approach of multiple strategies.

Example 3—Train the Trainer for Designers

The taxonomy approach also has been used in train-the-trainer programs for design specialists. These designers learned the taxonomy approach so that they could design highly engaging adult learning experiences for their internal organizations. In one case, a financial institution was about to launch a new learning institute facility for all of their employees. As part of the process of building the state-of-the-art learning institute, they decided they also needed a state-of-the-art design process for their learning programs. Their designers were taught how to design programs using the taxonomy approach. They used this approach to redesign courses on technical matters, such as credit applications and financial controls, as well as leadership courses, such as influencing, executive expression and implementing change. As a result, the financial institution had courses that were meaningful, dynamic and engaging. The course designs helped keep the participants' interest in the sessions and increased the adherence of the learning after the session.

Conclusion

A taxonomy approach to learning is a clear and understandable way to design learning. It is a very useful methodology to balance content with strategies of learning. It also is a very helpful technique for laying out a program and describing it to others. The taxonomy approach delivers proven results in the design of classroom learning and in the carryover of application of knowledge and skill to the workplace.

Article 3

Designing Instructional Strategies

A Cognitive Perspective

Kenneth H. Silber, Ph.D., and

Wellesley R. Foshay, Ph.D., CPT

Passion

What we have learned over the years is that there is no one best way to teach everything!

There has been a revolution in instructional design, based on current cognitive learning theory. Yet when we look at most training, whether platform or online, we find that it's still using the instructional models of forty years ago, based on behavioral learning theory. The result? Often, it's training that entertains and informs or that builds only low-level procedural skills. But the training fails to build deep understanding, and to teach people how to think and solve important business problems. Instructional designers should be using a wider range of more powerful instructional strategies, each suited to the types of knowledge required for deep understanding and real expertise.

The Cognitive Approach to Designing Instructional Strategies

Types of Knowledge

Before talking about how to teach, it's important to look at what we are teaching, because, not surprisingly, we teach different kinds of content differently.

When they discuss learning, cognitive psychologists often draw distinctions between different categories of knowledge. The biggest distinction is between *declarative* and *procedural* knowledge: *Declarative* knowledge is knowing *what,* and *procedural* knowledge is knowing *how.* (See Table 3.1.)

The basic difference between the two types of knowledge is that declarative knowledge tells you *how the world is,* while procedural knowledge tells you *how to do things in the world.* There are different types of declarative and procedural knowledge.

- Declarative knowledge includes facts such as names, concepts such as groups or categories, and principles and mental models, or how the world works.
- Procedural knowledge varies by *degree of structure,* from well-structured such as algorithmic knowledge, with fully defined inputs, processes and outputs, on a continuum to

Table 3.1. Strategies for Types of Knowledge

Type	Present Knowledge	Present Example	Practice
Declarative			
Facts	Facts in structures–**in relation** to one another	How the facts are used in the learners' real world	Repeat back facts in the structure, and relate to real world
Concepts	Attributes of the concept, **and** how all concepts relate to one another	One that is a "bulls-eye" example of each concept **and** examples that highlight differences among concepts	Classify examples of concepts
Principles	The laws by which things work ("if . . ., then . . .) statements) presented in a structure that relates them	Show how the principles operate in the learners real word	Give scenarios; learners explain or predict what would happen in the situation
Procedural			
Procedures	The steps in the procedure in a structure that makes sense (vs. just a list)	Show the procedure being done correctly and incorrectly	Give scenario; have learners both do the procedure **and** explain why they are doing it that way
Problem Solving	a. Sets of principles that relate to the problem; b. Set of heuristics (guidelines) for defining the problem and for solving it	a. Sample problems solved	a. Problems to solve; b. move from easier to harder; c. Lots of help (aka "scaffolding" as learners begin); d. Learners both solve and explain why they did what they did

ill-structured such as design knowledge, with undefined inputs, processes, and outputs.

The Model

The model for the cognitive approach to instructional design (Table 3.2) describes the five learning tasks learners have according

Table 3.2. The Cognitive Instructional Design Model

Learners have to do this to learn. . .	Trainers put these elements in lessons to help learners do it
Select the information to attend to: Heighten their attention and focus it on the new knowledge being taught because that new knowledge is seen as important and capable of being learned.	**Attention**. Gain and focus learners attention on the new knowledge; **WIIFM**. Tell learners What's In It For Me in the new knowledge; **YCDI**. Tell the learners You Can Do It in learning the new knowledge
Link the new information with existing knowledge. Put the new knowledge in an existing framework by recalling existing/old knowledge related to the new knowledge, and linking the new knowledge to the old.	**Recall**. Bring to the forefront the pre-requisite existing (old) knowledge that forms the base on which the new knowledge is built. **Relate**. Show similarities or differences between the new knowledge and old knowledge, so that the new knowledge is tied to the old
Organize the information: Organize new knowledge in a way which matches the organization already in mind for related existing knowledge to: make it easier to learn; cut mental processing; minimize confusion; stress only relevant information	**Structure of Content**. Present the boundaries and structure of the new knowledge, in a format that best represents the way the new knowledge itself is structured; **Objectives**. Specify both the desired behavior and the knowledge to be-learned; **Chunking**. Organize and limit the amount of new knowledge presented to match human information processing capacity; **Text Layout**. Organize text presentation to help learners organize new knowledge; **Illustrations**. Use well-designed illustrations to assist learners organization and assimilation of new knowledge
Assimilate the new knowledge into the existing knowledge: Integrate the new knowledge into the old knowledge so they combine to produce a new unified, expanded, and re-organized set of knowledge	**Present New Knowledge**. Using a different approach for each type of knowledge, present the new knowledge in a way that makes it easiest to understand; **Present Examples**. Demonstrate real-life examples of how the new knowledge works when it is applied
Strengthen the new knowledge in memory. Strengthen the new knowledge so that it will be remembered, and can be brought to bear in future job and learning situations	**Practice**. Involve learners by having them do something with the new knowledge; **Feedback**. Let learners know how well they've done in using the new knowledge, what problems they're having, and why; **Summary**. Present the structure of content again, including the entire structure of knowledge; **Test**. Have learners use the new knowledge again, this time to prove to themselves, you, and their employer that they have met the objectives of the training; **On-the-Job Application**. Have learners use new knowledge in a structured way on the job to ensure they "use it, not lose it."

The Trainer's Portable Mentor

to cognitive psychologists. For each learning task, it describes the two to five lesson elements trainers must put in their lessons to help learners accomplish the learning task. They provide the blueprint for the lesson structure modeled here.

The model is a way to:

- Synthesize and summarize the components of a well-designed lesson.
- Relate what learners have to do to learn to what you as a designer have to do to help them to learn.
- Present a general framework for instructional design up-front, with the notion that each subsequent component will teach how to apply this framework to teaching a certain type of knowledge.
- Provide a job aid that you can use as you design training.

The Cognitive ID Model, shown in Table 3.1, has two columns and five rows. The left column lists the five tasks learners have to do in learning, one in each row:

1. Select the information to attend to.
2. Link the new information with existing knowledge.
3. Organize the information.
4. Assimilate the new knowledge into the existing knowledge.
5. Strengthen the new knowledge in memory.

The right column lists the seventeen elements of a training lesson that you design to help learners accomplish those five learning tasks. In each row are brief descriptions of the lesson elements that relate to each of the five learning tasks.

Earlier, we said you teach different types of knowledge differently. For the purposes of this chapter (there are more differences highlighted in the references), the main areas of difference among types of knowledge are in Present New Knowledge, Present Examples, and Practice.

Conclusion

A basic principle of instructional design is that different types of knowledge are taught best with different types of instruction: there is no one best way to teach everything. Table 3.1 shows how a basic lesson structure can be adapted to teaching three types of declarative knowledge and the range of procedural knowledge structure. *In almost any business context, the most valuable capabilities involve well-developed mental models and ill-structured problem-solving.* Yet, training often stops at teaching facts and well-structured procedures—or tries to teach all types of knowledge using strategies that are effective only with these lowest-level knowledge types. It is also common, therefore, for well-designed instructional solutions to teach the knowledge types in combination. Taken together, we believe the strategies described here will result in maximally effective instruction which is also optimally efficient to design, develop, and use.

References

Foshay, W.R., Silber, K.H., & Stelnicki, M.B. (2003). *Writing training that works.* San Francisco, CA: Pfeiffer.

Silber, K.H., & Foshay, W.R. (2006). Using cognitive instructional strategies. In J. Pershing (Ed.), *Handbook of human performance technology* (3rd ed.). San Francisco, CA: Pfeiffer.

Article 4

Don't Be an Order Taker

Jane Bozarth, M.Ed.

Passion

I am passionate about my role in training. My job as a work-place learning and development professional is to solve problems and NOT to be an order taker. However, I see that in an effort to be responsive, and collaborative, and supportive, and keep our bosses happy, we trainers too often kowtow to the whims or mistakes of (probably) well-meaning managers.

"Yes, sir, Mr. Department Head, let me get you an order of team building with a side of stress management! Right away, sir!"

Experienced trainers all have war stories about misbegotten requests for training, most on one or all of the themes below:

- The Bad Hire, now being sent to "communication skills" training in hopes you will un-jerk him
- The Bad Supervisor, who's destroyed a formerly fine team and now wants the team to go through a "personality type" assessment workshop
- The Burned-Out Employee the boss wants to send to training because she wants the employee to hear "something motivational"
- The Manager who wants to send everyone to a "time management" workshop because staff spend all their time putting out fires—that the manager set
- The Executive who wants to implement an unpopular change—and wants the training department to play the role of unpopular messenger

While you may not always have the luxury of, or time for, a full-blown needs assessment, you often know in the course of the initial conversation that the manager's request won't do a thing toward solving the problem—and could even make it worse. Many perceived "performance problems" have nothing to do with skills, or knowledge, or attitude toward a job.

Here's a secret: Managers making a specific training request often don't even really want a workshop—they want a problem solved. YOU need to develop the skills in having conversations necessary to help move them from what they think will help (and you know will not) to what will really answer the problem. (Of course, this gets especially tricky when the manager *is* the problem.) Below are some tips for managing this conversation:

- Acknowledge, but don't blame: "You shouldn't have hired him" won't help the problem. Try: "I know it's awfully frustrating to bring someone on board and realize he's just not working out. . ."

- Watch your language. Saying, "That won't work" could get you into an arm-wrestling match with a manager who may well outrank you. Try: "I think you're on the right track, but I'm not sure that will really solve your problem."

- Offer alternatives: "Let's look at what else might help.", "Have you considered. . .?"

- Tell the manager the truth: "You know, all the training in the world won't un-jerk a jerk. We can work on the specific skills we've identified, but I want to be clear about what training realistically can do for this situation."

- Tell your boss the truth. You don't want to be reported for failing to do what the CEO says. While you may still sometimes just have to bite the bullet and deliver on the request intact, make sure your boss is aware of your concerns. And if you don't have "that kind" of relationship with your boss, cultivate it.

- Get educated. It is vital that you be able to articulate the appropriate uses of training, have sound knowledge of a number of needs assessment techniques, and be knowledgeable about possible approaches and solutions. Developing needs assessment and consulting skills in addition to training skills will put many more tools in your kit.

- Beware the four-letter fad. Cults grow up around team tools and personality assessment instruments (the most popular with the validity of, say, astrology), and little-animal management metaphors, and cheese. Be careful of jumping to deliver a packaged product for which the manager just happened to see an ad.

- Make the manager a partner. Do you hear beeping? That's the sound of a dump truck backing up and putting the problem on you to fix. Involve the manager in developing solutions and assessing performance once learners are back on the job. Put the final accountability in the manager's corner.

- Remember: You aren't a psychologist—or a referee. Be clear about your role.

Conclusion

Rushing to accommodate every request, without proper diagnosis, will not enhance the trainer's reputation. In the end, the trainer's—and ultimately the training department's—credibility is destroyed by failing to deliver on impossible promises. While it may be that the manager is your "customer," and it is your job to please him or her, realize that sometimes that may mean questioning, and challenging, and offering alternatives—the Edsel.

Article 5

Never Lose Sight of Your Audience

Jean Marrapodi, Ph.D., CPLP

Passion

Never lose sight of your audience or their goals. The rest almost takes care of itself. As simple as that sounds, I remind myself of the following basics every time I begin to design a program.

Whenever you are designing learning programs of any description, there are two key success factors. First, you are solving a specific problem for specific people with your program, whether it is a classroom program, e-learning module, webinars, or job aid. You need to know who you are designing for and what the problem is that the solution is intended to introduce or remediate. Once you have defined the problem, begin with the end state the solution should produce, and keep the end in mind as you work.

Who Are You Designing For?

Consider this: You have been asked to design an e-learning reading tutor program for beginning readers. Simple enough, right? Put up some ABCs, multimedia, flash tricks, make it Sesame-Street-like and voila!, you're done. Wait a minute though! That might work if your program is intended for kindergarteners, but what if your program is for older adult immigrants with no experience with books, paper, or pencils? What if it is intended for a juvenile corrections institution? How would your program differ in these scenarios? You must always consider the context of your learners, including their background and interests.

Adults learn best when they have a need to learn the information and when it is connected to something in their frame of reference. Take into account the learner population's education, background, life stage, prior experience, and interests. Think how a program intended for engineers would differ from one designed for call center customer service staff, or how a program for executives would differ from fast-food line workers. The content will be different, but your approach must also match the needs and style of the intended audience.

What's the Problem?

Training is intended to provide a solution to a problem. Part of your job is to define the exact problem and identify the training solution or intervention that will bring resolution. The goal should be stated as a single sentence, giving the big picture aim of the program. For example:

- This training is designed to introduce students to Microsoft PowerPoint and teach them to create basic presentations.
- This course is designed to give mid-level managers the skills to conduct behaviorally based interviews.

Knowing who your audience is helps you to determine what they already know and what they will need. Performance consultants attempt to determine the gap between the desired performance and the actual performance. To determine the existing performance, you need to meet with, interview, and observe end-users to understand what they already know. To determine the desired performance, you must listen carefully to your requester and the subject-matter expert(s) for the information that makes up the end state. As a training consultant, you bring the perspective of an objective observer who may see things that the requestors do not realize.

When the goal is to introduce something new, you can bring the novice's perspective to pinpoint concepts that beginning users will have difficulty with. Pay attention to your challenges as you learn what you will be teaching through your program and look to incorporate a resolution to those issues.

Another thing to be cognizant of is the difference between expert and novice perspectives. Subject-matter experts often want to include everything they know in a training program. As a training expert, you need to balance the "need to know" information with the "nice to know" information to avoid overwhelming the learners.

Keep the End in Mind

Once you have determined the gap and defined the goal the training will achieve, begin with the end in mind and keep it in the forefront of your thinking the entire time. Let's label the goal XYZ, and call the training ABC. After ABC, the student should be able to XYZ. In order to get to this point, you will need to chunk the information into the smaller areas that make up the big picture.

Begin by determining the sub-components of XYZ. What are the skills, knowledge, or attitudes necessary to achieve XYZ? As you list the skills and sub-skills, consider which of them the learners may already know. Build a hierarchy of steps for each task. In PowerPoint, for example, the student needs to know how to insert text before it can be formatted. As you build the steps, continue to ask yourself, "How will this meet the goal of XYZ?" If something is not directly related to achieving the goal of XYZ, it may fall into the "nice to know" category that can be eliminated when there is too much material.

Create objectives for each sub-area. An objective should be something specific and readily identifiable: "At the end of this section, learners will be able to cut and paste text." Look at each objective and see how it meets the goal of XYZ. All of the objectives should combine together, step-by-step to meet the end-state goal.

At this point, you will also want to consider how you will measure how the objectives will be met by the learners and measured. Will they demonstrate the new skill? Will they take a test at the end? Will the evaluation be participants' perceptions of the class at the end? Knowing how you will evaluate the success of the program at the design stage will help you to build in measures along the way to document success of the learner as well as the program.

After you have identified the objectives, create a tentative outline, listing the objectives in the order you believe they should be presented in and defining how they will be evaluated. Send the design plan to your subject-matter expert for approval. It is critical that you receive approval from the owner of the project before you begin to develop the materials to ensure you have accurately captured the intention of the program and the process to achieve the goal.

After you have the approved outline, you can begin to develop the content, including the exercises to achieve the goal.

Conclusion

By examining the audience, concisely defining the goals, objectives, and measures of success for the program; all the while keeping the end in mind, you can design learning programs that will effectively meet the needs of your participants.

Article 6

If You Don't Know Where You Are Going, You Will Probably End Up Somewhere Else

Toni Hodges DeTuncq

Passion

If you don't know where you are going you will end up some place you might not want to be. Instructional design is the art and science of building a roadmap that takes learners where they need to go.

The traditional method for training design is that the design is most often based on one of these premises:

- There is a performance gap that needs to be filled.
- The client wants a more trained workforce.
- The stakeholders enjoy training and want more.
- There was a previous program that was determined to be "successful" or popular and people want it again.

Once in a while there is an actual business need that will drive training. If that is the case, however, most often that need is not explicitly stated in terminology that can be translated into training requirements. Or the need is not diagnosed properly to determine exactly what solutions are required—whether they indeed are training needs or other performance-related solutions. But several organizations are beginning to realize the importance of doing this type of investigation, not only to improve performance successfully but also to prevent spending money on solutions that may not even be necessary. These best-practice organizations are putting into place systems and processes to equip their performance solution specialists with the tools they need to effectively target the correct solutions each time. If training is the only solution, or one of the solutions, data is then provided to the design team, who will then be able to design or select effective and efficient learning solutions that will not only provide the training needed but drive the performance required to meet the business needs.

This article and a subsequent follow-up article in the Measurement and Evaluation section of this book will describe a tool that the author has designed and many of these best practice organizations are using.

Objective Mapping®

Objective mapping (Hodges, 2002), requires that three distinct types of objectives be clearly identified, most ideally in the following order:

1. Business objectives are those objectives that identify the organizational need or problem that needs to be addressed. Table 6.1 provides examples of these types of objectives. The business objectives must be stated as goals with associated metrics. For example, if the business goal is increase sales, the goal should be quantified, say to increase sales by 30 percent. Or if the business objective is to improve employee morale, the extent for that improvement must be stated, for example to increase employee satisfaction index on the annual employee survey by 10 points.

2. Performance objectives are the performance requirement improvements needed from an identified group of employees to meet the stated business requirements. For example, to increase the sales, one performance improvement desired may be to diagnose customer requirements correctly. The criteria for which that performance will be

Table 6.1. Examples of Business Objectives

Produce Twice the Number of Units Each Week	Reduced Turnover Rate by 25 Percent	Generate 25 Percent New Accounts	Reduce Operating Costs by 50 Percent	Reduce Accident Rate by 20 Percent
Increase Shipments Incrementally each Month	Prevent Call Escalations by 30 Percent	Reduce Reject Rate by 35 percent	Increase Percent of Tasks Completed Properly	Reduce Absenteeism by 25 Percent
Reduce 20 Percent of Monthly Grievances in Each Department	Increase Number of Suggestions Submitted	Reduce 95 Percent of Safety Violations	Increase Job Satisfaction Index by 35 Percent	Increase New Hire Rate by 10 Percent

rated must be stated, such as, " using the online diagnostic checklist," or "90 percent of the time." If the business objective is to improve employee morale, one performance requirement may be for the supervisor to hold one-on-one meetings with their direct reports at least twice a month. There is normally more than one performance objective needed to meet each business objectives. But there must be *at least one* performance objective for each business objective. One performance objective may, however, help to meet more than one business objective.

3. Learning objectives are those with which most training designers are familiar. These are the ones that begin with, "at the end of this course, the participant will be able to . . ." Most often, learning objectives are developed from a vague notion of what is required. A task analysis may or may not have been conducted, for example. The objective mapping process requires that the learning objectives be developed based on the performance objectives. If the performance objective, for example, is that the performer must diagnose customer requirements correctly using the online diagnostic checklist, then some of the related learning objectives may be to: (1) access the online tool from the general menu; (2) type in the customer problems or concern in the correct area; and (3) press the "submit" button. As this example shows, there is normally more than one learning objective for each performance objective, but there must be at least one. And one learning objective may meet more than one performance objective. It is important to note that there should be NO learning objectives that are not linked to at least one performance objectives.

What you can see from the definitions and examples above is a clear link from the business requirement to the learning objectives. This direct linkage will ensure that the training program will ultimately solve the business and performance requirements and not provide unnecessary training. Very few organizations can afford to provide training for the fun of it. We can no longer provide training that is nice to have. We can only provide training that is truly needed. The objective mapping process will ensure that each aspect of the training is tied directly to the stated organizational needs.

Enablers and Barriers

We all know of situations in which, no matter how well our programs are designed, the performance we hoped for does not happen because of influences or "barriers" that are in the work environment that inhibit the use of the new skills learned. It is critical that these barriers be anticipated and recorded on the objective map so that the entire stakeholder group for the program can work toward eliminating them or reducing their influences and provide enablers in their place. Table 6.2 provides example business, performance and learning enablers, and barriers. Table 6.3 provides an example of an objective map for a sales/customer service training program.

Table 6.2. Examples of Enablers and Barriers for Meeting Objectives

Objective	Barriers	Enablers
Business	Market; Unemployment Rate; Competition; Manufacturing; Supply; Public Perception	New Product Line; Reorganization; Marketing Programs; Process Improvements; Incentive Programs
Performance	Lack of Management Support; Technology Not Ready; Workload; Insufficient Prerequisite Skills	On-the-Job Aids; Technology; Supervisor Reinforcement; Help Lines
Learning	Wrong Audience; Insufficient Time; Exercises Not Job Realistic; Program Materials Too Expensive; Job Distractions; Inconsistent Instruction	Exercises; Participant Selection; Prerequisite Work; Use of Media; Knowledgeable Instruction; Supervisor Support

Table 6.3. Sample Sales/Customer Service Training Program Objectives

1. Business Objective	2. Metric	3. Enablers/ Barriers	4. Performance Objective	5. Measurement Methodology	6. Enablers/ Barriers	7. Learning Objective	8. Measurement Methodology	9. Enablers/ Barriers
1. Improve Customer Satisfaction by 90%	Reduction in customer complaints	Enabler: New product line/ Barrier: Week market	1a. Opens call IAW established procedures; 1b. Demonstrates interest in caller's needs; 1c. Closes call with correct understanding of actions to be taken		Enablers: Training, job performance incentives;	1a1. Greet caller with standard company opening; 1a2. Introduces self; 1b1. Uses enthusiastic tone of voice (friendly, positive, non-monotone voice—happy, upbeat, cheery, pleasant); 1b2. Listens to customer without interrupting; 1c1. Conveys empathy; 1c2. Asks for customer's perspective; 1c3. Probes for agreement; 1c4. Restates agreed upon follow-up actions to be taken		Barrier: Lack of practice time/Enabler: realistic simulation

| 2. Reduce Escalations by 80% | Cost savings due to reduction in time required of team leader and processing clerk | 2a. Diagnosis customer's problem or need correctly; 2b. Gains customer agreement of follow-up actions that need to be taken; | Barrier: Lack of supervisor support | 2a1. Defines purpose of call; 2a2. Communicates what the initial plan will be; 2a3. Asks customer probing questions; 2a4. Uses company Problem Questions Checklist; 2a5. Asks what has been tried before in resolving problem; 2a6. Asks about timing issues; 2b1. Checks back with the customer to make sure rep understands issue/ confirms to ensure understanding; 2b2. Summarizes call; 2b3. Probe for agreement on any follow-up steps | Barrier: Lack of practice time/Enabler: realistic simulation |

To assist in establishing the linkage, an objective map can be initiated using the template provided on the website for this book. Column 1 provides the business objectives. Column 4 provides the associated performance objectives linked to each business objectives. And Column 7 provides the learning objectives linked to each performance objective. Note the numbering scheme. Business Objective 1 is linked to Performance Objectives 1a, 1b, and 1c. Performance Objective 1a is linked to Learning Objectives 1a1 and 1a2. The enablers and barriers for each objective are also noted in Columns 3, 6, and 9.

To see how each of these objectives should be measured to determine ultimately how successful the program was in meeting each of the stated objectives and to see the completed objective map for the Sales/Customer Service training program, please refer to Chapter 44 in the Measurement and Evaluation section of this book.

Conclusion

It is important that we ensure that the program we design helps the client to achieve desired business goals. There are sophisticated tools assessment tools that we can use to effectively identify real training needs and to provide training that returns an ROI in which organizations see value. I have confidence that the tools discussed in this article will help you write the kind of roadmaps that take you and the client to the desired destination. Enjoy the trip!

Reference

Hodges, T.K. (2002). *Linking learning and performance.* Boston, MA: Butterworth Heinemann.

Article 7

ISD—Faster/Better/ Easier*

Darryl L. Sink, Ed.D.

Passion

The instructional systems design (ISD) process and training are means, not ends. Focusing on results, rather than focusing on providing training, causes decisions to be made in very different ways. The training development organization needs to be project-driven vs. being process- and control-driven.

No, ISD is not dead. Recent criticism of ISD, however, is not without merit. Those who over-proceduralize ISD and

---

*This article has been adapted from *ISD—Faster, Better, Easier* by Darryl L. Sink pulished in the *Performance Improvement Journal*, 41 (7), 16-22.

concentrate on the process itself as an end, rather than as a means to an end, lose track of the fact that training and training development exist to help people do their jobs in ways that produce outcomes and results needed by their organizations. Unfortunately, many people have over-generalized the criticisms of ISD and make the assumption that ISD no longer is of value. In fact, ISD has and is evolving and changing to accommodate ever-increasing needs for rapid development, continuous content change, worldwide distribution needs, and cost savings.

This article is about the practice of ISD as it exists in the real world today and how it is being modified and used to produce training solutions that are *faster/better/easier*. Several areas of ISD are presented to illustrate how ISD has been adapted to meet real-world constraints and how it is best used with current delivery technologies, specifically web-based training. The article provides suggestions relating to some of the more important parts of the ISD process. The areas include needs assessment/analysis, content analysis, design strategies, try-out and revision strategies, and project management. General suggestions are given in each area, including a brief introduction, and followed by descriptions of useful techniques and practices that have emerged over time from the combination of research and the continuous striving by practitioners to find *better/faster/easier* ways to develop effective training interventions. Finally, concluding remarks and suggestions on the use of ISD in the field are provided.

In Figure 7.1 a simplified ISD model is presented, highlighting the areas that will be discussed.

The Needs Analysis Process—When to Use It and When Not

ISD is a problem-solving process. As a part of that problem-solving process, needs assessment and needs analysis are correctly

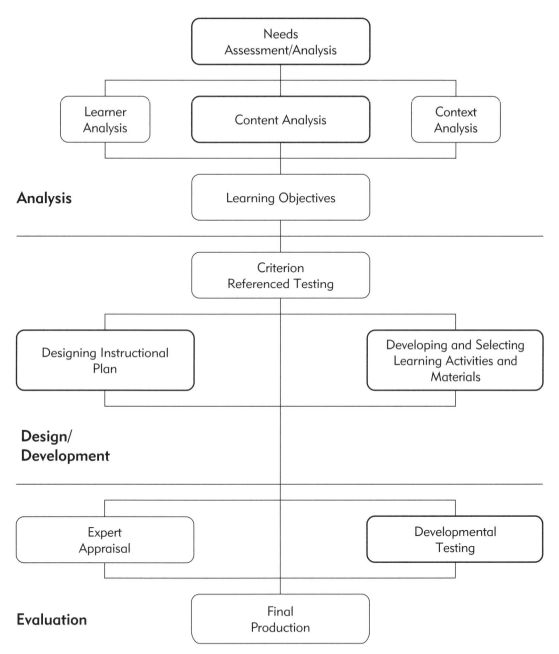

Analysis

Design/ Development

Evaluation

Figure 7.1. Analysis/Design/Evaluation Tree

considered the first steps. These analyses prevent development of training for issues that have nothing to do with real discrepancies in the knowledge, skills, and attitudes required of workers by the organization. Before providing an example of how to do needs assessments and needs analysis *faster/better/easier*, we share a note on when not to do one at all.

Needs analysis may *not* be necessary when training and the goal of that training are mandated or already clearly established. Regulatory training required by law (or required in order to be in compliance) is mandated training. New-hire job training may be another situation for which training is definitely required. This is especially true when it is not possible to hire enough people who already know how to do a job. Another situation in which a needs analysis may not be necessary is in when a complete and accurate job description and analysis exist. The training goals in this case may be established from the job analysis and with the help of master tradespersons, high performers, or subject-matter experts.

Needs analysis is the process of identifying problems and their causes, then matching solutions to the problems. Therefore, the formal needs analysis process is useful only when problems are not clearly identified or analyzed. Attention to the simple decision process illustrated in Table 7.1 may save time and embarrassment by avoiding the effort of a formal needs assessment and needs analysis when they are not necessary.

So it is important to recommend needs assessment and needs analysis when problems have not been clearly identified; and it is also important to intentionally avert this work when it is not necessary.

If there are performance issues and a needs analysis is in order, how can it be done *faster/better/easier*? Here is an example of one approach when conducting interviews is the chosen data gathering technique.

Table 7.1. What to Use Instead

If	Then
The training goal is clear or required as in mandatory training	Start with task analysis
You are training new hires to do a specific job	Start with job analysis then task analysis
New technologies, processes or programs are being introduced	Use subject-matter expert analysis
But if there seem to be performance issues, something other than not knowing how to do the job may be involved	Use needs assessment/needs analysis studies

Needs Assessment/Analysis Interviews— Faster/Better/Easier

One data-gathering technique used often in needs assessment/ analysis is the interview. Here is how interviews can be done *faster/better/easier.*

- Develop a list of standard questions and supplemental questions. The questions can be used repeatedly, if modified to address each particular situation.
- Use the standard and supplemental questions to identify gaps in the knowledge, performance, or attitude.
- Ask which gaps are most important to resolve.
- Ask questions about the root cause(s) of the interviewee's identified high-priority gaps (needs).
- Ask how the gaps can be closed (possible solutions to the problems identified).

By asking questions about the gaps, their root cause, and solutions, information for both the needs assessment and needs analysis is collected in the same interview.

To be more efficient and effective in collecting and handling the interview data, record the interviews and have them transcribed. A court reporting company or the services of a conference call center (if telephone interviews are used) will take the burden of transcription off the consultant and speed the process. The court reporters or the conference call centers will provide an electronic copy of the interview, as well as a hard copy, usually within forty-eight hours. Using this process, electronic copies of all interviews can be available within two days of the last interview.

Once the electronic copies are received, the comments can be sorted into problem categories. Comments are then summarized within each category. Recommendations are built from the summary information. This process makes the report more accurate *(better)* because what people actually said has been captured, rather than relying on notes. The process moves more quickly using transcription services *(faster)*, and it is certainly less time-consuming and laborious *(easier)*, compared to having instructional designers undertake all the work. The time and effort of instructional design professionals are saved for analysis, summarization, and recommendations.

What is the relationship between the needs analysis process and ISD? The needs analysis process is a preliminary step taken when it is not certain whether training is needed—or exactly what training is needed. If one of the outcomes of the needs analysis process is the identification of knowledge, skills, and attitudes that can be treated best as a training intervention, then it serves as input to the rest of the ISD process. If other interventions are selected, it serves for input to those non-training interventions.

Following are three more examples of how other parts of ISD can be done *faster/better/easier*. These three examples suffice to show how today's practitioner is able to effectively and efficiently apply ISD to accommodate increasing needs for speed, continuous content changes, and cost savings. The three areas of

ISD discussed are content analysis, instructional design strategies, and developmental testing. These three are common in one form or another in all ISD models.

Content Analysis—Faster/Better/Easier

Content analysis involves the use of various techniques to determine the knowledge, skills, and attitudes people need to meet a business need (problem or opportunity) or to do a specific job. For most practitioners, it is both the most difficult and the most important part of the ISD process.

No other area of analysis in ISD involves as many different techniques as content analysis.

An excellent book on content analysis is *Task Analysis Methods for Instructional Design* (Jonassen, Tessmer, & Hannum, 1999). The authors describe and illustrate twenty-six methods for task and job analysis. Three primary techniques widely used are hierarchical task analysis, procedural task analysis (covert and overt), and concept analysis.

- Hierarchical task analysis is used primarily for cognitive learning.
- Procedural task analysis (both overt and covert) is used for linear tasks. Overt procedural task analysis usually involves psychomotor behaviors, even when some cognitive processing may also be occurring. Covert procedural task analysis involves analyzing those procedures that are not directly observable, but are part of how people think through decisions.
- Concept analysis is used to identify the critical attributes of ideas and to identify examples and non-examples of the ideas for training purposes.

Here are some ideas for making this important and sometimes taxing process *better, faster,* and *easier.*

1. Content analysis should start with determining which kind of analysis is appropriate for a given training situation. If teaching topics have dependencies involving prerequisite learning, hierarchical analysis should be used. When teaching how to use a software program or how to operate something for which people push buttons and recognize cues, procedural task analysis is a better choice than hierarchical analysis. When teaching people to comprehend and use an *idea* (rather than a task), concept analysis should be used. There are many techniques for breaking content into usable chunks for teaching and learning. Using an appropriate technique based on the kind of learning undertaken will both speed the process and make it better in terms of identifying all the right content to be taught and learned.

2. Key to any content analysis is identifying all the necessary and sufficient knowledge, skills, and attitudes needed by a trainee to perform on the job. One of the most common learning reasons for non-performance is the lack of a prerequisite concept or skill. It is therefore important to ask content experts probing questions to be sure that all the necessary and sufficient content has been identified.

3. When conducting a concept analysis, divergent examples must be collected so that training can demonstrate the range of possibilities. Concept analysis should also identify non-examples that closely resemble the concept, but are not the concept. These close-in non-examples can be used in the training to help trainees avoid misunderstanding the concept.

4. To aid in the transfer of training and generalization of content to many situations, content experts should be asked for a wide range of examples when the learning task is hierarchical in nature or is a concept.

5. One technique for aiding content analysis is to use Post-it® Notes for displaying and sorting content. A separate task/topic is written on each note. The notes can then be

arranged and rearranged in different combinations to discover how the topics and tasks are interrelated. Additions and deletions can be quickly and easily made. It is also a fast and fun way to do a task analysis with content experts.

6. Content analysis is best performed by seeking the input of more than one content expert. This provides for multiple perspectives. This is particularly important with overt procedural tasks, since many high performers develop idiosyncratic behaviors over time that do not necessarily contribute to good performance.

These suggestions for making content analysis *faster/better/easier* can all help. However, it should be noted that content analysis is very important to most master developers. They devote considerable time and effort to ensure that all the necessary and sufficient content needed for acceptable learner performance on the job has been identified.

Design Strategies—Faster/Better/Easier

The design phase of ISD, like content analysis, involves the use of many different techniques. Most master instructional designers are familiar with a wide variety of design strategies. To design quickly and effectively, they select macro level designs based on the type of content, the target audience, and the context for the training. As they begin to work on the actual training modules, they think in terms of existing structures and formats (frames and SuperFrames™) that may be modified for reuse, then move on to the details. Below are some examples of macro-level design thinking and the use of frames and SuperFrames.

Software Training Development

An example of thinking at a macro level when designing instruction can be illustrated in what is a common scenario today—introduction of new software. Software is often developed for a specialized area. In one recent instructional design project, enterprise-wide software was created for managing a large company's real estate holdings. No user guide had been developed for the software, and performance-based training was needed to realize the anticipated value of the software as rapidly as possible. How was this done *faster/better/easier*?

- The user guide was created with the basic procedures for completing program functions at the same time training development was undertaken (*faster*).
- Separate from the user guide, performance-based exercises, demonstrations, and visual presentations were developed for the training. Keeping the exercises separate from the user guide allowed the user to have a streamlined user guide after the training, whether online or hard copy (*better*). By having performance-based exercises, the training simulated the job tasks users face in the real work world.
- To complete this macro-level design, a module at the beginning of the training was added that discussed how to maneuver though the software.

In this example the client received two for one: the user guide and the training program (*easier and better*).

Cognitive Processes and Approaches

In many training situations, there are cognitive processes and approaches to learn, usually related to problem solving. A fast macro approach to instructional design for such learning situations is to think in terms of the phases or steps required in the process/approach/methodology to be taught.

Some familiar examples of content that lends itself to this approach include training on ISD itself, or developing a course on change management, leadership, or teamwork. When faced with such topics, ask whether there is a process, a cycle things go through, or a methodology people will follow. If so, the phases required by the process, cycle, or methodology may be the general framework for a more detailed and complete hierarchical analysis. This is typically a *faster* way to start designing for topics that are hierarchical in nature. Each part of the process, cycle or methodology can then be formed into a training module. Each module can start with a definition of the phase or step in the process, followed by examples, case studies and worksheets.

SuperFrames

SuperFrames are an expansion of the concept of game or activity frames. SuperFrames provide fast and proven structures for learning. They consist of both a game/activity frame and imbedded job aids that are used during the activity and later on the job to promote training transfer. SuperFrames make the design/development process faster and promote performance based learning and transfer of training (*faster and better*). Because SuperFrames are based on existing activity structures, they are also *easier* to design and develop.

Most master developers carry several SuperFrames in their heads; they also refer to activity frame resources as needed. Here is an example of one SuperFrames that is helpful for teaching people to quickly and accurately use procedures online or in manuals.

The frame is similar to a scavenger hunt. The first step is presentation of job aids and brief explanations to show how the manuals or online reference systems work. If there are several manuals or systems, a job aid may even be developed to help the learner identify the right reference quickly. Other job aids are developed to illustrate the structure of the references.

Once the structure is apparent to the learner, an activity is used for practice and reinforcement—in this case, a scavenger hunt. Real scenarios are provided to the learner, which make the training performance-based. The learner uses the job aids previously presented to find the right procedures or policies quickly. The learner then answers two or three questions related to interpreting the procedure or policy. To conclude, the activity is debriefed. Such SuperFrames are fun, interesting, quick to develop, and performance-based, making them a *faster, easier,* and *better* way to design training in many situations.

The design phase of ISD can be accomplished *faster/better/easier* by macro level design and the use of frames and SuperFrames. Detailed techniques for teaching specific kinds of content (that is, facts, procedures, processes, principles, and concepts) are helpful too, but most master instructional developers think at a more macro design level to jump-start the overall development process.

Developmental Testing—Faster/Better/Easier

One of the keys to the systematic development of a training intervention (and non-training interventions as well) is to test the intervention prior to implementation. While few would disagree that testing training materials and programs before releasing the programs is important, this step in the ISD process—developmental testing—is nevertheless often diminished or skipped altogether.

Those with experience know that developmental testing is an essential step in terms of learning outcomes, as well as in program acceptance. Master developers know that just "going with it" is a formula for disaster. Consider the consequences of putting on a play without a dress rehearsal. A poor "opening night" can result in lowered attendance and possible cancellation. Training programs aren't much different, especially if learners have a choice in whether to attend the training or not. So how can materials be tested *faster/better/easier?*

Fortunately, much practical research exists in this area. Studies show that small group trials are as productive as large group trials in terms of collecting data for the purpose of improving an instructional program. Further, there appears to be no significant difference in the quality of information collected for the purpose of revision when testing a program on a very small number of people (or just one person), and testing the same version of the training material with larger groups of fifteen to twenty people. This is a great finding for practitioners! Of note is that the number of tryout and revision cycles the training programs are subjected to is more important for improvement purposes than the number of people in a single trial run. Therefore, using very small group trials as a strategy for developmental testing may not only be *faster* and *easier,* but it may be *better* as well, because more test and revision cycles are likely to be completed. It is also better because the risk of exposing the training program to many people before getting the bugs out of it is minimized. Remember, once the first class of fifteen to twenty students has been run, there are fifteen to twenty people who can function as either advocates for your program or as adversaries.

Thus far I have made suggestions about how the practice of ISD in the practical world is being conducted to make the process *faster/better/easier.* In the next section, I will demonstrate ISD's robust nature by showing how it is used in the exciting new world of e-learning and web-based training.

Project Management for ISD

As can be seen in the model in Figure 7.2, project management takes on a special significance in more complicated projects such as web-based training. Here I will provide suggestions for managing the ISD process *faster/better/easier.*

Instructional developers always face constraints that require them to develop training programs in an expedient manner. These constraints may vary, but they are always present to some extent. Some of the constraints besides time are money, location, access to people, and access to equipment. How can the

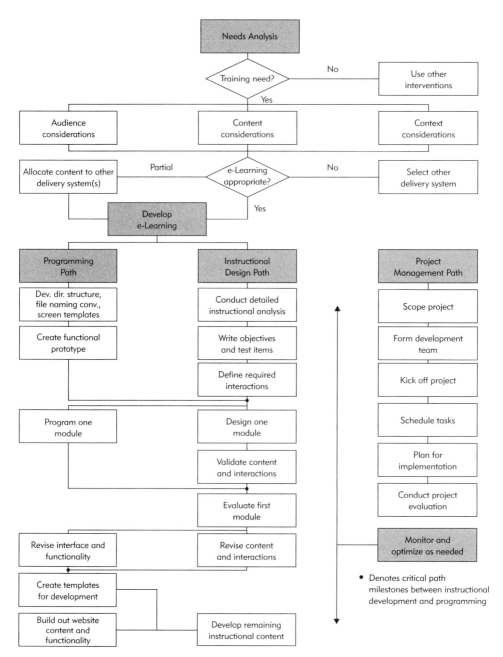

Figure 7.2. Project Management Model

The Trainer's Portable Mentor

systematic instructional development process be maintained under these circumstances? What can be done to organize ISD work and manage projects in today's fast-paced, cost-conscious environment, yet still obtain the outcomes and results desired? Here are ten ways to organize and manage ISD projects *faster/better/easier:*

1. Team selection and formation for any given project may be the most critical factor in project success. Team selection should be based primarily on capability and reliability. Too often, the primary selection criterion is availability.

2. Large projects should be jump-started with an extensive kick-off meeting (virtual or live) in which project goals, the business need driving the project, the deliverables, milestones, means of communication, and methods for tracking progress throughout the project are clearly communicated.

3. To make "shorter time to completion" a way of thinking and acting, limit the number of projects developers are assigned to, but hold developers accountable for project deliverables and completion times.

4. Provide an environment that supports uninterrupted time every day for instructional developers to work on their projects. Mornings should be quiet time in an instructional development work environment; staff meetings and other routine interruptions and activities should be scheduled for late afternoon.

5. To avoid setting unnecessary controls and procedures that may distract from the primary effort of developing the instructional program, determine the fewest number of milestones that require approval.

6. Organize projects for speed and customer results (instead of organizing for process and control). Do not over-proceduralize the ISD process; doing so makes it longer and less effective.

7. Use technology to increase effectiveness and efficiency in communications and productivity: email, transcription services, and online file sharing are all examples of technologies that can help.

8. Ask all personnel to keep track of time on projects. Use experience/statistics from completed projects to do a better job estimating resources for future projects.

9. Consider using a lead developer with experience as the project manager to help anticipate bottlenecks and determine how to keep them from slowing the development process.

10. Provide production assistance and coordination to instructional developers toward the end of the project. Consider using production services that can provide a fast turnaround time, allowing more time for the instructional developers to create the final product.

Conclusion

So what can be done to keep focused on this primary goal of customer outcomes and results? Here are some recommendations:

- As a training organization, focus on helping customers obtain the results they want. This requires the training development organization to be project-driven versus being process- and control-driven. The training organization should let customers know they have a process for helping them with their issues, and then move on to focusing on the customer's issues and needed results. The ISD process should be secondary to a focus that is results-driven.

- When the training organization is process- and control-driven, they often make a big deal out of something that can be easily and quickly resolved. One way to help make sure this does not happen is to take a minimalist approach with customers. Give a simple solution when something doesn't really require a full ISD approach. For example, instead of developing a formal training program, it may be sufficient to produce a simple job aid, provide some structured on-the-job training, provide a briefing on a new tool (if the audience already possesses the necessary prerequisites to use the tool), design a well-articulated communication (when trying to implement a change), or produce better user documentation when existing directions aren't clear. While some of these examples may be considered non-training solutions, the training organization can often provide these services because the skills necessary for providing these solutions are within the ISD skill set.

References

Fleming, M., & Levie, W.H. (1978). *Instructional message design.* Englewood Cliffs, NJ: Educational Technology Publications, Inc.

Gordon, J., & Zemke, R. (2000). The attack on ISD. *Training,* pp. 43–53.

Jonassen, D.H., Tessmer, M., & Hannum, W.H. (1999). *Task analysis methods for instructional design.* Mahwah, NJ: Lawrence Erlbaum Associates.

Kaufman, R., Rojas, A.M., & Mayer, H. (1993). *Needs assessment: A user's guide.* Englewood Cliffs, NJ: Educational Technology Publications, Inc.

Silberman, M. (1998). *Active training: A handbook of techniques, designs, case examples, and tips* (2nd ed.). San Francisco, CA: Pfeiffer.

Silberman, M. (1999). *The 1999 training and performance sourcebook.* New York: McGraw-Hill.

Sink, D.L. (2001). *Designing instruction for web-based training.* Monterey, CA: Darryl L. Sink & Associates, Inc.

Sink, D.L. (2001). *Project management for instructional development.* Monterey, CA: Darryl L. Sink & Associates, Inc.

Sink, D.L. (2001). *The course developer workshop.* Monterey, CA: Darryl L. Sink & Associates, Inc.

Sink, D.L. (2001). *The needs analysis workshop*. Monterey, CA: Darryl L. Sink & Associates, Inc.

Thiagarajan, S. (1997). *Framegames by Thiagi* (7th ed.). Bloomington, IN: Workshops by Thiagi, Inc.

Zemke, R., & Rossett, R. (2002). A hard look at ISD. *Training*, pp. 27–33.

Article 8

Front–End Analysis, Implementation Planning, and Evaluation*

Escaping the Pamela Syndrome

Harold D. Stolovitch, Ph.D.

Passion

We have a professional responsibility to our sponsors and clients.

Not too long ago, I was invited to a friend's home for dinner. I watched, intrigued, as their four-year-old daughter,

---

*A version of this chapter appeared in *Performance Improvement*, 2002, *41*(4), 7–9, Reused and updated with permission of the International Society for Performance Improvement.

Pamela, painstakingly put together a hundred-piece puzzle. The concentration, the frustration, the energy. The attempts to match color, shape, and pattern. Finally, the transcendent joy of success as Pamela triumphantly fit in the last piece. After a long and arduous struggle, she had finally succeeded in achieving her goal, despite all obstacles and adversity. As Pamela sat gazing at her completed puzzle, I leaned over and gently inquired what she was going to do with it. She stared at me for a few moments, blinked, and then, with a patient sigh—due, no doubt, to my obvious ignorance—informed me in a patronizing manner, "It'll go back in the box and onto my puzzle shelf." Marrying action to word, she pulled apart the puzzle she had been working on for so long and with so much effort, stuffed chunks of it into the box, placed it on her special puzzle shelf, drew another one down, and began afresh.

There is something inherently fascinating about putting things together. In the field of learning and performance, this attraction manifests itself very obviously in the time, effort, and resources we expend to create and build interventions. There is the rush and thrill we experience when we receive the green light to develop the training, create the performance-support tools, produce the job aid, or design the new curriculum. The work is intense. Drawing together all the disparate elements is a challenging, frustrating, yet in the end, exhilarating experience. We analyze, design, redesign, develop, try out, revise, and finally produce our learning or performance products. We have succeeded! We have completed the puzzle. Then, like Pamela, too often we place our latest masterpiece on the shelf (aka catalogue or LMS), where, after a short time, we abandon it in the frenzy of the next new challenge.

On Front-End Analysis, Implementation Planning, and Evaluation

One of the toughest tasks I encounter is persuading clients, and sometimes even colleagues, to focus on what appear to be the less-glamorous activities of performance improvement: front-end analysis, implementation planning, and evaluation. Of course, we all acknowledge how important these are. After all, every design and development model includes these three key elements. Yet when the new project is launched, we often find little more than lip service paid to these critical activities. Let's spend a moment on each of them.

Front-End Analysis

Is there any learning and performance professional who does not insist that the front-end analysis (FEA), the initial systematic diagnosis of "the gap," is an essential step? Yet after more than forty years in the learning and performance support field, I rarely encounter well-executed FEAs. Why is it such a hard sell, such a pitched battle to convince clients—and often trainers—of the critical importance of this vital set of activities? After all, it is FEA that establishes in a data-based way whether there is a gap between desired and actual performance, how this gap relates to business needs, and how important the gap is (magnitude, value, urgency). FEA identifies the factors affecting the gap and appropriate economical, feasible, acceptable solutions for eliminating it.

After much investigating and soul searching, I have come up with the answer to this apparent conundrum. It is because of client impatience to get the job done (and our fear that if we do not get busy doing it, the client will go elsewhere) and it is not as immediately reinforcing as developing an intervention. Like puzzles, it is more overtly rewarding to build the thing than to qualify and quantify gaps. At the end of an FEA, you have uncovered a great deal of information. Often you find out that making something, usually training, is either not necessary (dangerous conclusion) or insufficient (annoying conclusion). What joy and excitement is there in that? Certainly not as much as in designing and developing an electronic product complete with color and animation. In addition, not only do training groups, clients, and managers acquire a palpable product, but they also get to check off boxes showing that the planned-for learning and performance interventions have been completed. FEA simply does not seem to offer the same thrill.

Implementation Planning

Like FEA, implementation planning does not usually elicit a rush of creative excitement. This step focuses on the nuts and bolts of smoothly operationalizing whatever has been created. A number of years ago, I watched in fascinated horror as an automotive manufacturing company poured millions of dollars into a computer-based learning system that stumbled and finally crashed and burned.

That may have been the most dramatically poor implementation planning case I ever experienced. Nevertheless, I am consistently amazed at the enthusiasm and effort everyone is willing to expend on creating "things." I rarely encounter the same level of excitement toward planning and preparing for their implementation. Somehow, figuring out schedules, calculating available hours, counting manuals, and determining storage facilities or equipment requirements does not arouse the same level of emotional commitment that making a training video, an electronic performance support system, or an e-learning program does. Yet, when we analyze why our incredibly appropriate, creative solutions are not being used, we soon discover the myriad implementation obstacles we had not foreseen: production quota pressures, personnel cutbacks, new business priorities, insufficient equipment, equipment incompatibilities, technical snafus, travel restrictions, lack of supervisor preparation, and many more. Keep in mind that even the best training program poorly implemented has a lower probability of success than a not-so-well-designed program brilliantly implemented. This is also true for any performance intervention.

Evaluation

The only reason we create learning and performance tools, materials, or systems is to produce desired accomplishments efficiently. But how do we know when we have achieved success? The answer: through evaluation.

Every time we read a study or report about the evaluation of training or performance interventions, we learn (or at least rediscover) that, other than using smile sheets, very little of what we produce and implement is properly evaluated. The most recent industry reports from the American Society for Training and Development (ASTD) suggests that less than 5 percent of all workplace training receives any form of payoff evaluation. From my examination of the literature and review of so-called impact and return-on-investment studies, I would estimate the percentage to be significantly lower, since the ASTD data are derived from self-reports. In my own projects, evaluation is a tough sell. Cost, time, resources, management pressures, and lack of understanding of the benefits that evaluation data can provide are the main reasons for not committing to a thorough investigation of what our creative learning and performance interventions produce. Then, of course, there is always the magnetic draw of the next looming project.

What to Do

Despite this somewhat jaded portrait I have been painting, there is a great deal we should and can be doing. Allow me to continue on a more upbeat, optimistic note. I begin with my list of *"shoulds."*

Should–Dos

1. **Accept responsibility.** If too much attention is being placed on building interventions and not enough on

FEA, implementation planning, and evaluation, I contend that we as workplace learning and performance professionals are largely to blame. Business-minded people know that prior to investing in any venture, they have to conduct research and create a business case. So do we in the workplace learning and performance arena. It is our responsibility to provide our clients with clear arguments, precedents, and examples of the value of FEA, implementation planning, and evaluation. We have to turn our own inclinations away from the exciting design and development events and, while not neglecting them, raise our own motivation to emphasize the less-glamorous, but often more critical ones we have ignored.

2. **Educate ourselves.** I was partly horrified, partly amused, when I designed and ran an FEA at a large real estate corporation some years back. The client asked me to involve a half-dozen of his instructional designers in the effort as a learning experience. They all had master's degrees in instructional technology or human resource development. They were intrigued by the process and soon became very excited about it. In one of our early meetings, they all agreed that they had learned of such activities in their university curricula, but had not thought people actually did this "in the real world." Several had been working in industry for a dozen years or more!

   Surveys of learning and performance practitioners demonstrate over and over again how few of us really know how to conduct proper FEAs, build effective implementation plans, or carry out comprehensive evaluations. As a major "should," it is time we became more informed about what we are supposed to know and do.

3. **Fight for more respect.** As a professional group, we are often brought very late into a corporate project, given limited budgets and mandates, and then shackled with

impossible deadlines. This is not done out of malice, but out of a lack of understanding and even a lack of respect for our perceived contributions. We are viewed tactically rather than strategically. It is time we demonstrate what we can do beyond merely building things. It is time to show, with data, that we have the potential to contribute far beyond what many of our clients imagine.

4. **Seek out opportunities.** We all know the expression, "If you always do what you've always done, you'll always get what you've always got." We have not pushed hard enough to identify opportunities to perform FEAs, to insist on devising strong implementation plans, or to integrate sound evaluation methods and worth/ROI calculations for what we create. Every project has the potential to stretch further in these three areas. It is up to us to seek the opportunities and make the most of them.

5. **Demonstrate results.** Long ago, we established our ability to create intriguing training and performance products. We have shown that we can leap from one medium and delivery system to the next with ease. Recently, I sorted through boxes of materials my associates and I had developed over the years. I found among our archival treasures programmed instruction manuals, audiovisual training programs, audio- and video-based packages, interactive telephone testing kits, computer-based learning software, multimedia, intelligent tutoring modules, board games, simulation and role-play kits, and, of most recent vintage, webinars and e-learning modules that integrated a variety of interactive, synchronous, and asynchronous components. So many of us can demonstrate our abilities to design and develop wonderful interventions. When it comes to accompanying our marvelous creations with data on results, however, how quickly our pile of artifacts shrinks!

Can-Dos

With respect to what we can do, here is my starter list of recommendations:

1. **Seize the initiative on projects whether we are internal to the organization or an external resource.** Critically examine work requests, early project plans, and requests for proposals to identify weaknesses in the front-end logic and opportunities to demonstrate the value of strong implementation planning. Emphasize the steps beyond design and development that lead to desired performance results. Assume the responsibility of project success, but insist on all the necessary activities that will ensure desired results.

2. **Support and participate in professional development.** We need to build strength and expertise in ourselves and/or our organizations in FEA, implementation planning, and evaluation. Read, attend seminars, meet with specialists, collect credible cases, and identify mentors who can help you progress in your professional capabilities.

3. **Seek out articles and studies that demonstrate the relationship between solid FEA, implementation planning and evaluation, and valued accomplishments.** Highlight the salient parts of these publications and circulate them to clients and decision-makers. Proactively identify performance gaps or potential projects and demonstrate interest to become involved from the start. Gather and disseminate data early in a project's life. Demonstrate how we can contribute to initial decision making in valued ways. Leverage internal and external cases to show how, through early analysis, careful implementation, and systematic evaluation, we can make a major difference to the bottom line.

4. **Adopt an "account management" approach to clients.** Identify opportunities to improve performance by

conducting informal FEAs. Demonstrate how past implementation inadequacies decreased results or increased costs. Offer planning methods for avoiding these problems on new projects. Identify efficient, "natural" means for gathering evaluation data and show how this enhances the project's accomplishments.

5. **Emphasize results more than the characteristics of a solution.** Speak the language of business. Using FEA, build business cases for our learning and performance solutions. Use process and outcome evaluation methods to strengthen interventions and to show what the investment in learning and performance effort has produced.

Conclusion

Pamela is only four years old. She is right to invest energy and attention into making puzzles. Her job is one of discovering and learning. Her accomplishment is in putting the pieces together. She is not expected to close gaps or produce more efficient and effective results. After all, she is only four years old and her puzzle building is a form of creative play.

Like Pamela, we must never lose our childlike fascination with creation. However, unlike Pamela, we are learning and performance professionals. Our mission is to produce desired results. We cannot afford the luxury of endlessly building artifacts that will sit on shelves.

Resources

Combs, W.L., & Falletta, S.L. (2000). *The targeted evaluation process.* Alexandria, VA: ASTD Press.

Stolovitch, H.D., & Keeps, E.J. (2002). *Engineering effective learning.* San Francisco, CA: Pfeiffer.

Stolovitch, H.D., & Keeps, E.J. (2004). *Front-end analysis and return on investment.* San Francisco, CA: Pfeiffer.

Article 9

Creativity, Emergence, and the Design of Learning Experiences

Peter C. Honebein, Ph.D.

Passion

"Wow!" That's what I say when my students, whether they be undergraduates or working professionals, do something in class that is truly revolutionary and inspiring. When it happens, I know that the learning experience was well designed.

If you are reading this article, then perhaps you are stuck. Maybe you've got writer's block. Perhaps your motivation is low.

Perhaps you are just plain tired of redoing and repackaging what you did last month into yet another vanilla-flavored, template-based, cookie-cutter training course that earns 4.0 on the smile-sheet evaluations, where 5 equals extremely satisfied. In other words, you've entered a rut in which good training courses are just accepted, even though your heart yearns for the opportunity to design great training courses. And you don't know how to escape from that rut.

This article is about how to get unstuck from the same old patterns of course design. The ideas that I'll explore don't come from the left-brain, logical, ADDIE-driven instructional design processes. Innovation rarely comes from looking inward like this. Rather, I'll be taking you on a journey that explores ideas outside the stagnant field of training that can breathe life into your training designs. We'll explore how the principles of learning experiences and emergence blend with good-old systematic design.

A Brief History of Instructional Design

Why is it that our learners, the people we care deeply about in terms helping improve their performance, often have such low expectations about the training experience?

The answer lies in our recent history. The past hundred years or so have seen the exponential rise of numerous technologies by which we can communicate, and hence learn. Many of these technologies have been proffered as modern-day Nuremberg Funnels, the mythical device that enables teachers to "pour" knowledge into students' heads. Just as the ideals of the industrial age were to mass produce goods, training strategies evolved to mass produce competent performers. The emphasis was on systematic, left-brain methodologies designed to produce efficient training. Some enterprising instructional designers thought the process was so systematic that they created software programs, such as Designer's Edge, to help trainers do training design.

What we ultimately ended up with was good training. And we now have good tools to create good training: The ADDIE model, Mager's method for writing instructional objectives, Gagné's nine steps for sequencing instruction, Kirkpatrick's four levels of evaluation, and the list goes on. These tools are so well documented and discussed that you really don't need to buy the books—a quick search online should provide you a solid foundation.

However, the mindset you need to have is that the "good" training design tools we have now aren't enough to create "great" training. You need to bring something else into the mix.

Learning Experiences

After diligently studying the habits of creative people, University of Chicago psychology professor Mihaly Csikszentmihalyi succinctly captured the essence of creativity in a single sentence: "Creativity generally involves crossing the boundaries of domains." What this means is that if we are to move from being able to create "good" training to "great" training, we have to seek inspiration outside the world of instructional design. In fact, the science of instructional design was originally cobbled together from the ideas of a variety of different disciplines and domains. But as our design methods evolved, so did the barriers to entry for new ideas.

The same challenge was being experienced in the field of marketing. For years, the mantra of Product, Price, Promotion, and Place (the 4P's) guided marketers like blinders on a horse. Eventually, the ability to differentiate products and target them to specific market segments became more and more difficult. Products lost their uniqueness and became victim to commoditization, where price was the only difference.

So marketers turned to the domain of theater for inspiration. And from this domain was born the idea of *customer experiences.* What marketers found was that when you blended the core utility of a product with Joseph Pine's and James Gilmore's ideas of entertainment, education, esthetics, and escapism qualities, you could significantly differentiate the product and increase the product's economic value—the amount of money customers would pay for it.

I believe that these same ideas can be leveraged to the design of training. Rather than creating *courses*, you need to think of yourself as someone who is creating *learning experiences*. These learning experiences would blend the experience realms of entertainment, education, esthetics, and escapism into a compelling, economically rich solution. The economic value wouldn't necessarily be measured in price (although it could be, if your business is selling training), but rather the motivational value the course has on changing behavior and performance. Some current examples of these kinds of learning experiences include corporate theater, storytelling, even cooking. In 2006, 67,000 people paid to take learning experiences at the Viking Cooking School, a customer education program produced by the folks who manufacture the high-end Viking Range cooking appliances. The classes involve some entertainment (the banter of the professional chef teaching the class), education (culinary methods), escapism (the role of "chef" that students play during the class), and esthetics (the design of the kitchen classroom where the training takes place).

The creation of learning experiences requires some creative thinking about instructional strategies. For example, you might assign learners to play certain authentic roles in the course to satisfy the *escapism* quality. You might integrate into the course videos, fishbowl-style activities (like debates), and rich storytelling to address the *entertainment* quality. The quality of the furnishings, the art on the walls, the instructional graphics, the user interface, the clothes the instructor wears, even the music that's played, contributes to enhancing *esthetics* in the course. And performance-oriented content that is generated, sequenced, and presented using time-tested instructional design methods would provide the *education* in the course.

Encouraging the Wow! Factor

Another idea that I've found helpful in designing great learning experiences is that of *emergence*. Emergence is a design technique that fosters an environment in which learners can create tangible and innovative work products that cause instructors to say "Wow!" "Wow!" is what I say when my students, whether they be undergraduates or working professionals, do something in class that is truly revolutionary and inspiring. It may be projects they complete, the questions they ask, or statements of perspective they make. Whatever it is, I (and most likely the other students in my class) sit in silence for a moment while the full impact of what we've just witnessed is absorbed. It is brilliant, enlightening, and provocative. I say to myself, "That's way better than even I could have done."

Like learning experiences, the principles that enable emergent learning come from outside the instructional design domain, namely through a South African philosopher named Paul Cilliers. They are based on his work defining the qualitative attributes of complexity. Thus, a learning experience has a greater potential for emergence when it has the following qualities:

1. There are lots books, resources, and materials available to learners, and there are perhaps even a lot of learners (note that the instructor is also a considered a learner in emergent learning experiences).
2. The learners can communicate freely with one another, at any time.
3. Lots of information can be shared among learners.
4. What learners communicate is not predictable, and communication is not scheduled.

5. Most communication occurs at the person-to-person, one-to-one level.
6. Feedback is able to move freely between the learners.
7. New ideas, elements, and resources can enter the learning experience at any time.
8. The learning experience can change forms, such as from instructor-led to e-learning.
9. The learning experience keeps track of time, actions, events, and other data, and uses that data to manage interactions.
10. No single element, not even the instructor, holds the key to the purpose, behavior, or structure of the whole learning experience.

I have found that fully embracing the ideals of emergent learning really requires a learning experience to be blended. That means that it combines both instructor-led experiences and e-learning experience. A lot of the interactions and history can be facilitated on discussion boards available in most modern learning management systems (LMS). And the instructor-led experiences provide the context for feedback loops and face-to-face interactions. Some other ways that I have incorporated emergent learning into my learning experiences include:

1. Incorporating discussion boards into both instructor-led, e-learning, and blended training solutions. This enables greater interaction between learners, enhances the richness of those interactions, and keeps the learning experience "open."
2. Providing students examples and knowledge generated from previous classes. I call this "work product recycling." For one class I teach, I write detailed one-page critiques of student presentations. These critiques are then organized in a .pdf file and given to students in subsequent courses as an additional set of readings (now forty-five pages and

growing). This history captures and communicates a lot of the emergent knowledge that occurs in the course.

3. Engaging students in collecting and summarizing articles about a topic or content domain. To do this, I use an activity called "Knowledge Base" in learning experiences. For a given period of time, students must find articles related to course content, presentations, or readings. They then summarize and post that article to a discussion board. This engages students to be co-creators of knowledge by increasing the number of elements, articles and readings, available in the class. And, these article summaries become recycled work products for subsequent classes.

Conclusion

To design great learning experiences, you must go beyond the tried-and-true methods of instructional design. Creatively designing your courses as learning experiences and integrating the principles of emergent learning gives your learners an environment in which they can innovate, explore, and perform. The result is something that is much more than the sum of the parts, since it offers the possibility of amazing breakthroughs in the creation of new ideas and knowledge.

Article 10

Creating Sacred Space

Michael Milano

Passion

What a great challenge: a passion statement! On reflection, I realized I knew my passion long before I named it. Until eight years ago I knew in an intuitive way that I was drawn to training and to organization development because I love creating opportunities for people to tap into what they already know. Whether as a designer or facilitator, I was always more interested in the process of engaging learners than I was the specific content of the learning event. I loved finding ways to ask the right questions to open learners to something new; the right questions for them to apply what they already knew about the subject, about life, and about learning; the right questions to invite learners to determine the value of what was being learned.

> "The kind of teaching that transforms people does not happen if the student's inward teacher is ignored."
>
> **Parker J. Palmer (1998)**

Eight years ago I did some serious work creating that kind of space for myself in order to listen to and articulate my mission. To my great delight I discovered that my mission speaks directly to what I love—creating sacred space—that space in which people tell and really listen to their stories—that space in which people hear the voices of their inner wisdom. It became clear to me that this mission has always been guiding and undergirding my work. However, now that this is clear to me, it guides my work in a much more conscious way. Let me say more.

In our book, *Designing Powerful Training* (Milano & Ullius, 1998), Diane Ullius and I talk about three key characteristics of powerful training. We say powerful training is Effective, Efficient, and Engaging. I would like to briefly reflect on each of these characteristics, with special emphasis on Engaging, in the light of creating sacred space.

Effective

When we say that powerful training is *effective,* we mean that it impacts the learners' success on the job and/or in life. Designing effective goals and objectives helps learners to apply what they learn in the classroom to their lives. When we, as designers, think about what success means in any endeavor, we have to go beyond books, theory, and subject-matter experts—we have to consider the sacred space of the learners. We have to talk to people who are successful and trust that they know what is required. This isn't to say that we don't rely heavily on content experts to inform us, but we have to listen to real stories to know what is and is not essential. In addition, it means that when we articulate goals and objectives, we have to test them out with our learners: Do they resonate with what they understand to be their needs? If not, we need to listen more to what learners do understand as their needs. We need to trust their knowing.

Efficient

When we say that powerful training is *efficient,* we have a very simple measure for this: the learning isn't any more uncomfortable than it has to be. Learning often involves some necessary discomfort. To take in some new concept or skill, we might first have to struggle with old ones that bring us comfort by their familiarity. And, if we are honest as designers and facilitators, some unnecessary discomfort comes from poorly designed instruction. We can become so attached to a learning activity or technology that we *have* to include it in the design, even though the connection between the activity and what is essential to learn may be strained. To consider sacred space in relation to efficiency means taking learner evaluations seriously. It means asking honest questions about the learning itself and then using that data to redesign, even if it means letting go of our favorite activity. The questions can be pretty simple: What was that activity like for you? What do you see as the connection between that activity and the objectives/your work?

Engaging

It is the *engaging* characteristic of powerful training that I would most like to talk about, for this is where I believe the call and opportunity to create sacred space is strongest. Engaging, in our terms, means not only engagement between learners and facilitator and learners with each other but also the more subtle and more potent aspect of engagement, engagement between the learner and the content. And this engagement takes three main forms: cognitive, psychomotor, and affective engagement—all three aspects of the learner's inner wisdom. Malcolm Knowles taught us all well that the single thing that differentiates adult learners from younger learners is their experience. To paraphrase Knowles (1990): Adults do not just have their experience, they are their experience. Their experience is their story, and all new information has to find its way through the story experience if it is to have a place to be stored.

It is the designer's task to find ways to invite learners to dance with the new content, to engage the two realities, the personal and the new, so that real learning can take place. Those times when a learner says, "I'm uncomfortable doing this new step. It feels awkward" mean that on some level he or she realizes that he or she is being asked to change. Learning is happening and, rather than providing the correct answer to cut short the conversation about what the new content should mean to the learners, we must make space for it in our designs. The learner is saying: "I am going to have to let go of something I've held onto until now in order to make room for this new information. I have to decide whether I am willing to do that." Powerful design explicitly plans in moments and activities, sacred space, to foster this kind of personal and sometimes communal awareness and reflection.

It is the designer's job to create activities that bring the experience of the learner and the new content face to face. Even if the content is entirely new, the designer still has to engage the learners' capacity to know/learn. To me, this is the scared space in design because it invites the learner to be a teacher and to embrace the dance between inner wisdom and the learning event. Sacred space in design invites and engages learners' inner wisdom, and inner teachers. Sacred space invites learners to become active participants in the learning event.

There are some specific ways to engage learners in sacred space, and I'd like to end by spending a bit of time on three of them. First, back to objectives. Sacred-space objectives convey their respect for the learners. They honor what learners bring to the event and the simple truth that learners will make the final decisions about what meaning the learning has for them. Often we feel the urge to "sell" things to learners: new policies, practices, leadership skills. Yet we know that adult learners are independent; they are continually passing judgments about the utility of what is being presented—whether or not they voice those judgments. By formulating honest, sacred-space objectives, we begin the design process by committing to creating the space wherein learners will be invited to listen carefully to and honor their judgments. We write objectives like: "By the end of this training you will be able to name what most excites you and most concerns you about being responsible for implementing this new policy." And, once we have committed to that objective, we are bound to create learning activities that support it. We find ourselves creating discussions and worksheets that ask people to stop throughout the training and reflect—i.e., to listen to their inner wisdom interacting with what they are learning.

And that is the second way designers create sacred space in learning: by explicitly including two kinds of activities. In the first, the activities bring together what learners already know and the new content. They ask learners to bring their information processing to consciousness and to compare and contrast, to name what is going on. In addition, they send a powerful signal that it is okay to talk about this process in sacred space. The second kind of activity gives learners time and tools to reflect on the meaning of what they are learning: these activities invite inner teachers to give voice to their wisdom.

Finally, the questions we design to initiate the kinds of learning activities just described are powerful ways to create sacred space. By avoiding using leading questions we send clear signals that we are not looking for the *right answer*. Even more powerful is designing specific questions that ask learners to compare what they are learning with what they already know, or to listen to what the new learning means to them. For example, the designer might build a discussion into a customer-service skills class that begins with: "Imagine yourself using this new skill with a very difficult customer. What will come easily to you? What will be challenging? How do you imagine you will feel?" And, in the spirit of sacred space, the design could call for personal reflection followed by sharing for those who wish to do so.

Sounds idealistic? It is, and I believe deeply that it works. We know people are more likely to transfer from the learning event to real life what they believe will be useful and that which fits their values. In that sense creating sacred space is effective. However, to me the more evocative and compelling reason for creating sacred space as designers is counter-cultural and deeply spiritual. We are, every day, bombarded by new information, messages about who we have to be to be successful. Sacred space invites people to listen to what they already know about the world and themselves, to see themselves as teachers—not just in this particular learning moment but in their lives. We so often hear about empowerment as if someone is empowering someone else, giving them power. Sacred space empowers by inviting learners into their own wisdom, their own power. Imagine the freedom of coming to trust your own inner teachers as a source of wisdom.

Conclusion

I encourage you to try this: Read through a few designs through the lens of sacred space. Where do you see evidence that learners are being invited to integrate their experiences with what is being presented, listen to their reactions and judgments, and, maybe even voice those out loud so that the communal story with all its diversity might be heard? And then listen to your own inner wisdom, your teachers, about what this means to you. Namaste!

References

Knowles, M.S. (1990). *The adult learner: A neglected species.* Houston, TX: Gulf.

Milano, M., & Ullius, D. (1998). *Designing powerful training: The sequential-iterative model.* San Francisco, CA: Pfeiffer.

Palmer, P.J. (1998). *The courage to teach: Exploring the inner landscape of a teacher's life.* San Francisco, CA: Jossey-Bass.

e–Learning Content— Sorting Through the Tonnage

A Quick Anatomy Lesson for Those on the "Buy" Side

Steve D. Bordonaro, M.Ed., and

Frank P. Bordonaro, Ph.D.

Passion

One key to successful talent development is to provide your people with the best learning assets you can find for the price. Your quest for quality is complicated by a need to master e– and blended learning solutions, where content proliferates and varies widely in quality. We think we can help!

Many talent management and learning staffs have an irreducible mountain of e-content to review and evaluate. No sooner do they stock the LMS than another batch of courses comes on the market. Quality is uneven; titles proliferate with little expansion of coverage; promising topics flatten at the desktop; the gems are there, but where? Shopping can be inefficient and frustrating.

Alignment between learning and performance requirements (competencies, transferable skills, knowledge, and technical mastery) is the first screen, but there remains the huge issue of *content effectiveness and quality.* We asked ourselves: How can we help talent and learning professionals quickly get a grip on the most important features of e-learning content so that they can sort through and choose well?

The trick is to go underneath the surface and look at the learning structure itself. *The basic unit of e-content is called a learning object.* There are usually multiple learning objects/units/modules/lessons within a course. But the tried-and-true makeup, or building block components of a *complete* learning object, is powerful and something that one can evaluate fairly easily.

Specifically, learning objects have *five components*, appearing in any order, sometimes overlapping, and even sometimes repeating, but always easy to recognize: They are:

1. Tell
2. Show
3. Do
4. Review
5. Assess

Take a few minutes to dive into each component until you understand the basic purpose and know what to look for. After assessing a few learning assets, you will find these basic elements easy to spot—or detect that they are missing!

Tell

This element usually leads off the content with an overview of the whole learning object (or lesson).

A good learning object **"tell . . ."** is usually found on some sort of home page and:

- Briefly introduces an area or series of topics, including the content's boundaries
- Sets expectations for learning via the content to follow
- Provides clear objectives or asks essential questions that are relevant to the entire learning object
- Associates the student's participation/performance expectations with a specific timeframe (or duration)
- Engages the learner's intellect by explaining why the broader topic is important

Examples of *engaging learners via a Tell:* For a course in *Accounting*: "In a recent poll of major CEOs say a grasp of finance has become required knowledge in choosing the next generation of company leaders."

For a course in *Oral Communications*: "Wall Street analysts say they rely increasingly on conference call presentations in valuing stocks."

Show

The "show" comes early and is often adjacent to the "lesson's tell" or combined with it. The purposes of "show" are to deepen intellectual engagement and to evoke emotional energy toward the topic. Humans are powerfully affected by connections to issues and experiences they already understand.

Therefore, a good "**show**". . .

- Uses a compelling metaphor, analogy, example, or short story that places the essence of the topic in a context

   Examples: For that course in *Accounting: "Look* at the twelve photos above. What do these people all have in common? They served as CEOs for Fortune 500 companies. All were fired or resigned after a string of inaccurate earnings projections. Managers who served them did not accurately grasp the financial impact of day-to-day decisions."

   For that course in *Oral Communications*: Crowd shots showing protest demonstrations from around the world. "Who is always present when ordinary people do extraordinary things? The person at the podium, on the soap box, with the bullhorn, in front of the pack. Speaking skills—the leader's indispensable asset."

Do

This component is at the core of the learning sequence, designed to help the learner make a transition from simply absorbing to interacting with the material. It is a low-pressure ramp-up, in which the learner is asked to recall, interpret, or extrapolate content from the "tell" and the "show."

A number of on-screen devices may be used to allow interaction with content (from simple *click and drag* of items into categories, to *type-in* recall that completes the content, to creating and sharing documents, to discussing topics via asynchronous/synchronous text messages sent to co-learners or instructors). If the learning object is advanced, the "do" might require production of actual (or simulated) work, and the feedback may be in the form of guidance or checkpoints for the learner to self-assess or receive feedback from a live "coach."

Regardless of form, a good "**do**"...

- Is a fun or intriguing content/people interaction (activity)—a warm-up, sometimes with a game-like quality
- Describes boundaries, rules, or criteria by which the student (player) will score
- Provides an interactive environment that tests early mastery without stressing the learner
- Builds knowledge and confidence for the elements to follow

Examples: *Accounting course:* "In the left column, you see a list of items that have a dollar value assigned to them (rent, materials and supplies, shipping fees, accounts receivable, etc.). Drag each item to the columns at the right to form your P&L statement. After you have placed all items, click on Submit to see how you did. This exercise allows you to repeat your assignment until you have all items placed correctly. Need more explanation? Just roll your cursor over any item to learn why a certain item belongs where it does."

Oral Communications course: "Below, you see three possible opening paragraphs for a speech called We Need to Eat More Green Beans! Each paragraph is written to have a distinct effect on the audience. After each paragraph, choose from the list of intended effects boxed above (as 'appeal to health concerns,' 'invoke national pride,' 'sell flavor and eating pleasure,' etc.). Drag the purpose you think is best served by that paragraph. At the end, click on Professor Bean, who will talk to you about the correct answers and tell you some examples from great speeches in history."

Review

Think of this component as the natural counterpoint to the "tell." Its purpose is to reinforce the main topics promised in the "tell."

In a "teacher-led" online environment, the review may be class participation to review the previous "do." If the object is strictly digital, the review may be handled with simple bullet points or may be more visually engaging. Often, the "do" and "review" are repeated until the student or class is ready to move on to the assessment.

A good **"review"**. . .

- Repeats all of the main points in the "tell," with language and visual consistency to strengthen the association
- Enriches the original main points to bring in material that was delivered in the "tell," "show," and "do."
- Shows examples of successful performance, parallel to the learning objectives promised in the "tell."
- Provides (when possible) a forum for conversation, such as a threaded discussion, to allow students and instructor to regroup on all topics and subtopics covered in the "tell," "show," and "do." Main points and details are hashed out and clarified for all, before moving on to the final assessment.

Examples: *Accounting:* "Now that we've covered our lesson on financial decision making and you've had a chance to work through the case study, what would you argue is most important to the financial decision makers at the Healthy Beverages Company: Cost of Goods Sold, Return on Assets, Cash Flow? You decide. Respond to this topic in the threaded discussion, and then provide your reactions to two of your peers' responses."

Oral Communication: "After completing all of the practice items, let's review the main elements of a strong, persuasive argument. They are. . . ."

Assess

This final component is a measure of retention and comprehension. Assessments are keyed to observable measures that can be clearly spotted by software or (if more qualitative), by online instructor.

A good "**assessment**"...

- Tests for the *level* of student performance promised in the *"tell's"* objective (for example, if an *application* was mentioned in the objective, the assessment tests for application, rather than simple recognition of concepts)
- Covers all of the main elements listed in the Review
- Provides clear and specific feedback revealing gaps in mastery, with opportunities to remediate

Examples: *Accounting* (from the "tell"): "Analyze the accuracy of the department's forecasted budget."

Accounting Assessment: "Compare your actual department performance to the forecasted budget benchmarks."

Oral Communication Objective (from the "tell"): "Write engaging and mission-relevant slide notes."

Oral Communication Assessment: "Use Professor Flat's slide presentation in the lesson's example and replace his flat dialogue with an active voice that (1) speaks clearly to the topic, (2) informs, and (3) engages your audience."

No matter how loose or tight, the correlation between objective and assessment brings the learning object full circle.

Do you find cases in which the "assess" is left out of the learning object? That probably means the designer is counting on a final, larger test that will cover all of the learning objects for a particular course. We disagree; assessment should be included within each learning object, because it offers two advantages (1) content flexibility—the learning object becomes "stand-alone," and "reusable" to new contexts with little or no rework and (2) performance visibility—each assessment represents an individual student record of performance, a data point that can be tracked, queried, and used to assess not only the student but the test, course, instructor, and program performance over time. That way, areas of the content are easily retrieved and fine tuned as needed.

Below is a simple checklist that summarized all of the elements we have discussed. You can use this to review any learning object. As a shortcut, we recommend a quick pass to check for completeness. If an object does not include treatment of any one element, and you can't easily supply it, drop that asset and move on.

Tell

- Topic and boundaries
- What learner will learn
- Why important

Show

- Deepens intellectual interest in topic
- Engages learner emotionally

Do

- Is fun
- Provides low-stress practice
- Builds knowledge/confidence

Review

- Repeats "tell"
- Enriches "tell" with "show" and "do" material
- Gives examples of positive performance versus learning objectives

Assess

- Tests at level promised in "tell"
- Covers all elements in "review"
- Provides feedback and remediation

Conclusion

One key to successful talent development is to provide your people with the best learning assets you can find for the price. Your quest for quality is complicated by a need to master e- and blended learning solutions, where content proliferates and varies widely in quality. We've provided a **structural view** of the learning object, the basic unit of content. We've also offered some value judgments about what content should be better than others. With factors such as technical compliance, reliable tracking, and alignment with your learning agenda, you have enough to wrestle with. Meanwhile, your job as content reviewer can now be a bit easier and more rewarding.

Blended Learning Strategies for Knowledge Workers That Work

Deborah Stone, CPT, Steve Villachica, Ph.D., CPT, and John Endicott

Passion

Make invisible problem-solving skills visible, through real-world practice, in authentic situations, modeled by living, breathing experts, is easier than you think.

We are junkies for expertise. Cognitive mojo, instinct, voodoo . . . whatever you call it, it's the mental stuff in the heads of people whose jobs consist of consist of novelty, creative decision making, and problem solving. It surrounds us in expected and unexpected places—from Columbo, the raincoat-clad detective, mumbling the last question that nails the perp, to the mechanic who can diagnose your car just by listening to the engine, to the master chef who, through judicious mixing and application of heat, can magically transform raw ingredients into a gourmet delicacy.

But as anyone who has tried to obtain a recipe from a chef can tell you, capturing expertise can be an interesting. Much of what experts know is automatic and invisible, so they often are unable to articulate what makes them experts. And traditional classroom approaches lead to knowledge that learners possess but cannot apply.

So how do people learn how to think? One way is through blended learning: a "big tent" approach to training that mixes classroom and technology-based delivery, online and offline components, and formal and informal learning experiences. And while blended learning is an excellent approach for teaching problem-solving skills, too many designers focus exclusively on the technologies. While the technology delivered training offers increased access and efficiencies, instructional strategies add the "bang" to blended learning for knowledge workers. In this article, we will show you some powerful instructional strategies—which some ivory-tower folks and the gurus at the *Harvard Business Review* label "cognitive apprenticeship." These strategies work together as a system to make your novices think and perform more like experts.

Model Expert Performance Using Role Plays, Video, and/or Audio

As sandlot philosopher Yogi Berra observed, "You can observe a lot just by watching." Showing learners what you want them to do is much more effective than telling them. You can use streaming audio and video, comic-strip sequences, guest presenters, or simulated role plays to show an expert thinking out loud about a situation, making a decision, and experiencing the consequences of that decision. In short, modeling lets your learners see how to "talk the talk" and "walk the walk."

Figure 12.1 shows an example of training DLS created for managing partners of a large insurance company. In addition to ensuring high sales volume and overseeing compliance, these managing partners had to defuse delicate interpersonal conflicts. Using experts to interpret conflicting compliance issues and actors to model correct and incorrect ways of responding to compliance issues while at the same time dealing with a host of

Figure 12.1. Sample DLS

interpersonal conflicts, resulted in a powerful training that "rang true" to the managing partners.

Of course, who you choose as your models makes all the difference in the world—which brings us to the next strategy.

Use Experts as Coaching "Narrators"

When you need to model a process or procedure, there's no substitute for letting your students learn from the best. The message simply has a greater impact and authenticity when it is derived from actual experts in the field—ideally opinion leaders in your organization or industry whose reputations precede them.

Figure 12.2 shows how we used "virtual experts" in a course designed to teach pharmaceutical sales reps how to set up a speaker's program. Top performers at the client organization were chosen to narrate the training, introduce lessons, pose questions, and provide feedback to student responses.

Of course, for every expert there is an equal and opposite expert. If your organization wants to standardize an approach, use a steering committee to work with the dueling experts. If there are multiple acceptable ways to accomplish a task, then let the complexity of the topic drive the way you apply this instructional strategy. Use separate experts or virtual coaches for basic content to novices; use multiple experts or teams higher-level courses. But regardless of the complexity of the content, you can add relevance and interest by using seasoned experts.

Situate Learning and Performance in Authentic Settings

The U.S. military has a saying: "Train how you fight; fight how you train." That is, learners need to practice new skills in the same contexts in which they will apply them on the job.

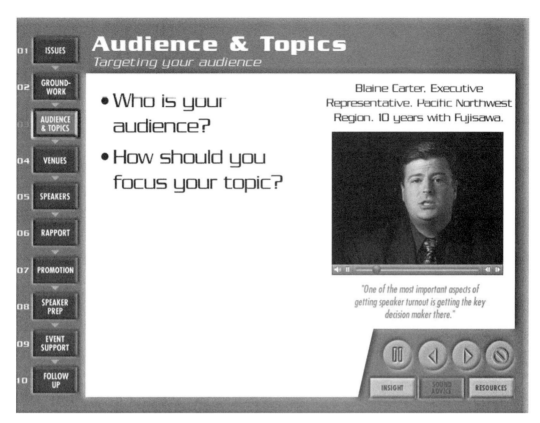

Figure 12.2. Sample "Virtual Expert"

Regardless of the medium, you can build situated practices into your training through vignettes, simulations, or embedded case studies whereby learners solve a real problem that resembles, as closely as possible, the ones they will encounter on the job. Ideally, such case studies should be based on events that actually happened.

The training DLS created for examiners of a regulatory organization who audit securities firms used situated learning extensively. When examiners in the real world conduct exams, they spend a lot of time creating and reviewing files. Our e-learning required them to do the same: opening an online "file cabinet" to review relevant information. As Figure 12.3 shows,

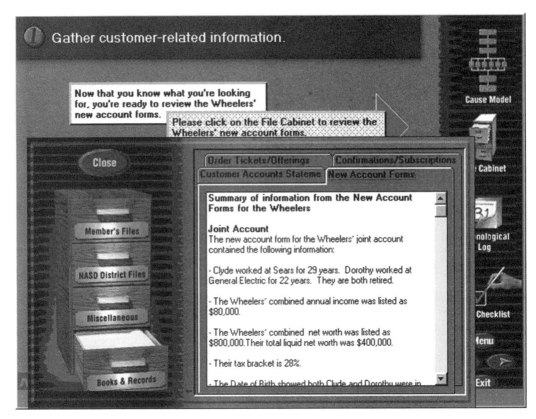

Figure 12.3. Online File Cabinet

the files in our online file cabinet were organized the same way examiners would see them during a real exam. Over the course of a lesson, the contents of the file cabinet grew as new information is uncovered.

There is nothing like the expressions that appear on learners' faces when they apply their skills for the first time, working through a real-life case with the same resources and processes they will encounter on the job. Only when they've practiced solving problems and making decisions have they really learned how to do it.

Teach the Mental Models, "Rules of Thumb," and Process Controls That Guide Expert Performance

Part of what makes teaching knowledge work so interesting is the invisible nature of the skills experts employ. But you can make these skills visible through such techniques as mental models: graphic depictions of what experts do in their minds. These mental models often include "rules of thumb" (heuristics) and process controls ("What do I do next?") that experts cannot articulate, even though they use them automatically, on a daily basis. By representing these ethereal thought processes and decisions graphically, via a flowchart, table, or diagram, you can make them come to life. Even your experts may learn something!

For the examiner training, DLS modeled the process examiners employ when auditing securities firms. To generate this model spoke with managers and project stakeholders, interviewed twenty subject-matter experts (SMEs), and conducted focus groups with less-experienced examiners to identify gaps in their knowledge and skills from those of the experts.

By the time we were finished, we'd spoken with 103 examiners, comprising approximately one-third of the total population. But we had something to show for our efforts: a powerful visual tool that gave our training the points of reference it desperately needed to organize training on an inherently messy process.

Figure 12.4 shows how this process was used to organize the major lesson objectives. These objectives remained the same for each of the six lessons, which helped learners integrate with and build on what they'd learned in earlier lessons.

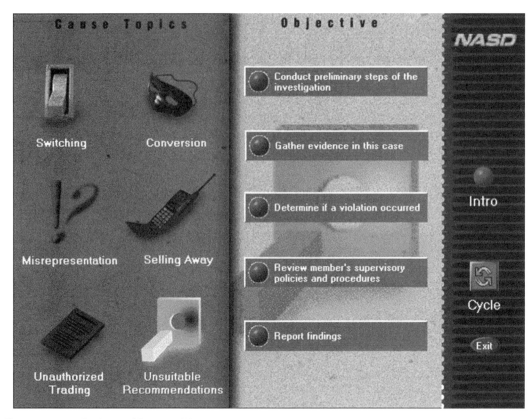

Figure 12.4. Outline of Major Objectives

Use Articulation and Reflection Loops

Give your learners first-hand reasoning experience by having them think through problems out loud (articulation), then compare their thinking to that of an expert (reflection). You can use this strategy regardless of the medium. For online training, you can add open-ended questions comparing what the learner would do to the expert's response. For offline training, you can apply the same process in a coaching and mentoring session via "think-alouds." Having learners put their thinking into words gives them a deeper insight into their assumptions and reasoning—which they can then improve by comparing their responses to those of an expert. Figure 12.5 shows articulation and reflection loops incorporated into training for analysts.

Employ Scaffolding to Enable Learners to Perform Real Tasks Until They Master Them

When you first learned to ride a bicycle, you probably had the aid of a pedagogical resource known as "training wheels." Attached to the rear of your shiny cruiser, these training wheels let you practice riding before you had fully mastered the motor skills or balance you needed to ride unassisted. After a little

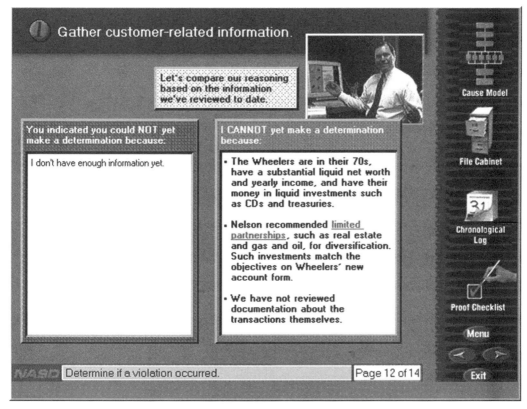

Figure 12.5. Articulation and Reflection Loops

practice, you were ready to adjust the wheels so that only one supported you at a time. Finally, you could remove the wheels altogether.

Simply put, scaffolding is a way of providing "training wheels" for the mind in the form of pacing, job aids, cue cards, or even "novice" views of software. These mental training wheels give learners confidence in their abilities and let them practice with increased complexity and diversity, over time. As they develop their skills and master the content, you can gradually "fade" (remove) the scaffolding—just as the scaffolding for a building is removed once the building can stand by itself.

We built scaffolding into a performance support system created for a securities regulator. Designed to support examiners as they investigate securities firms, the tool includes a built-in training component that stepped novice examiners through the exam process, from front to back. As Figure 12.6 shows, novices can display pop-up support for each field they complete in the software: in this case, an exam number.

Novices who need more scaffolding support can use the "coach" function. This additional layer provides more information about the details of preparing an exam, as if an expert were looking over your shoulder, ready with quick explanations and details. As novices become more competent and experienced, they can remove the training wheels by "turning off" one or both levels of scaffolding.

Conclusion

Translating the problem-solving and decision-making skills experts employ on the job to the less experienced employees is critical to the future of today's workforce. Short of a Vulcan mind meld, there is no magic bullet. But by incorporating this chapter's simple, yet powerful instructional strategies for making these invisible skills visible to others, you can enable your learners to think more like experts and create the bang in your training.

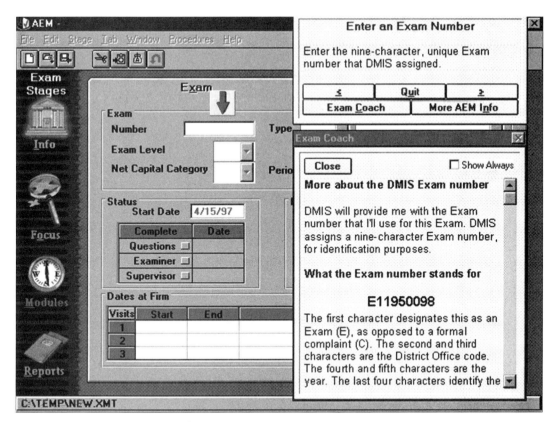

Figure 12.6. Pop-Up Support for a Field

Confessions of a Gamer

I See Games

Steve Sugar

Passion

Have you ever seen a learning game that gets participants so energized, so involved, so committed to game play that they experience the topic from the inside? HIS is my payoff! THIS is what drives me to write the next game.

"I saw an angel in the marble and worked to set him free."
Michelangelo Buonarroti

My Passion, Defined

George Balanchine, the great ballet master, was asked whether he could predict future greatness by simply observing the performance of a five-year-old student dancing ballet.

"Why, yes," he replied, "I think I can."

"Is it the child's grace or athletic ability?" asked the interviewer.

"Not at all," replied the ballet master. "I simply look at those students who fling themselves about the room without any concerns for how they look to others. It is those students who are willing to do anything, even fail, who become the great ones."

Like that young ballet student, I have no problem in 'flinging' myself into each new game—no matter how foolish I may look to checkout clerks; no matter that I resemble a "bag man" as I drag bags of assorted game paraphernalia across campus and into the classroom. My payoff is watching passive participants become active players, players so wrapped up in the game that they experience the topic first-hand.

In my thirty years of creating classroom games, the most frequently asked question is: "Where do you get ideas for games?" My response is simply this: "I 'see' games." That is, when inspired by a "prompt"—an object, catch phrase, or event—I envision developing a pattern of play around the prompt into a game. My goal is to present the topic from a different perspective; ultimately, to create a new learning experience that allows the student to see the key learning points, again, for the very first time.

My creative process is more of a trial-and-error process than of instant discovery. First, I am inspired by a prompt, such as an object (ugly plate), catch phrase (RAT Race), or event (movie scene). This prompt initiates an ongoing write, review, and rewrite process that culminates in a game readied for classroom play. Then the real work begins as I bring my newly designed game before a live audience. From observations of the quality of play and from participant feedback, I begin a triage of saving or discarding parts or all of the game. If saved, the game is prepared for another pilot run. In other words, you don't have to be crazy to write games, you have to be crazy and persistent.

Still confused? Then please allow me to present three cases of how I see and then develop games.

Case One: Object (the Ugly Plate)

The Prompt

While visiting a local L.L. Bean store, I saw an ugly plate appropriately sitting in the "clearance" section. My inspiration was a 14-inch round plastic "chip and dip" serving platter, ringed with alternating patriotic red, white, and blue stripes. I assumed this little beauty was left over from the recent July 4th holiday. But, where the average customer saw an ugly plate, I "saw" a target throw game.

I carried the entire stock of six plates to the register, where the two checkout clerks looked at each other, as if to say: "Can you believe what this idiot is buying?!" In retrospect, they were right! These six plates were ugly enough to offend even the most patriotic citizen.

The Process

What I "saw"' in the plate was the basis for a qualify-and-score review game. And so I began working on the review game, *Champions*, as a test preview game for my college classroom—an undergraduate management class at the University of Maryland Baltimore County (UMBC). My plan or game flow was: (1) players qualified by correctly answering topic questions, (2) each correct answer earned a target throw, and (3) players take target throws to earn points. After write-ups and many revisions, the game was ready for play.

The Game

Champions (Sugar & Willett, 2005)

- Divide class into three or more teams.
- Distribute a five-question quiz to each team.
- Have teams take the quiz and hand in their quiz sheets.
- Award one target throw (at the ugly plate) for each correct response.
- Have each team select a throwing "champ" to take the earned target tosses.
- Score as follows:
  - Each throw into the bull's eye (dip portion of plate) = 5 points
  - Each throw into target area (edge of plate) = 2 points
  - Each throw not in target area (off the plate) = 0 points
- All rounds are played the same.
- The team with the most points wins.

The Outcome

The response to *Champions* was immediate. Heretofore "sit-and-stare" students now scrutinized each question, critically aware of the difference(s) between correct and incorrect responses. Then interest turned to frenzy as students cheered on every target throw. *Champions* seemed to tap into that reservoir of energy college students left at the classroom door. From its impressive debut, *Champions* has become the most popular game in the course.

Case Two: Event (the Movie Scene)

The Prompt

For the past two Bucknell reunion dinners, I have conducted the well-known icebreaker, *Autograph*—the "find-someone-who" signature hunt in which players obtain the signatures of those who fulfill the requirements, such as finding someone who "owns a sports car," etc. This all-too-familiar game, however, is oft used in business, school, and church orientation programs. When a classmate commented that this game went much better than her previous experience, I knew it was time to re-invent the game.

While watching the 1936 movie, *My Man Godfrey* (Carole Lombard and William Powell), I marveled at the energy created by the opening scavenger hunt scene. This inspired me to begin adapting Autographs into a scavenger hunt that was conducted from the participants' table.

The Process

My first step was to use the familiar Bingo matrix as the game sheet. Within each square I wrote a clue for an item that had to be "resourced" (found or produced) at the table. Many of the clues were written in a way that encouraged players to create OR find the item.

- "Type of pie" could be a bakery item OR a pie-chart created on a napkin.
- "Something clubby" could be a piece of wood or a membership card.
- "Something musical" could be the ring of a cell phone or a group song.

I created the game sheets on 5 × 5 tables and produced one sheet for each team.

The Game

Scavenger Bingo (Sugar & Willett, 2005)

- Divide class into three or more teams.
- Distribute one game sheet to each team.

- Have teams produce items that meet the criteria for each space.
- Have teams cover spaces on the game sheet when they have located the specified item.
- The team with the most spaces covered wins.

The Outcome

I found this game worked equally well as an icebreaker or creativity exercise. Players automatically grouped around their game sheets and then began the team-like process of assigning roles—some players foraging for items, other players huddled in problem-solving groups. I am always impressed with the increased energy level and delighted by the creativity and quality of the items produced in response to the game sheet clues.

Case Three: The Catch Phrase (RAT Race)

The Prompt

Perhaps you have taken Dr. Sarnoff Mednick's "**R**emote **A**ssociation **T**est" (or *RAT*) used by MENSA to measure creativity and problem-solving in their candidate screening. The *RAT* process—the main attraction of the game—requires the candidate to associate different remote word-concepts through the use of a fourth or "link" word.

For example, solve this RAT by finding a "link" word that can be placed before OR after each of these three words

➔ ___lip___   ___yard____   ____shift____.

Solution: stick—lipstick, yard stick, stick shift

The Process

My first generation RAT Race involved teams negotiating an estimate (time contracts) of how long it would take them to solve a set of five RATs. Then the teams raced the clock to meet their contract and solve their RATs. Later, team builder George Takacs refocused this game into a team-learning event by establishing a fixed contract time (ninety seconds) and introducing a facilitation process used between rounds of play.

The Game

RAT Race (Sugar & Takacs, 2000)

- Divide class into teams of five or six players.
- Distribute a set of five RAT puzzles to each team.
- Have teams solve all five RAT puzzles within ninety seconds.
- *Score the game in the following way:*
  - Award 13 points to each team that solves all five RATs.
  - Deduct 8 points to each team that do not solve all five RATs.
- All rounds are played the same.
- The team with the most points wins.

The Outcome

RAT Race produces an unusual "love-hate" relationship with players. Players love the mini-successes of solving each RAT; but, teams hate the punitive scoring—an 8-point penalty if you do not solve ALL five RATs. In ten years of conducting this game, I have found that it is this lack of scoring that drives teams to revisit their individual and group behaviors, creating a rich and instructive dialogue about team learning.

Conclusion

My question to you is: How might you surprise your classroom participants or individual clients and have them experience a topic from the inside out? In other words, how might you create the space wherein they learn something as if for the "very first time?" Have fun in the classroom—take risks—learn how to fling yourself across the room with no regard on how you look to others!

References

Sugar, S., & Takacs, G. (2000). *Games that teach teams.* San Francisco, CA: Pfeiffer.

Sugar, S., & Willett, C. (2005). *Games that boost performance.* San Francisco, CA: Pfeiffer.

Conclusion to Section One

So you've just had a whirlwind tour of passion, ideas, and practices.

I hope this foray into instructional design has stirred your pot. In fact take a few minutes and write down your instructional design passion statement and then email it to me at terrence@ makingstories.net.

Inquiring minds like mine need to know. I've learned so much speaking with this great group of folks that I'm all revved up to write a new course for one of my clients.

However, there are days when I swear I will never write another course. I just want to throw the materials out. That turns out not to be a bad idea; at least in spirit. What happens when a group of learners assembles is sacred. One thing's for sure; it's never the same. If what we design can act more as a guide than a literal map, I believe we come closer to actualizing the organizational and personal imperative of real-time learning. If we were public training companies forced to repeat the same learning experience over and over again with little to no variation between events, I might have more tolerance for a more controlled approach to instructional design. That's just not the case for most of us. Even when we need to train specific behavioral responses there is more latitude to how we can move folks from point A to point B.

That being said, it's an exciting and humbling time in the field of instructional design. Never before have we been faced with so many wonderful technologies, delivery strategies, and increasing research to help us understand how we learn.

There are no right answers but here are a few of the questions that keep me up at night:

1. How will instructional design change over the next ten years? What can we learn from the field of complexity that can we apply to learning? How will advances in neuroscience and cognitive science change our field?
2. Will the pace of information and the technologies we use to communicate learning substantively change the process and principles we use, or will the same principles hold for different delivery mediums and or a decrease in development time?
3. Do we really need to design courses at all?
4. What if design were done in real-time, where course are co-created by participants? For what sort of topics would this approach work for? Which ones would it not work for? What sort of skills would trainers need to have?
5. Given the diversity of topics and performance results we are asked to produce learning for, is it realistic to think instructional design is a robust and flexible enough disciplines to guide us? What other disciplines can we use to inform us?

Here is a list of other books and resources for you to explore. In the next section we will look at delivering training.

Designing Training Resources

Articles on the Web

Locating "Project Management" Inside the Instructional Design Process by Charlene Muir Benjamin, M.S.

Talent Development Solutions—A Buyer's Checklist by Frank P. Bordonaro, Ph.D.

Further Reading on Designing Training

Austin, R. (2002). Managing knowledge workers: Evolving practices and trends. *Science: Next Wave.* Retrieved 2/16/2007, from http: // sciencecareers.sciencemag.org/career_development/previous_issues/ articles/1470/managing_knowledge_workers.

Beruvides, M.G., & Sumanth, D.J. (1987). Knowledge work: A conceptual analysis and structure. In *Productivity Management Frontiers-I* (pp. 127–138). London: Elsevier Science.

Brown, J.S., Collins, A., & Duguid, P. (1989). Situated cognition and the culture of learning. *Educational Researcher, 18*(1), 32–42.

Casey, C. (1996). Incorporating cognitive apprenticeship in multi-media. *Educational Technology Research & Development, 44*(1), 71–84.

Claburn, T. (2006). Wikis, blogs slow the mail avalanche. InformationWeek, 1113, 58–59.

Clark, R.E. (1994). Media will never influence learning. *Educational Technology, Research & Development, 42*(2), 21–29.

Clark, R.E., & Blake, S.B. (1997). Designing training for novel problem-solving transfer. In R.D. Tennyson, F. Schott, N.M. Seel, & S. Kijkstra (Eds.), *Instructional design perspectives. volume 1: Theory, research, and models* (pp. 183–214). Mahwah, NJ: Lawrence Erlbaum Associates.

Collins, A., Brown, J.S., & Holum, A.(1991). Cognitive apprenticeship: Making thinking visible. *American Educator: The Professional Journal of the American Federation of Teachers, 15*(3), 6–11, 38–46.

Cross, R., Laseter. T., Parker., A., & Velasquez, G. (2006). Using social network analysis to improve communities of practice. *California Management Review, 49*(1), 32–60.

Curtis, R, Leon, D., David Leon Partnership, & Miller, R. (2002, November/December). Supporting knowledge work with physical design. *Knowledge Management Review, 5*(5), 27–29.

Davenport, T. (2002). Can you boost knowledge work's impact on the bottom line? *Harvard Management Update, 7*(12), 3–4.

Davenport, T. (2005). *Thinking for a living.* Boston, MA: Harvard Business School Press.

Davenport, T., Thomas, R.J., & Cantrell, S. (2002). The mysterious art and science of knowledge-worker performance. *MIT Sloan Management Review, 44*(1), 23–30.

Drucker, P. (1974). *Management.* New York: Harper & Row.

Drucker, P. (2002, October). Knowledge work. *Executive Excellence, 19*(10), 12.

Ericsson, K.A., & Charness, N. (1994). Expert performance: Its structure and acquisition. *American Psychologist, 49,* 725–747.

Gargiulo, T.L. (2007). *Once upon a time: Using story-based activities to develop breakthrough communication skills.* San Francisco, CA: Pfeiffer.

Graham, C. L. (1996). Conceptual learning processes in physical therapy students. *Physical Therapy, 76,* 856–864.

Hammer, M., Leonard, D., & Davenport, T. (2004). Why don't we know more about knowledge? *MIT Sloan Management Review, 45*(4), pp. 14–18.

Harris, P. (2006). Beware of the boomer brain drain. *T+D, 60*(1), 30–33.

Jacobsen, A., & Prusak, L. (2006). The cost of knowledge. *Harvard Business Review, 84*(11), 34.

Lesgold, A., Lajoie, S., Brunzo, M., & Eggan, G. (1992). A coached practice environment for an electronics troubleshooting job. In J. Larkin & R. Chabay (Eds.), *Computer assisted instruction and intelligent tutoring systems: Establishing communications and collaboration* (pp. 201–38). Mahwah, NJ: Lawrence Erlbaum Associates.

Lesgold, A., Lajoie, S., Logan, D., & Eggan, G. (1990). Applying cognitive task analysis and research methods to assessment. In N. Frederiksen, R. Glaser, A. Lesgold, & M.G. Shafto (Eds.), *Diagnostic monitoring of skill and knowledge acquisition.* Mahwah, NJ: Lawrence Erlbaum Associates.

O'Byrne, K., Clark, R., & Malakuti, E. (1997). Expert and novice performance: Implications for clinical training. *Educational Psychology Review, 9,* 321–332.

Pulichino, J. (2004). *The trends in blended learning research report.* Santa Rosa, CA: The eLearning Guild.

Reich, R. (2005, April). Plenty of knowledge work to go around. *Harvard Business Review, 83*(4), 17.

Reigeluth, C.M. (1999). The elaboration theory: Guidance for scope and sequence decisions. In C.M. Reigeluth (Ed.), *Instructional-design theories and models—volume II: A new paradigm of instructional theory* (pp. 425–453). Mahwah, NJ: Lawrence Erlbaum Associates.

Ritchie, S.M., & Rigano, D.L. (1996). Laboratory apprenticeship through a student research project. *Journal of Research in Science Teaching, 33,* 799–815.

Roach, S. (1991, September/October) Services under siege: The restructuring imperative. *Harvard Business Review,* pp. 82–83.

Savery, J.R., & Duffy, T.M. (1996). Problem-based learning: An instructional model and its constructivist framework. In B.G. Wilson (Ed.), *Constructivist learning environments: Case studies in instructional design* (pp. 135–148). Englewood, Cliffs, NJ: Educational Technology.

Spira, J. (2005, February). Services under siege: In praise of knowledge workers. *KM World, 1,* 26–27.

Thurm, S. (2006, January 23). Companies struggle to pass on workers' knowledge. *Wall Street Journal,* p. B1.

Villachica, S.W., & Stone, D.L. (1998). CornerStone: A case study of a large-scale performance support system. In P.J. Dean & D.E. Ripley (Eds.), *Performance improvement interventions: Performance technologies in the workplace* (pp. 437–460). Washington, DC: International Society for Performance Improvement.

Villachica, S.W., & Stone, D.L. (2007). *Ten ways to better blended learning for knowledge workers.* Paper presented at the at the 2007 International Society of Performance Improvement International Conference, San Francisco, California. Retrieved 5/7/2007 from www.dls.com/1164_Blended_Learning.pdf.

Walker, D. (2006). Wiki-wild world. *Information Age.* Retrieved 2/14/2007 from www.information-age.com/article/2006/january/wiki-wild_world.

Williams, S.M. (1992). Putting case-based instruction into context: Examples from legal and medical education. *The Journal of the Learning Sciences, 2,* 367–427.

Wilson, B.G. & Cole, P. (1996). Cognitive teaching models. In D.H. Jonassen (Ed.), Handbook of research for educational communications and technology: *A project of the Association for Educational Communications and Technology* (pp. 601–621). New York: Macmillan Library Reference USA.

Wolff, E. (2005). The growth of information workers in the U.S. economy, 1950–1990: The role of technological change, computerization, and structural change. *Communications of the ACM, 48*(10), 38–42.

SECTION TWO

Delivering Training

Introduction to Section Two

I'm convinced that one of the fastest ways to become an effective trainer is not to know what you are doing. Maybe that's what people mean as "beginner's mind"? When I think back to some of my earliest experiences of delivering training, I didn't have a clue what I was doing or how I was supposed to do it. I contend this was responsible for developing me into the seasoned pro I am today.

A background in performing arts made me gutsy or perhaps foolish enough to stand in front of a group in a state of ignorant bliss; the rest I owe to all the groups that endured my awkward fits and starts. You see the groups taught me how to be a trainer. I let them teach themselves. It was an accident—I had no other choice. I stumbled upon a style that is now termed by some as "participant collaboration." By involving the group in an almost ceaseless stream of questions, I took the pressure off of myself and let the class teach itself. This is not sustainable, nor is it a substitute for developing the skills of a trainer, but it quickly taught me that training is more about enabling than anything else. I began to see myself as a conductor molding the sounds and tempos of the group. I was being paid more to be the eyes, ears, and heartbeat of the group than a single shining point of knowledge. And here is my first pearl of wisdom I have to share: Keen listening and sensitive observational skills are two of the most essential attributes of a successful trainer.

In hindsight it all makes sense. I've always been a passionate, relentless learner but hated school. I was the sort of kid who preferred to put cotton in my ears while the math teacher explained the steps involved in solving a certain kind of problem so I could go home at night and have the joy of figuring it out myself. Even if I couldn't figure it completely, I wanted the freedom to explore. I've become more sophisticated since then, if not more stubborn. I still like to figure things out; although if someone had handed me a manual with my two beautiful children, I swear I would've read it.

I've gained better appreciation for all the different learning styles and modes of learning. One of the challenges in our field is the vast array of significant and effective learning tools and techniques available to us. Training is not a one-size-fits-all industry. This makes it very tough on consulting guys like me who need to hang our hats on a single peg to collect our industry badge of expertise and win great consulting gigs.

In this section you are in for a real treat. We've assembled a first-rate crew of folks to act as navigators as we find our way through a rich field of possibilities. Let's take a peak at what you'll find in this section. There are twelve articles:

14. Make Adult Learning Come to Life
15. Making Workshops Work: Lessons from an Old Pro
16. Incredible Credibility
17. Enlarging the Pool of Participants at the Beginning of Any Training Event

18. How Learners Are Motivated
19. Applying Self-Determination to Training
20. The Best Training I Never Did
21. Some Basics from a Couple of Training Pros: Training Is More Than What You Say
22. The Synergy of Co-Facilitation: Creating Powerful Learning Experiences
23. Learnertainment®
24. Seven Strategies on How to Use Stories to Increase Learning and Facilitate Training
25. Dealing with Difficult Issues in Training

Preview of the Articles

Our first contributor has been a central super-star in our field. Jean Barbazette really knows how to tap into people's talents and make them shine. When I asked her for one sentence to sum up training delivery she said, "*Make adult learning come alive!*"

Our next contributor has a unique gift. I've watched Dr. Hal Kane in action dozens of time. Somehow he manages to develop amazing connections with everyone in his workshops, and yet he does so in a way that never violates people's personal space nor makes them feel uncomfortable. On the contrary, people open up and in the process he makes learning real. I think he's a magician at heart.

As I thought about what Hal shared with me, I felt compelled to add my two cents to the conversation. So the next article builds on Hal's ideas of connecting with our audience. I discuss how our challenge lies in winning the trust and respect of those in the classroom and how we need to be accessible to our attendees, sensitive to their needs, and responsive to their learning objectives.

Mel Silberman's groundbreaking work in active and experiential learning will long inform our work in the field. Mel insists that your training session will not spark active learning unless participants are eager to participate. And he give us simple easy advice on how to engage people right from the beginning.

Our next two articles deal with the often mysterious box of our learners. What do They want? What do they really need? Matthew Richter of The Thiagi Group is one of the few guys out there I know and trust to offer some very illuminating insights into this strange realm. In a two-part article Matthew gives us a handle on how to work with motivation to engage learners to achieve performance objectives. He helps us understand how we can create an intrinsically motivating environment for learners.

Our next contributor did not have any industry jargon to describe what he discovered—so what if Action Learning has been around for a while. Goes right back to what I was saying in the front of this introduction. It's really what all of the articles in this section in one way or another say— *"Deliver training in a way that enables people to drive the learning process for themselves as much as possible."* Glenn Smeaton's article titled "The Best Training I Never Did" could be turned into a jingle and become our industry top-forty hit song. What do you think?

Robb Murray and I team up to share five basic but powerful techniques for being effective with groups. Robb Murray is one of the brightest and most positive people I've ever met. His mind is a sponge. Given the opportunity, he aims his fascination at a subject or person and dives in with reckless intellectual abandonment. Robb's style of instruction follows suit. He shares a few of his techniques for how he spices up his classroom with both verbal and non-verbal responses to participants.

According to Dr. Vince Molinaro, co-facilitation is a dynamic way to enhance the learning experience for participants. Although it can be a challenging experience, when it goes well, it's one of the most rewarding peak experiences you will have. It is very gratifying to work with a trusted colleague to create synergy that leads to powerful learning outcomes for learners.

This next guy really knows how to marry learning with entertainment. If you haven't heard about Lenn Millbower already, I'm thrilled to introduce this dynamic luminary to you. He'll put a smile on your face and a jig in your step. Lenn shares with us the core principles of his training delivery philosophy in his article. When I asked him to be serious, he offered me the following summary of his passion: "*Entertainment-based content relaxes the right hemisphere, in effect, baby-sitting it, keeping it busy with things it likes: cartoons, music, games, activities, visuals. Once the right hemisphere is playfully engaged, learning can commence without negative blocking emotions. Attention is riveted on the positive aspects of learning.*"

Lenn got me all worked up. Stories are one of my specialties. I have found some very interesting and unconventional ways to use stories in training. If you haven't run out and bought all my books yet, than go take a look at my latest, *Once Upon a Time: Using Story-Based Activities to Develop Breakthrough Communication Skills*. There are some powerful story-based tools, techniques, and activities in the book. In the meantime, my article offers you seven strategies for using stories in training.

I wrap up our section on delivering training with a discussion of how to handle difficult issues when they come up during a training event.

So what are you waiting for? Dive right in and sample this smorgasbord of delectable training wisdom.

Article 14

Make Adult Learning Come to Life*

Jean Barbazette

Passion

Make adult learning come to life!

Many trainers are familiar with an experiential learning model that takes learners through a series of steps to process a learning activity such as a simulation. This type of debriefing discussion is helpful and appropriate for any type of learning activity. Here is a general description of what takes place during the

---

*Used with permission from *The Art of Great Training Delivery*, Chapter 1. San Francisco, CA: Pfeiffer. © 2006 Jean Barbazette.

five steps of adult learning. The successful trainer or facilitator guides adult learners through these five steps to gain the most from any learning activity used to achieve the learning objective. These five steps are similar to many experiential learning models.

1. Set Up the Learning Activity by Telling What, Why, and How

Set up the learning activity so that the participants understand *what* they are going to do (for example, read a case study and individually prepare answers for a discussion) and why they are doing it (learn about how to give a performance review). Adult learners become motivated when they understand the benefit to them of learning something new or the importance of objective for themselves. To understand *how* the objective will be met, give directions and ground rules regarding how the learning activity is to be conducted. The setup of a learning activity can include such things as:

- Tell participants the purpose of the learning activity and why they are going to learn from the activity without giving away what is to be "discovered"
- Explain what the participants are going to do
- Review the written directions and answer questions about the activity
- Divide participants into small groups or explain the amount of time to prepare individually for a group activity
- Assign small group roles such as recorder, reporter, small group discussion leader
- Give other ground rules

2. Learners Participate in a Learning Activity

For a learning activity to be successful, involve learners as much as possible. Consider how learning from a learning activity will appeal to different learning styles. This step might includes individual reading of a case study, reading background information for a simulation, or other preparation, such as following the written directions given at the beginning of the activity. This step might include reading questions to be answered as the class watches a video. Following the learners' discussion, ask a reporter from each small group to share each group's answers.

3. Learners Share and Interpret Their Reactions to the Case

This step is essential to help conclude the small group discussions and gives learners the opportunity to identify what happened in different small group discussion. Ask the group additional questions to help the learners analyze the discussion and then develop individual and group reactions to the activity. Learners share their reactions by identifying what happened to themselves and others, and how his or her behavior affected others during the small group discussion. Sample facilitator processing questions are:

- "What made it easy or difficult to find a solution to this problem?"
- "What helped or hindered the progress of the discussion?"
- "Let's summarize the key points from the case study."

Sometimes, it is appropriate to have participants individually write down their reaction to the learning activity so that another person does not influence their thinking before sharing reactions to a learning activity. Reactions come from the learners, not the facilitator, so the learners can discover the concept behind the learning activity.

Sharing a reaction is the beginning step of developing a pattern. If some participants do not share their reactions, it is difficult to end the activity and "get out of the learning activity." If this step is not completed, learners may prolong some unfinished business that spills over into other activities during a workshop.

4. Have Learners Identify Concepts from Their Reactions

In this step, have learners move away from the specific situation or learning activity. This is the "So what did I learn from the activity?" step. Questions that help learners develop concepts, include:

- "What did you learn about how to conduct an interview, discipline a subordinate, teach a new job, etc., from this learning activity?"
- "What is appropriate behavior for a new supervisor?"

If this step is left out, then learning will be incomplete and the objective might not be reached. Up to this point, participants have been actively learning from a specific situation, and may not be able to apply new learning to similar situations outside the classroom. When concepts are inferred from a discussion of the learning activity, adult learners are ready to apply these newly learned or recently confirmed concepts to future situations. For "discovery learning" to take place, ask questions to elicit concepts from the learners, rather than tell them the concepts they should have found in the learning activity.

5. Help Learners Apply Concepts to Their Situation

This is the "So what now?" step in the adult learning process. Ask participants how they can use and apply the new information they have learned from the learning activity. Ask questions like:

- "How will you use this skill the next time a subordinate asks you for a favor?"
- "What are some situations in which you would be more effective if you used this technique?"

If this step is left out, the learner may not see the relationship between the learning activity and his/her job or situation and consider what others learned as not useful to him/her. This step stresses practical application and helps the learner get a personal benefit from the learning activity.

To effectively facilitate a case study discussion, ask the learners questions about the learning activity, rather than tell them suggested applications. Following are Facilitator Processing Questions to elicit discovery learning using Steps 3, 4, and 5.

Facilitator Processing Questions**

Questions for Step 3: Learners Share and Interpret Their Reactions to the Activity

- "What happened when you tried out that function/step as part of the case?"
- "What surprised you?"
- "What part was easy? Difficult? What made it easy? Difficult?"
- "What did you notice/observe? How was that significant?"
- "How was that positive/negative?"
- "What struck you most about that?"
- "How do these pieces fit together?"

**Adapted with permission from J. William Pfeiffer (Ed). (1988). *UA Training Technologies 7: Presentation & Evaluation Skills in Human Resource Development* (pp. 66–68). San Francisco, CA: Pfeiffer.

Questions for Step 4: Learners Identify Concepts from their Reactions

- "How does this relate to other parts of the process?"
- "What might we conclude from that?"
- "What did you learn/relearn?"
- "What processes/steps are similar to this one?"
- "What else is this step/process like?"
- "What does that suggest to you about _____ in general?"
- "What's important to remember about this step/function?"
- "What other options/ways do you have for completing this step/function?"
- "How can you integrate this step into the larger process?"
- "What other functions are impacted by this step?"

Questions for Step 5: The Learners Apply Concepts to Their Situation

- "How can you use this?"
- "What is the value of this step/function?"
- "What would be the consequence of doing/not doing this?"
- "What changes can you make to help it work for you?"
- "How does that fit with your experience?"

After considering how to process an adult learning activity using the five steps, the next consideration is how to pace a variety of training activities for maximum attention and retention.

How Training Methods Are Paced to Maintain Attention and Improve Retention

The tool at the end of this article is a Methods Variety Scale that is based on the assumption that most adults have at least an attention span of about fifteen minutes. Learners born after 1960 and "raised on television" may have an attention span closer to seven minutes, since that is the programming time between commercial messages. Learners raised in the United Kingdom watching the British Broadcasting Corporation (BBC) may have an attention span of twenty minutes, since that is the typical length of programming.

The vertical axis of the Methods Variety Scale in Exhibit 14.1 shows what the learner does on a scale of 0 to 10, with 0 a low level of activity that requires little interaction with others. Most of the terms are self-evident; however, the difference between a lecture and a participative lecture is for the learner to answer a few large group questions during a participative lecture to increase learner involvement. A *return demonstration* is also called practice and usually follows a demonstration by the trainer (which is the same rating as watching a lecture or a film/video). A *structured experience* is also called a simulation.

The horizontal axis of the Methods Variety Scale is divided into hours by solid lines and dotted lines for every fifteen-minute portion of class time. The directions for using the Methods Variety Scale suggest that you plot the level of the learner's participation and identify whether the pace changes at least every fifteen minutes. Also, check to be sure that the learner's level of activity is at least over the level of 5 once an hour or more. If these two criteria are not met, then learner attention and retention can be increased by increasing the variety of learning activities as well as getting the level of participation over "5" at least once an hour. For full-day workshops, try getting the level of participation over "5" at least twice an hour after lunch when some participants would prefer to take a nap than pay attention.

Many software training sessions can enhance retention by using this scale. In particular, the variety of methods is often limited to demonstration (level 2) and a return demonstration (level 9). Following the practice a two or three return demonstrations, which is using only the first two steps in the five steps of the adult learning model, try having a large or small group

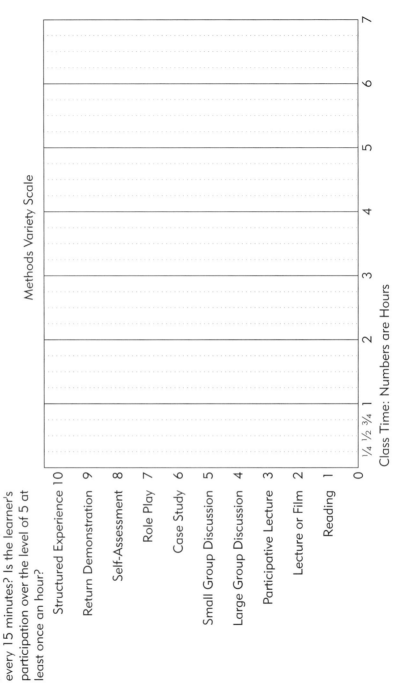

Directions: Plot learner's level of participation. Does activity vary every 15 minutes? Is the learner's participation over the level of 5 at least once an hour?

Methods Variety Scale

Class Time: Numbers are Hours

What The Learner Does

Structured Experience 10
Return Demonstration 9
Self-Assessment 8
Role Play 7
Case Study 6
Small Group Discussion 5
Large Group Discussion 4
Participative Lecture 3
Lecture or Film 2
Reading 1

Exhibit 14.1. Methods Variety Scale

© 1986. 2nd Edition The Training Clinic, 645 Seabreeze Drive, Seal Beach, CA 90740 (213) 430–2484. Copies available for purchase.

instruction for the learners to share and interpret their reactions to what they have been practicing. Then ask them the concept they have discovered by practicing this software process, and finally ask them how they can apply what they have learned in their own work. Breaking up practice sessions by using a variety of methods can avoid overloading participants with too much information in a compressed period of time. Use the Methods Variety Scale to plot the results.

Conclusion

I hope you have enjoyed this overview of how learning professionals help participants gain the most from their learning activity. The added dimension for all of these suggestions is that the learner has a limited attention span. Understanding that learning needs to be chunked and focused within a seven-, fifteen-, or twenty-minute cycle will also enhance your effectiveness as a trainer. Now, how long did it take you to read this article?

Article 15

Making Workshops Work

Lessons from an Old Pro

Hal Kane, Ph.D.

Passion

I love meetings!

Workshops and meetings are one of the more important means of communicating in organizations. As such, they should never be perceived as a waste of time. Rather, they should be experienced as an opportunity to share information, address sensitive issues, and tackle problems with colleagues who are prepared and motivated to spend their time doing good work. If you are in a workshop or a meeting and experiencing none of the above, please walk out.

Let me share what contributes to running a good meeting. In my experience you can extrapolate these ideas to running workshops and other group meetings

Get Agreement on the Ground Rules Before You Launch Your Agenda

People don't automatically concern themselves with Robert's Rules of Order or any other form of professional arrangements, and may need to be reminded that a self-generated set of rules for conduct will go a long way toward ensuring that the needs of all attendees are met.

Spend no more than five to ten minutes either creating these rules or refreshing the previously constructed rules. These are rules for both meeting the content objectives and respecting the process, are agreed to by all the members present, and reflect the organization's working culture ("Don't over-talk others" or "Wait your turn"). This is particularly valuable when skill and knowledge transfer needs to happen in a short period of time, without interruptions.

Near the conclusion of the workshop leave time to evaluate how well the rules were followed and, as needed, calibrate the rules until they accurately reflect the reality of the workshop or meeting. For instance, if sensitive issues were kept on the sidelines, ask whether there is a way to bring them forward without destroying the meeting. Similarly, if one or more egos tend to dominate the conversation, ask whether there is a better way to listen to capture everyone's concerns. Finally, if the material was used to enhance the audience's ability to do the job, was that point emphasized, captured, and placed in a repository that can be readily accessed.

Draw Up a List of Objectives to Be Accomplished and Gain Agreement Before You Meet

Nothing saps energy more than the lack of concrete issues to be discussed and things to be accomplished. Ideally, the objectives are circulated as part of the meeting or workshop agenda a good week in advance so that everyone has the opportunity to reflect on the issues and add value to the discussion. If the objectives of the workshop fell short, document why that happened and select suggestions for improvement.

Another useful tactic is to seek additional objectives from the attendees while ratifying your submissions. It puts the meeting on an even keel and makes everyone feel like a full participant. In addition, the ownership of issues is spread across the meeting, making action planning an obvious as well as a necessary component. After all, why propose something that you have no intention of doing anything about? If you're running a workshop, make sure that everyone got something out of the experience by asking them to align the workshop objectives with their own reasons for being there.

Spend Sufficient Time Eliciting Input and Tracking Input in Relation to the Objectives as They Are Discussed

Use an enamel board or flip chart to publish the results. People like to see progress, especially if they're committed to the issue at hand. If you're using brainstorming, the use of Post-it Notes can facilitate a rapid discussion of what's in and what's out. If needed, subgroup the larger meeting and let the smaller groups come up with suggestions and solutions, then "pitch" these to the larger group.

If you're too busy keeping one eye on process and the other on content, appoint a recorder to document and archive all the information generated in the meeting. People become irritated when they see or sense that their suggestions are being ignored. By accurately recording their contributions, you reinforce your ability to draw out their thoughts and feelings as the meeting progresses. In a workshop environment, process and content are nearly one and the same, and you need to be alert to changes in volume, tone, pitch, and body language—yours and theirs.

Organize Your Thoughts in Advance, But Stay Open and Flexible

You have to exercise your leadership skills and take charge, but you also must show that you're light on your feet and can handle any extracurricular material that pops up. Having a sense of humor goes a long way in reducing tension if things become sidetracked or get personal. You could also generate a spontaneous discussion ranging from the macro (organizational issues) to the micro (specific personalities) by framing it as an agenda item called "Word on the Street," a grab bag of anything that bothers the group, or as a handle on the rumor mill. Time box this item but don't ignore the possibility that people harbor strong feelings about what is normally unspoken but lies directly underneath the surface. Tell the group how and when you will deal with the items.

Keep Focused and Don't Allow Any Mid-Course Deviations

There's always the temptation to pick up a juicy topic not on the agenda, particularly when you are facilitating an information meeting that suddenly segues into a problem-solving session.

It certainly helps to identify the purpose of the meeting in the agenda, but if that wasn't done, the meeting leader should announce it to the assembled at the front end and publicly vow to maintain the focus.

As needed, a "parking lot" or issues log can house spontaneously generated topics. Careful handling of these is important so as to ensure that sufficient time is put aside to address them, or at least suggest ways to handle them in the future. Once again, people's ideas have to be taken seriously for them to respond in kind; otherwise they fall into dependency patterns and rely on the omniscient "them" (meaning management) to do all the thinking.

Listen Closely to Your Supporters; Listen Even More Closely to Your Opponents

Not everyone in the room is automatically on your side of every issue, nor should they be. You probably didn't become a leader through an election process, and now that you've been appointed you eventually discover that you can't please everyone. Good. Don't try.

Meetings and workshops are forms of discovery, possibly even self-discovery. Here's your chance to experience one-off and even contrary ideas. If you handle them well, through active listening, you're bound to develop a more holistic appreciation of the situation. By showing that you can handle different perspectives and contradictions in a mature manner, you'll gain the respect of even those who feel that they should be in your job.

People like to be listened to, and letting them know that you understand their concerns will win you a reputation as an honest broker. It's not a question of winning friends so much as winning the right to be the final arbiter, based on a balanced perception of all sides of the issue. If you are not a subject-matter expert on an issue, it's fine to admit it, provided you show your audience that you are a resource for them, that you can find and connect the missing dots, or show them how to do that for themselves.

Conclusion

If you can practice doing these simple but important steps in managing meetings and facilitating workshops, you can reduce the coefficient of grief that everyone inherits when they get into a managerial role. Management of others is the hardest job on the planet, and we're still learning how to do it better. In the meantime, give yourself and your people a break and spend time becoming a partner in their need to do a good job. Run better meetings and group sessions, and watch the frowns turn into smiles.

Article 16

Incredible Credibility

Terrence L. Gargiulo

Passion

We already have the authority; standing in front of a group naturally grants us a certain position. Now our challenge lies in winning the trust and respect of others. We need to be accessible to our attendees, sensitive to their needs, and responsive to satisfying their learning objectives.

There's that moment at the beginning of every class when we think to ourselves, "Quick, say something to prove to these folks that you belong up here." Everyone needs to establish credibility with a group. Our credibility is about our believability. We already have the authority; standing in front of a group naturally grants us a certain position. Now our challenge lies in winning the trust and respect of others. We need to be accessible to our attendees, sensitive to their needs, and responsive to satisfying their learning objectives.

Here are a few things I have found to be helpful:

Be a Good Host

Your credibility begins the moment you interact with attendees. First impressions are the most important ones. Do everything you can to make people feel comfortable. Little things make a big difference. I can remember lots of times when I have gone out of my way to find a more comfortable chair for an injured person.

Be Personable

Smiles are a wonderful way to break the ice. They will relax you and encourage people to interact with you before an event begins. There is nothing worse than walking into a training venue and mistaking it for a library. Encourage conversation by taking an interest in people. When appropriate, share a little tidbit about yourself without dominating the conversation.

Set Aside Your Credentials

Leave the certifications and diplomas on the wall. What you have accomplished is very important; however, how you share it, when you share it, and what you share are the challenges. Every training context is different. Think of it as "Just-Enough-Just-in-Time Credentials."

It's All in the Doing

Attendees grant credibility based on your performance. To quote a favorite cliché, "actions speak louder than words." Treat every interaction and question asked as an opportunity to demonstrate competency. Let your expertise shine through your command of the material.

Tell a Story

People love stories. Use a story to share an experience. It provides people with a concrete example of the material being learned and gives you an outlet to build credibility.

Discover Participants' Learning Objectives

It's all about them. Uncover an attendee's needs, demonstrate your capability to fulfill those needs, and you will win his or her respect every time. Our credibility as trainers is linked directly to the learning objectives of attendees. When we help them achieve their learning objectives, we both stand to win.

Manage Your Learning Commitments

Disappointment hurts. I have to temper my enthusiasm to transfer as much learning as I can with an honest evaluation of what is possible, given the constraints of the training. Be sure to under-promise and over-deliver. Treat learning commitments as liabilities. Pay them off diligently, and your assets of credibility will never be in danger.

Give Credit to Others

You look good when you make others look good. Nobody likes a know-it-all, and nobody can know everything. Be willing to share the podium figuratively and, if necessary, literally. Your credibility will be enhanced by the company you keep.

Conclusion

If you can put into practice even a few of these ideas you will be well along your way to Incredible Credibility!

Enlarging the Pool of Participation at the Beginning of Any Training Session

Mel Silberman, Ph.D.

Passion

Your training session will not spark active learning unless participants are eager to participate.

The bad news is that only a small minority will actively participate (raise their hands, volunteer, ask questions, and so forth) unless you do something to increase the number of participants right from the start. Once the frequent participators are established, it's very difficult to increase the pool of participation.

Many trainers assume that several participants do not participate because they are shy, insecure, or disinterested. Of course, that's true for some participants, but hardly the majority. Rates of participation are much more influenced by the trainer than determined by the participants. I have observed time and again that trainers have a habit that they are unaware of. This habit leads to lower participation and needs to be changed. Are you curious what habit I'm referring to?

Assuming the trainer asks interesting questions, sets a non-threatening climate, and encourages participant response, the one problematic behavior I often see is that trainers *call on the first participant whose hand is raised.* The reason this occurs is that it seems rude not to do so, especially if the participant in question does not volunteer constantly. In addition, many trainers are grateful that the participant is raising his or her hand when the rest of the class seems disinterested or afraid. The problem that arises is that participants (and trainers) get used to a single volunteer (or maybe just a few), and the pattern and rate of participation are set. Sooner or later, a small minority of participants fill the role of responding to trainer requests for participation.

Without realizing it, most trainers even use language that promotes a small pool of participants. They say things like "*Who* wants to give his views next?" "Can *anyone* tell me what's the solution here?" "I'm looking for *someone* to. . . ."

Here are five guaranteed ways to increase the pool of participation. You don't need to do all of them, but you should get in the habit, as soon as possible, of employing some of them. Also, don't expect great results the very first time you use the techniques you select. The good news is that, once the participants get the hang of what you are doing, even after one exposure, they will start to respond with greater frequency.

1. Create the Opportunity for "Pre-Discussion"

Pose a question and invite participants to discuss it with others seated near them. Say: "Take a few minutes to discuss this question with your partner before we open the floor for discussion."

Next, ask the question again for a total group discussion.

2. Obtain a Commitment to Participate

Pose a question and ask: "How many of you have some thoughts about this?"

Encourage several participants to raise their hands before you call on any participant.

Call on participants who have not volunteered so far or, if time is available, call on all the hands raised.

3. Specify How Many You Wish to Participate

Ask a question and open it up to the entire group.

Say: "I'd like to ask four or five participants to give me their opinions."

4. Establish a "New" Participant Rule

Pose a question.

Say: "I'd like some new participants this time. Which of you haven't shared your ideas yet?"

5. Use a "Call on the Next Speaker" Format

Ask participants to raise their hands when they want to share their views and request that the present speaker in the class call on the next speaker (rather than the trainer performing this role).

Say: "When you are the speaker, please talk to other participants rather than addressing me."

Planning Sheet

Enlarge the pool of participation at the very beginning. *Use the following checklist to implement this strategy.*

Technique: check one or more:

☐ Create the opportunity for "pre-discussion"

☐ Obtain a commitment to participate

☐ Specify how many you wish to participate

☐ Establish a "new" participant rule

☐ Use the "call on the next speaker" format

My Plan:

Conclusion

As learning professionals, we want to create an environment in which clients learn how to effectively participate in training. The intention of the ideas in this article is to spark your own creativity to find ways to actively engage participants in exciting and effective learning experiences.

Article 18

How Learners Are Motivated

Matthew S. Richter

Passion

Get participants to truly connect to the value of what they are learning!

Use activities to facilitate higher levels of competence and engagement to offer participants the opportunities to discover their own value. Implementing an intrinsically motivating environment to a training situation requires a complete understanding of multiple factors, such as the goal of the training, how participants perceive the training, the logistics of the training, learning styles, trainer skills, etc. When you create opportunities to expand participant autonomy and engage them phenomenal learning can occur.

I am a trainer. I have been a trainer for just about all of my career. I started in the early 1990s and was inundated with all sorts of training games that used rubber balls, funny sounds emanating from trainers to participants, and est-like connections to humanistic approaches in business. Frankly, this stuff drove me crazy and I was somewhat embarrassed to admit I was a trainer.

It was at this time that I met a guy named Thiagi. Thiagi was renowned as the *game guy*. All of my colleagues used his games and half the games I infused into my delivery came from him—and I didn't even know it. I should say, however, that my friends and I were all misapplying his activities. And we all had the misinterpretation that training games should be fun first. When I met him, Thiagi explained that fun was not what he and his activities were about. In fact, his goal was to facilitate engagement toward a performance objective. Now today, this all makes sense—but remember that fifteen years ago, it was all about funny sounds and hopping around like a chicken. Thiagi talked about relevance to performance, and how every activity needed to be congruent with every performance goal. And every performance goal should have a link back to a business objective. Essentially, Thiagi was talking about getting participants to truly connect to the value of what they were learning. And he used activities to facilitate higher levels of competence and used engagement as a way of offering opportunities for participants to freely engage and find their own value.

Thiagi was teaching trainers to create motivating environments that had significance. I was hooked.

I had transitioned from a naïve practitioner to someone who could do the moves properly. I had technique but no reason why Thiagi's way of doing things worked. I probably should have just asked him. Then I was introduced to a model that explained why we do what we do. A mentor of mine handed me a book called just that, *Why We Do What We Do*, by Edward L. Deci. It explained how and why people were motivated, intrinsically and extrinsically, to perform. The more fluent I became in applying

Deci's model to what Thiagi had taught me, the more convinced I became that life had meaning.

Introduction to Motivation

Motivation is the energy that accelerates behavior. Often trainers and instructional designers devote a lot of effort in designing reward strategies, convinced that finding the right reward for the right participant will endow the participant with the motivation to learn. Many of us think of motivation as a "carrot and stick" kind of enterprise, with the mechanism influencing motivation located externally. This chapter will help trainers to choose whether to use reward strategies, and if so, how to use them wisely, with a greater understanding of the consequences of their choices.

The goal of most trainers is to get their participants to engage in the program as productively as possible. Many prescriptive models of motivation have been developed to help educators achieve this objective, but we will only focus on only one. Self-determination theory (from the work of Edward L. Deci and Richard M. Ryan, both of the University of Rochester) is an especially useful model.[*] When applied appropriately, this model can help trainers and designers achieve effective results.

Throughout the ensuing discussion on the application of rewards versus creating a more intrinsically motivated learning environment, I'll focus on the vital role of relevance; where the more effective goal is to move participants along a continuum from being a motivated or apathetic to becoming passionate learners.

---

[*]While at the University of Rochester, I had the opportunity to spend several semesters of study with Deci and Ryan. It was a marvelous and life-changing experience. This paper is my interpretation of their work applied to the workplace. Any value offered here is derived from their research and any incorrect application is due to my own misinterpretation.

These are the major purposes of this article:

- Discuss the role of motivation in the training situation
- Help leverage the use of rewards and reinforcement systems when they are advantageous
- Explore alternatives to reward/reinforcement motivation strategies
- Encourage careful analysis of the intention with which you approach training.

Components of motivation include a sense of relatedness, a sense of competence, and a sense of autonomy.

These factors influence how a person's motivation is realized, or in other words, what mechanisms drive a person to feel completely apathetic toward learning, capable, but forced to learn, or passionate to learn. Here's the crucial point for trainers to remember: the participant's *perception* of each component is what counts. For example, a participant may come to you with a diagram that is totally incomprehensible. Your first reaction is to tell the participant how great it is. The participant walks away with glee, believing he (or she) is a fantastic graphics person. You and I both know the diagram is objectively hideous. That is real competence. The participant has perceived competence. Motivationally, that perceived competence is what counts.

- *Competence:* Competence is the need to perceive oneself as successful at achieving a task or an activity. To feel competent, a person must believe he has the knowledge and skill to perform the task, as well as the environmental support and structure to do it. A sense of competence must be present for a person to be intrinsically or extrinsically motivated. Competence is both the capability (knowledge and skills) to do something, and the capacity (time and resources) to do it. So in a classroom setting, this means participants believe they have the knowledge and skill to learn your topic and the necessary tools and appropriate activities to practice.

- *Autonomy/Control:* Autonomy is the perception that one has a choice in performing a task and is not influenced by any other source to do it. A sense of autonomy must be present for intrinsic motivation to occur. Control is the opposite of autonomy. Control occurs when the participant feels he doesn't have a choice in his learning or is influenced by some external source. Clearly, if he feels forced to do an activity or memorize some silly facts, he is less likely to feel either pleasure or passion in engaging the process. So even if he feels competent to learn, if he feels controlled, he will be only extrinsically motivated to perform. A form of reinforcement is then necessary.

- *Relatedness:* Relatedness is the feeling that one is emotionally tied to significant others in one's life. Relatedness is engendered when participants feel "we're in this together." The more we can make the learning relevant to learners, the more engaged and purposeful the training will be.

Rewarding Desired Behavior

Often I'm called into an organization to deliver training programs that I have designed. I often don't have a long-term relationship with the participants. I'll be with them for perhaps a day or two. I've found it useful in these situations to hand out dollar bills—lots of them. I tell participants that I'm going to pay them for saying anything I deem to be profound or useful or smart-alecky or that might be considered heckling. Clearly, I'm rewarding them for participation. I'm offering an immediate reward, a reinforcing consequence to get them to perform a desired behavior. This is quite effective when given the fact that the majority of participants are assigned the course and have no desire to be there. It helps bridge the initial apathy with potential intrigue.

I find handing out dollar bills to be very effective. Participants compete to answer questions, leap to their feet to volunteer, and keenly listen for any opportunity to show what they're learning. Knowing I'm out of there after a day or two enables me to punish them, publicly humiliate them, pay them off, or reward them in any way I want to. I get a real short-term bang for my buck. Literally. In a recent Change Management course I taught, I handed out $250 in one-dollar bills and rewarded one team a $300 cash prize for winning a game. Great for me. Great for the participants. Right?

Or are you appalled, thinking, "I train these people again and again over the course of a year. How can I afford that kind of reward system?" The downside is actually worse than that. Hang on.

The day after our Change Management workshop, a friend and fellow trainer was scheduled to lead the same twenty-five participants in a workshop on hard-core performance management—a fill-out-the-form type of performance appraisal training (the dead, dull boring stuff). My friend's real problem, however, was that she had the misfortune of following me the day after I was handing out cash. After a day of money rewards, the participants were fully expecting a great payout from her, especially when I had teed her up as an exciting, awesome trainer and friend. Imagine the reaction, then, when she informed them she had no money with her to reward them. Given how completely motivated they were to earn the money, the participants joked around a lot at first. Unintentionally, I'd set her up to fail.

In relying solely on rewards, then, I set up two problems: (1) I established unrealistic expectations in our participants for external rewards from every future training situation and (2) I oriented them to value the reward and not the learning (or its application on the job).

Consequences of Rewards

In deciding to use one motivation strategy with (or over) another, we need to know the consequences of that strategy. It's easy enough to pump participants up in the moment with a reward, whether it's a dollar, an A, a gold star, or an award. What's the *consequence*? We're not arguing that rewards are ineffective. In fact, they are extremely effective (as is punishment). Remember how well our dollar bills worked? The consequences, however, concern the *consistency* of the desired behavior and the *quality* of the behavior when it's demonstrated. When the reward is withdrawn, often so is the behavior. If consistent behavior is required in a system of rewards, the reward must be consistent, too. This means you have to be ready, willing, and able to cough up the dough every single time. As an outside consultant, that is more likely to be possible than if I am an inside guy.

So we may see consistent behaviors if we keep the dollars coming, but what of the *quality* of the behavior? Edward L. Deci, in his book *Why We Do What We Do* tells the story of Lisa, a six-year-old girl, whose violin teacher awarded her a gold star for every practice session Lisa completed. When Lisa had collected enough gold stars, the teacher gave her a "treasure." Lisa's parents discovered, much to their dismay, that while Lisa completed every minute of her practice sessions, she did no more than was required to receive the star, watching the clock the whole time. Worse yet, her effort and diligence in learning new songs and correct fingering were all but non-existent. Remember, she wasn't rewarded for *quality* practicing, just for *consistent* practicing. Clearly, the consequences of the reward system inadvertently sabotaged the goal of learning. Instead of being motivated by the pleasure of playing music (and playing well), she was fixated on the gold stars. In fact, she became quite stressed out at the possibility of not meeting the expectation. Stress became the overriding emotion rather than pleasure.

Context plays its part on motivation, too. Many years ago, I taught a course at Nazareth College, near Rochester, New York, called Intrinsic Motivation in the Workplace. Since I considered it hypocritical to award grades in a course designed to teach people to see the inherent value in what they're doing,

I arranged with the dean to *not* give traditional grades at the end of the course, but to indicate "pass" or "fail" on the students' transcripts. I had a rebellion. The students were furious. They wanted their As. They complained that the class just couldn't be worthwhile if they didn't earn a grade. In what might be the ironic *coup de grace*, they wondered how they would know if they'd worked hard enough if they didn't get a grade. The system of motivation in place on campus was so overwhelmingly skewed toward rewards (i.e., grades) that the students tolerated no single exception to the system. On a grander scale, we have to ask how motivation is affected by the system in which it's embedded.

From the Outside In: Moving Participants Toward Seeing a Value Proposition

Most motivational strategies are applied from the outside to the individual, as in the reward strategies discussed above. When the strategy is applied from the outside, it is perceived as (and, in fact, is) controlling. Whenever a participant is controlled, influenced, manipulated, or coerced, long-term, negative consequences arise. Money, grades, and other rewards can be manipulative. So, too, are value systems, cultural concepts, and organizational structures. When a motivation strategy is controlling, its benefits are only of a short duration. Yes, their effect can be measured quickly, but reward strategies distract the participants' attention from what's really in it for them, replacing the intrinsic value of the learner with the "value" of the reward. The result is lowered intrinsic motivation. Our goal as trainers should be to come as close as possible to creating an *intrinsically motivating environment*. Along the way, learners are led to see the value of the training proposition, to them and to the organization.

What's Your Intention?

If we begin by asking ourselves *why* we're offering training, we're bound to uncover our intention. Each decision we make is informed by our intention, so we might as well come clean with ourselves right up-front. Say we're scheduled to deliver training in a compliance topic, such as sexual harassment or an ethics policy (which is often just an excuse to cudgel people not to disclose company secrets). Is it fair to say our participants sometimes feel a little punished and resentful, just to be dragged into the training? *So why are we doing it*? If our answer is, "It's mandated," what does this mean for our participants? From the get-go, our intention is not about them. It's about us, the mandate, and our butts. The training is a waste of time, then, from a *learning standpoint*, especially if participants consider themselves compliant already, of if they consider the training useless on the job, or if the material is dead, dull, boring, and painful. Simply put, the training isn't relevant to them. Then we're stuck trying to get them to learn in spite of themselves.

Self-Determination Theory

If we decide the training is about helping our participants to *see the value* in the training, to *feel competent* and *autonomous* to use compliant behavior, and to know we're *in this together*, then the training is more about the participants and their learning. Our intention, then, will drive design and training decisions. We had better ask ourselves, "What's the goal of this training?" If we link the learning objectives to business results, we're half-way home. If we link the business results to a value proposition to participants, even better.

Now we're going to look at a theory of motivation that looks at the factors of *competence, autonomy,* and *relatedness*: Self-Determination Theory, when applied appropriately, can help trainers achieve greater results than reward strategies alone.

Where does motivation come from?

The idea of *internal* and *external* motivation is easy to grasp. If I raise my hand and answer questions correctly in a training session because I'm $1 richer for doing so, I have been *externally* motivated. If I answer the question because it makes me proud of myself or because I take great pleasure in responding, I have been *internally* motivated. However, the difference between *intrinsic* and *extrinsic* motivation is trickier—and more useful.

When you are motivated, you are motivated in one of two ways (see Figure 18.1):

- *Intrinsically:* Intrinsic motivation occurs when you are passionate about a task and perform it for the sheer pleasure of doing it. The motivator resides within you. *Not all internal motivators are intrinsic.*
- *Extrinsically:* Extrinsic motivation occurs when you perform a task because some force, either external to you (money, rewards, grades, punishment) or internal to you (a value or belief that impacts your self-worth) drives to you perform.

	Intrinsic	Extrinsic
External		Money Bonus Punishment Praise
Internal	When you have a passion for performing a task. When you perform a task for the sheer pleasure of it. When you freely choose to perform a task.	Guilt Ego Gratification Seeing the Value of a Task

Figure 18.1. Intrinsic vs. Extrinsic Motivation

The Mechanisms of Motivation

We've been discussing extrinsic motivation quite a bit in this chapter, thus far. Whenever we discuss rewards and recognition strategies in a system (or training session), we're referring to external motivation. Extrinsic motivation, however, can also arise *within* the individual. Figure 18.2 is a variation of what Deci and Ryan call the Mechanism of Motivation.

Apathy

Have you ever been in front of a classroom and seen long faces, disheartened souls, and completely miserable participants? Usually this occurs in highly technical programs for highly non-technical people, or highly flaky (interpersonal) topics for people who have a great aversion to members of humanity. Essentially, apathy, or *amotivation,* as Deci and Ryan refer to it, occurs when participants are forced to learn material they believe they have no competence to learn. Let me give you an example. I can't ski. If you put me up on the top of a mountain, slap some skis on me, and put a gun to my head, forcing me down the slope, I will

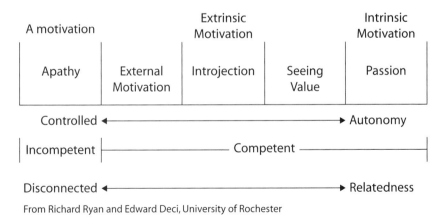

From Richard Ryan and Edward Deci, University of Rochester

Figure 18.2. The Mechanism of Motivation

do it, knowing full well that the likelihood of my dying is only slightly lower than dying from a bullet to the head. I feel utterly and completely incompetent—no skill, no ability, and certainly no knowledge to ski down a mountain, and yet I would be compelled to do so. That visceral feeling of hopelessness and helplessness in the face of doing something that feels completely impossible is amotivation. Learners don't face their own mortality in the classroom, but being forced to learn something they feel incompetent to learn is no less frustrating or scary. When participants fall into this frustration zone, it's our job as trainers to get them out of it as quickly as possible. This is an appropriate time to offer rewards as a way of introducing the possibility of competence. Remember, competence is all about the learner's perception of it.

Rewards, Punishment, and Other Controlling Factors

We've said a lot about the effects of rewards and can't emphasize enough the often detrimental effects rewards have on a learner's intrinsic motivation. So let's just summarize. Rewards:

- Devalue the focus on learning for learning's sake
- Demotivate all those who don't achieve them
- Crowd out other possible focal points
- Reinforce a Machiavellian approach to learning and reroute the goal to achieving the reward, and not the learning objective
- Require the continuation of subsequent rewards

External motivation means just that. The reinforcement comes from outside of the person and controls, forces, or strongly influences participant behavior. I can't emphasize enough how powerful this is when the goal is short-term behavioral change.

That's the obvious reason why parent, teachers, bosses, government officials, and animals rely on external motivation as the most efficient catalyst for behavior. Long-term, however, the shortcomings are often perilous to authenticity.

Introjection, the Guilt Factor, the Ego Thing, the "Should" Factor, and KFKD

Extrinsic Motivation from Within: According to Deci and Ryan, sometimes we are motivated by an internal factor that is not truly intrinsic, which they call introjection. Call it guilt. Call it ego. Call it, as Anne Lamott does, a radio station inside her head, tuned to the most judgmental critic and nag imaginable. (She calls it "KFKD.") We don't want to do something, but because we believe we should, we do. Our self-esteem and self-worth are threatened or stroked, depending on what we think of our behavior. You recognize this motivator in your training session when a participant has forced herself to volunteer for something when she's clearly uncomfortable. She may be telling herself that she's bound to fail, but because her boss has sent her to this training, she feels she should volunteer. She's been motivated by a factor extrinsic to her self (the boss's expectations) expressed from within. As a motivator, introjection can be powerful, but it doesn't often result in excellence. For example, my three-year-old Lia came up to me with tears in her eyes. She said, "Daddy. You're going to die. I don't want to be a porphan." I looked at her, quite confused, and asked what she meant by all this. She told me very seriously that I was fat, and that I ate too much, and needed to pexercise. Then she sobbed and asked me not to leave her alone. My three-year-old looks nothing like me, and thankfully takes after my wife, which makes her impossible to resist. That afternoon, we went to an exercise equipment store and purchased a treadmill. The first week, she would sit right next to me as I walked, urging me to go faster and insuring that I completed my forty-five minutes. By the second week, she would only get me started before she explained that she had other things to do. By the third week, the treadmill was in the basement. This is a good example of the long-term effects (or lack thereof) of introjection on behavior. While ego gratification, seeking approval, or guilt may have a longer effect than rewards, the long-term effect is still negligible.

Seeing the Value

Extrinsic Motivation Further Along the Continuum: Another extrinsic motivator is the ability to see value. Although you are not doing the task because you freely choose to and you passionately want to, you have internalized its overall importance. This type of motivation is actually quite close to intrinsic motivation. However, seeing value is still extrinsic, because the sense of importance originates from an outside source. For example, a man might quit smoking, because he knows it is good for his health. He knows he will have more energy. And he knows he will save money on dry cleaning. You've noticed the participants in your training sessions who see value in what you're doing. They're not dying to be there, but they appreciate that it's good for them. Helping your participants see what's in it for them is a good strategy for trainers to employ. Making training relevant moves them along the continuum toward intrinsic motivation, where passion motivates behavior.

Intrinsic Motivation

Intrinsic motivation is synonymous with passion. As a trainer and an instructional designer, I have seen passionate learners in corporate settings. Frankly, this is rare. Intrinsic motivation means that your participants have freely chosen to engage in the learning opportunity and completely believe they can do what it is they're learning. I use simulations and games frequently as a way to engage learners to a degree that they no longer think about or reflect on their competence. Essentially, when they're having fun or are engaged, they don't perceive their own incompetence. The more relevant and applicable the activity (game or simulation), the more likely the participants see value or, if I'm lucky, freely choose to do it.

Conclusion

Motivation is trickier than it looks. If a trainer wants to increase participation and decides that in order to do so, she will hand out dollar bills, she must know that she is doing so at the expense of increased learning retention and relevance, substituting extrinsic motivation for intrinsic. Money, rewards structures, and gold stars do influence behavior, but they focus behavior on getting the external reward, not on really improving at the task at hand. In a technologically rapid world, sometimes it is necessary to push behavioral modification through quickly. However, acknowledge to the employee what you're doing, and strive to create, in parallel, a more intrinsically motivating training environment.

Making the training *relevant* is of paramount importance. When a trainer focuses on improving the opportunities for people to meet their psychological needs (competence, autonomy, and relatedness), it is more likely that the trainer will attain higher levels of satisfaction and morale, and foster a mastery-orientation among the participants, demonstrated by increased resourcefulness, concentration, creativity, and intuition. Creating a motivating environment takes more than just throwing money at the problem.

Article 19

Applying Self-Determination to Training

Matthew S. Richter

Passion

I am passionate about creating environments wherein participants not only feel respected but freely engage in learning activities and increase their competence—and confidence!

In the previous article, I looked at how learners are motivated. Now let's take a look at the specifics of when and how to create an intrinsically motivating environment. In this article, I will focus on three components:

1. When to create an intrinsically motivating environment
2. Examples from both a design and delivery perspective
3. Tips for implementing an intrinsically motivating environment

We're not about to tell you that you should only strive toward creating an intrinsically motivating environment in your training sessions. Sometimes your participants are just too resistant, jaded, demoralized, or resentful to be intrinsically motivated. Sometimes the system is so entrenched in extrinsic reward systems that, given the choice, participants would rather go with what's familiar and comfortable. Perhaps the short-term goals are so pressing that you must rely on extrinsic motivators, such as rewards or punishments. All this is to say, know what your intention is, know what your goals and constraints are, and choose deliberately, understanding the consequences of your choices. Sometimes you will choose a reward strategy.

The ideal, from my point of view, is a strategy that enables intrinsic motivation to be possible. When participants are intrinsically motivated, their learning is more energized, creative, self-directed, and durable. Not only is the session itself more effective and engaging, but you'll notice greater retention and application of the learning back on the job.

1. When to Create an Intrinsically Motivating Environment

Some key indicators that a motivation system intervention is needed are:

- When a participant doesn't believe she's capable of completing a task, either stemming from an inability (she doesn't have the knowledge or skills) to perform, or an incapacity (she doesn't have enough time or resources) to perform the task. She might complain, "I don't know how to do this" or "You didn't give us enough time to finish."

- When a participant doesn't believe he has any choice in whether to perform the task or how to get it done. He might complain, "I know this part. Do I have to listen again?" or "I hate to do everything in a team. Why can't I work alone on this?"
- When a participant doesn't feel that she belongs in the training session or the organization. She might complain, "I don't belong here" or "No one here respects me" or "I don't fit in."
- When a participant believes that nothing he's learning is going to make any difference on the job. He might complain, "What does this matter?" or "No one cares what I do around here. Why should I bother?"
- When a participant doesn't receive any kind of feedback about her performance. She might complain, "I don't even know if I'm doing this right" or "Do we get a grade or what?"
- When a participant is more concerned with compensation and pay. He might complain, "Are we getting a bonus for learning this junk?" or "If we do this, what do we get?"
- When a participant is more concerned about peer approval, managerial approval, or your approval. She might complain, "I'll do this as long as no one thinks I look stupid," or she might constantly seek out your opinion.

2. Examples Both from a Design and Delivery Perspective

Principle 1	Component of Intrinsic Motivation
Begin building from the highest level.	AUTONOMY: The more people see the link to what they're doing in training to what they value on the job, the more they will choose to learn
Answer the question, "What is the ROI of this training?"	
Align the goals of training with the overall goals of the business.	
Be certain participants see the value in terms of business results.	Make it relevant to them.

Application or Activity

I like to use a game developed by my mentor and partner, Thiagi, called the "HELLO" game. The trainer begins by asking participants about their goals for learning, their expectations for session, their questions, etc. This allows participants to name their own goals and perspectives. This allows the trainer to debrief the activity by connecting to alignment with ROI. (All games described herein can be found in greater depth at our website, www.thiagi.com or by emailing me at matthew@thiagi.com.)

Principle 2	Component of Intrinsic Motivation
Use a dose of reality for the performance test. If the final test is a "real world" example of what they'll actually do at work, participants will be able to prove they can apply the task in context. Many learners need feedback on actual performance to retain the learning.	COMPETENCE: By proving to themselves they can do what you're training them to do, they leave with a sense of competence.

Application or Activity

In this case, simulations or case studies work very well. It's important that these be drawn from real job activities and contexts. Again, with all training decisions, the choices must be relevant to the learners' work performance.

Principle 3	Component of Intrinsic Motivation
Don't design the content; design activities. Content is abundant. The trainer should prioritize	AUTONOMY: Participants see value in activities that allow them to practice and learn what they need to do/

activities that help the participants toward performance goals by using the content.

All activities must be relevant.

Keep the goal of the training in mind at all times: performance outcomes.

Locate primary content sources, and select and adapt suitable activities to explore the content.

know at work. They choose to participate.

COMPETENCE: Participants discover they can do what they need to do.

RELATEDNESS: Activities require interaction, especially when the activities are games.

Application or Activity

"35" is a wonderful activity that facilitates content stemming from the participants. In this structured sharing game, participants discuss and evaluate ideas from other (anonymous) members of the group, assigning relative value to the ideas by giving points. The highest (best) idea could earn 35 points. As they play this game, they are reviewing content, adding their own viewpoints and opinions.

Principle 4	Component of Intrinsic Motivation
Build the airplane while you fly it. Create an outline or prototype. Improvise your training delivery. In this way, trainers avoid predetermined, controlling boundaries, allowing the needs of the participants *in the moment* to dictate the session. Come prepared with five or six activities per module, so you can be flexible and responsive.	AUTONOMY: Participants understand that they are choosing what comes next.

Application or Activity

This is an application, in a way, of historian James MacGregor Burns' observation, "Leaders are great when they follow the followers."

Principle 5	Component of Intrinsic Motivation
Let the inmates run the asylum. Have the participants design content elements. Arrange for them to teach or coach one another. Have participants test and evaluate each other.	AUTONOMY: They have choice in each element of the session. COMPETENCE: They prove their capability when they lead the way. RELATEDNESS: Interdependence of participants engenders unity.

Application or Activity

I like to use an improv game called "The World's Worst." In this game, participants improvise the "worst" examples of sales techniques (for example), in order to develop lists of successful techniques and a list of pitfalls to avoid. This game draws on the collective knowledge of the group, honoring what some already know.

Principle 6	Component of Intrinsic Motivation
Don't reinvent the wheel. Trainers waste time creating stuff that already exists. The design and materials are not as important as hitting the outcome. All focus should be on participants reaching performance goals.	COMPETENCE: When the focus is squarely on the participants and activities, trainers teach to the test, enhancing participants' sense of competence.

Application or Activity

Very simple. Content is everywhere. Leverage videos, manuals, published books, podcasts, blogs, etc. There are, I believe, at last count over nine trillion training activities that are frames that can be used to facilitate your participants to the end result.

Principle 7	Component of Intrinsic Motivation
Open minds with open questions. Ask authentic open questions. Use alternative approaches to providing feedback, such as checklists, peer feedback, expert feedback, and real-world feedback. Align all questions with the performance test.	AUTONOMY. Participants make connections and are involved, allowing them to see value in the work themselves. COMPETENCE. Participants feel a sense of being right and of being able to answer questions.

Application or Activity

Use case studies with no clear right and wrong answers. These provide participants with a lot of flexibility to explore and chance being wrong. The opportunity for learning is really in the debriefing and dialogue how and why participants made their choices. Simulations also provide the opportunity for participants to take risks safely and learn from their mistakes. And, of course, you can always use games with multiple and varied strategies or approaches.

Principle 8	Component of Intrinsic Motivation
Mix up everything. Remember to accommodate different learning styles. Use a variety of media. Remember that both active and passive learning can be of value.	AUTONOMY: Participants choose which modality is best for their individual learning styles. COMPETENCE: Participants are bound to perform in a way that suits their strengths,

Allow people to work in teams at times and on their own at other times. Allow them to take different roles in the activities.

Consider which sensory mode to work in.

allowing for a greater sense of competence.

Application or Activity

Any of the activities listed above, or any learning approaches at all work well when trying to leverage variety. At last count, we have identified sixty-six different interactive strategies that can by applied. The trick is to never do an activity for the sake of the activity. Always have a purpose and goal in mind. The sixty-six are listed and described on our website, specifically at www. thiagi.com/interactive-stratgies.html.

3. Tips for Implementing an Intrinsically Motivating Environment

Above are tips for creating a motivating environment, but what do you do once you have initiated a set of strategies? Below are some tips for implementing your strategies:

- *Make known the "facts of life."* Inform participants up-front what is expected of them and what boundaries, constraints, rules, goals, and measures are inherent in the training. Explain why you're there, and what's in it for them.
- *Provide choices.* Given the "fact of life," engage the participants in determining how to learn what is expected, how to contribute what they know and want to know, and how to establish their own measures of success.
- *Establish a variety of avenues for learning.* Participants must perceive their own competence. Provide learning opportunities that serve a variety of learning styles.

- *Be accessible and ensure that participants feel comfortable asking for help when they need it.* Not everyone is comfortable revealing ignorance.
- *Constantly engage the participants.* Be sure to know what they're thinking, wondering about, and wanting next. Ask them for input at each juncture. Involve them in creating activities or in setting goals or in selecting resources.
- *Evaluate.* Obviously you will have metrics from "up above" that determine how you and the participants will be measured. These metrics must be communicated as "facts of life," and you have to use them in the session to show participants how well they're doing. Think of evaluation as a support mechanism for enhancing their perceived competence. Remove any link between these evaluations to compensation, and focus on individual development and growth. Use any standards developed by the participants as an evaluation tool, too. (You'll often find that when they're intrinsically motivated, participants develop much more stringent "yardsticks" of success than you or their managers may have.)

One Example of a Design Flow
History

We recently worked with a high-tech software company that had several new products coming out and very little processed (nicely documented) material that could be used in training their customers on how to use the products. Given the state of software development, the organization didn't want to spend a fortune designing training programs that would only become obsolete within a year when the next version came out. And most importantly, the company had to deliver training yesterday, not in three months after a complete needs analysis was done.

Process

Step 1: A little analysis: Check in with your customer or with management

In partnership with management, we determined what skills and knowledge participants should exhibit at the end of the workshop, focusing on what participants had to be able to do to perform on the job as it pertained to the content of the class. Our focus was on increased competence and alignment with business goals, both of great relevance to the participants. This seeded our design with the potential for seeing value in the workshop.

Step 2: A little more analysis: Check in with your potential participants

Step 2 correlates with our design philosophy of being learner-focused. We determined *participant expectations* and matched those to the organizational objectives. This step incorporated learners' choices and preferences, in an autonomy-supportive way.

Step 3: Design the test

Once we determined and fleshed out expectations, we designed a final test that evaluated the participants' ability to perform the skills and apply the knowledge of the content on the job. We used real-life (i.e., work context) simulations and materials. We designed a test that would have participants writing code for and using the software they were learning. Each participant on a team would take a portion of the test, sequentially. The participants would rely on other team members as "lifelines." Each team member would build on the success of the previous members' work. Passing the test would be determined by the successful completion of the simulation by all participants. As you can see, we built in opportunities for developing competence and relatedness. Since the work would be largely self-directed, participants would choose strategies and next steps. In this way, we supported their autonomy. Knowing the end point (the test), we backfilled the necessary content and activities to support participants' capacity for success.

Step 4: Gather content

Once content from the test design was determined, we gathered it in its raw form. Through manuals, documentation, interviews, and videos of subject-matter experts, we constructed a data file of the targeted content. Remember, the focus wasn't on reinventing the wheel or creating impressive manuals. Content is always abundant. We just gathered it and used our energy to design activities.

Step 5: Translate content

We translated the raw content into a coherent layout for the simulation, encapsulating it in several formats: manuals, videos, performing tasks, one-hour mini-lectures and demonstrations, consultants, web-based resources, and practice work stations. We put participants into teams of four or five and gave them play money with which to purchase resources. They were given the test and told to plot out their learning strategy for passing the test. Once they passed the test, they could leave. Responsible for their own learning, they chose the strategies that supported their competencies. This autonomous supportive approach relieved us from having to predict all learning styles, questions, problems, and strategies in advance, allowing us to be flexible and respond to participants' immediate needs and preferences.

Step 6: Prepare to play

We customized the simulation to the number of teams, the "cost" of each resource (paid in play money), time of the training session, and other details specific to the program. Now it was time to play. It's nearly impossible to feel incompetent when you're engaged in a game. Participants "designed" their own training with the game structure created for them, supporting their autonomy, competence, and relatedness along the way.

Conclusion

Motivation is tricky stuff. Implementing an intrinsically motivating environment to a training situation requires a complete understanding of multiple factors, such as the goal of the training, how participants perceive the training, the logistics of the training, learning styles, trainer skills, etc. By focusing on good, old-fashioned instructional design principles and creating opportunities to expand participant autonomy, engage them, and increase overall competence, learning can truly be achieved.

References

Baard, P.P., Deci, E.L., & Ryan, R.M. (2004). Intrinsic need satisfaction: A motivational basis of performance and well-being in two work settings. *Journal of Applied Social Psychology, 34,* 2045–2068.

Bandura, A. (1996). *Self-efficacy: The exercise of control.* New York: Freeman.

Burns, J.M. (2003) *Transforming leadership: The pursuit of happiness.* New York: Atlantic Monthly Press.

Connell, J.P., & Wellborn, J.G. (1991). Competence, autonomy, and relatedness: A motivational analysis of self-system processes. In M.R. Gunnar & L. A. Sproufe (Eds.), *Minnesota symposium on child psychology* (Vol. 23). Mahwah, NJ: Lawrence Erlbaum Associates.

Cskiszentmihalyi, M. (1990). *Flow.* New York: Harper and Row.

Deci, E.L. (1980). *The psychology of self-determination.* Lexington, MA: D.C. Heath.

Deci, E.L., Connell, J.P., & Ryan, R.M. (1989). Self-determination in a work organization. *Journal of Applied Psychology, 74,* 580–590.

Deci, E.L., & Flaste, R. (1996). *Why we do what we do: Understanding self-motivation.* New York: Penguin.

Deci, E.L., Koestner, R., & Ryan, R M. (1999a). A meta-analytic review of experiments examining the effects of extrinsic rewards on intrinsic motivation. *Psychological Bulletin, 125.*

Deci, E.L., & Ryan, R M. (1985b). *Intrinsic motivation and self-determination in human behavior.* New York: Plenum Press.

Deci, E.L., & Ryan, R. M. (2000). The "what" and "why" of goal pursuits: Human needs and the self-determination of behavior. *Psychological Inquiry, 11,* 227–268.

Deci, E.L., & Ryan, R.M. (2002). Overview of self-determination theory: An organismic dialectical perspective. In E.L. Deci & R.M. Ryan (Eds.), *Handbook of self-determination research* (pp. 4–33). Rochester, NY: University of Rochester Press.

Deci, E.L., & Ryan, R.M. (Eds.), (2002). *Handbook of self-determination research.* Rochester, NY: University of Rochester Press.

Deci, E.L., & Ryan, R.M. (2002). The paradox of achievement: The harder you push, the worse it gets. In J. Aronson (Ed.), *Improving academic achievement: Contributions of social psychology* (pp. 59–85). New York: Academic Press.

Dweck, C.S. (1999). *Self theories: Their role in motivation, personality, and development.* Philadelphia, PA: Psychology Press.

Elliot, A.J., & Church, M.A. (1997). A hierarchical model of approach and avoidance achievement motivation. *Journal of Personality and Social Psychology, 72,* 218–232.

Elliot, A.J., & Dweck, C.S. (2005). H*andbook of competence and motivation.* New York, NY: The Guilford Press.

Elliot, A.J., McGregor, H.A., & Thrash, T.M. (2002). The need for competence. In E.L. Deci & R.M. Ryan (Eds.), *Handbook of self-determination research* (pp. 361–387). Rochester, NY: University of Rochester Press.

Gagné, M., & Deci, E.L. (2005). Self-determination theory and work motivation. *Journal of Organizational Behavior, 26,* 331–362.

Hull, C.L. (1943). *Principles of behavior: An introduction to behavior theory.* New York: Appleton–Century–Crofts.

Kohn, A. (1993). *Punished by rewards.* Boston, MA: Houghton Mifflin.

Lamott, A. (1994). *Bird by bird: Some instructions on writing and life.* New York: Pantheon.

Maslow, A.H. (1943). A theory of human motivation. *Psychological Review, 50,* 370–396.

McClelland, D.C. (1985). *Human motivation.* Glenview, IL: Scott, Foresman.

Ryan, R.M., & Deci, E.L. (2000). Intrinsic and extrinsic motivations: Classic definitions and new directions. *Contemporary Educational Psychology, 25,* 54–67.

Ryan, R.M., & Lynch, M.F. (2003). Philosophies of motivation and classroom management. In R. Curren (Ed.), *Blackwell companions to philosophy: A companion to the philosophy of education* (pp. 260–271). New York: Blackwell.

Skinner, B.F. (1953). *Science and human behavior.* New York: Macmillan.

Thomas, K.W. (2000). *Intrinsic motivation at work: Building energy and commitment.* San Francisco, CA: Berrett-Koehler.

Vansteenkiste, M., Simons, J., Lens, W., Sheldon, K., & Deci, E.L. (2004). Motivating learning, performance, and persistence: The synergistic effects of intrinsic goal contents and autonomy-supportive contexts. *Journal of Personality and Social Psychology, 87,* 246–260.

Vansteenkiste, M., & Deci, E.L. (2003). Competitively contingent rewards and intrinsic motivation: Can losers remain motivated? *Motivation and Emotion, 27,* 273–299.

Vroom, V.H. (1964). *Work and motivation.* Hoboken, NJ: John Wiley & Sons.

White, R.W. (1959). Motivation reconsidered: The concept of competence. *Psychological Review, 66,* 297–333.

The Best Training I Never Did!

Glenn Smeaton

Passion

Don't get me wrong, I have nothing against teachers, and trainers. I have seen some very effective trainers and have admired their organization and presentational skills. Teaching and training are good strategies to obtain specific results. Often, however, the desired results are not achievable by formal teaching or training. A glass of water, for instance, can be life– saving if the problem is thirst. It is not much use, however, if the problem is drowning! I offer three stories to illustrate my point, and although this article relates to technical training, its concepts and steps can also be applied to non-technical training.

1. Training Wasn't Working—Or Was It?

It was a warm day in May. My slide projector motor was running hypnotically. I was in a frenzy trying to make a particular course interesting. (You try discussing cationic versus anionic polymers with non-chemists on a warm spring day.) One student, always the same student, was leaning slightly off vertical and his eyes were rolled up so all that I saw was white. I called a break and met with the individual. I asked what I could do to make the class more useful to him. He said that it wasn't the class but that he was so tired. I wondered out loud since the class wasn't required why he couldn't skip class and go out to his car and take a nap.

He explained, "I am the local cop as well as the water and wastewater operator in my town." Two nights ago, somebody called at 2 A.M. to report a rabid dog—it wasn't. Last night there was a fire and I had to make sure the volunteer firemen had enough water. As soon as I got back to my bed, the phone rang reporting a potentially violent marital quarrel. I am afraid to go to my car because they can reach me there by radio.

He pretty much finished by saying he had to go to my class because he needed the sleep! The particular class I taught ran for six hours. It covered most aspects of feeding chemicals in waste-water treatment. Since it covered a wide range of chemicals and equipment, my average student may have only needed about five minutes out of the entire six hours. Think of it, five hours and fifty-five minutes of filler and five minutes of useful information. I changed my approach to training in the morning and touring the facilities of my participants in the afternoon. On tour, they discussed their problems and the other participants offered suggestions. It wasn't very flattering, but *I soon discovered that most of the learning was taking place when I wasn't in front of the room!*

2. A Compliment at a Conference

While attending an annual wastewater operator's association conference I received a compliment. These conferences are interesting in that there are a lot of high-powered speakers presenting valuable information to the audience. Virtually all of the real learning that takes place, however, occurs during the breaks! Operators get together to talk trade with other operators. You hear terms like nocardia, cavitation, filamentous, centrifugal, and positive displacement. If they try this line of conversation on any of their family, friends, or neighbors, they are sure to receive a glassy-eyed stare and a polite frozen smile. So at their conference they unload a year's worth of questions, strategies, and shared information. In one of those sessions an operator came to me and said, "Glenn, I want to thank you for your idea—it really works!" I couldn't remember the conversation or my suggestion so I asked, "How did you implement it?" As he explained, I started remembering our original conversation.

He asked me about a thick layer of norcardial (a threadlike microorganism) scum on his aeration tanks. It was preventing necessary oxygen transfer in his tanks.

I asked, "What have you tried so far?"

"Chlorine"

"Did it work?"

"No."

"What happened?"

"The chlorine didn't reach the scum floating on top."

"What do you think you should try next?"

"I'm thinking of spraying it on top but the chlorine will probably eat through the piping."

"Where have you worked with chlorine before?"

"In our pump house."

"What kind of piping do you use for chlorine in your pump house?"

"PVC"

"Do you think that might work for your spray system?"

"It should. I will give it a try."

So where was the idea I gave him in all this? It was really his idea! What I helped him learn was to have more confidence in his own problem solving skills. I could have suggested a similar approach, but then I would have enforced his *lack of confidence* in his problem-solving skills. Then I accidentally said the right thing, "You identified and solved that problem by yourself—you must really take pride in that!" He stood up straight and said, "You're right—thank you!"

I learned that formal teaching and training essentially reinforce parent/child dynamics. If you need your participants to assume an adult or leadership role, you can't get there by being a parent. You have to work with them as adult to adults as they identify problems, develop strategies, implement solutions, and reflect on what was learned. This may seem slow and inefficient, but it is the quickest way to achieve lasting performance improvement.

3. The Spark

Consultants Thomas Mickelson of ALG Incorporated and Bob Hegg were conducting an operator training program in northern Wisconsin on a treatment process called, "activated sludge." They were working harder and harder, but nothing was happening. They asked the participants at the morning break, "What can we do to make your training more effective?" It turned out that none of the participants needed any information about activated sludge—they were all pond operators (a very different process). They were just attending to complete their continuing education requirements to renew their state wastewater operating licenses.

Mickelson decided to stop teaching about activated sludge for the rest of that course. Instead, he asked, "What problems are you working on solving at your plants?" He changed the focus from the presenters to the participants. His participants were working to solve real problems. That was the spark that lit the room. Later, many of the participants came up and said that that was the best *learning* experience they ever had. That was the beginning of what is now identified by Hegg and Mickelson as, "Implementation Training." What made this process differ from typical "trouble shooting" courses was that it was participant-centered. Coaching and training were imbedded into the activities only when needed as part of the problem-solving process.

Mickelson learned that adults don't want to be "trained"; they want to be given the tools they need to solve their own problems. If you hand a wrench to a mechanic working on a job when he needs it, he will use it. If we hand information to our participants when they need it, they will use it. If they use a particular tool or procedure three or four times, they will remember it when they need to use it again. This process is called "imbedded training." Imbedded training is the heart of what Hegg and Mickelson call "Implementation Training."

Mickelson worked with Glenn Smeaton to help Madison Metropolitan Sewerage District adopt "Implementation Training" as its central learning and performance support strategy. In an effort to better describe the intent of "Implementation Training," we renamed the process, "Learn While You Work Leadership Development (LWYW)."

Later, I met author Michael Marquardt (*Action Learning* and of *Optimizing the Power of Action Learning)* at an ASTD International Conference. Although Madison Metropolitan Sewerage District's LWYW process evolved independently of Marquardt, what we arrived at can qualify as "Action Learning." Whether you call it "Implementation Training" or "Learn While You Work," or "Action Learning," it works! If you want to try it yourself, here is how:

1. **Start with careful project selection.** Your project should be regarded by the directors and by the participants as an important project. Your project should have inherent learning opportunity. Your project should be conducive to a cross-functional learning team approach.

2. **Draft a specific statement of the problem to solve or opportunity to capture.** Your "project charge" should be $\underline{S}$pecific, $\underline{M}$easurable, $\underline{A}$ttainable, $\underline{R}$ealistic, and $\underline{T}$ime-bound (SMART).
3. **Carefully plan for both the project's implementation and the related learning opportunities.** This involves attention to a detailed checklist. (Remember that time spent in project identification and planning is much less costly than time spent with a room full of project participants.)
4. **Follow specific procedures for the implementation phase (This is not significantly different from effective project management).** Start-up of this process should be very formal and outlined on a task list. Once the project is started, however, the facilitator must be very flexible and only provide assistance and training when needed and requested by the participants.
5. **Allow time at the end of each project for celebration, reflection, and action planning.** (The reflection process is what reinforces what was learned in the implementation phase. It also is what distinguishes this process from standard project management.) Celebrate early and often, but make sure you take the time to reflect on what was learned (Our work culture likes going out for lunch or ordering pizza as their celebration).

Conclusion

Be sure to ask:

1. What went well?
2. What lessons were learned?
3. How can we use this information in future efforts?

If you follow this process carefully, you will solve problems of strategic importance while building organizational capacity to address future problems. How's that for ROI?

Some Basics from a Couple of Training Pro's

Training Is More Than What You Say

Terrence L. Gargiulo and Robb Murray

Passion

We are instruments of learning and it's critical to honestly examine our basic assumptions about how people learn.

How much do people learn through didactic explications? If people learn more through making associations, then we must use less "instruction" and more stimulation. We'll examine five simple ways to stimulate learners and provide more effective verbal and non-verbal feedback to keep people engaged and constantly learning.

Take a moment and try to recall teaching experiences when you communicated well and learning ones when you felt engaged. Consider the following questions:

- How do you convey complex concepts without lecturing?
- What role did active participation play?

Here are five techniques to try:

1. Give Up Control

We want to be the experts. At the end of a session we hope for glowing accolades and fulfilled students. Is it possible to have even greater control over the learning experience by not focusing on these things? How far can we meander from the course materials and still hit our objectives? It all depends on our willingness to give up a certain amount of control. It's important not to pay just lip service to the notion of participation. Exhibit a willingness to learn from others. Whenever I stand in front of a group, I remind myself that the collective knowledge and experience of it is far greater than my own. If I build good rapport with a group and create an environment where sharing is encouraged, everyone stands to win.

2. Use Questions

Create a path of questions. For each concept or learning objective, develop a set of questions you can use to guide people. Lead them to the concept through associations. Even the most complex concepts can be explained in this way and in a shorter amount of time than through traditional lecturing. A lecture follows a single stream of ideas. Often there are parts of a concept that are self-evident. Let the participants state these for you and move past them quickly. When there is too much information, use rhetorical questions. These plant seeds in a people's minds for making future connections.

3. Think Fast on Your Feet

Scripts are easy to follow. What do you do when there is no script to follow? As we allow more room for flexibility in our sessions, we need to think quickly on our feet. As you ask questions, you will not always get the same responses. Be prepared to move in any direction. You may be surprised by a person's answer or comment. Tune into how various people are synthesizing the information you are presenting, and adjust your questions and tact accordingly.

4. Visualize the Group

What do we know about a group, it's personalities, and dynamics before we meet them? Try to identify the type of language or metaphors that people will respond to and understand. Prepare examples that use concepts from their areas of expertise and utilize anecdotes and stories whenever possible.

5. Make People Work

Do you find it easier to passively listen than actively participate? Most of us prefer to quietly sit and listen to someone else. People may not like to be bombarded with questions, but it forces them to think. Set the ground rules from the beginning. Let people know they will need to participate and work in order to learn.

So once you begin stimulating learning, you need to find ways to encourage people as they start contributing more and become more engaged. I would encourage all trainers to add color to the black-and-white way in which we sometimes acknowledge desired student responses in class: spice up the verbal with the nonverbal. Both you and your students may achieve more. Here's what I mean:

Most trainers know and use "verbal reinforcement." When a student gives a desired response by voicing a correct answer, or trying a procedure that has heretofore been a source of trepidation, a trainer may respond with "Right!" "That's it!" "Good job!" "Way to go!" "You got it!" or some other word of praise.

Such "reinforcers" warm up the class atmosphere and tend to bring out more involvement from learners. These verbal reassurances show the moral alignment of the trainer with learner progress, and may thereby bring out trust, a reduction of tension, and group solidarity.

Now let us observe something important here: it can be the way in which these reinforcers are delivered that gives them their power. Two truths we know:

- "Actions speak louder than words."
- "Enthusiasm makes the difference."

Delivery Is Key

Ergo, we have the power to boost our laudations by varying the ways in which we deliver them.

If we reinforce with believable enthusiasm, gusto, and sincerity, our little tributes are more interesting and motivating. If we speak them dramatically, humorously, self-deprecatingly, with surprise, or with an onward-rushing acceleration or pitch build, we make happen a mini-scene that students *feel, remember, and absorb* at a gut level.

We can also add a hand clap to the varieties of pitch and vocal pacing. A finger snap. A professional finger, raised in surprise, as if to say, "Eureka!" A high-five, thumbs-up, or raised fist of victory. A lifted eyebrow or a tilt of the head. A shake of instructor's papers we are holding. A gasp of happy, comic surprise. These all bring the moment of student praise into high relief. If the energy build fits, you may even stomp your foot as you make an exclamation, or slap a desk. And as though out of control, you can tap the white board with a pointer in animalian excitement.

"That's Good Training"

Is there any among us who doesn't remember a favorite teacher from the past who used techniques of this sort? Didn't this teacher usually command attention and achieve effective progress with a class?

Yes?

"Good! [hand clap] Hey, ya *got it* [finger snap]!"

Conclusion

Using these five basic guidelines for stimulating learners and becoming more aware of how we use verbal and non-verbal adornments improve students' enjoyment of training and enhances the learning environment.

It is often said that a trainer may be "a frustrated actor." Yet the drama of education, a utilitarian craft by comparison to the art world, has its own beauty and power. When it is well done, a well-taught training could leave many an actor in the frustrated role, because its positive purpose and after-class benefits to its audience are so undeniable. "So useful—and yet so fun!" That's good training.

The Synergy of Co–Facilitation

Creating Powerful Learning Experiences

Dr. Vince Molinaro

Passion

Co-facilitation is a dynamic way to enhance the learning experience for participants. I am passionate about the "aha" moment—when learners gain new insights that open up creative opportunities for future growth and success.

Co-facilitating any learning session with another trainer can be tricky and at times fraught with problems. This article explores the benefits of co-facilitation, reviews some of the potential pitfalls, and provides a proven set of steps to ensure your next co-facilitation experience delivers great results for your learners.

Co-Facilitation: The Benefits

Co-facilitating sessions has the potential to offer many benefits:

- Co-facilitators bring different perspectives to the session. This makes the learning experience richer.
- Co-facilitation can increase participant attention and retention.
- With two facilitators in a room, both can better focus on their parts without having to pay attention to myriad classroom dynamics. This results in a better learning experience.
- Two facilitators can better spot and manage group dynamic issues when they surface and support each other as they address them.
- When two facilitators co-facilitate well, it creates a unique synergy that is greater than would have been achieved with only one facilitator in the room. The synergy exists between the facilitators and among the learners as well.

Co-Facilitation: The Potential Pitfalls

Co-facilitation has many pitfalls, let's examine some of the most prevalent:

- *The Self-Absorbed Facilitators:* The first pitfall is when facilitators focus on themselves instead of on their participants. Perhaps you've had this experience as a participant of a learning program: As you entered the room, you saw the two facilitators at the front talking and laughing and clearly having such a good time that they forgot to attend to their participants.

- *Clash of Egos:* Another common pitfall of co-facilitation is the clash of egos that can lead to what I call "dueling-facilitators." The co-facilitators compete with each other—trying to outdo each other and show who is smarter or better. In the end, this behavior serves to undermine the credibility of both facilitators and fails to create synergy.

- *Lack of Preparation:* Many times co-facilitation fails because the facilitators do not take the time to prepare adequately. This usually happens because some trainers are in fact master facilitators on their own. They then assume they can merely walk into a room and achieve the same great results with a co-facilitator that they accomplish when they facilitate by themselves. However, this approach is a recipe for disaster. One facilitator may appear ready, while the other doesn't. In other cases, neither is ready, and it seems as if they are making things up as the go along. The bottom line is that credibility is undermined, and the learning experience is not as strong as it should be.

- *Lack of Modeling:* Years ago, I took part in a two-day training program on conflict management that was led by two facilitators. For most of the two days, the atmosphere was professional, but it was clear that the two were not getting along. Finally, in the afternoon of the final day, the two facilitators began to have an open conflict. As their voices began to rise, it became quite uncomfortable in the room. More importantly, it was clearly evident that the facilitators were not applying the same conflict management skills they were teaching.

As you review this list of pitfalls, it is important to keep in mind that learners are very astute, and they pick up on all these issues. Don't ever think you are fooling anyone in the classroom.

Co-Facilitation: Proven Strategies

Below are some proven strategies gained through countless co-facilitation experiences. I've also provided a checklist in Exhibit 22.1 at the end of the article to ensure successful outcomes for your next co-facilitation opportunity.

1. Prepare for the Session with Your Co-Facilitator

Learning to work together with a colleague will take some time, so pre-session preparation is a critical success factor. Here are some steps to ensure that sufficient pre-session preparation takes place:

- Develop a set of ground rules that will govern how you will work together while co-facilitating. These ground rules will cover all sorts of issues, such as how decisions are made in real time, how to resolve conflicts, etc.
- Designate one facilitator as the "lead" facilitator for the day or program to ensure that logistics, dynamics, and the overall session flow well.
- Consider who is best suited to deliver each section.
- Discuss a back-up plan in the event that one of you becomes ill or is unable to deliver the session.
- Discuss how you will introduce yourselves to your participants. Make sure to explain your roles as co-facilitators. I have found that one facilitator should act as a "master of ceremonies" to begin the workshop and welcome the participants and other facilitator.

2. Create Synergy in the Classroom

Below are some important ideas to keep in mind when you are about to facilitate your session:

- Check your egos at the door, and focus your collective energies on generating optimal outcomes for your learners. Your participants will appreciate you both for it.
- Plan to rotate sections every couple of hours or so. This helps increase the participants' retention and attentiveness. Look for logical breaks in the session for making transitions. Practice your transitions so that your participants feel the learning is seamless.
- Set up a facilitators' table at the back of the room. This way, when one facilitator is presenting, the other can be at the back of the room observing group dynamics and his or her colleague.
- When a facilitator is presenting a section, it is important that the co-facilitator remain alert and attentive. This is a critical time to model good learning behavior to participants.
- Identify clearly with each other how you want to handle issues throughout the day. Discuss how comfortable you and your partner are with each of you giving input during sessions, and build guidelines in advance.
- Look for subtle ways to provide real-time feedback to each other. One of the strategies I have used is to create index cards with various symbols. One card has a drawing of a smiley face that a co-facilitator can use to remind the other facilitator at the front of the room to smile. Another card has a symbol of an ear to encourage the facilitator to speak more loudly. Other cards use symbols to indicate picking up the pace, slowing down the pace, etc.
- Avoid interrupting your partner while he or she is leading a section. This can diminish the facilitator's credibility and take the focus away from the session. If you want to add an important learning point, wait until your partner is leading a group discussion and then raise your hand to indicate you have something to add.

- Keep on time. If you run over your allotted time, it can be more difficult for your co-facilitator to do his or her job well. Give each other time reminders. Also, discuss when it is okay to go over time, and develop contingency plans on how to adjust the agenda.
- The key to great co-facilitation is to establish an open, honest, and trusting relationship. If you are both getting along and having fun, your participants will feed off this. If you are both tense and in conflict, this will also affect your participants.
- Remember to model what you are teaching. For example, I was facilitating a week-long leadership program with a colleague. At the end of the week, several participants came up to us and said, "Both of you don't just teach this stuff, you model it in how you work together. It was great seeing you in action and how you both supported each other during the week." This is one of the gratifying aspects of co-facilitation. It points to the fact that while trainers are co-facilitating, they are not merely imparting skills and knowledge, they are modeling good teamwork and leadership to learners—and the learners appreciate it.

3. Debrief After the Session

Another good practice is to meet with your co-facilitator after your session to debrief the experience. Here are some ideas.

- A useful approach is for the facilitators to identify something they were proud they accomplished and then identify something their partners accomplished. Then each identifies something he or she can do better next time and something they feel their partners can do better.
- Review participant feedback sheets, and highlight the strengths and areas of development. Wrap up the meeting by discussing how you and the other facilitator will work more effectively in future sessions you will deliver together.

You will find a sample of the co-facilitation strategies checklist in Exhibit 22.1. I have included a ready-to-use template of the checklist on the website.

Exhibit 22.1. Co-Facilitation Strategies Checklist

1. Prepare for the Session

☐ We have developed a set of ground rules that will govern how we will work together while co-facilitating.

☐ We have designated one facilitator as the "lead" facilitator to ensure that logistics, dynamics, and the overall session flow well.

☐ We have determined who is best-suited to deliver each section.

☐ We have a back-up plan in the event of that one facilitator is not able to attend.

☐ We have determined who will introduce the team, explain our roles, and act as "master of ceremonies."

2. Create Synergy in the Classroom

☐ We will check our egos at the door and focus our collective energies on generating optimal outcomes for our learners.

☐ We have a plan to rotate sections every couple of hours.

☐ We have set up a facilitators' table at the back of the room.

☐ We agree to remain alert and attentive throughout.

☐ We have discussed how we will handle issues as they arise and how we intend to provide one another with feedback.

☐ We have a plan on how to provide real-time feedback to each other.

☐ We agree not to interrupt one another.

☐ We commit to do our best to keep the program on time.

(Continued)

- [ ] We have established an open, honest, and trusting relationship.

- [ ] We will model good teamwork.

3. Debrief After the Session

- [ ] We will meet after our session to identify strengths and areas of development and to provide each other with meaningful feedback.

- [ ] We will review participant feedback sheets to identify strengths and areas for development.

- [ ] We will develop a plan for how we will build on our strengths and address development areas the next time we co-facilitate.

Conclusion

Co-facilitation can be a challenging experience. When it goes well, it will be one of the most rewarding peak experiences you will have. It is very gratifying to work with a trusted colleague to create synergy that leads to powerful learning outcomes for learners.

Article 23

Learnertainment®

Lenn Millbower

Passion

As Louis Mercier said, "What we learn with pleasure, we never forget."

I remember one particularly difficult college class I taught, and the two students who were likely to fail. They, like many in a growing segment of learners, had short attention spans. They expected more value in less time, but wouldn't listen well enough to find that value. Instead, they would become bored, and ignore the learning.

One day, I heard the two praising James Cameron's movie *Titanic* (1997). Immediately, an incongruity hit me. *Titanic* is three hours long! Those would have mutinied if I attempted a three-hour lecture. To make matters more galling, they PAID to see *Titanic*. REPEATEDLY! Both students were destined to repeat this class, but would not have willingly paid for the opportunity. Hollywood had succeeded in capturing and maintaining those two learners' attention, where I had not.

Their *Titanic* comments led me back to my prior career as a professional entertainer, and the entertainment techniques I had learned while performing music, magic, and comedy. I identified two commonalties that the training and entertainment communities share. (1) Both disciplines require a professional delivery. If the delivery is amateurish, the entertainer is booed, and the trainer is ignored. (2) Both must attract attention, and fail if attention is not captured, or worse, lost after it is gained. If no one notices the selected playing card, the magician's production of it has no magic. If no one hears the learning point, that point cannot be remembered.

I next began looking for entertainment techniques I could apply to my classroom. Each time I added an entertaining element, the learners responded, so I'd add another. I soon noticed that test and class evaluation scores rose. The more entertainment techniques I employed, the more effective the learning became. And then, one day, one of those former learners, now repeating my class, approached me. She asked if she could attend one of my classes again! That's when I knew that entertainment-based learning works.

In this article, I share with you the theory that resulted from my journey. It offers a different way to think about learning and a method for increasing retention while simultaneously making learning engaging and fun. It is a combination of learning and entertainment I call *Learnertainment*®.

To Leave or Learn?

The searchlight is always on. It scans the landscape, looking first left then right, ever vigilant for signs of danger. This searchlight is unusual in its sophistication. Like all searchlights, it scans visually. But in addition, it listens, it uses its sense of smell, it reaches out to touch unknown items, and on occasion, it tastes the stimuli in question. Perhaps the most amazing fact about this searchlight is that humans didn't invent it. It predates science. It's the human brain.

When the human brain sees potential danger, it stops searching. It blocks out all extraneous stimuli and focuses tightly on the perceived threat. Even those higher-order components of the brain responsible for logic and the arts pitch in, refocusing their energies in an "all hands on deck" effort survive. If the threat turns out to be minor, the various brain components resume their normal activities . . . until the next time the searchlight calls.

This dynamic is continuous; twenty-four hours a day, seven days a week, below the level of awareness, but always dictating human behavior. And as such, the searchlight cannot be ignored. Ideas, and the intellectual application of those ideas, are important, but are of little consequence to a brain that feels threatened.

Fortunately for trainers, teachers, facilitators, and other learning professionals, the brain has a secondary favorite input: pleasure. In humans, survival and pleasure exist side by side. They are the Yin and Yang, the left and right, the balancing forces of our existence, and they are driven by the searchlight of emotion. (See Figure 23.1.)

Emotion Creates Attention

The word emotion comes from the Latin *exmovere*, meaning "to move out of," "to agitate." Aristotle believed that people are persuaded not just by logic, but also through emotion. Plato agreed when he said, "All learning has an emotional base." And Carl Jung added, "There can be no transforming of darkness into

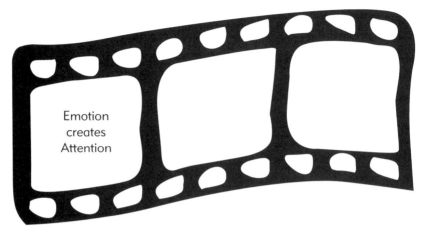

Figure 23.1. The Learnertainment® Chain

light and of apathy into movement without emotion." They were all correct. Emotions start a chain of events that lead to learning.

For centuries, folklore stated that emotion was a creature of the heart. As science gained ascendancy over folklore, emotions were thought to be a function of the brain. Recent research demonstrates that both folklore and science had it right. Emotion is generated in the brain AND the body.

Emotions affect our whole body, including our heart, lungs, stomach, skin, and immune and endocrine systems. If you think back through your own life experience, you instinctively know this to be true. We have all felt the goosebumps of fear, the sweat of nervousness, and the rapid breathing that comes from excitement. A "gut" reaction is just that, an emotional signal from the gut.

The wisdom of gut reactions makes sense when you consider that the heart starts beating in a human fetus before the brain is formed, and that, as the brain develops, it begins with the brain stem. From the brain stem, the emotional limbic system emerges. Next, the thinking brain grows out of the emotional regions. Perhaps as a result, more neural connections go from the

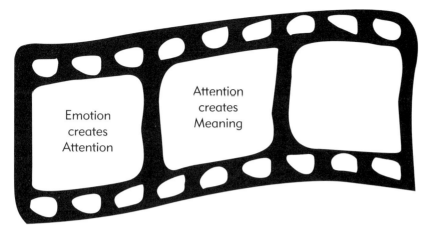

Figure 23.2. The Learnertainment® Chain, Part 2

limbic system to the cortex than the other way around. Certainly as a result, emotional reactions occur before we think. We feel first, and think later.

The body's up-front focus on feelings is critical to our survival. In situations in which life or death stands in the balance, split-second responses are essential. Emotion serves the purpose of identifying general threat levels. The emotional meaning of the situation captures the brain's attention and helps it make snap fight-or-flight decisions. This response is automatic. Although people may be able rationalize their emotions, the truth is emotions control them. Even when people overpower emotions with logic, the feelings that created the emotion remain, often forever. (See Figure 23.2.)

Attention Creates Meaning

Once emotion has taken hold, the brain shifts into a heightened level of attention. This heightened level is stressful. It cannot be maintained for long. To protect itself from overload and to free up capacity for the next potential threat, the brain quickly determines the meaning of the emotion. It explores its memories, searching for something comparable. Once a comparison is found, the brain concocts a mental concept or model to explain the emotion. It then uses this explanation to determine an appropriate response. This is not to suggest that the brain has made an intellectual decision. Rather, it has captured the general meaning of what has happened and selects a correct response accordingly.

During this process, the initial stimulus is held in short-term memory. Short-term memory is that portion of memory devoted to the things that must be remembered in the moment, but may not be significant in the future. Short-term memory has finite capacity and can only store items for around thirty seconds. Consequently, the brain quickly determines the meaning of the information, and its potential future importance. (See Figure 23.3.)

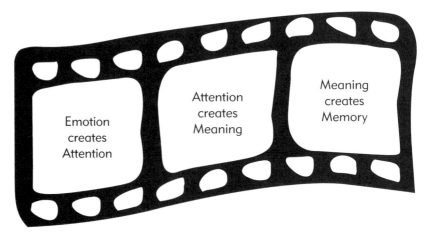

Figure 23.3. The Learnertainment® Chain, Part 3

Meaning Creates Memory

With an item's meaning defined, the event is codified. Information of little long-term value is discarded. Information that is, or may be, meaningful in the future, is forwarded into long-term memory.

It is in the long-term memory where learning, if successful, resides. Unlike short-term memory, long term memory has an almost infinite capacity. Once an item has passed into the brain's long-term memory, it remains on file, waiting for the searchlight's call. The item, although nearly forgotten, remains so potent that the correct emotional stimuli—a song, a smell, a visual, or a combination of sensory inputs—can bring it flooding back into conscious memory. And often the memory returns so vividly that it seems as if the event just occurred!

This depth of memory provides learning professionals with an advantage. Knowing that an emotional stimulus remains powerful when locked in the memory, it's in the instructor's best interest to tie learning to emotion. All that is required is a strong, emotional trigger . . . like entertainment. (See Figure 23.4.)

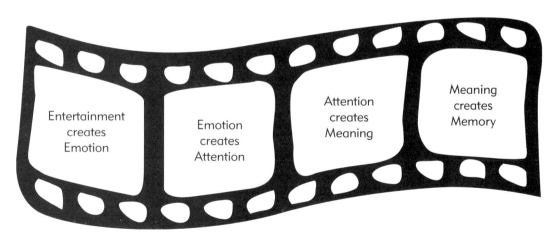

Figure 23.4. The Learnertainment® Chain, Part 4

Entertainment Creates Emotion

In today's world, entertainment is everywhere. We see it in advertising, in news programming, in "reality" television, in TV-based education, and in businesses ranging from restaurants to retail stores to theme parks.

We have become a society obsessed with entertainment. In the United States, on average, we spend 5.1 percent of our income on it. That figure is comparable to our spending on health care (5.3 percent), and is more than we spend on clothing (4.7 percent).

What those figures don't represent is the rise in entertainment spending through the years. In 1935–1936, we spent just 3.3 percent of our income on entertainment, 4.4 percent on health care, and 10.4 percent on clothing.

Where spending on entertainment is at a high, the rate of personal savings is at a low, under 3 percent. After housing (32.6 percent), transportation (19.0 percent), and food (13.6 percent), enjoyment trumps all. And the percentage of income spent on food is misleading, because 5.7 percent of that category is dining out costs, and a significant success factor in the food service industry is the entertainment value (atmosphere, theme, and food presentation) a restaurant provides.

It's not an accident that entertainment rules. As survival concerns receded from the foreground, people became individually focused. In past generations, assembly-line style orderliness and a "Yes Sir!" willingness to follow commands were valued. Today, people instead focus on their individuals needs, with little adherence to the dictates of others. They expect to be catered to, and will patronize organizations that provide enjoyment.

In response, many organizations have entertainmentized their products. The result is a culture in which the lines between entertainment and non-entertainment are evaporating. Entertainment content is becoming the norm. Shakespeare was correct before his time. The world IS a stage.

Learnertainment®

It is appropriate that the world is a stage. The entertainment arts were created to complement the brain's searchlight quest for danger. At the dawn of human history, pleasure, although secondary to survival, was always present. Pleasure had a survival function. Food, sex, and sleep were required for survival, and thus were pleasurable. The brain also required excess capacity for emergencies, but excess capacity had to be exercised. The entertainment arts provided the exercise regimen.

Eventually survival was assured, but the excess capacity remained. Fortunately, the portion of the brain that processes negative emotions, the right hemisphere, is also attracted to the entertainment arts. People began to refocus this region on pleasurable experiences.

Whether the forum was a nighttime cave fire, the Greek coliseum, the Elizabethan stage, the vaudeville palace, Broadway, the movies, television, or most recently, the Internet, a straight line can be traced from the receding of survival needs and the ascension of emotionally based entertainment.

In this context then, the learning professional's challenge is to match society; to make classroom instruction equal in entertainment value; to lift classroom instruction from expected to exceptional, from required to desired, from painful to pleasurable; in short, to make it fun!

The key to fun is the solicitation of positive learner emotions. As we have discovered, negative emotion rarely sleeps: especially in the classroom. When the brain focuses on survival, it focuses completely. Worse yet, learning requires the exploration of unfamiliar territory, and when the incoming information doesn't fit any recognizable pattern, the brain tags the information as a potential threat. The searchlight stops and learning is blocked. Smart learning professionals draw the searchlight towards positive emotional energy.

Conclusion

Here's where Learnertainment® can help. Entertainment-based content relaxes the right hemisphere, in effect, *babysitting it*, keeping it busy with things it likes: cartoons, music, games, activities, visuals. Once the right hemisphere is playfully engaged, learning can commence without negative blocking emotions. *Attention is riveted on the positive aspects of learning.* In short, Learnertainment® distracts them so that you can slip some learning in on them.

So the searchlight scans, never to stop. It's no matter. Learnertainment® welcomes the spotlight. It beckons that light, it draws it in, entices it to stop and performs for it, demanding it pay attention. And with attention secured the spotlight shines where it should, on learning.

Seven Strategies on How to Use Stories to Increase Learning and Facilitate Training

Terrence L. Gargiulo

Passion

Stories are how we communicate, learn, and think. Trainers have many opportunities during the course of a learning event to use stories for more than just entertainment or illustration of points.

Stories come in all different forms, including personal experiences, anecdotes, metaphors, analogies, or jokes. The guiding rule for using stories in trainings or workshops is to be sensitive to the group. By staying tuned in to the group's ever-changing needs, you will be able to find the right stories to tell at the right time, elicit group member's stories, and increase learning.

Here are some ideas on how to start.

1. Answer People's Questions with a Story

Questions are good. It means people are thinking. Get people to draw parallels between the story you tell and the questions they are asking. Provide analysis and insights about the story when people become stuck.

Example

There are times when a group doubts the message you are charged with delivering. This is evident in the number, tone, and intensity of questions raised by the group. I remember one session when the barrage of questions about the restructuring of a company's sales territories and bonus structures were faster than I could field them. It turned out that after extensive research the current structure that had been in place for over ten years was promoting unproductive competition between sales representatives. This was resulting in a loss of business to the organization, especially of larger, more lucrative accounts that had higher profit margins. In the long run, the company's gain in revenue and profits and the bonuses people would receive from these increases would offset the short-term loss of individual contributors' commissions. I shifted gears and told about an experience I had as a competitive fencer during a crucial team match in which I purposely lost a bout to set up a strategic situation for the team. I shared with the group my reluctance to make this personal sacrifice and the tremendous leap of faith it required. In the case of the fencing match, the strategy paid off handsomely and resulted in our winning a match against a stronger team.

My personal story gave many people a chance in the group to momentarily suspend their concerns and consider the motives of their company from a broader perspective.

2. Elicit Stories from the Group

Try to tie people's comments together. Ask them to be specific and give examples. They will end up sharing personal experiences in the form of stories. Synthesize their comments with their experiences to make new points and to reinforce previous ones.

Example

I was facilitating a project management workshop. Many people in the group were concerned about the amount of documentation that was going to be expected of them. So when we started a discussion about writing a communication plan (a document that describes how members of a project team intend to share information with stakeholders, in what form, and with what frequency) people became visibly agitated. Rather than trying to provide any further rational justification as to the importance of writing a communication plan, I asked people to share some of their experiences around difficult project dynamics. One story led to a flood of others. With a little probing, people began to see a common theme of breakdown in communications emerge as one of the greatest problems. When I asked the group how any of these communication problems might have been averted, it naturally led us back to the concept of a communication plan.

3. Use a Metaphor or an Analogy

Help people to visualize the idea or concept you are trying to explain by applying a metaphor or analogy from another domain. After you provide one, ask them to think of another one. This solidifies the concept for them and gives them confidence. It also allows you to make sure they have grasped the concept.

Example

I was heading up a team of instructional designers and trainers to create an information technology orientation program for global senior human resources executives of a Fortune 10 company. Conversations with stakeholders had already alerted me to the reality that almost all of these executives had little to no technical background. Even worse, one of the chief reasons behind the program's creation was the impatient and intolerant attitude these executives exhibited toward information technology. Before the project kickoff meeting with my team, I made a huge list of technical terms and concepts. After some introductory activities with the team, I broke them up into groups and gave each group a list of technical terms. I instructed them to come up with analogies and metaphors apropos to the company and human resources concepts. We wove these examples into all of the materials and created a cheat book for trainers with all of the metaphors and analogies in it. After we ran the first program, the evaluations were filled with comments about how the course materials and trainers had made technical mumbo jumbo so easy to understand and fun to learn. I got my greatest satisfaction when I was walking the down the hall one day and I heard one of the executives explaining a technical concept with one of the analogies my team had written.

4. Tell a Story to Change the Group's Energy

There are natural ebbs and flows to a group's energy. A story can stimulate and revitalize a group. Likewise, stories can help a group relax and become centered.

Example

We've all experienced it before; it's afternoon and despite our best efforts, the group resembles a herd of comatose cattle. One of the first times I experienced this truly terrifying phenomenon as a trainer I was fortunate to have a copy of one of the *Chicken Soup for the Soul* books. In an act of desperation I gave people a ten-minute stretch break, and as they filtered back into the room, I observed that they still seemed exhausted. I reached for the book and opened it at random and read a few stories. It was as if I had given them a blast of cool air conditioning in a heat-drenched room. From that day forward, I began to build a repertoire of stories I could either read or tell to groups.

5. Validate and Transform Emotions with a Story; Tell a Story with Your Voice and Body Language

Tell a story that mirrors the emotions you sense in the group in a non-didactic and unpatronizing way. This validates unspoken emotions and allows people to move past them. Once negative feelings are acknowledged, they can be examined safely through the story and even transformed into more positive ones.

When you tell a story, match the tone and body language of individuals in the group. People will become more aware of what they are saying through their bodies and begin to modify their body language. As they do so, there will be subtle shifts in their perceptions and emotions.

Example

I came back after a lunch break and noticed a curious change in the group's energy. Some people were exhibiting a nervous, agitated state, while others were noticeably quiet and sullen. With a little probing I learned that the organizational group these folks belonged to was being tasked with a very challenging and visible project that many people felt was destined to fail. Folks were feeling like guinea pigs. So I told them and enacted the story behind the cliché, "a canary in a coal mine." The contrast of a bright yellow canary with a dark coal mine is a striking image. Miners in coal mines used to carry canaries in cages on their shoulders. If a canary died, they knew the air in the mine was not safe. I used a tone of voice that I felt empathized with the uneasy feelings of the team. Right or wrong, many of them believed that the business was setting them up for failure. I used the story to validate emotions and articulate possibilities. We talked about how people could work with the negative emotions of fear and resentment about being set up for failure to positive ones of excitement about the challenge that lies ahead of them. I used the story to engage their imaginations to discover that the story can be rewritten. Why not give the story a new spin? The canary neither has to die nor be stuck in a cage. We discovered that, unlike canaries, the team is free to make choices to avoid disaster. Show how the team will be brave pioneers for the business.

6. Tell a Story to Change a Group's Perspective

Stories can be used as tools to encourage thinking. A group becomes stuck when it is unable to imagine other possibilities. Stories can be rich sources of irony and paradox. These, in turn, challenge a group's current thinking and can move them in new directions.

Example

I was having a heck of time helping a client streamline its help desk processes. There was a lot of resistance to imagining any changes.

The support group had spent a lot of money on a web-based tool for tracking and resolving trouble tickets. The issue, of course, was not the tool, but I had an idea. I pulled the director of the group aside and asked him to give me an hour and a half with his team. After a little cajoling, he agreed. I went through the trouble ticket database and selected five recent tickets. Next, I invited the internal customers who had submitted the tickets to meet with us and share their stories with the group. The day arrived for the meeting, and people had no idea what we were going to do. After warming the group up and getting them relaxed, I informed them that we were going to review five recent trouble ticket stories from two perspectives. First from the customer's and then from the engineer's who had been responsible for resolving it. In order to facilitate open communication, I asked the engineer associated with the ticket being discussed to leave the room. Likewise, I asked each customer to leave the room when the engineers shared their stories. As was to be expected, there was some defensive face saving, but the stories yielded lots of rich information. The group was able to shift its thinking and see new opportunities for improving its processes. And customers had a chance to understand what goes on behind the scenes and give their thoughts, ideas, and suggestions.

7. Use a Joke or Tangent

Jokes are a great tool for getting people to be less analytical. Jokes are like little epiphanies. A joke is funny because the punch line is unexpected. It hits us as a surprise. Telling a joke or leaving the subject at hand to go off on a tangent will help a group become less analytical and more creative.

Example

I'm really not that funny of a guy. My wife tells me all the time that I have wonderful gifts and attributes, but that humor is not among them. As a trainer I have worked hard to develop wit on the fly and quirky, instant repartee with a group to provide levity when necessary. I'm not one to tell a long, drawn-out joke, but I will use humor in mid-sentence to shake up a group. One common device I use is asking the group to be my laugh track. I confess my struggles as a funny guy and ask the group to humor me if I try to say something funny. I give them the task of giving me a courtesy laugh every time I pull my ear after I've tried to say something funny. This works like a charm. I can distract the group for a moment, stir things up, and then pull them right back into the topic at hand without getting sidetracked for any length of time.

Conclusion

Stories are the most powerful low-tech virtual reality simulators we can ever use in training. People respond to stories and, given the opportunity, people will share stories and draw connections between the topic at hand, their experiences, and the experiences of others. Look for new ways to use stories for more than just reinforcing a point. The seven strategies discussed in this article offer some subtle but very effective ways to use stories to encourage stimulate learning.

Note: For an in-depth discussion of how to work with stories, see my new book *Once Upon a Time: Using Story-Based Activities to Develop Breakthrough Communication Skills* and *Stories Trainers Tell* by Mark Wacker and Lori Silverman.

Dealing with Difficult Issues in Training

Terrence L. Gargiulo

Passion

Navigating through challenging waters while facilitating a training class is the kind of adventure that I have grown to enjoy. This is not to say that dealing with difficult issues in training is easy stuff or that we can follow any ready-made formula for how to deal with them, but responsibly leading a group through difficult issues is one of the most reward-ing, humbling, and deepening experiences we can have as trainers.

Imagine the following scenario . . .

You have been contracted by upper management to teach a communications and team-building workshop to a group of disgruntled union employees you have never worked with before. Morale is low. The union is in dispute with management. People are being laid off left and right, and there is a good chance that the plant will be closed.

How about this one?

You find out minutes before you are to begin a workshop that one of the attendees has just died. He or she was a long-time employee at this company and well-known by the people attending your session.

Before you read on, take a moment and reflect on these situations and similar ones you may have found yourself in. What would you do? How did you handle the situation?

Some Guiding Principles

This is by no means an exhaustive list, but here are a few guiding principles I have found useful over the years:

1. *Make No Assumptions*

Avoid making assumptions. For instance, do not assume people want to discuss a difficult topic. People may have already spent enough time discussing it and not view the training session as the appropriate time or place. Avoid assuming you know how people feel. There will be a variety of feelings. Avoid assuming you know all the details of a given situation. Most importantly, do not assume you can either solve the problem or change the way people are feeling. Remember that you are there to teach a workshop that has specific learning outcomes. Ask yourself: What do I need to do to stand the best chance of achieving those objectives and make the most productive learning environment?

2. Create an Open Environment of Trust and Vulnerability

In order for people to feel comfortable sharing what's on their minds, we must make them feel safe. If the group does not know you, this can be a real challenge. You have very little time to create an open environment. In all likelihood you will have to find a genuine way of demonstrating some vulnerability and sensitivity with the group. A short personal story well told and well timed can be very effective. For example, in the first situation from above, you might tell a short anecdote of a recent experience that made you feel powerless. Maybe recount a humorous but poignant customer service encounter. The combination of humor, frustration, and the similarities of an emotional experience that will resonate with their own is likely to loosen up a group. Don't forget that our non-verbal gestures are as important as anything we say. Be confident to act and speak extemporaneously. Precanned speeches and behaviors have the danger of coming across as hollow; or worse yet, even in genuine.

3. Validate Emotions

Find ways to validate people's feelings. There is a natural inclination to question feelings, probe for reasons why those feelings are there in the first place, or to offer explanations; however; none of these well-intentioned interventions help the situation. Even negative emotions can be transformed into potentially positive perceptions if we honor people's feelings. Try to get people to speak more from their hearts, emotions, and imaginations than from their heads. When a person begins to explain his or her feelings he or she will usually start from the head. The person is working from a mental transcript. Certain words and phrases have habituated the person's thinking processes and catalyzed his or her feelings. Act as a guide by probing the stories and images behind these abstractions. Ask the person to provide a narrative re-experiencing of events that have formed these thoughts. Allow people to work off of one another. One person's telling of an experience will trigger a telling from someone else. Soon you will be in a fertile field of imagination. We must be willing to invoke the irrational in order to reveal the ironies, paradoxes, and inconsistencies of our bold and deliberate rationalities.

4. Poll the Group

Here is a technique I sometime use at the beginning of a session to get a quick gauge on a group's feelings. Ask everyone to take a piece of paper and write down an adjective or two that describes how he or she is currently feeling. Collect all the pieces of paper and read the words out loud. You can also capture words on a flip chart. This has two clear benefits. First it allows people to express their feelings in a safe way. Second, people will realize that others have similar feelings. This can be a great way to lead into a discussion or decide to forego one, depending on the type of responses you receive.

5. Be Flexible with Your Timeline

Training sessions are never long enough. Allocating time to topics other than those on our agenda is bound to get us in time trouble. If you decide to tackle a sensitive topic, be prepared to give it enough time. Find other places in the agenda where you can cut. As long as you manage expectations and let people know that certain items on the agenda will not be covered, most people will not have a problem with the changes. Be sure to point out the value of the discussion and, if possible, relate it in some way back to the session's learning objectives.

6. Be Opinion-Less

While vulnerability may be important to establish with a group, we must be careful to leave our opinions and strong ideas at the door. Take the time to be aware of your own feelings prior to a session. During the session, watch and observe your own feelings, but be careful of how you expose them. Remember that whatever processing of emotions and discussion might ensue during a session is for the participants and not for you. On more than one occasion I have had to catch myself and refrain from expressing a strong opinion. This is not to say that you should never bring your ideas or opinions to the group, but do so with utmost care, caution, and respect for the group and its needs.

Back to Our Scenarios

Let's take a moment and apply some of these principles to the opening scenarios in this article. When faced with a group of employees involved in labor disputes and massive layoffs, I made it a priority to give people a chance to vent. I did not want to silence their voices and I did not want to shape or constrain their feedback. My first job was to earn people's trust. I did not want to take sides, but I also did not want to be perceived as a puppet of management. So without letting the session turn into a gripe session, I asked people to share their experiences. I had an unspoken ground rule that I reinforced with my facilitation behavior. Broad sweeping complaints were not allowed. I made people share their personal experiences in narratives. This allowed people to build a mosaic of experiences and feel validated while minimizing the negative energy of editorialized attacks. Some of the stories were horrific, so I had to be very vigilant about not being pulled into them while still experiencing the stories in a visceral way to gain people's trust and increase my understanding of what they were feeling. The session became a safe place for people to explore their questions about the future. I was careful not to offer rosy visions or try to put a positive spin on the situation. I just stayed focused on helping people voice their fears and connect with each other.

In our second scenario of a sudden death of someone in the company known well by members of the group, I asked the group for permission to veer from our agenda. I carved out a piece from our schedule and let the group design a mini ritual to honor the person. This turned into forty-five minutes of testimonials. I gave people a short break during which they could write down a few memories they wished to share with the group. One person even went to this person's desk and brought back some personal objects to share with the group. The group decided to pass along some of the stories to Human Resources and Corporate Communications to use in any of its communiqués.

Conclusion

Difficult situations are inevitable in training. Our response to them is less predictable. We need to be prepared to be open and spontaneous. Keeping in mind these six principles will help you handle these situations with professionalism and personal grace.

Conclusion to Section Two

Haven't we all found ourselves fumbling nervously before a group of trainees arrive? We take a few deep breaths and run through a quick mental rehearsal.

It is so simple but easy to forget. Trainers catalyze learning. We have to suspend all of our other agendas, especially ones tied up with our egos. Looking good, sounding smart, and getting great evaluations are at best ancillary to our core charter. Here is a key phrase I use to keep myself centered as a trainer: "Proactive Learning . . . Reactive Teaching."

Proactive Learning

Would you agree there is not one path to any concept, information, or insight? PowerPoint slides, pre-canned modules, scripts, etc., are certainly important, but we must remember that they are only guidelines. We should never let structure get in the way of learning. What things do we do to actively engage each learner in the room? We need to be "Pro"fessionals at making learning active. I try to give up the urge to be a single bit stream of information. I enjoy being the center of attention and standing on my soapbox, but it does not promote proactive learning. Make every learner work. Although technique and style will differ from trainer to trainer, identify methods for engaging learners. I find there is a relationship between the number of questions I ask, the number of comments I elicit, and the number of metaphors I use with the quality of learning. Don't wait for people to leave before they have an opportunity to synthesize new information. Give them a chance and medium to gain insights while they are with you. That is the heart of *"proactive learning."*

Reactive Teaching

Be ready for a roller-coaster ride. Every time I ask a question to a group of learners, I hold my breath. I have no idea what they will say. Or worse yet, how I might need to respond to their answers, or manage the group's reaction to it. We may be looking for a certain answer but *"reactive teaching"* challenges us to find a way to transform any response so that it energizes the group and affirms the contributor. The image of a potter is helpful here. Each comment or interaction, verbal and non-verbal, is like a piece of clay that needs to be molded and shaped. In order to make this happen, we must be like the potter and let the wheel spin vigorously and get wet, sticky clay all over our hands. Our potting wheel is the group, and its interaction with us is the wet, sticky clay on our hands that are the personalities, learning styles, and needs of each person. Be fearless. I enjoy training because I love to learn and I love to watch others experience the joy of their epiphanies.

Is it time for the curtain call already? Are you ready to go out and assimilate some of the things you have gained from our cast of mentors?

Before we go, here are a few questions on my mind:

1. Do you know your strengths and assets as a trainer? Everyone has a unique style, but are you sure your style is consciously based on your strengths?
2. Are there instructional styles better suited for certain audiences and topics?
3. If you could change anything about your style on instruction, what would it be?
4. When was the last time you tried something totally new as a trainer?
5. What would be on your top ten list of must-have skills as a facilitator? How do you rate against your own list?

Be sure to put together an action plan for yourself. Introduce changes to your training routine slowly, but never stop looking for new ways to spruce up your act. Find your unique style, respect it, and look for techniques that are well aligned with your strengths. When we keep our eye on the participants, it's hard to go wrong. They shouldn't even know what we have done to create a productive learning event. To be an unsung hero may be one of best litmus tests of success. If we are tired, people's performance changes as a result of the training, and most of the participants do not know what we have done other than that we have attained a level of mastery that I hope all of us achieve during our careers.

Delivering Training Resources

Forms and Worksheets on the Web

"Methods Variety Scale" from Article 14: Make Adult Learning
  Come to Life by Jean Barbazette

"Planning Sheet" from Article 17: Enlarging the Pool of Participants at the Beginning of Any Training Event by Mel Silberman

"Co-Facilitation Strategies Checklist" from Article 22: The Synergy of Co-Facilitation: Creating Powerful Learning Experiences by Dr. Vince Molinaro

Further Reading on Delivering Training

Arch, D., & Meiss, R. (2000). *Warming up the crowd!* 57 pre-session training activities. San Francisco, CA: Pfeiffer.

Barbazette, J. (2005). *The trainer's journey to competence.* San Francisco, CA: Pfeiffer.

Barbazette, J, (2007). *The art of great training delivery.* San Francisco, CA: Pfeiffer.

Bozarth, J. (2008). *From analysis to evaluation: Tools, tips, and techniques for trainers.* San Francisco, CA: Pfeiffer.

Carliner, S. (2002). *Designing e-learning: Learn to adapt your ISD skills and blend solutions to ensure learning sticks.* Alexandria, VA:, ASTD Press.

Gargiulo, T.L. (2005). *The strategic use of stories in organizational communication and learning.* New York: M.E. Sharpe.

Gargiulo, T.L. (2006). *Stories at work: Using stories to improve communications and build relationships.* Westport, CT: Praeger.

Gargiulo, T.L. (2007). *Once upon a time: Using story-based activities to develop breakthrough communication skills.* San Francisco, CA: Pfeiffer.

Hodell, C. (2006). *ISD from the ground up: A no-nonsense approach to instructional design.* Alexandria, VA: ASTD Press.

Kirby, A. (1992). *The encyclopedia of games for trainers.* Amherst, MA: HRD Press.

Lowe R. (2000). Improvisation, Inc. *Harnessing spontaneity to engage.* San Francisco, CA: Pfeiffer.

Marquardt, M.J. (1999). *Action learning in action.* Palo Alto, CA: Davies-Black.

Meier, D. (2000). *The accelerated learning handbook.* New York: McGraw-Hill.

Millbower, L, (2003). *Show biz training: Fun and effective business training techniques from the worlds of stage, screen, and song.* New York: AMACOM.

Newby, A.C. (1992). *Training evaluation handbook.* San Francisco, CA: Pfeiffer.

Parry, S.B. (2000). *Training for results: Key tools and techniques to sharpen trainers' skills.* Alexandria, VA: ASTD Press.

Pike, B., & Busse, C. (1995). *101 games for trainers.* Minneapolis, MN: Lakewood Books.

Pike, B., & Solem, L. (1997). *50 creative training closers.* San Francisco, CA: Pfeiffer.

Pike B., & Solem, L. (2000). *50 creative training openers and energizers.* San Francisco, CA: Pfeiffer.

Pike, B., Solem, L., & Arch, D. (2000). *One-on-one training: How to effectively train one person at a time.* San Francisco, CA: Pfeiffer.

Scannell, E. (1994). *The complete book of games trainers play.* New York: McGraw-Hill.

Silberman M. (1995). *101 ways to make training active.* San Francisco, CA: Pfeiffer.

Silberman M. (2007). *Active training* (3rd ed.). San Francisco, CA: Pfeiffer.

Silberman, M. (2007). *Training the active training way.* San Francisco, CA: Pfeiffer.

Stolovitch, H.D., & Keeps, E.J. (2002). *Telling ain't training.* Alexandria, VA: ASTD Press.

Stolovitch, H.D., & Keeps, E.J. (2004). *Training ain't performance.* Alexandria, VA: ASTD Press.

Sugar, S. (2004). *Games that boost performance.* San Francisco, CA: Pfeiffer.

Thiagarajan, S. (2006). *Thiagi's 100 favorite games.* San Francisco, CA: Pfeiffer.

Thiagarajan, S. (2005). *Thiagi's interactive lectures,* Alexandria, VA: ASTD Press.

Ukens, L.L. (2000). *Energize your audience! 75 quick activities that get them started . . . and keep them going.* San Francisco, CA: Pfeiffer.

SECTION THREE

Workplace Performance and Learning

Introduction to Section Three

How do we define Workplace Learning and Performance? One accepted definition defines it as "the integrated use of learning and other interventions for the purpose of improving human performance and addressing individual and organizational needs. It uses a systematic process of analyzing and responding to individual, group, and organizational performance issues. It creates positive, progressive change within organizations by balancing humanistic and ethical considerations" (Rothwell, Sanders, & Soper, 1999, p. 121).

This definition clearly states the significance learning and performance impacts the workplace. Learning is now at the forefront of building organizational strategies. Profit or non-profit, public or private, small or large, organizations of all types are recognizing the contribution workplace learning and performance has on helping to achieve specific objectives. Building a sustainable learning environment is more than simply following an "insert training here" mentality. Organizations must begin early clearly defining what it means to be a learning organization and how it connects to "business" results.

Through a well-developed workplace learning and performance strategy, every organization can become a learning organization. Keep in mind that the terms "workplace learning and performance" and "learning organization" have evolved considerably since their inception into our lexicon approximately eight years ago. Workplace learning and performance commonly referred to as WLP and quickly becoming known as talent management (TM), is something that is gaining significant attention from those not directly involved in learning but who are directly responsible for the operations and growth of the organization. This is where the evolution in WLP takes root.

Thanks to those actively involved in the evaluation of learning, the learning community and its professionals have been actively striving to connect learning to what we often refer to Kirkpatrick Level 3—the participants' change in behavior or, more appropriately, the application to their responsibilities. As such, WLP has been truly connected to the performance side of the organization. In recent times, resulting from the need of organizational leaders outside of the learning sphere to become more competitive, WLP is now regarded as an opportunity to gain and sustain a competitive advantage.

Although anecdotal, we are increasingly hearing about organizations becoming more innovative and creative. Where does this stem from? It comes from knowing what your people already know, what they need to know, and leveraging their skills, knowledge, and competencies for the future. Still not convinced? Look at who the market and industry leaders currently are. You can almost count them on one hand. They are the General Electric's, the Apple Inc.'s, the Microsoft's, the Wal-Mart's, the Toyota's, and the Google's, to name a few. What do they have in common? They know what their people know, clearly know where they want to go, and are able to reconcile both to make things happen. What are the outcomes? Great and innovative products and services! This is what the public recognizes them for, but these results came from effectively capitalizing on the knowledge their people possess. Let's face it, in the end every organization is about its people, not about who has the most assets.

The increasing importance for WLP is connected to another motivating reason. We are living in the "information age." Unlike the industrial age for the majority of the 20th century, the 21st century for industrialized nations is truly about knowledge and information sharing and capitalization. It has become so prevalent and important to our economies, that information is being valued as much as any other tangible monetary attributable measures of the past such as gold. Some may claim that knowledge and information are even more valuable than any rare natural resource.

What does this mean for professionals in WLP? A shift in our economic thinking requires that learning and talent management professionals become more accountable for the solutions they develop in how it directly connects knowledge and information to organizational performance. We can probably say that WLP's role is secure for the immediate future as it will, and is already, playing an ever-increasing role in decision making and shaping of futures.

Here you will discover the passion for WLP, especially toward performance, from some of the leading experts in our field. They are driven and have a sincere passion for not just what we need to do but for what we need to become.

In their articles, they are challenging you to be open to the new ways of connecting your learning solutions, not just to application of skills to the job (Kirkpatrick Level 3), and to take on the role of ensuring that performance is a the center of every initiative you are mandated with.

The ten passionate articles that you will find in the Workplace Performance and Learning section include:

26. Capturing Learning Opportunities Within Your Organization, by Ajay M. Pangarkar and Teresa Kirkwood
27. New Accountabilities: Non-Financial Measures of Performance, by Ajay M. Pangarkar and Teresa Kirkwood
28. Discovery Learning: The Driving Force Behind Achieving Real Organizational Change, by Catherine J. Rezak
29. The Integrated Approach to Leadership Development, by Dr. Vince Molinaro and Dr. David S. Weiss
30. Independent Means: Taking Control of Internal Knowledge and Minimizing Dependency on External Expertise, by Ajay M. Pangarkar and Teresa Kirkwood
31. Return on Intelligence: The New ROI, by Ann Herrmann-Nehdi
32. Turnover—Slaying the Monster One Touch at a Time, by Dr. Frank P. Bordonaro
33. Creating Credibility with Senior Management: A Simple Approach for Connecting Training to the Business, by Timothy P. Mooney and Robert O. Brinkerhoff, Ed.D.
34. Workplace Learning—Beyond the Classroom, by Ajay M. Pangarkar and Teresa Kirkwood
35. A Business Approach to Learning: Increasing Profits Through Marketing Methodologies, by Ajay M. Pangarkar and Teresa Kirkwood

Read the passion of these contributors and recognized WLP experts. Take away as much as you can to make your workplace a learning and performance environment.

Preview of the Articles

As we mentioned in our article, "Capturing Learning Opportunities Within Your Organization," successful knowledge-enabled organizations strive to harness the knowledge existing within their extended value chains. Leveraging learning leading to performance requires organizations to reorient themselves to capitalize on the knowledge existing in their environments, match the learning requirements of the organization to the personal learning needs of employees, develop a learning environment to maximize overall performance and value, and properly structure and organize learning tools and environments to directly contribute to the strategic goals of the organization.

Harold Stolovich is adamant that our role as learning and performance professionals is to produce results, not just interventions. As Harold puts it, "When we don't analyze to determine whether what we do is necessary or sufficient, don't ensure proper implementation, and don't measure results credibly, we fail in that mission." The key to obtaining these results is that we must not take shortcuts to the solution. We tend to not focus on what appear to be the less-glamorous activities of performance improvement. Harold has seen too many ineffective front-end analysis. In fact, we all have and may have contributed to the problem as well. The second type of failure is a lack of implementation planning, as figuring out the logistic or the "nuts and bolts" of implementing our solutions will not win us the kudos we expect from developing our learning initiatives. The third failing for effective performance is the lack of proper evaluations of learning solutions. Very little of what we produce and implement is properly evaluated.

Catherine Rezak's vision of connecting learning to workplace performance challenges our preconceptions. She presents to us that it is not "How do we get employees to learn?" but rather, "How do we create a context in which they can tap into their own powerful and innate abilities to experience, reflect, connect, and test." Notice the important difference between the two orientations. Organizational learning ceases to be something we do *to* employees. Instead, facilitators become stewards of a latent, collective power that may be harnessed and directed toward our organizations' shared goals and aspirations. For Catherine, unlocking the power of widespread transformation means simply embracing some new assumptions. Immerse learners in experiences. Welcome mistakes. Discover what works. Apply your discovery to reality.

Ann Hermann-Nehdi's view of performance is linked to ROI but not ROI in the traditional sense, but rather return on intelligence. Her view of performance is similar to beauty, in that performance, like anything else, is in the eye *of the person defining it.* Understanding your definition of performance is key to attaining truly successful business outcomes. An immediate implication for the workplace performance and learning profession is that our assumptions about the learner must now be completely reconsidered. As the concept of return on intelligence demonstrates, intelligence is no longer one-dimensional, but rather includes the notion of "multiple intelligences," as Howard Gardner describes it. When you truly consider each individual as a unique learner with learning preferences different from other learners' preferences, it becomes clear that learning design and delivery, organization development, reward and recognition, and all communication must attempt to reach each learner in a way that is best suited to his or her needs.

Tim Mooney and Robert Brinkerhoff remind us what performance is about for the rest of the organization if we are enveloped with learning. They ask you to imagine the CEO asking you something like: "We are investing millions of dollars in this strategy, and we see the training as an important piece of this initiative. The training *must* work. Can you guarantee it will work?" However, the challenge that we have as L&D professionals is that it is difficult to get the attention of senior and line management in these activities. All too often, we approach the task from a training perspective, rather than from a business perspective. As a consequence, our message gets lost in the "L&D speak." We expect managers to view the world from our perspective—after all we are the training experts; we know the "ins and outs" of the field and what it takes to make training work. Unfortunately, when we go into our explanations and talk about what we need or what will make the training work, eyes glaze over or we are politely dismissed. Often we are not viewed as an equal partner at the planning table and hence we do not truly connect WL to the P.

Once again, Teresa and I discuss what it means to become a learning organization and to move beyond the classroom. A learning organization is capable of aligning its strategic objectives and vision with the capabilities, competencies, and ideas of its employees. Managers within a learning organization seek to create an environment in which employees can realize their maximum potential. Employees who receive additional knowledge are only one part of a complete learning strategy. To gain employee commitment, managers must include and align their employees' personal goals with the corporate vision. They must also develop the competencies and knowledge lacking in the team to attain their strategic objectives. As this learning culture is supported and fostered by management, employees seek out and solve problems, becoming more entrepreneurial and more willing to take risks.

We continue to feel for all learning professionals and their efforts to gaining support for their WLP initiatives. Training managers are challenged to "sell" the benefits of an intangible need to those wanting tangible results. External consultants understand this obstacle; however, when those responsible for training propose training solutions, they often encounter significant resistance. Senior managers recognize the importance for training but, with limited resources, they are also concerned with accountability and results. T&D is also challenged by other stakeholders, employees and management alike, to overcome indifference and skepticism of any proposed learning initiative.

The perception of learning is changing and the need is growing. If real change is to take hold, learning professionals must find effective ways to ensure that true learning leads to results, which translates to performance. Learning is about developing abilities and knowledge that translate into sustained performance within the workplace. Building organizational requirements and employee needs into the training solutions is essential to gain acceptance at every level. It is time for T&D to shift their thinking to business and strategic orientations focusing on workplace learning and performance and results to gain credibility and facilitate buy-in. Training and development must realize they are an integral component to the business, not an organizational footnote.

Reference

Rothwell, W.J., Sanders, E.S., & Soper, J.G. (1999). *ASTD models for workplace learning and performance: Roles, competencies, and outputs* (p. 121). Alexandria, VA: ASTD Press.

Article 26

Capturing Learning Opportunities Within Your Organization

Ajay M. Pangarkar, CTDP, and

Teresa Kirkwood, CTDP

Passion

Supporting our clients may call upon more than our technical skills and can include the powers of persuasion. Are we ready for that role?

As learning professionals, we know the importance of people to an organization's success. There are times, however, when senior executives may not share that understanding. This is the time when presenting a business case for development may be persuasive. This article presents such a case written as a letter to a business leader. We are confident that you will extrapolate the key ideas to use as you have conversations within your own organizations.

Dear Business Leader,

How you use and develop employee knowledge will determine your level of success in a knowledge-based world.

Business people often ask learning professionals what it takes to survive and profit in competitive and volatile market conditions. The common answer is to offer improved products and services. This is partially true; however, improvements are only the expected results not the source of competitive advantage. Improved products develop through innovation, which arises from the knowledge and experiences of your employees, customers, and suppliers.

Business survival is not solely based on products and services, but rather it is dependent on the knowledge of people. Leveraging and maintaining the knowledge and competencies of your staff and transitioning from a product or service orientation to a learning organization is the first step. Other critical factors to becoming knowledge-enabled include developing an environment with an efficient infrastructure and leadership that encourages learning to take place.

Employee Competencies and Technology Working Together

Growing organizations face many challenges and opportunities. Globalization, deregulation, technology, and competition empower businesses and consumers. These rapid and continuous changes are forcing all businesses to respond and meet market demands faster and with more innovative solutions than was the case in the past.

By effectively managing operational concerns, knowledge and information flow freely within the organization and are accessible to the right people. Current technology provides "virtual" environments to accomplish this. Virtual integration creates efficiencies in operational structures while maximizing employee knowledge and critical information. Integrating a virtual process to capture, develop, and manage knowledge takes full advantage of your organization's most valuable asset, its people.

A Holistic Approach to Organizational Learning

Change is an integral component for surviving the knowledge economy. Managing change requires that you focus on what you do best. This is why many organizations delegate non-core parts of their value chain to strategic partners. Involving strategic partners in the value chain (from suppliers through to customers) creates a flexible extended enterprise with access to the most current knowledge. This is known in business as "patching" and/or "clustering." This is important for growing companies to understand, because they are in a position to virtually integrate this extended structure and harness the knowledge available to them.

At the core of the extended enterprise are the people that create its primary value. Again, this value is derived from the intellectual capital that drives product innovation and organizational flexibility and not necessarily what the company offers. Building a knowledge-economy business requires shifting your strategic focus internally while still being aware, but not overly concerned, about external competitive environments. This is because the extended enterprise involves and integrates their external partners knowledge into their fold.

Many growing organizations are beginning to place a significant amount of effort into developing comprehensive employee knowledge development and management processes. They focus on people and acquire the tools to facilitate the transfer of knowledge within their value chain. How employee knowledge and abilities is managed, developed and leveraged within the context of the organizations strategic imperatives is essential.

Developing Your People's Knowledge

Leading organizations learn early the importance of developing and managing employee knowledge. It becomes everyone's responsibility, not just that of the human resource manager or training director. This allows management to develop and deploy their employees' competencies in the same way they integrate other parts of their value chain. Developing your people in this manner results in:

- Quicker information and knowledge transfer through out the value chain
- Alignment of employee objectives and supplier needs
- Reduction in down time and wasted efforts
- An increase in customer satisfaction
- Gaining, training, retaining, and motivating the right people for your organization
- Possessing the right competencies to ensure performance objectives

As simple as this may sound, successfully deploying a learning development strategy requires a clear understanding of its impact within your value chain.

What You Need to Address

According to Harvard Business School Professor Michael Porter, "Competition in today's economy is far more dynamic . . . Competitive advantage rests on making more productive use of inputs, which require continual innovation" (porter, 1998). Business strategies must continually innovate and be flexible to respond to change. According to Porter, "Companies today must forge close linkages with buyers, suppliers, and other institutions." This shared responsibility is important, as your customers and competition is not only local but also global.

The problem is that, even though the business environment is changing dramatically, businesses maintain outdated business strategies and old-style HR attitudes toward training. These barriers are still prevalent. Organizations that make large investments in learning and developing their people outpace their competition consistently as evidenced in studies conducted by the American Society for Training and Development (www.ASTD.org).

Successful knowledge-economy businesses clearly understand the dynamics involved in this environment. They avoid "commoditizing" their products and services by maintaining and fostering their people's skills and abilities. In return, their people are capable of contributing significantly more to the objectives of the organization. Management focuses on:

- **Employee empowerment**—Empowerment gives employees more autonomy and power over the decision-making process within their work environment and allows them to understand how they contribute and fit into the organizations "big picture."
- **Technology management**—Knowledge-economy businesses use technology as a tool to create efficiencies and build relationships. But most importantly, they allow their people to communicate and have access to information, helping them to make smarter and faster decisions.
- **Management leadership**—Top management leads by example. They are the first to show their commitment and enthusiasm to new ideas and processes. Managers are expected to become directly involved and the first to initiate and integrate the new values within their business environment.

What's Involved in a Learning Development Strategy?

When you include recruiting, hiring, on-the-job training, and salaries, people become an organization's greatest investment. Many businesses, however, focus their efforts on acquiring and managing traditional fixed assets rather than on maximizing the most important and vested asset in their extended organization— the value and knowledge of their workers and value chain.

Through effective use of your employees' knowledge, you maximize the value of your products or services, creating a loyal customer-base. It is important to involve your customers' insights and knowledge to capitalize on market opportunities and develop innovative solutions. This fosters beneficial and profitable relationships while reducing the effect of competitive forces on your company.

Creating a learning development strategy begins with the fundamental aspects involved in developing employee knowledge. At the most basic level, a learning development strategy involves:

- Discerning what your people know and how they use their knowledge
- Being capable of further developing their knowledge and skills
- Leveraging this knowledge through out the extended organization
- Managing and maximizing the contribution obtained from this knowledge base

Incorporating a learning development strategy requires your organization possess a clear vision and solid infrastructure. To build this strategy your organization should:

Reorient Strategically

Becoming a knowledge-economy business requires a shift in thinking. Business models that once worked have difficulty keeping up with the current volatile environment. The learning organization is flexible and promotes innovation and creativity. It also redefines how an organization is structured and fits within the value chain.

Manage Learning

Managing learning requires matching the learning requirements of the organization to the personal learning needs of employees. It encompasses every aspect related to the learning and development of your knowledge workforce. Learning management involves determining learning needs, developing knowledge capacity, selecting appropriate and viable learning formats, and producing timely management reports and evaluations.

For some global organizations, accurate reporting is becoming compulsory. Governments are increasingly looking at ways to legislating workforce development laws, requiring businesses to meet strict reporting guidelines.

Technology, specifically a learning management solution, enables you to manage your employees' knowledge and effectively administer various facets of your workforce's learning requirements.

Manage Performance

The primary purpose of developing a learning environment is to maximize the organization's overall performance and value. This is attained by setting clear strategic objectives, measuring comparative benchmarks against objectives, establishing a process for continuous feedback, and offering opportunities to take risks.

Effective performance management offers a way for you to measure the return on your learning investments and the development of employee competencies. This is important if learning is to contribute to the profitability and viability of your knowledge-enabled organization

Manage Learning Events and Content

Learning takes place both formally and informally in growing knowledge-economy businesses. Their strength comes from properly structuring and organizing learning tools and environments so they directly contribute to the strategic goals of the organization.

Developing, sourcing, and deploying appropriate training material requires both internal and external expertise. Most learning is not neatly structured in a course format. It comes through various forms of material and communication networks within your extended enterprise. The key is ensuring that the right content gets to the right people at the right time. It is critical that you acquire the experience, expertise, and technology to help you package and manage this learning content effectively.

Increasingly, employee development and management is playing a major role in the growth of the knowledge-economy enterprise, displacing outdated perceptions and strategies. Successful knowledge-enabled organizations strive to harness the knowledge existing within their extended value chains. Managers are beginning to shift their focus from internal employees to a broader knowledge partnership perspective.

The impact of technology and the rise of the Internet provide new opportunities to integrate seamless learning management solutions within growing organizations. Driven by strong vision and leadership, the virtually integrated, knowledge-enabled enterprise empowers employees and brings together various elements of critical to the organization ready to capitalize on new market opportunities. We are here to support you in your learning endeavors.

Your Learning Professional

Reference

Porter, M.E. (1998, November/December). Clusters and the new economics of competition. *Harvard Business Review.*

Article 27

New Accountabilities

Non-Financial Measures of Performance

Ajay M. Pangarkar, CTDP, and

Teresa Kirkwood, CTDP

Passion

As learning professionals there are times when we wish that we had a crystal ball to look into the future. Don't you?

Where everything changes immediately, there is little time to wait to see what happened (financial outcomes). Decision-makers need to make things happen *now*, and the only way is through performance measures that provide a glimpse of future expectations and results.

Mention the word "performance" and many managers immediately shift their thinking to measures related to some type of financial result. This is how many managers are formally trained, and they believe measuring performance through financial accountability provides the most relevant and simple way to demonstrate progress and productivity.

It is true that financial outcomes are tangible, immediate, and relevant, but their strength lies in measuring short-term objectives. In recent years, however, corporate America has had it share of downfalls relating to the manipulation of financial performance measures. So much so that shareholders and the public are demanding that performance measures be independent from financial outcomes and deliver a longer-term outlook. This outcry has led organizations down a more enlightened path of developing and including more non-financially based measures.

The challenges with financial based performance measures are two-fold. First, financial measures are often overused and extensively relied upon. Managers of companies face a tremendous amount of pressure to perform and to demonstrate results quickly. The most convenient method to show their results is through financial metrics. These measurements are fast and familiar for managers. They also provide for a very narrow focus of a larger perspective of the organization's impact in the marketplace. Secondly, financial-based measures do not reflect true performance drivers against intangible outcomes. For example, how does a manager quantify customer satisfaction or intellectual capacity in a financial context? In several organizational studies, there is often an over-emphasis of financial metrics such as shareholder value, profitability, and expense reduction over non-financial measures such as customer satisfaction, quality, and innovation.

In recent years, many companies are finding that measuring performance based on financial results is at times relevant, but that having a more inclusive and holistic approach to performance measurement is necessary. It is increasingly important that performance be directly linked to the strategic objective of the organization. Financial performance metrics provide results related to short-term outcomes. But when dealing with organizational strategy, however, a long-term approach is required and maximizes the impact of non financial performance measures.

Many non-financial factors have demonstrated that they contribute to and have a lasting impact on a company's market value. Since these non-financial measures are more forward-looking and are linked to operational activities, they help to focus a manager's efforts and better evaluate employee performance.

The current economic environment is placing increasing importance on intangible factors such as employee knowledge, continuous process improvement, innovative capabilities, and intellectual capital. In recent years, strategic frameworks have developed "dashboards" for management to balance both financial and non-financial performance indicators. The most common type of framework is the "balanced scorecard." It translates corporate strategy through performance measures, allowing managers to make more appropriate decisions.

The Growing Need for Non-Financial Accountability

Why are non-financial measures gaining prominence within the business environment over financial metrics? It is because these measures provide a direct correlation to strategic objectives. Most financial measures focus on short-term accountabilities and leave out intangible factors that directly affect the customer, supplier, and employee. The same financial results lead to situations narrow in focus and set up adversarial environments based on irrelevant data. Financial measures can also be manipulated to meet the outcomes desired by the party reporting them.

Numbers are not the most complete or appropriate measure to demonstrate organizational performance. These results do not address non-financial factors that help organizations attain their strategic objectives leading to improved financial performance. Take for example a company expanding product research and development. This non-financial objective goes against traditional financial performance measures, negatively affecting financial indicators, increasing expenses, and reducing bottom-line results. But the company will attain its long-term objective of becoming market leaders in its product space, resulting in improved financial performance.

Managers can no longer afford to hang on to preconceived notions of using financial measures as the holy grail of organizational accountability. Integrating non-financial measures regarding the strategic performance of the organization will help to communicate objectives, assist in the effective implementation of strategic plans, and provide incentive for management to address long-term strategy.

The use of non-financial factors is gaining importance as our economy evolves into a knowledge-dependent environment. Critics of financial measures argue that the success drivers for many industries lie in intangible assets such as human capital and innovative capability, rather than traditional measures of hard assets represented in a company's balance sheet. Managers must avoid reverting to traditional financial thinking. The real value of non-financial measures is the qualitative value of the firm's intangible assets and its indirect relationship to quantitative results.

Many studies examine how non-financial performance measures of intangible assets (employee knowledge, innovation, etc.) lead to differences in U.S. companies' stock market values. These studies commonly find that measures related to innovation, management capability, employee relations, quality, and brand recognition are major contributing factors to a company's overall value. By excluding these intangible assets, financially oriented measures can lead managers to make poor and risky decisions.

The evidence demonstrating that non-financial based measures are better indicators of a company's financial performance is significant. Financial results traditionally do not take into account or capture long-term benefits, even when trying to maximize financial performance. Under current laws, many expenses and costs are usually declared in the period they are incurred, reflecting poor performance. But if the expenditures are justified, the benefits would be seen as improved future profitability along with other intangible benefits. For example, let's say you want to extensively develop your employees' skill base and foster a more cohesive workplace. This would require a significant investment in training, coaching, and other methods of support. In the near term, financial performance would be negatively affected, but the longer-term non-financial benefit would result in innovative ideas and products, leadership in market presence, increased productivity, and improved reputation through reduction in errors and defects. These intangible results will lead to many financial benefits such as increased demand and sales for products, increasing profit margins, and increasing future cash flows, to name a few.

An additional benefit non-financial measures offer is the ability to balance factors within and beyond your control. External factors are wild cards in performance measurement. Financial accountability is often impacted by external concerns such as economic or market changes that play havoc with forecasts. The greatest benefit of non-financial factors is the focus on actions that are in the organization's control. What does this mean for you and the company? It means that (1) the company is less susceptible to external changes, (2) managers are able to direct their efforts on issues directly related to strategic objectives, and (3) both employees and managers can fairly evaluate and improve their performance as required.

Limitations to Non-Financial Performance Measures

Changing the rules on evaluating performance in an organization is a challenge. Financial-based measures are ingrained. New forms of performance evaluation are often seen with skepticism, especially as organizations introduce "flavors of the month" when it comes to management trends and techniques. The first hurdle for integrating non-financial based measures is resistance from all levels of the organization.

Another major drawback of non-financial performance measures is the perceived time and expense needed. Too often the cost and time developing a performance management system can easily exceed expected benefits. Excessive development and implementation time, incorrect selection, inconsistent application of measures, and significant time involved in selling the solution to employees often leave many performance-based measurement systems orphaned.

Consistency is crucial if any type of performance measurement system, financial or non-financial, is to be effective. Too many times managers attempt to balance existing performance measures, usually financial, with new, non-financial based measures. This not only takes more time, but also causes confusion among those using the measures.

Performance measurement is linked to results—not to constant evaluation. In theory this makes complete sense, but look around and you will find too many organizations making any performance measurement process an exercise in futility, continually discussing, evaluating, and reporting performance results rather than capitalizing on the results. With increasing competitive pressures and changing economic conditions, there is no time for extensive discussions of performance results. Constant discussion takes valuable resources away from more relevant issues such as meeting customer needs. If your performance evaluation metrics, especially non-financial ones, require a significant amount of time, then it is time for you to rethink your performance criteria and how they are evaluated. Begin by reducing the indicators used, minimize reporting processes, and reduce meetings to discuss outcomes.

A significant disadvantage of non-financial measures over its financial counterpart is the need for a common base for measurement. Non-financial performance data can be measured in many ways. As difficult as it may be, what is important for managers to realize is ensuring there is a common measure and a common understanding of the measurement. How is this done? Each organization is unique, and this dictates how non-financial performance measures are established. Some develop measures in relation to strategic priorities and rank their importance to the overall objectives through a weighted average approach, whereas others arbitrarily assign subjective measures on a random basis.

Your goal is to minimize randomness and subjectivity of the measures, making them tangible and relevant to the employees and organization. To minimize resistance and reduce skepticism, it is essential to ensure that real and critical links are made to the non-financial measures you implement. Too often managers adopt a non-financial measure without demonstrating the relationships between the measure and the tangible indicator to performance like shareholder value, market share, or earnings per share. A weak correlation to a tangible result could lead to a dead end.

Another mistake often made applying non-financial measures is attempting to implement too many indicators. In this case more is not necessarily better. Utilizing a multitude of performance indicators can lead to a dilution of the information and a loss of data integrity. The main indicators are lost among many others that do not provide any true value to the organization and have managers trying to interpret irrelevant data rather than the main drivers. Bell Canada Enterprises developed a structured approach, clearly knowing that their strategic objective is built on customer experiences. Their performance strategy differentiates between internal and external factors and clearly defines relevant key performance indicators (KPI). The company's KPIs are directly linked backed to the strategic objective and deliver tangible results. When measuring the performance of call center representatives, for example, BCE utilizes leading indicators such as revenue per person hour.

What Drives Performance?

Developing effective performance measures begins with understanding objectives and values. These factors contribute to the overall success of the organization and help to translate strategic vision into specific actions. See Figure 27.1.

Although this seems like common sense, managers still tend to miss the mark and develop measures that are irrelevant or overly complex. Developing non-financial based indicators begins by first understanding what you are attempting to address strategically. BCE, for example, does not link its performance to traditional industry measures but rather to customer experiences and satisfaction. Once the values are identified, you are in an advantageous position to develop the requisite performance drivers that directly link back to the overall objectives and, hence, link to tangible financial-based results.

Another method for developing performance measures is to identify key industry benchmarks. Competitors, suppliers, and industry clients possess a significant amount of reference data on current and past performance. This type of benchmarking can equally extend to an internal comparison of historical performance. In either case, caution is required, because comparing performance measures, especially non-financial ones, can lead to significant discrepancies as objectives and cultures vary from one organization to another.

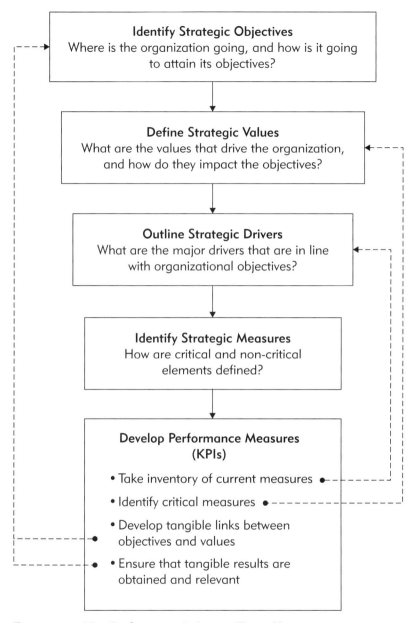

Figure 27.1. Key Performance Indicator Flow Chart

One of the most reliable methods of measuring non-financial performance is through the relationship of intangible measures to numerical data-driven performance. At BCE, performance indicators of call centers representatives is based on how they perform based on the customer experience; however, the results are based on average call handle time and first call resolution.

Keeping Performance Simple Keeps It Real

Usually, larger organizations tend to develop more complex non-financial measures. First, take inventory of the non-financial indicators currently used and identify those that are effective in their application. It is important to begin from the top (strategic orientation and objective) and work your way down to the value drivers of the organization. Discard all measures that do not deliver any value and develop new metrics addressing issues critical to advancing the organization towards its goals. Two things are important to remember: (1) not all performance indicators have to be identical for each task and (2) simplicity in your measures is usually most effective.

The next step is to integrate the measures through transparent and easily accessible processes facilitating reporting and evaluation. The choice of performance measures should not be taken lightly, as they will impact all levels of the organization and employee performance.

Conclusion

Each non-financial performance measure is as unique as each organization seeking to implement an effective performance management process. As direct and simple as financial performance measures can be, they do not reflect organizational strategy holistically. The true value of non-financial measures is dependent on the selection of appropriate objectives related directly to organizational strategy. But it is important to keep in mind that any performance management solution is a dynamic process and that choices made today may not reflect the direction taken tomorrow. Your performance management process must evolve with your organizational strategy and changes in the nature of the environment.

Discovery Learning

The Driving Force Behind Achieving Real Organizational Change

Catherine J. Rezak

Passion

Today, the promise of sustainable change hinges on the human beings who comprise the organization; their knowledge, under-standing, and learning are the organization's most sacred assets. People have always been, and continue to be, the true answer to change.

Let's begin our story of organizational transformation—not in the walnut-paneled office of a Fortune 500 firm, but in the ancient Greek city of Syracuse.

Archimedes had just been tasked with discerning whether the gold in the king's new crown was pure or mixed with silver alloy by a dishonest goldsmith. How could Archimedes know without actually melting down the crown?

He wrestled intensely with the problem for many days, but produced few answers. One evening, still consumed by the puzzle, he filled his bathtub with too much water. When he stepped inside, water spilled over the edge. In that instant, it occurred to Archimedes that objects displace water equal to their volumes and masses. He cried out, "Ah-hah! I have it!" Thus, he designed a simple water displacement experiment that confirmed that the volume of gold in the king's crown was less than the amount originally given to the goldsmith.

Now, flash forward 2,000 years to a corporate training room anywhere in the United States, where employees of any company can be heard chattering excitedly about current business concepts. Supply-chain optimization, cost shifts, and capacity restraints are being dissected with the enthusiasm usually reserved for sporting events. The room is buzzing, and employees are having a blast. Organizational leaders are observing the learning event, stunned. Just a couple of months ago, this would have been impossible. In fact, despite their best efforts to initiate any dialogue regarding company issues, it was a confusing concept and fell on deaf ears.

And now, this.

Awareness. Understanding. Excitement. What made this engagement possible?

There are plenty of other organizational leaders who would like to know. Among organizations, the quest for employee-driven change has reached a near-feverish pitch. After all, most organizations have felt the sting of change, as well as the pressure to mobilize, flex, improve, deliver value, and innovate. Where else is there to turn in these matters but to their employees?

Today, the promise of sustainable change hinges on the human beings who comprise the organization; their knowledge, understanding, and learning are the organization's sacred assets. When it comes to breathing life into strategic initiatives, employees are the ones who hold the power.

Traditional Training Breakdown

Here's the hook: Creating a learning organization to fulfill these training and communication needs has proven to be devilishly difficult. Many have looked to learning technologies, such as computer-based delivery with streaming video, as the hope for change. But in the corporate communications suite and the training room, the initial intoxication over these technologies is giving way to a more sober perspective.

Sure, such tools are enticing and their economic efficiencies are compelling. But they are, after all, merely tools that offer no magic on their own. They can't generate knowledge, commitment, or enthusiasm. For deliverance, corporate agents of change need to begin elsewhere.

Instructivism and the Nurnberg Funnel

Leverage may be found in reaffirming what we already know intuitively about organizational learning and change. In 1990, learning theorist John M. Carroll presented his argument against ineffective instructional methods in a book called *The Nurnberg Funnel*. The title is a reference to the ridiculous image of the Funnel of Nurnberg, a nonsensical device that allowed vast amounts of knowledge to be poured directly into a learner via a funnel inserted into the brain. We may laugh at the absurd image, but take a stroll around some training and corporate communications suites, and you'll find the principle is still alive.

Carroll deconstructs learning methods that rely heavily on such activities a listening, recording, memorizing, and regurgitating, but very little on personal connection or application. This approach to learning is called instructivism, and in his book, Carroll takes a critical look at many of the assumptions of the persistent Nurnberg-like approach. Specifically, we find that instructivism assumes that:

- Everyone learns best by listening and receiving information. ("Tell 'em what you're going to tell 'em, then tell 'em what you just told 'em.")
- People will naturally make the bridge from theory to application. ("Here's a graphic of our four-quadrant model. Hang it up in your office so you'll remember to apply it.")
- Knowledge transfer is a passive process in which awareness is transferred from teacher to student. ("Listen up. I'm the expert.")

Of course, it is old news that the approach is flawed. This is confirmed time and again. In the 1980s, for example, an experiment was conducted at the IBM Watson Research Center. In it, two groups of participants were tasked with learning how to operate the IBM DisplayWrite system. The first group was given the system's ninety-four-page instruction manual. The second was given a set of twenty-five cards that contained no step-by-step procedures. Rather, they featured challenges to complete specific tasks by directly manipulating and experimenting with the DisplayWrite system. Further, key parts of those cards were left blank, so the learners would have to fill in the details as they explored the equipment.

The results of the experiment were dramatic. By flipping through the twenty-five challenge cards (in no particular order, mind you), the second "guided-exploration" group attained the desired level of proficiency in less than three hours. The "instruction manual group" took more than eight hours. Furthermore, the guided-exploration group learned many additional aspects of the system that weren't even part of the assigned task.

When it comes to learning—we are reminded again and again—experience matters.

Experiential Training: The "Discovery Learning" Approach

The idea of participant-centered discovery/experiential learning has been around a long time and is well documented, explains Dr. Pat Gill Webber, a consultant, coach, and facilitator, who specializes in organizational change and transformation. "The idea of experiential learning can be traced back to John Dewey, founder of Teacher's College at Columbia in the 1920s," says Webber. "[Dewey] first presented the concept of people's learning and constructing meaning from their experiences." Since then, the body of theory has mushroomed, with many of the most significant developments in experiential and discovery learning emerging since the 1980s. Dr. Webber cites three in particular:

- **Adults learn differently than children.** "Our observations about pedagogy, or childhood learning, cannot be uniformly transferred to adult learning," says Dr. Webber. "Research now confirms that andragogy, or adult learning, is unique in many important ways." (See Knowles, 1980)
- **Adults are self-directed.** "Unlike children, who are instructor-focused in their learning, adults learn effectively when they have control within the learning environments," says Webber. (See Houle, 1961, and Tough, 1971 and 1979.)
- **Adults are capable of perspective transformation.** Dr. Webber explains: "According to [learning theorist] Mezirow, the hallmark of adult learning is the ability to consider our own presuppositions, recognize how they affect our experiences of the world, and make changes to our actions to create new possibilities." (Mezirow, 1990)

In traditional organizations, the instructor-centered, peda-gogic approach can still be found. This approach is appropriate in a world in which there is little complexity and the future is largely predictable. However, few of us recognize that world and are more accustomed to a context that is marked by change and unpredict-ability, where the creativity and innovation of people are needed. In this world, the andragogic, experience-based approach is essen-tial. Today, the promise of sustainable change hinges on the human beings who comprise the organization; their knowledge, understanding, and learning are the organization's sacred assets.

Experience, Reflect, Connect, and Test

A review of the many theories of adult learning is intriguing—not so much for their differences, but for their similarities. Today, we recognize that most theorists define at least three dis-tinct phases of experiential learning.

Whenever we go about our daily work tasks, we are learning—naturally and intuitively. In fact, much of the time when we are learning, we don't stop to think, "Hey, I'm learning!" We simply fall back on the hard wiring of our brains to experience, reflect, connect, and test. The challenge, then, is to create an environ-ment for intentional and directed natural discovery throughout the organization.

Let's look again at the stages of experiential learning and consider its application in the context of organizational change.

- **The experiential phase** is fostered by providing the mem-bers with concrete experiences composed of elements they may manipulate. This may consist of games, simulations, props, case-study materials, or any means that mentally and physically engages each learner.
- **The reflective phase** is facilitated by providing learners with new models and new vocabulary to help them make

sense of what they just experienced and create new conceptual "buckets" for categorizing the memories. For this task, there's a lot of power to be leveraged by using metaphors, stories, images, and music to help the learner embrace and internalize concepts.

- **The testing phase** is where the learner identifies new contexts—specifically, within his or her business reality—and applies new awareness of these contexts, thus beginning the learning process all over again.

Most important during this process is the idea that teachers don't teach. Rather, learning is propelled by the learner. The role of the change agent is merely to facilitate an environment, or context, in which people become safely and confidently immersed in the process of experiencing, reflecting, and testing.

Conclusion: Reflections on the Future of Learning

The challenge, then, is not "How do we get employees to learn?" Rather, it is "How do we create a context in which they can tap into their own powerful and innate abilities to experience, reflect, connect, and test?" Notice the important difference between the two orientations. Organizational learning ceases to be something we do *to* employees. Instead, facilitators become stewards of a latent, collective power that may be harnessed and directed toward our organization's shared goals and aspirations.

The equation is simple.

To unlock the power of widespread transformation, simply embrace some new assumptions. Immerse learners in experiences. Welcome mistakes. Discover what works. Apply your discovery to reality.

And if, like Archimedes, a little water gets splashed all over the floor, its all the better.

References

Carroll, J.M. (1990). *The Nurnberg funnel.* Cambridge, MA: MIT Press.

Houle, C.O. (1961). *The inquiring mind.* Madison, WI: University of Wisconsin Press.

Knowles, M. (1980). *The modern practice of adult education.* Englewood Cliffs, NJ: Prentice Hall.

Mezirow, J. (1990). *Fostering critical reflection in adulthood.* San Francisco, CA: Jossey-Bass.

Tough, A. (1971, 1979). *The adult's learning concepts.* Houston, TX: Learning Concepts.

The Integrated Approach to Leadership Development

Dr. Vince Molinaro and Dr. David Weiss

Passion

How do we build strong leadership capacity?

Building leadership capacity is mission critical in organizations today. Many are experiencing a significant leadership gap. One of the ways to close the gap is to take a more integrated approach to leadership development. In this article we will discuss why an integrated approach is important and present the eight steps to help you implement this kind of approach in your organization.

The Evolution of Leadership Development

Over the past few years, the field of leadership development has been undergoing a fundamental evolution, which is reflected in the image in Figure 29.1.

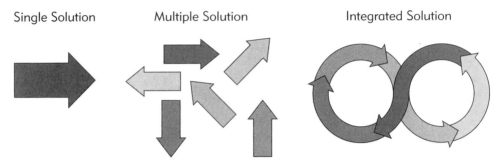

Figure 29.1. The Evolution in Leadership Development

The Single–Solution Approach

Traditionally, the most common and extensively used approach to building leadership capacity has been what we refer to as the "single-solution" approach. Many organizations implement this type of approach because they assume there is one answer (e.g., classroom-based leadership programs), a so-called "silver bullet" that will develop leadership. However, the single-solution approach has limitations and is not sufficient. Although many such programs provide value, increasingly, they are seen as too time-consuming. Leaders today are too busy to attend leadership programs that ask them to sit in a classroom for long periods of time.

The Multiple–Solution Approach

As a result many astute organizations implement a more evolved approach—what we call a "multiple-solution approach." This approach consists of utilizing an array of leadership development options, such as assessment, coaching, learning programs, and job experiences. However, we find that many times these development options are implemented in a fragmented manner. For example, the multiple-solution approach may not be guided by an overall strategy. This leads to a lack of coordination and a disjointed approach to leadership development. Ultimately, leaders within the organization become confused as they experience a hodgepodge of discrete developmental options that do not appear to add value to each other.

The Integrated—Solution Approach

Several factors are creating a new sense of urgency for organizations to evolve to an integrated solution to leadership development.

- First, the business environment is more complex, and, therefore, leadership development in today's world needs to be more integrated and sophisticated to deal with greater complexity.
- Second, trainers and OD practitioners need to deliver results on many levels, such as transferring vital skills and ideas to leaders, enhancing performance, reinforcing corporate culture and values, driving business results and adapting to changing business realities.
- Finally, leaders who are the participants of leadership development have extremely high expectations and want their organizations to implement integrated and high-value leadership development options. Consequently, trainers and leadership development practitioners are under tremendous pressure to deliver results.

Therefore, we believe organizations must implement an "integrated-solution" approach to leadership development. We define this approach as one that brings together and unites an array of development options that adds value to one another. The integrated-solution approach is more comprehensive, rigorous, and long-term in focus. It is also more complex and requires greater commitment from organizations. In the end, it is also the most effective approach to building leadership capacity and overcoming the leadership gap. There are three reasons for this that can be summarized in three "S's":

1. *Strategic:* The integrated-solution ensures that all development options are focused on helping the organization gain competitive advantage. This approach involves creating a comprehensive strategy for leadership development and implementing the strategy effectively.
2. *Synergistic:* Instead of implementing a hodgepodge of discrete development options, the integrated-solution approach is more synergistic. It strives to select and implement development options in a seamless manner so that they add value to one another.
3. *Sustainable:* The integrated-solution approach is sustainable in that it takes a long-term perspective to leadership development. It recognizes that leadership development today is an emergent and iterative process that needs constant attention, focus and resources. It is not work to be delegated to a training or OD department, but, rather, it needs to become an organizational priority.

The Eight Steps to Implementing an Integrated-Solution Approach to Leadership Development

Below we explore the eight steps to successfully implement an integrated-solution approach to leadership development:

1. Develop a comprehensive strategy for integrated leadership development.

2. Connect leadership development to the organization's environmental challenges.
3. Use the leadership story to set the context for development.
4. Balance global enterprise-wide needs with local individual needs.
5. Employ emergent design and implementation.
6. Ensure that development options fit the culture.
7. Focus on critical moments of the leadership life cycle.
8. Apply a blended methodology.

Step 1: Develop a Comprehensive Strategy for Integrated Leadership Development

The integrated solution approach begins with the development of a comprehensive strategy. Organizations do not have unlimited resources; therefore, they need to develop a strategy for integrated leadership development that optimizes the available resources in a way that delivers sustainable competitive advantage. Organizations must also ensure that the strategy mitigates risk to the business that might emerge from existing leadership gaps. In addition, the strategy must ensure that development options are relevant, align to business needs, and add value to leaders.

Step 2: Connect Leadership Development to the Organization's Environmental Challenges

The integrated-solution approach is effective because it connects leadership development to the organization's new environmental challenges. It focuses on helping leaders develop the capacity needed to lead effectively in future business environments.

Step 3: Use the Leadership Story to Set the Context for Development

An organization needs to have a compelling story that communicates its philosophy and leadership approach to its employees. The story becomes part of the folklore of the organization and creates an expectation that leadership will behave consistently with the story and its message. An integrated-solution approach to leadership development uses the leadership story to set the context for development. The story tells the organization's employees why leadership is important and how leaders will be developed. The story also creates a well-delineated leadership model that clearly articulates what leadership means to the organization. The model then serves as a focal point for defining development options.

Step 4: Balance Global Enterprise–Wide Needs with Local Individual Needs

An organization must strive to balance its global and enterprise-wide development needs with local responsiveness to a leader's individual development needs. Therefore, the organization identifies development options needed by all its leaders—such as creating a common leadership culture, enhancing core leadership competencies, and responding to changes in the business environment. The organization must also identify development options that target individual needs either on the part of key talent, future incumbents for critical positions, or specific departments and business units.

Step 5: Employ an Emergent Way to Design and Implement Leadership Development

Organizations must continually be in touch with what is happening in their businesses and be ready to respond. They must constantly be looking for opportunities to improve development options because leaders learn through a continuous process of learning, relearning and unlearning. Therefore, the design and implementation of leadership development needs to be emergent rather than static—and also flexible and fast because the business world moves quickly, and leadership solutions must keep up.

Step 6: Ensure That Development Options Fit the Culture

At times organizations fail at building leadership capacity because they implement development options that do not fit their culture. For example, the solutions that would work in a financial services company with a strong results- and numbers-driven performance culture would be different than those that would work in a public-sector organization. Both have different cultures reflective of their sectors, and both would require development options that fit their own unique organizations.

Step 7: Focus on Critical Moments of the Leadership Lifecycle

The integrated-solution approach also focuses its attention on critical moments along a leader's life cycle. These are times when a leader transitions to a new role, such as the first time an employee becomes a manager or a leader becomes an executive. Each transition presents new challenges and pressures. To succeed, new leaders need to develop new ways of thinking about their roles. These are moments when leaders are at the greatest risk of failing or derailing. The integrated-solution approach supports leaders through the critical transition points in leadership roles.

Step 8: Apply a Blended Methodology

An organization uses a blended methodology when it selects development options from assessment, coaching, learning, and experience and organizes them so that they are aligned, seamlessly adding value to one another. These development options should not be separate and distinct from one another, but rather part of an overall integrated approach to leadership development. This does not mean that all development options have to be blended. However, increasingly we are seeing organizations take a blended approach to leadership development and create robust offerings that blend some form of assessment, coaching, learning, and experience.

Conclusion

Trainers and OD practitioners are being called on to help their organizations build strong leadership capacity. The eight steps discussed in this article provide a powerful roadmap for future success.

Independent Means

Taking Control of Internal Knowledge and Minimizing Dependency on External Expertise

Ajay M. Pangarkar, CTDP, and

Teresa Kirkwood, CTDP

Passion

Think outside the box. Your clients want to enhance employees' knowledge and also save costs. How can you help them achieve both goals? In our experience, helping your organization take control of internal knowledge will help them minimize their dependency on external expertise.

During economically turbulent times, many organizations have a greater need for training. At the same time, however, training budgets are slashed, questions arise about the training's real value, people want different types of personal and professional development, and management holds HR accountable to attain a certain return on investment benchmarks while leveraging employee knowledge.

Many companies depend on the external expertise of consultants to implement and facilitate the training requirements of their organizations. But when budgets are reduced, consultants, and anything associated with training, are the first cost-cutting casualties.

Companies still have to support the development needs of their employees even without the expertise of external training professionals and organizations. The challenge is figuring out how to do it.

Internalized Training

An effective way to alleviate budget cutbacks and continue to support critical training is to build an internal team of training specialists equipped with essential learning transfer skills. This "train-the-trainers" alternative presents organizations, especially growing ones, with tangible advantages, including reducing their dependency on external consultants and lower overall training costs. This wealth of internal knowledge and expertise also places the company in a favourable competitive position.

Cost savings are at the top of every manager's list but the primary business advantages of "train-the-trainer" include building internal expertise, empowering employees, and protecting proprietary knowledge. This is especially important for larger organizations that use the services of external consultants who, once they complete their mandate, end up leaving with the accumulated knowledge and valued expertise.

Internal trainers also impact an organization's profitability. It's proven that a properly implemented train-the-trainer program saves companies thousands, potentially millions, of dollars annually through improving productivity and lowering external costs.

There are, however, other factors to consider when evaluating the overall cost savings of this approach. You need to factor opportunity costs and time lost when your internal trainers, composed of subject-matter experts and managers, are instructing and assisting others, rather than working on their primary responsibilities. Other unforeseen costs may include the need to hire additional employees to accommodate already overworked managers. In the long term, a well-trained staff is certainly beneficial, but it requires the organization's dedication to a well-developed learning strategy.

The question that management will ask becomes: "Can we effectively leverage the employees we have without having to sacrifice other issues within the company or should we develop an independent team of internal trainers?" Our job is to help them think through the issue and reach a satisfactory solution.

Team Building

Former U.S. Federal Reserve Chairman Alan Greenspan recently stated, "Workers today must be equipped not simply with technical know-how but also with the ability to create, analyze, and transform information and to interact effectively with others." This is important for a company seriously considering a train-the-trainer strategy. Providing managers with quick training for training others involves more than making sure they understand the subject thoroughly. Many individuals are unequipped in some fundamental skills such as public speaking and organizing simple training sessions.

Note that training is not an intuitive skill. True learning comes from individuals who possess fundamental skills and character traits.

Apart from knowing their subject extremely well, successful trainers have a friendly personality, excellent interpersonal abilities, and a high degree of patience. One often overlooked but very important skill when selecting potential trainers is their ability to review the basics of a subject and be able to repeat it as often as necessary. Many subject-matter experts find these last two points difficult, but they are essential if the program is to work. This is when incorporating a comprehensive external train-the-trainers program provides the tools and techniques to appropriately and effectively develop your internal team.

When evaluating potential subject matter with employees and managers, evaluate whether they can communicate ideas and concepts in a logical manner and whether they are perceived as a credible source by their co-workers. Be demanding in your selection process and allow the potential candidates to communicate their concerns and needs with you. First, determine whether they want to become trainers. Then conduct a thorough pre-assessment of their abilities and knowledge. Observe how they communicate with co-workers and ask them to explain how they go about attaining their work objectives. Be extremely diligent when selecting potential trainers.

Key Competencies

Now that you have selected your internal training team, determine what they need to become effective trainers. According to the American Society for Training and Development (ASTD), good trainers require four primary competencies:

1. *Training needs and assessment:* Performing a proper needs assessment allows a trainer to clearly identify whether training will resolve a situation or whether an alternative solution would be more appropriate.
2. *Design:* Training design is not a common ability and most trainers are formally trained to do this effectively. They

are capable of designing and structuring the information in a learnable format that even the most inexperienced participant will understand.

3. *Delivery:* Delivery is more than reciting information to an audience in the hope they assimilate some of it. Effective delivery skills include the ability for a trainer to:
   - Manage the training information;
   - Understand and quickly respond to the needs of the participants;
   - Provide a safe environment that allows for risk-taking and mistakes, and
   - Ensure that the participants are able to apply what is presented in the workplace;

   The expert is much more than a trainer. Experts must act as facilitators to initiate group discussions, manage questions, and act as mediators to mitigate conflicts and disagreements. Also, they should have proper public presentation skills to assure credibility and to connect with the audience.

4. *Evaluation:* Evaluate the effectiveness of the training conducted. Depending on the organization's expectations, various measures and benchmarks can be set, including how the participant has applied the newly acquired knowledge on the job or how much productivity/profitability has improved as a result of the training.

Guaranteed Success?

Simply selecting subject-matter experts and attempting to teach them training skills will not guarantee effective trainers. Developing new trainers should begin by having them pass a train-the-trainer certification course and providing them with an experienced training professional who can act as a coach and mentor. It's critical that they experience training in front of a sample audience—acting not only as a trainer but also as a student. This allows them to work out weak spots, build synergy, and refine their strengths.

Training is about giving people new knowledge, skills, or attitudes. An effective train-the-trainer program will give your trainers the tools to help ensure that learning takes place, and it will also measure the extent of that learning. A proper training program must be highly interactive and designed to be a model for participants in how to plan, design, and deliver training in a professional environment. It should provide and use a wide variety of instructional techniques to allow people with different learning styles to gain maximum benefit from the material.

Conclusion

Evaluate all possible alternatives available fairly when it involves the intellectual development of your client's employees. Even though building an internal training team provides many advantages, including developing in-house expertise, accessing critical information, and increasing productivity and profitability, it's best to find a balance between external expertise and internal needs. Whatever the size of your client organization, an internal team of trainers is an appropriate solution that will provide consistency in learning, dedication to organizational needs, and a significant reduction in cost and dependency on external consultants.

Return on Intelligence

The New ROI

Ann Herrmann-Nehdi

Passion

Return on intelligence is your ultimate job. In order to achieve it we must use all that we know about the brain.

Much of the focus in recent years in the world of workforce learning has been the challenge of demonstrating "ROI", usually defined as return on *investment*. An entire body of work and consulting business has spawned around this effort. As such the focus on *performance* has become the driving force of our industry. This is not new. Harold Geneen, CEO of International

Telephone and Telegraph, said it this way early in the 20th century:

> "I think it is an immutable law in business that words are words, explanations are explanations, promises are promises—but only performance is reality."

Without performance outcomes, what is the purpose of training and learning design? The ultimate objective is to become very clear on the task at hand by defining exactly what results we seek to achieve. How each of us defines, measures and tracks performance is critical to the success of each project we engage in.

How do you measure successful performance? Take a moment to think about it. Would your definition of successful performance be any different than that of your co-workers? Your customers? Your boss? Your family? Your senior-level leader's definition of performance might be very different from yours. Performance, like anything else, is in the eye *of the person defining it.* Understanding your definition of performance is key to attaining truly successful business outcomes.

As I have worked with individuals in different organizations around the globe, I have seen a multitude of different definitions of performance, often with a wide range of criteria. For one organization, the "bottom line" saving of $500,000 as a result of their "program" was the indicator of performance (even though one of the stated initial objectives had been "culture change"). This was in contrast to another organization that had initiated a program that significantly improved customer relationships. The long-term impact would certainly impact their finances, but this huge success had been more difficult to quantify in financial terms. Yet another organization had experienced fewer job-related injuries with a series of process improvements that would lead to incremental performance outcomes. Then there was the large greeting card company that had greatly improved the "robustness" of their ideas, improving the innovative output of their target teams.

In many cases, the ultimate objective is improved business success. So where does the performance come from?

Is performance the return on investment we seek? Workplace performance is a human endeavor. I believe a more appropriate framing of ROI in the world of learning is to think of it as "Return on Intelligence."

With that definition in mind, I have found it clarifying to describe the "I" in ROI in four different ways: Investment, Implementation, Interaction, and Innovation.

- **Return on Investment:** This is measuring performance based on quantifiable outcomes, most frequently articulated in financial outcomes or relevant numerical data related to the *purpose*. Those among us who prefer quantitative, mathematical, logical, analytical, and rational thinking naturally define success on the basis of quantifiable data, looking for the value received for money or time invested. This constitutes "proof" that the investment was worthwhile. When outcomes cannot be articulated in these terms, this type of thinker may conclude that there is no return at all. He or she might ask: "What is the bottom-line outcome?" "How much was invested?" "When will we see the return?" "Is the analysis sound?"

- **Return on Implementation:** When evaluating return in this case, performance is often linked to execution and *process*. Individuals, who prefer organized, sequential, structured, and detailed thinking tend to measure success in terms of successful execution and completion of an initiative. Questions might include: "Did it happen the way it was supposed to? Efficiently? On budget?" "Were the proper steps followed and completed?" "Was it legal and ethical?"

- **Return on Interaction:** As one might expect in the world of human performance, here the focus is on *people-oriented* results. Individuals who prefer an interpersonal, emotional, feeling, and humanistic way of thinking would often be satisfied with softer, less data-driven measures of success. Questions they might ask include: "Were relationships improved?" "Did meaningful communication take place?" "Was learning achieved?" "Was help provided?" "Was happiness achieved?"

- **Return on Innovation:** The focus here is getting the most out of the *possibilities* that are available in terms of new ideas, products, processes, markets, and customers. Those who prefer conceptual, imaginative, intuitive, and holistic modes of thinking would typically measure success in terms of solutions and achieving breakthrough concepts and ideas. They would value achievements that were unique, future-oriented, and global. Taking risks and surmounting them is often part of the equation and the path to success and performance outcomes. This approach will have questions such as: "Is it new and unique?" "Is it future-oriented?" "Will it provide competitive advantage?" "Are there global benefits?" "Is it cutting edge?"

Unleashing Learning in the Brain

Over the past fifteen years I have asked every audience what percentage of brain power they believe is actually used in their organization. What would your answer be? Consistently, responses have ranged from 5 to 25 percent. We tend to go in with very low expectations, which gives us a rational for why performance may be lacking. Much has been written about the deluge of change and information that is impacting everyone in the workforce. This has put even more pressure on our profession to deliver more effective means to make learning happen. The most obvious solution is to look at how we can accelerate and optimize each learning opportunity by understanding what is happening in our heads and brains.

We have learned from ongoing brain research that each brain is unique and that brains in general are *specialized*. While experts argue about the degree of specialization and the specificity of location, there is general agreement on the fact that our brains are designed with specialization in mind. Thus our thinking and learning naturally are also specialized. We are designed with a general *asymmetry:* each of us has a preference for which hand we use most, which eye, foot, ear, and specialized parts of our brains. We all have access to all of theses specialized modes of thinking and learning. Understanding the implications of specialization and preference are critical to unleashing more of the brain power that is available in your organization.

Consider your own experience throughout your personal learning history: Didn't you do much better in some subjects than in others? Respond much more to some teaching methods than others? We all know we retain some material more accurately and for a longer period of time than other material delivered in a different way. I personally remember the three or four teachers I found to be "brilliant and outstanding," but have forgotten many others who were not as effective for me. I do, of course, remember those teachers who were *so different* that I did not perform well. The reason is that our personal uniqueness and individual learning styles differentiate us from others. The way we react to information, content, delivery, learning environment, and teaching techniques will all be impacted by our unique learning styles.

An immediate implication for the workplace performance and learning profession is that our assumptions about the learner must now be completely reconsidered. As the concept of return on intelligence demonstrates, intelligence is no longer one-dimensional, but rather includes the notion of "multiple intelligences"—as Howard Gardner describes it. When you truly consider each individual as a unique learner with learning preferences different from other learners, it becomes clear that learning design and delivery, organization development, reward and recognition, and all communication must attempt to reach each individual learner in a way that is best suited to his or her needs. This way, the subject matter and message will be equally understood by all the participants in the experience, not only in terms of comprehension, but also in terms of intended outcomes and performance. Using a "whole brain teaching and learning" approach provides the basis for bridging the gap between the unique individual learner and the design and delivery of the learning. A chart of instructional strategies that best address the needs of each quadrant is provided in Figure 31.1.

Whole Brain Learning Considerations

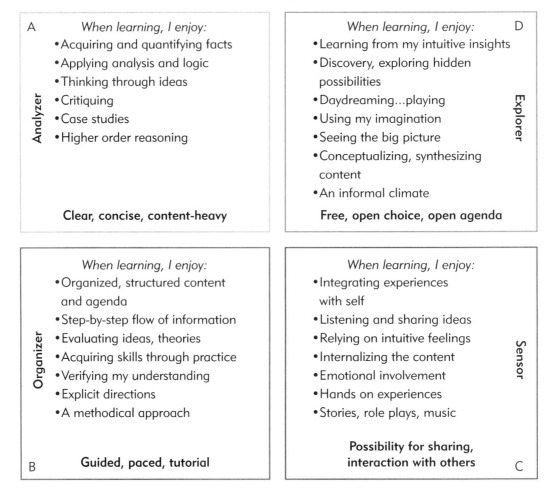

A   *When learning, I enjoy:*
Analyzer
- Acquiring and quantifying facts
- Applying analysis and logic
- Thinking through ideas
- Critiquing
- Case studies
- Higher order reasoning

Clear, concise, content-heavy

When learning, I enjoy: D
Explorer
- Learning from my intuitive insights
- Discovery, exploring hidden possibilities
- Daydreaming...playing
- Using my imagination
- Seeing the big picture
- Conceptualizing, synthesizing content
- An informal climate

Free, open choice, open agenda

When learning, I enjoy:
Organizer
- Organized, structured content and agenda
- Step-by-step flow of information
- Evaluating ideas, theories
- Acquiring skills through practice
- Verifying my understanding
- Explicit directions
- A methodical approach

B   **Guided, paced, tutorial**

When learning, I enjoy:
Sensor
- Integrating experiences with self
- Listening and sharing ideas
- Relying on intuitive feelings
- Internalizing the content
- Emotional involvement
- Hands on experiences
- Stories, role plays, music

Possibility for sharing, interaction with others   C

Figure 31.1. Learning Styles Considerations Model
Source: Herrmann International.

The Trainer's Portable Mentor

Leveraging Your Company's Brains for Accelerated Learning and Performance

A frequent complaint I hear from many in our profession is that senior management doesn't "get" the value of learning. An ASTD/IBM study in January 2006 on the Strategic Value of Learning provides some good news, revealing CLOs and other C-level executives (CXOs) agreed on the following:

- Learning provides strategic value at the enterprise, business unit, and individual capability level of an organization.
- Learning's value contribution is seen primarily in business outcomes and human capital.
- It is difficult to isolate and measure learning's value contribution to business outcomes.
- Perceptions of stakeholders (employees, business unit leaders, and executives) are a key indicator of learning's value.
- Learning's alignment with business needs is indicated by integration, proactivity, and responsiveness.

So what? We cannot use lack of management support as an excuse! Clearly, workplace performance and learning have never been as critical to organization success. In order to get the return on intelligence we need, it is essential to:

1. Clearly define the performance outcomes of each learning initiative as you see them.
2. Use a whole brain approach to identify and articulate those outcomes: investment, implementation, interaction, and innovation.
3. Beware of the impact your own thinking and learning preferences may have on your view of the world—get outside input from those who think differently than you do.

4. Understand the definition of success as defined by your customers, both the sponsor and the end-user using the same approach.
5. If necessary, translate those outcomes into a different mode and language to obtain buy-in.
6. Evaluate the thinking and learning preferences of all involved so you can ensure successful learning transfer occurs and design with the whole brain in mind.
7. Seek support from functions in your organization that can help you measure current state (essential!), and then track and measure progress against those outcomes (e.g., finance, administration, HR, R&D).
8. Use the Whole Brain Model as a framework to think through your outcomes. How did preferences impact the success?

Conclusion

Return on intelligence is your ultimate job. Thus, in order to achieve it, use all that you know and can learn about the brain. Seek help from others who look at the world differently than you do and learn from them. As Woodrow Wilson put it: "I use not only all the brain that I have, but all the brain I can borrow." The return on your intelligence will transform.

Turnover—Slaying the Monster One Touch at a Time

Dr. Frank P. Bordonaro

Passion

Put on your armor. Find your shield. Get ready for battle!

As a "talent management" executive, you are in a uniquely advantaged field position for slaying one of the great cost monsters in all of business, turnover. Because your role encompasses the whole range of talent touch points, you can use them all to surround and subdue the problem. Turnover is a place where cost reduction and improved talent converge to form opportunity.

Turnover is a monster alright. It chomps huge chunks out of company profits, disrupts business operations, undermines morale, disconnects you from your customers, and runs your people ragged. It's no wonder so much has already been written about it. As a talent management executive, what can **you** do about it?

This article is written to help you take advantage of your unique perspective: your daily concern with multiple ways in which the organization "touches" people. For you, the key to helping your organization defeat turnover is to redefine the battlefield and surround the problem. In this chapter, we take a look at **ten** potential angles of attack, all within the purview of talent management.

Easy to Justify

First let me get your attention with a little ROI demonstration.

- **Background:** The departure of an employee triggers a well-documented array of expenses. Researcher Hinkin and Tracy (2000) cite cost items for: separation; recruiting and attracting replacements; selection; hiring; and lost productivity. Companies vary widely, from .25 to 2.5 time's annual compensation. (Turnover calculators are easy to find via your browser, so you can come up with your own estimate.)
- **Live Example:** Here is a quick example, adapted from one of my client cases, in which a talent management investment of about $200K was proposed. (*Note:* This example uses a multiplier of $1 \times$ annual wages and benefits)

  Population targeted for turnover reduction initiative: 3,000
  Average wages, 30K, with a benefits load of 25 percent
  Total payroll = $112,500,000 (3,000 $\times$ 30,000 $\times$ 1.25)
  Annual turnover rate = 15 percent

Size of population turning over = 450

Annual turnover cost = $16,875,000 (112.5 million × .15 × 1) or (1 × 37.5K × 450)

Cost of initiative = $200,000

Cost of initiative as a percentage of turnover cost = 1.12 percent ($200K/$16.875 million)

Turnover saves needed to fund the initiative = about 5 (450 × .0112)

- **The ROI-Based Sale:** *Voiceover:* "Based on cost estimates and company payroll records, turnover in the Widget division is costing us about seventeen million dollars a year. The source of this cost is a "risk pool" of 450 employees who are, at any given moment, in the process of leaving us. We propose investing two hundred thousand dollars to reduce this cost. In order to completely offset the investment, only five of the 450 at-risk employees would need to be converted to "saves." In other words, even if the investment fails at a rate of about 99 percent, it pays for itself. Where else in the company do we have nine-figure cost items that can be reduced without losing assets? What other investments do we have that are self- funding at 1 percent effectiveness"?

- **A Tip:** By all means, use your best calculations to measure the actual *results* of your turnover reduction strategy. However, when it comes to *justifying* such strategies, you can afford conservative assumptions. Payroll is such a huge portion of overall operations costs that *almost any multiplier and any success rate are compelling.*

With solid reasoning and conservative assumptions, you will seldom get an argument from your CEO over the importance of reducing turnover and keeping it low. However, sheer numbers do not a proposal make; you are left with the problem of where to make investments and how those investments are connected to the turnover problem. To understand this better, it helps to reflect on the reasons why turnover isn't so easy for organizations to defeat.

. . . But Difficult to Do

You may have wondered why turnover hasn't been solved on your organization, simply by providing management with incentives to drive the problem away. After all, don't we already know the major dissatisfactions that produce turnover? Yes, but the issue is more likely one of capacity and ability to focus, rather than lack of knowledge or will. Once turnover reaches a certain level, the organization's ability to fight it is reduced, creating a momentum effect. The "soft" costs, such as staff time, loss of tacit knowledge, and reduced morale are drains on organization capacity, and there is little energy left to correct the root causes. Commonly, the pressure to cope falls on those charged with replacing people, as they frantically try to plug holes.

The turnover problem is then redefined as an operating problem: "We don't have enough people—let's hire more people, fast!" Hiring managers are forced to lower standards of entry. The result is a talent "throughput machine" that spends most of its time recruiting in and processing out. Under such conditions, managers and their harried HR staffs can hardly be expected to innovate solutions. In your more strategic role, you can help them.

Running on limited capacity, companies often try the "rifle shot" approach, pinpointing one kind of change and hoping they've hit the target.

- Hold supervisors more accountable for employee morale and retention!
- Address selected employee survey items like "connection to mission")!
- Raise wages or give people "stay" bonuses!
- Train first-line supervisors! Etc.

Because these solution attempts are only partial, they generally have a minor impact on the problem. Yet, they are hard to argue with, so are likely to become institutionalized. After all, who wants to cancel employee surveys or performance management? Collectively, they can further weigh down the organization in a bevy of annualized activities. The unintended consequence: supervisors overloaded with processes to manage, which they view as the "flavor of the month." That's not a recipe for success.

Use Your Perspective to Advantage

The only way to reverse the situation is to cut off the monster's food and air supplies. Below, we'll talk about ten *touch points*, areas of action that, when managed well, can stifle turnover.

Start with the premise that each touch point is a potential contributor to or reducer of turnover. If not working at maximum effectiveness today, that touch point needs to be strengthened. Let's look at each of the ten, explore why it can contribute to lower turnover and what might be done to improve it:

1. *Pre-Source Talent*

This is basically a way of tilting the supply/demand equation more in your favor, by increasing the number of people who will seek employment in your company. On campuses, you will have little trouble finding companies that have retained undergraduates as "reps" who take wages to promote a corporation as a "great place to work." Companies are also providing chat sites of their own or sponsoring intercampus chat facilities. Employment advertising firms are using the Internet to reach hard-to-find talent pockets (such as nursing) and creating relationships with them to facilitate communications when actual openings occur.

Take a look at the way your company does pre-sourcing today. Look for new ways to make your firm look more compelling as a place to work. The more people you have clamoring to get in, the more advantage you have in finding those who will join and stay.

2. Source Talent

Soliciting applicants for specific positions or for a menu of jobs is prevalent practice. Sourcing has long ago migrated to the Internet. Your company recruitment site is probably several years old by now and may need updating. Companies regularly post openings on job boards, but may have difficulty evaluating those boards from the viewpoint of the applicant. Tuning into Pete Weddle's periodic reviews, surveys, and tips to job seekers may provide insights.

Take the time to sample your portals of job application entry from the viewpoint of an outsider looking in. Challenge your company to make applications for jobs convenient and the jobs themselves intriguing.

3. Refine the Candidate Pool (Screening Out)

There are basically three dimensions for screening talent: (1) what is the person's track record of relevant experiences and accomplishments, (2) what are the person's acquired skills and knowledge, and (3) who is the person, in terms of type and temperament, work passions, and interests. The screening out process is most commonly done without direct contact with candidates—the funnel top is too large for close inspection, so it's logical that the most common screen is the resume, and that is essentially Dimension 1 above, with some insights into Dimension 2. Least visible at this stage is Dimension 3. However, this may be changing. The online world is beginning to develop tools for prospective applicants to screen themselves in and out of job pools based on work they enjoy/don't enjoy.

Evaluate the screening out process for Dimensions 1 and 2. Explore tools and methods for self- screening by applicants. The employee who sticks will usually have a personal connection to the company and the work.

4. Select (Screen In)

Kenneth Nowack (2007) of Envisia Learning is correct in pointing out that no one dimension of assessment is going to yield the bulk of predictive power in most jobs. Two ideas receiving more attention these days are interpersonal competence and job fit. Paying attention to interpersonal savvy simply serves to rebalance our wacky overdependence on cognitive abilities and "IQ" to predict job success. My own work with all kinds of managers leads to the conclusion that more than 80 percent turnover from performance failure stems, in turn, from interpersonal issues like consideration for others, teamwork, ability to communicate, and perceived ethics.

Work passions, enjoyed transferable skills, and ideal work environments comprise Dimension 3 above. Interest here is growing, arising from a 21st century workforce and the understanding that passion at work is a huge factor driving employee engagement. Progressive companies are spending more effort on this third dimension of applicant "fit." They know their success is going to depend on discretionary effort put out by employees who enjoy their work.

Review the screening in process on a simple basis of balance among (1) know-how/education, (2) track record (including demonstrated soft skills), and (3) personal preference/interests/passionately enjoyed skills. Seek balance; the employee who stays is most likely one who has a good degree of fit on all dimensions.

5. Support Orientation/On-Boarding

How important is it that your employees get a good start at the company and in their first jobs? Since almost all of us vividly remember our first few days on any job, it seems common sense that our survival antennae were up there for a reason! Huge sections of the economy put a heavy weight on successful startups for survival in the job. To take one example, sales forces funded mainly by commissions are notorious for high flunkout rates early on, with gradual, then dramatic retention improvements in the out years. Recent data from the insurance and financial services fields show retention after four years to be under 10 percent! Insurance companies respond with a bevy of measures to encourage early success. Similar emphasis is found in a number of businesses in which preparation for success is fundamental. If you question your call center support person following a *positive* service experience, as I did recently, you will typically find that the person on the other end spent a month or so in simulation drills before coming on the line live.

At higher levels, on-boarding is often a form of coaching provided by internal or external experts. They cover the elements and timeline for a good job start (learn the boss's priorities, meet your top ten internal clients, form your strategy, prepare for your first budget and personnel reviews, etc.). When on-boarding involves a group move to a new parent organization, as with mergers and acquisitions, adaptation to a new culture can be treated directly. Both GE and S.C. Johnson gave arriving employees a chance to measure old and new cultures and work with supervisors on adaptation plans. Retention improves under such practices.

Talk to a few start-up employees in different jobs. Ask them about the first sixty days on the job. When you find best practices, leverage them. Where turnover is high today, insist on an overhaul (or introduction) of the on-boarding process.

6. *Manage Performance*

This touch point is often in the target zone of those working on turnover. Suffice it to say that the more helpful processed do a few things well:

- Work expectations are clear.
- Feedback is frequent—and if there are problems—early!
- Performance covers "soft" skills as well as operating results.
- Employees receive lots of support as they work on improvements.

You are already on this page. Your best bet is to help your organization understand that performance management is a weapon against turnover—and assure the above "few things" are actually happening.

7. Provide Career Development

Give talented employees and future employees a chance to ask one question in order to evaluate you as an employer. Chances are good the most frequent inquiry will be: "What can you do to help me become more valuable in the job market?" Talent management experts know that they have a fundamental challenge here. Promotion opportunities seldom crop up in appropriate timing or quantity to continuously stretch even your best talent. Hence, the creative work of finding opportunities for "within job growth, horizontal career paths," special assignments, innovation, and action learning teams, etc.

Accept the premise that too much of your turnover arises from talent who have concluded they aren't growing fast enough. Your "stay" incentive often rests on the expected values of a future paycheck and the rewards of a better position.

8. Provide Feedback and Guidance

Chances are that you are scrambling in this area. Organizations are trapped in a tradition of relying on tutorial/coaching role for the supervisor, where the boss was expected to "bring people along." Yet, most managers today, be they chief surgeons, first-line production managers, financial executives, etc., work within a reality that does not really support much coaching and mentoring. Many executives now rely on outsourcing, external suppliers, independent service providers, and their personal electronic devices to run a function; there are few people left to coach! Just as difficult is the reality of the managers who do have direct reports, because there are so many of them. Span of control, where it exists, is usually too wide to allow individual attention.

These developments help explain the dramatic rise of the (internal or external) business coach. Additional resources, such as the online follow-up tools provided by Fort Hill Company, indicate there will be online solutions to help fill the vacuum. Yet trying new skills at work under supervision remains at the top of the learning hierarchy. Moreover, surveys routinely find that "opportunities to develop my skills" is a top determiner of "intent to stay" with an organization. In short, you can't beat on-the-job development as an attack on turnover.

Accept the premise that development resources are often overspent in areas in which turnover is least likely. Cast a critical eye on the coaching/feedback and development happening in pockets where your turnover is highest. Explore shifting some coaching resources and online development tools to those spots.

9. *Plan for Succession*

This is well-plowed ground for talent management executives. A concern for turnover might prompt you to change your focus, however. Most succession planning is concerned with contingency planning *after* turnover occurs. Preventive succession planning focuses more on the events that spike turnover. Here are a few vulnerable points:

The week after Person B learns he is not in line for a position he wanted

The fourth year individuals have been in assignments initially planned as "developmental slots"

Individuals who are considered good performers but are not in line for advancement and are in "career drift"

Revisit the results of your last corporate-wide succession plan, this time focusing exclusively on the non-successors and non-movers. Use management communications, compensation, or special career coaching to re-engage the keepers.

10. Outplace

Why would outplacement have anything to do with retention? Consider the mental landscape of the valued employee who "hears footsteps" that suggest a RIF, relocation, reorganization, or acquisition may impact them. This is a prime time for quiet looking at the job market. It is wise to focus preemptively on the nervous talent in your ranks and to initiate the contact with them. Second, if the outplacement plans are well-thought-out and done with class and quality, you make it easier for the desired turnover to happen, placing less pressure on headcount overall. In short, outplacement is both a harbinger of turnover and a tool for controlling turnover for least net loss of needed talent.

Review your outplacement process and support resources. Pay close attention to spots in the organization where outplacement is being considered—if you know about it, your talent does too. Consider good outplacement as a threat reducer for those who will be leaving and for those you don't want to slip away. Work to improve communications with survivors and benefits for those leaving. How your company treats people in these situations will impact your reputation as a place to work, which affects pre-sourcing (back to touch point 1!)

Conclusion

Like most huge opportunities in business, turnover reduction requires a shift in perspective and approach. Talent management is a role made for this battle. Access as any touch points as you can, and use them to get your organization, and your talent, a win.

References

Hinkin, T., & Tracey, J.B. (2000). The cost of turnover: Putting a price on the learning curve. *Cornell Hotel and Restaurant Quarterly, 41,* 14.

Nowack, K.M. (2007, February). Predicting the future success of T, in talent management. *Mediatec, 1*(3).

Creating Credibility with Senior Management

A Simple Approach for Connecting Training to the Business

Timothy P. Mooney and

Robert O. Brinkerhoff, Ed.D.

Passion

Effective training is not about good intentions. It's about results!

Most learning and development departments provide good training events that are well-intended, well-designed, and well-liked. Yet, they fail to produce meaningful business impact for the organization most of the time. The problem doesn't lie in the training itself, but in how organizations implement the training. The problem will only be solved by educating the whole organization (executives, managers, and employees) on how to turn training into business results and then building accountability for making this happen.

I want you to imagine yourself in this scenario: You are busy working away at your desk planning a major training implementation to support an important and new organization business initiative. In walks the CEO who says to you, "This initiative is vitally important to our business strategy. We are investing millions of dollars in this strategy and we see the training as an important piece of this initiative. The training *must* work. Can you guarantee that it will work?"

In that brief second that your career begins to flash before your eyes, you begin thinking about all the things that can cause training to fail that are outside of your control; for example:

- The training participants who may not really be motivated or grasp the importance of the change initiative
- The large number of participants who probably won't even use the new skills back on the job
- The managers who may not be willing or able to coach or support the new skills
- Various senior execs who may not be committed to the success of this effort

And while you're thinking, the CEO says, "And one more thing; would you be willing to bet your paycheck on it?"

What would you do in this situation? What steps would you take, if the training absolutely, positively had to work and lead to business results?

PAUSE FOR A MOMENT AND FORMULATE YOUR OWN ANSWER BEFORE CONTINUING TO READ

Most HRD professionals would probably respond with something like the following:

- Do a thorough needs analysis to determine what skill or competencies were needed
- Talk to senior management to better understand their goals for the training
- Search the marketplace for the best training programs available that address those skills or competencies
- Involve line management in the decision making on the training
- Build or buy the best training program possible (for the funds available)
- Build in training reinforcement tools or refreshers
- Work to get senior management to endorse and kick off the training
- Work to get first-line managers to support, reinforce, and coach the training
- Use evaluations to identify how well the training worked and then make adjustments to the training as needed

All of the aforementioned steps are valuable and good. They are like "motherhood" and "apple pie." It is hard to argue against any of them. However, as seasoned learning and development (L&D) professionals, we recognize that one task (among all these noble steps) rises to the top. Building management support, especially executive support, is critical to success.

However, the challenge that we have as L&D professionals is that it is difficult to get the attention of senior and line management to be involved in these activities. Why does that happen? Sometimes we are our own worst enemies. All too often we approach the task from a training perspective. We don't approach it from a business perspective. As a consequence, our message gets lost in the "L&D speak." We expect managers to view the world from our perspective—after all, we are the training experts; we know the "ins and outs" of the field and what it takes to make training work. Unfortunately, when we go into our explanations and talk about what we need or what will make the training work, eyes glaze over or we are politely dismissed. Often we are not viewed as an equal partner at the planning table.

Revisit those steps that I mentioned at the beginning of this chapter. For the most part, they all have training as the central element.

- Why do you want the training?
- What do you want people to learn in the training?
- What competencies should this training address?
- What are your objectives for the training?
- What do you want people to do better after the training?
- How much time are you willing to devote for the training?

Training! Training! Training! It's no wonder line managers' eyes glaze over when we start down this path.

Most managers order training as they would order a pizza: "Give me a one-day strategic leadership course and hold the role plays." As ineffective and frustrating as that is, the worst part is that we in L&D let them do it and even encourage this behavior: "Do you want pre-work (extra cheese) with that?"

They do this because—as we have lamented all along—they don't understand how training works. Our job is to help them connect the training to the business goals. This connection can't just be a superficial or nominal connection, such as: "We need to do customer service training, so we can improve customer loyalty and retention."

Instead, we need to establish a clear and step-by-step linkage that connects the training, the job, and specific results.

In order to identify these types of linkages, we need to come at things from the perspective of the business, not our training programs. Instead of asking questions about the training, we should be asking questions like those below:

- What are the two or three business outcomes you are really trying to achieve?
- What time frame do you have to achieve these goals?
- Where are you currently against these goals?
- What would achieving these goals be worth to the business?
- Which roles in the organization can deliver the goals you have just identified?
- What makes these jobs/teams critical to the business goals?
- What outcomes must the team job/team produce to achieve your business goals?
- How do these job/teams deliver these business results?
- How might we measure these job/team results?
- What are the three to five things these jobs must do well in order to deliver these results?
- Does the organization have the skills/knowledge to produce these results?

The goal of asking these types of questions is not just to get smart about the business. The goal is to be smart so that we can create a clear and concise "line of sight" from the training room door through the field or plant to the boardroom door. This line of sight would describe in specific terms the connection between each of these elements:

- The key organization goals/strategy the training is intended to support
- The team or individual results that need to be achieved that contribute to those goals

- The most critical on-the-job situations ("moments of truth") where better performance will lead to better team or individual results
- The learning outcomes from the training that will equip trainees to be effective in those on-the-job situations

An example of a single "line of sight" for a customer service rep role that connects customer service training to a business goal of improving customer loyalty is depicted in Figure 33.1.

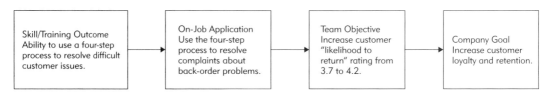

Figure 33.1. Example of Line of Sight

A training program would involve multiple "lines of sight" for people in each position attending the training.

One of our most important roles as L&D or performance consultants is to be able to articulate this line of sight to all levels in the organization. If **we** can't clearly and specifically articulate it—as designers, facilitators, consultants, and leaders of training—how can we expect learners or line managers to make the connection between the training, the application back on the job, and results? And if they can't make the connection, how can we expect them to do the things we need them to do, such as setting expectations for using the new behaviors and holding their direct reports accountable?

Admittedly, to ensure that training absolutely, positively leads to business results, there are other factors that need to be built into the design. However, getting all levels of management aligned on the "line of sight" is critical for starting off in the right direction and gaining senior management's active commitment.

Organizations that have taken this approach have seen several important benefits. First and foremost, aligning all the key players (senior executives, line managers, participants, and the L&D organization) typically leads to greater use of the important new skills back on the job and consequently to improved business results.

In addition, L&D professionals have realized several benefits that have raised their stock in the eyes of the company:

1. They develop fluency about the business and its issues; as a consequence they are able to have a different type of conversation with business leaders from other functions.
2. They are viewed differently by line management and senior executives. They are seen as partners in the business and not "providers of training events."
3. They are able to produce more value around the business objective by more effectively designing and delivering training that hits the bulls-eye.
4. Training budgets are approved more readily and recognized as being integral to the business' success.

Conclusion

A lot of companies provide good training, but enlightened L&D professionals understand that it's not about the training. It's about the business and the results they can deliver!

Readers who would like to learn more about how to build a line of sight that connects training to the business goals, should go to www.AdvantagePerformance.com.

Work Learning—
Beyond the Classroom

Ajay M. Pangarkar, CTDP, and

Teresa Kirkwood, CTDP

Passion

How an effective learning environment empowers employees to develop imaginative strategies and innovative practices is the key to an organization's success in the marketplace.

Albert Einstein was once quoted as saying, "The significant problems we have cannot be solved at the same level of thinking with which we created them." Even though he was speaking about the state of the world, his statement is equally important for businesses striving to succeed in this ever-changing and extremely competitive economic environment. Whether you are a manufacturer or provide a service, your industry requires a dynamic learning strategy that harnesses the knowledge of its people and is an integral component of the firm's strategic plan. Now more than ever before, businesses must learn from their experiences and adapt to changes to survive and prosper.

To build a lasting learning environment, organizations must begin early by clearly defining what it means to be a learning organization. Growing entrepreneurial companies have a distinct advantage in this regard because their existence hinges on active learning and constant knowledge acquisition. This means that they learn faster and avoid confronting bigger problems later. Although unstructured, these firms have what it takes to build a strong learning culture. What they lack is a clear and functional method of learning, with easy-to-apply management guidelines. Many businesses don't understand how to learn and either fail or remain marginal competitors. Companies that successfully implement learning strategies have the best chance to thrive.

A learning organization is capable of aligning its strategic objectives and vision with the capabilities, competencies, and ideas of its employees. Managers within a learning organization seek to create an environment in which their employees realize their maximum potential. Employees who receive additional knowledge are only one part of a complete learning strategy. To gain employee commitment, managers must include and align their employees' personal goals with the corporate vision. They also need to develop the competencies and knowledge lacking in the team to attain their strategic objectives. As this learning culture is supported and fostered by management, employees seek out and solve problems, become more entrepreneurial, and are more willing to take risks.

Training Is Not Learning

Businesspeople often, mistakenly, equate training with learning. Although these terms are often used interchangeably, they are distinct concepts. Training is instruction for learning a specific task. Learning, on the other hand, is a continuous process. Training is one of the many tools used to build a learning environment. Learning encompasses an individual's acquisition and assimilation of experiences, information, and daily activities.

Training can only provide information to employees. This information can only be converted to knowledge if employees are capable of applying it to their jobs. Learning takes place when the person applies these skills through practice and reinforcement. To ensure that the new skills are learned and applied managers must:

- Take responsibility for their employees' and their own learning activities;
- Provide employees with a continuous learning environment;
- Allow employees to take risks and make mistakes; and
- Reinforce learning as employees experiment with their new skills

Managers often view training as a separate function from the employees' work activity. This negative perception is further entrenched as employees take time away from their jobs. Once the employee returns to his job, the new skills are often not integrated or encouraged in his daily activities, which makes the training simply an expense rather than a useful tool. Learning must be viewed differently.

Ask yourself what it will take for your company to survive in a changing economy. You must understand what your organization's capacity and capabilities are before confronting external factors and competitors. This important exercise (balanced scorecard or SWOT analysis) results in ultimately knowing your organization's strengths, weaknesses, and the direction required to reach your goals.

All companies want to attain superior performance and through it an identifiable competitive advantage. Success is attained when organizations answer one question: "How can we use our existing resources to develop our workers' intellectual capacity to attain our vision and cannot be copied by others?"

A Case for Learning

When learning becomes an integral component of the corporate strategy, is part of the daily activities, and contributes to the development of workers, the organization possesses a sustainable competitive advantage that cannot be copied.

Significant and noticeable advantages of learning organizations include:

- *A reduction in errors and mistakes.* When workers recognize and learn from mistakes early, they can quickly adapt to change, resulting in an increase in productivity and morale.
- *Improved quality and innovations.* A byproduct of learning from mistakes is the impact that it has on the workers' responsibilities and how it improves the organization. People begin to improve the quality of their output and become increasingly innovative since the consequences of their efforts can only help the company.
- *Having a better understanding of the business.* Many employees we speak to say to us, "We do not understand how we fit into the organization's vision." A dynamic learning strategy allows every employee to connect to the business and clearly see how the pieces of the puzzle fit together. The result: Every employee is able to more effectively serve the client and identify opportunities for improvement.
- *Empowered employees.* Learning allows employees to take on more responsibility and insight into the company and thus improve their professional and personal well-being. Empowerment results in workers showing more initiative,

becoming increasingly creative, and promoting a different way of viewing business processes.

Becoming a Learning Organization

It's perceived that the job of creating learning cultures is best left to those with large budgets and extensive resources. This myth unnecessarily holds back smaller companies from considering and investing in developing a learning organization. But it doesn't have to be expensive. Follow these basic points and you're on your way to a more effective working environment.

- **Step 1. Keep it simple.** The first rule in building a learning culture is to keep things simple. The most effective strategy is one that makes certain that everyone clearly understands what is involved and what is expected from employees and managers.
- **Step 2. Clearly define your strategic objectives.** This is a critical step. It will ensure that your learning strategy is effective. Bring your management team and advisors together to clearly define the company's vision and, working backward, outline the critical steps required to attain it. You need to know where you want to go, how you are going to get there, and the resources needed in the process.
- **Step 3. Set up a learning committee and policy.** Bring together employees and managers who appropriately represent the scope of the organization. Ideally, the committee should be composed of no more than five to eight individuals, and each should have an equal say in the development and implementation of the training policies.
- **Step 4. Take inventory of existing knowledge and competencies.** This is an involved two-step process. First, identify each position in your company and then determine the

skills and competencies required to effectively complete the responsibilities. Second, document the skills and competencies of the employees currently in these positions.

- **Step 5. Identify the skills and competency gaps.** Once you complete the knowledge inventory, determine the knowledge gaps that exist between the employees' competencies and the skills required to reach your strategic objectives.
- **Step 6. Determine your employees' personal goals.** Talk to each employee individually. Build a dialogue with them to determine what their personal aspirations are within the organization and in life. Help them help you accommodate their needs. You will gain a dedicated and motivated worker. Also, this will help you figure out whether each individual is a good fit for the company.
- **Step 7. Develop a training plan.** At this point you know where you want to go and what competencies you need to get there. With this information you are now able to source appropriate training to resolve the identified knowledge and competency gaps.
- **Step 8. Integrate learning into daily activities.** Learning is a continuous process. Implement tactical methods to encourage learning among employees and to support employees with new or more complex responsibilities. Coaching and mentoring are two ways to make the learning process more interesting and an integral part of the company's strategy. Continue to measure, document and manage the results of these processes.

There is no question that a learning organization provides a safe place to take risks and to develop new ideas, behaviors, and the challenge to stretch beyond perceived limits. Everyone's opinions are valued and the number of people who can contribute isn't determined by the position they occupy in the organization. Employees at all levels will find it more enjoyable to work in and on the business because it provides a basis for creative ideas and gives people more control of outcomes and the ability to make things better.

Conclusion

A well-developed and effective strategic and competitive advantage is an elusive objective for many businesses. It requires workers to be creative, knowledgeable, and innovative. They have to do this faster and more efficiently than their competitors. More importantly, managers must begin to view knowledge and human capital as the organization's most valuable and volatile resource. By continuously developing and leveraging your employees' knowledge, you will be capable of handling every situation that arises and be strategically equipped to become an industry leader.

A Business Approach to Learning

Increasing Profits Through Marketing Methodologies

Ajay M. Pangarkar, CTDP, and

Teresa Kirkwood, CTDP

Passion

Like every other investment a company makes, training must be sold to those unconvinced of its true benefits. Proving the worth of WLP is essential if you are to gain the buy–in and internal support if you are to make your learning initiatives a success.

Training managers are challenged to "sell" the benefits of an intangible need to those wanting tangible results. External consultants understand this obstacle; however, when those responsible for training propose training solutions they often encounter significant resistance. Senior managers recognize the importance for training but, with limited resources, they are also concerned with accountability and results. Training and Development (T&D) is also challenged by other stakeholders, employees, and management alike, to overcome indifference and skepticism of any proposed learning initiative.

The days when T&D managers were able to convince senior management that training could not be measured tangibly or financially are over. Managers of training departments must make a radical shift in their thinking to gain support for learning initiatives. As training budgets increase, senior managers expect to see some type of tangible return on their budget allocations as they do from any other operational or functional activity. Increasingly, stakeholders at all levels want to see tangible outcomes as they relate to their functions and environments.

The mistake T&D managers often make is attempting to position training as an essential need. *Secret 1: Nothing is an absolute need to senior management.* T&D believes they must convince senior management of the benefits and to actually invest funds to make proposed initiatives a reality. Doing this is a mistake and places T&D in a defensive position. *Secret 2: Most senior managers are already sold on the need and the necessity for training.* The buy-in is not about whether they want to have training, it is about which training initiative presents the most benefits and tangible results to the organization at all levels.

T&D has grown up in the last few years; where once it sat at the "kiddie table," today it is invited to sit with the adults. When an organization commits a seat at the executive table they are clearly stating to T&D, "Sell us on what training will do for the organization in business and strategic terms we understand."

Chief learning officers (CLOs) must prepare themselves with answers for questions such as:

- How is the learning strategy inline with the organizations overall vision/direction?
- What are the expected and tangible outcomes/benefits of the learning strategy?
- How will it be marketed within the organization?
- How will we gain the buy-in from the affected departments/individuals?
- How will T&D justify the cost and investment for the training?
- What is the business metrics to measure organizational impact?

This is not an exhaustive list of senior management questions but it is a starting point for CLOs to demonstrate to their senior counterparts and stakeholders how T&D initiatives impact the organization through tangible business measures. It requires taking a "business" approach to proving T&D's worth.

1. Proving T&D's Worth

Management is primarily concerned with profitability. Every business unit is expected to be profit centers or, at the very least, demonstrate profitability in some way. For traditional cost centers such as T&D, this is a highly debated topic. The question often raised is, "How can T&D be profitable?" As much as we would like to provide you with a magic solution to this question, each approach is as unique as the organization itself.

In a *CLO* article Zeinstra (2004) speaks about cost recovery as an alternative measure of T&D's profitability. He states, "Package the outcome to your stakeholders not as seeking profit, but as seeking cost recovery." Cost recovery is not a new concept but offers a "softer" approach to operational profitability. It does not make a corporate support division appear as "making money" off of its employees.

Another method to profit center thinking is getting T&D to become an internal consulting group for the learning needs of other business units. This gets T&D to think through consultative approaches in terms of solutions, results, and meeting client (other business units) expectations the same way if the organization sourced external consultants.

Positioning T&D as a consulting group helps it to:

- Answer the specific and targeted needs of business unit clients
- Deliver tangible business results
- Deliver focused solutions in line with organizational strategy
- Be accountable to costing, pricing, and profitability
- Facilitate "buy-in" within the organization
- Develop effective solutions

Like every other business function, training's worth is determined by its contribution in helping the organization reach strategic objectives. But to do this, T&D must actually see itself as its own business and be fully accountable. This can be accomplished if T&D possesses a holistic approach to learning and performance rather than simply focusing on the training function itself. This requires those responsible for training to possess not only expertise in training but also to have a basic comprehension of business and strategy.

This orientation positions training and development as a strategic partner helping stakeholders at all levels attain desired objectives and specific results. This is how T&D will facilitate "buy-in" of training initiatives throughout the organization.

2. Knowing Your Audience: Gaining Buy-In

As T&D managers develop their knowledge and understanding of organizational objectives in business terms, they increase opportunities in delivering the right message to their customers—the organization and its business units. The greatest failure is not knowing, understanding, or clearly communicating what the customer wants. An effective marketing and communication strategy for T&D requires demonstrating tangible results to those expected to benefit from the training.

Marketing and selling your training internally is all about being prepared, involving the appropriate and affected individuals, and clearly understanding what executive management wants to hear. After all, we are basically talking about applying fundamental sales, marketing, and people skills. But to establish true credibility in the eyes of management, it is critical to demonstrate a clear relationship to business and strategic objectives. No matter how effective you are in developing an effective marketing strategy for training initiatives, there will always be critics trying to challenge your assumptions.

Marketing Mistake 1: Focusing on Features

The focus of any training must be on the benefits and not on the features. For example, if you are proposing a customer service program for front-line workers, one feature would be resolving client problems for which the benefit would be an increase in customer satisfaction or an increase in repeat sales. These are the tangible results senior managers want to see. Too many times we see organizations jump quickly on the "new business trend" bandwagon. This is another example of features taking precedence over benefits. Because a topic is gaining popularity, it does not mean that it is appropriate for your staff or organization. Business decisions are based on deliverables in line with strategic objectives, not on appeal. Applying the feature/benefit principal will help prepare you to move your cause forward with those that are most resistant.

Marketing Mistake 2: Focusing on One Level of Decision Making

Apart from only focusing features, when seeking "buy-in" for training related projects training managers tend to focus on obtaining support from the highest-level of decision makers, senior management. There are only two outcomes from this approach. Either management approves or they reject the training project. If it is approved, then congratulations, but only one level of decision makers are sold on the idea. At this point the proposed initiative, more often than not, is doomed to fail because those directly affected were not involved or consulted. Like wildfire, resistance spreads quickly leading to non-acceptance of the training initiative, eventually jeopardizing and, possibly, killing the project. Hence, management blames the training manager for the failure and lack of results, further propagating the belief that training is an expense and reinforcing to participants that training is a waste of time and money.

Marketing Mistake 3: Not Knowing Your "Buyers"

Training managers who successfully gain internal acceptance for training recognize early who they need to approach and quickly gain an appreciation for the concerns and needs of those directly or indirectly involved. These managers also have an understanding of the fundamental marketing philosophies, "know your audience" and "sell the buyers what they want to buy; not what you want to sell" (see Table 35.1). Essentially, there are three groups to address: training participants (or employees); mid-level managers; and senior management.

Table 35.1. Defining Your Target Audience and Their Needs

Internal Target Audience	Internal Target Audience Concerns
Senior Management, including:	
• C-level management	⇒ Strategic alignment (balanced scorecard)
• Divisional executives (presidents)	⇒ Budget requirements
• Senior vice presidents	⇒ Cost involvements
• Senior operational managers	⇒ Financial outcomes/analysis
• Senior functional managers	⇒ Tangible results
	⇒ Intangible benefits
	⇒ Business impact (level 4)
	⇒ Return on investment (level 5)
	⇒ Project justification to the board/shareholders (major investments)
Mid-Level Management, including:	
• Business unit managers	⇒ Attain business objectives/prescribed benchmarks
• Operational managers	
• Functional area managers	⇒ Meet budget allocations
• Divisional/operational coordinators	⇒ Cost impact to budget
• Department/staff supervisors	⇒ Staff time requirements
• Controllers	⇒ Alternative learning possibilities
	⇒ Respect of current resources
	⇒ Tangible business-unit results
	⇒ Intangible business-unit benefits
	⇒ Immediate application of skills (Level 3)
	⇒ Direct relationship to tasks/jobs

(Continued)

Internal Target Audience	Internal Target Audience Concerns
Training Participants, including:	
• Operational staff	⇒ Correlation to their jobs/tasks
• Functional staff	⇒ Benefits to their jobs/tasks
• Support staff	⇒ Time required/away from job
• Any training participants	⇒ Contribution to personal growth
	⇒ Contribution to professional development
	⇒ Know what they need to know (pre-assessment and Level 2 assessment)
	⇒ Support to new skills acquisition (Level 3)
	⇒ Other available options to training
	⇒ Personal financial benefits

Training participants will usually accept any training if it provides them with value-added resources and does not take time away from their immediate responsibilities. The training must be easy for them to absorb and incorporate into their daily activities if it is to change behavior. Changing behavior and attitudes of participants is at the core on how training will impact business results. It is important to balance the needs of the participant with the need for performance improvement. Effectively doing this aligns the participants' goals with the needs of business managers and broadens access to other possible alternatives.

When dealing with business unit managers, it is important to recognize their specific requirements. They are often challenged to leverage their employees' ability to achieve specific departmental or production objectives with the demands of senior management. At this level, managers are involved in budget planning and the allocation of funds directly affecting their environment. Being directly on the front lines of business, they are accountable to attain preset performance benchmarks on many levels placing extensive demand on their resources. Taking these concerns into account, business managers have little patience or time for training solutions that do not produce immediate results and take their employees away from their daily responsibilities

Decision making at the senior level focuses on attaining strategic objectives, increasing profitability, and maximizing shareholder value. At this level, managers want to create an environment that increases sales and revenue through improving product quality and customer and employee satisfaction. Their objective is to optimize the return on their investment in every business-related activity, especially when investing in employees. In the knowledge economy, ideas, innovation, and synergy are critical to long-term success. Every training investment must ensure that the performance of the organization improves by developing a knowledgeable team of employees to effectively serve clients and to capitalize on new opportunities. It is usually at this level that many training managers pitch their proposals—often ignoring other levels of decision-making involvement.

3. Answering the Seven Essential Questions

You will certainly encounter critics and individuals at every level of management challenging your reasons. Being prepared for the "critical" questions is essential if you are to sell your solution. The following are some examples of questions often asked. These questions will help you face the challenges you may encounter when proposing T&D solutions.

1. Is There Really a Need for Training?

Training professionals often overestimate the value training can provide. If the perception of training is to change, then training managers need to be honest with its effectiveness. There are many instances in which a formal training solution is unnecessary. For example, your company has recently upgraded existing software. Is there a need for training or are they capable of learning it on their own? Perhaps they only require coaching in some of the new features of the software.

2. Do All Employees Have to Be Trained?

Management believes the myth that all employees must pass through training if they are to maximize their investment. The impact of training is realized if the right individuals are involved. Focus your training efforts on the people with the need and those who will benefit most, and clearly demonstrate to management the impact this focus will have on the organization. For example, if you are introducing a new product, then the production team may require training in quality procedures, whereas customer service employees would require training on the use of the product.

3. What Are the Expected Outcomes?

You will be asked this question. Training professionals often misdiagnose the problem the required training is supposed to solve. Training's primary goal is to improve on existing processes and outcomes. This leads back to the benefits mentioned earlier. When attempting to build a case for training, you must ensure that the benefits answer the needs of your audience and the investment delivers on the actual expected returns.

4. How Will the Training Move Us Closer to Our Goals?

Executive managers expect that every business decision move them closer to a desired goal. Training investments are not exempted from this rule. Managers recognize that their people are the key to their success or failure. Even more importantly, they also recognize that the investment they make in people is also unpredictable and volatile. Your responsibility is to assure and show management that the proposed training solution will lead them one step closer to their goals. Clearly show tangible links to operational and organizational strategic objectives.

5. What Are Management's Expectations?

Each level of management has certain expectations from the investment. Clearly understanding what they are will help in your marketing efforts. Senior managers expect to see links between productivity and profitability. Setting up clear "benchmarks" against both internal and industry measure will certainly improve your case for training. Mid-managers want to see immediate outcomes and results. Work closely with them to develop an implementation plan that minimizes workplace disruption and equips their staff with the skills that will move them closer to their immediate objectives.

6. What Resources Will the Training Require?

All organizations are constrained by limited resources. Many managers also believe that there are more critical issues to resolve with these resources before they will commit to training. To avoid this objection, you want to know what resources are required. Do not underestimate your needs and be prepared to justify your position. Then present this case to the decision makers and those who are affected by the training.

7. What Will the Training Cost?

Cost-benefit and profit-loss are terms that are not always familiar to training professionals. If not handled carefully, this question can be a trap. The key to selling your training internally is to speak in terms that management understands. Prove to them that training employees is an investment that will result in measurable and profitable outcomes. Clearly determine direct and unforeseen costs and related to expected results. Remember, talk to them in business terms, not training terms.

Your success depends on how you address the concerns at each level of decision making and whether the individuals affected participated in developing the proposed training solution. It requires an understanding of the benefits related to the needs of the employees and organization. Knowing your audience is essential to gaining support and the first step to selling training solutions internally.

Conclusion

The perception of training is changing and the need is growing. If real change is to take hold, training professionals must find effective ways to ensure true learning leads to results. Training is about developing abilities and knowledge that translate into sustained performance. Building organizational requirements and employee needs into the training solutions is essential to gain acceptance at every level. It is time for T&D to shift their thinking to business and strategic orientations focusing on performance and results to gain credibility and facilitate buy-in. Training and development must realize that they are an integral component to the business not an organizational footnote.

Reference

Zeinstra, R. (2004, December). Converting from a training department to a profit center. *CLO*.

Conclusion to Section Three

We have always been strong believers that we can learn from others. These experts provide us with valuable information and knowledge we can take away and build on and make it our own. Each learning performance professional has his or her own unique perspective on the information provided, and no two perspectives are alike. These articles are a resource to help and, at times, guide, support, and even to teach you things you might not know you didn't know.

Some of the key elements to take away from reading these articles are some ways to help you to produce results and to remember not to take shortcuts to solutions. People tend to focus on the glamorous activities of performance improvement and ignore the rest. Your goal is to become holistic in your approach to workplace performance and learning. The other point to take away is the need for more implementation planning, specifically figuring out how the logistic or the "nuts and bolts" of implementing your solutions will win you praise from developing result-oriented learning initiatives. The third point to effective performance is the lack of proper evaluations of learning solutions. Very little of what we produce and implement is properly evaluated.

What can we conclude from the articles written by of some of the more recognized industry experts presented in this section? It is clear that for them workplace learning is directly correlated to organizational performance, and it is also clear that they expect those involved with learning to make their efforts connect with the objectives of the organization.

As mentioned in the article "Capturing Learning Opportunities Within Your Organization," successful knowledge-enabled organizations strive to harness the knowledge existing within their extended value chain. Leveraging learning leading to performance requires organizations to reorient themselves to capitalize on the knowledge existing in their environment, match the learning requirements of the organization to the personal learning needs of employees, develop a learning environment to maximize overall performance and value, and properly structure and organize learning tools and environments that directly contribute to the strategic goals of the organization.

Once again, we discussed what it means to become a learning organization and to move beyond the classroom. A learning organization is capable of aligning its strategic objectives and vision with the capabilities, competencies, and ideas of its employees. Managers within a learning organization seek to create an environment in which their employees realize their maximum potential. Employees who receive additional knowledge are only one part of a complete learning strategy. To gain employee commitment, managers must include and align their employees' personal goals with the corporate vision. They also must develop the competencies and knowledge lacking in the team to attain their strategic objectives. As this learning culture is supported and fostered by management, employees seek out and solve problems, become more entrepreneurial, and are more willing to take risks.

We feel for all learning professionals in their struggles to gain support for their workplace performance and learning initiatives. Training managers are challenged to "sell" the benefits of an intangible need to those wanting tangible results. External consultants understand this obstacle; however, when those responsible for training propose training solutions, they often encounter significant resistance. Senior managers recognize the importance for training but, with limited resources, they are also concerned with accountability and results. T&D is also challenged by other stakeholders, employees and management alike, to overcome indifference and skepticism of any proposed learning initiative.

The perception of learning is changing, and the need is growing. If real change is to take hold, learning professionals must find effective ways to ensure that true learning leads to results that translates to performance. Learning is about developing abilities and knowledge that translate into sustained performance within the workplace. Building organizational requirements and employee needs into the training solutions is essential to gain acceptance at every level. It is time for T&D to shift their thinking to business and strategic orientations focusing on workplace learning and performance and results to gain credibility and facilitate buy-in. Training and development must realize they are an integral component to the business, not an organizational footnote.

SECTION FOUR

Measurement and Evaluation

Introduction to Section Four

Measurement and evaluation—these are two words that learning professionals quickly recognize as essential for every learning initiative developed. But it also sends chills to many who do not possess a thorough understanding of what it really is about. Bersin and Associates conducted a 2006 survey on the most challenging areas in training, and 92 percent of the respondents claimed that measurement was at the top of the list.

In recent years those of us responsible for learning have been focused on effective measurement and evaluation solutions. This is a result of the increasing demands from organizational leadership for learning to be accountable for resource investments, specifically monetary resources. We have been overwhelmed with a wealth of philosophies, techniques, and technologies to help the learning community communicate the outcomes of their learning initiatives. From Kirkpatrick to Phillips to Brinkerhoff and many others, we recognize the worth of the work of these experts, but the holy grail of connecting the outcomes of learning still remain elusive for many in the learning profession.

The good news is that the measurement and evaluation of learning is evolving and is being recognized as an integrated component in the design, development, and implementation of our learning solutions. Although the ADDIE model (assessment, design, develop, implement, and evaluation) remains a valid framework, having evaluation, or the "E" at the end of the process is misleading. Evaluation and results are not only becoming more integrated in the learning design and development process, but they are increasingly being correlated to business objectives and strategic outcomes or the organization.

This is why learning professionals are living in very interesting times in our profession. As mentioned in earlier articles in this book, we are currently living in a knowledge-based economy. As such, learning's role is propelled to the forefront of organizational thinking and becoming part of the strategic context of many organizations. We did say this was good news, although you still may not think so if you are newly accountable to senior decision makers of your organization. But this is your opportunity to prove training's worth to those who for many years perceived it as the soft side of the business and a necessary evil to keep employees happy.

This is one of the most exciting sections of the book, and we believe you will also find it quite insightful. We sought out some of the industry's leading experts specializing in measurement and evaluation and asked them to not only write about what is taking place in learning but to "step it up" and help you to see how you should evaluate the outcomes of your learning initiatives.

The passionate articles that you will find in the workplace learning and performance chapter include:

36. Beyond ROI: To Boldly Go Where No Training Evaluation Has Gone Before by Ajay M. Pangarkar and Teresa Kirwood

37. Linking Learning Strategy to the Balanced Scorecard by Ajay M. Pangarkar and Teresa Kirwood

38. Taking a Strategic Approach to Evaluation: Proving and Improving the Value of Training by Timothy P. Mooney and Robert O. Brinkeroff

39. Measure and Optimize Training's Impact by W. Boyce Byerly

40. Formative Evaluation: Getting It Right the First Time by Donald L. Kirkey and Gary A. Depaul

41. Measuring the Impact of Leadership: Fact or Fiction? by Ajay M. Pangarkar and Teresa Kirwood

42. Transition Planning: Steps for Building and Sustaining a Results-Based Learning Focus by Holly Burkett

43. Demonstrating Your Worth to Management with Credible, Business-Focused Results by Harold D. Stolovitch and Paul Flynn

44. We Know We Got There by Toni Hodges De Tuncq

45. A Four-Part Strategy for Communicating Business Value by Theresa L. Seagraves

46. Measuring Time to Proficiency by Steven C. Rosenbaum

47. Making "Cents" from Your Training ROI: How Organizations Can Make Training Accountable by Ajay M. Pangarkar and Teresa Kirwood

Preview of the Articles

In the first article you will read about how Ajay Pangarkar and Teresa Kirkwood challenge the preconception of evaluating training based on monetary figures, specifically return on investment (ROI). They challenge you to move beyond ROI and boldly move toward non-financial performance-based measures. The workplace learning and performance sector is convinced that measuring return on investment of learning initiatives is what will convince organizational decision makers to invest more in training. These authors say it is time for workplace learning and performance to value itself more than simplifying its results down to financial figures such as return on investment. Workplace learning and performance (WLP) professionals need to start thinking "outside of the course" and think in terms that connect with the business concerns and strategy objectives. This will facilitate the process of developing the right performance measures in a way that is inexpensive, relevant, and moves them beyond ROI.

The same authors then challenge you to further move past business impact and ROI once again and connect your learning to organizational strategy. Why? Because organizational leaders want to achieve their objectives, and in a knowledge-base world they view learning as the enabler that will help them do this. This is very apparent in the strategic tool of choice, the "balanced scorecard." More than ever before, this has become one of the most widely accepted strategic and performance management tools. It helps WLP to gain significant credibility, contribute directly to performance, and become a catalyst and enabler of the primary operational concerns of the organization. Learn about what you need to know to link your learning strategies to the balanced scorecard.

In their article, Tim Mooney and Robert Brinkeroff once again take us past the traditional context of measurement and evaluation and continue toward the strategic approach of evaluating learning. The real power of their evaluation strategy is not in proving the value of past training, but in improving the value of future training.

In Boyce Byerly's contribution, "Measure and Optimize Training's Impact," he asks the simple question, "Why does your organization train?" to begin your evaluation process. Most training relates to the bottom line, helping employees to gain the skills and motivation to improve performance on some business process. If business processes are improving, data should reflect it. So why are we tallying questionnaires to find out whether trainees liked their lunches? Most measurement techniques were developed in the Sixties and Seventies. Using corporate data is the most accurate and powerful way to measure training. Doing an ROI study that measures *and* optimizes your training is in your grasp. The steps involved include: picking quantitative metrics and collecting the data; ensuring your metrics have business importance and have a plausible connection with training; representing your results clearly, and over time; breaking down the information by demographics—and always considering your audience.

Donald L. Kirkey and Gary A. DePaul take us back to the roots of evaluation, emphasizing the importance of conducting formative evaluations and not stressing on the final, or summative, evaluations. Most of what you read and hear focuses on checking "after the fact," that is, verifying that the training had the desired personal and business impact. This is known as summative evaluation. While summative evaluation is critical, their passion is building training right the first time and implementing without major problems. One method to ensure flawless training execution is to subject it to formative evaluation.

Workplace learning and performance professionals have been taught to speak the language of performance. After all, helping others improve their performance is what WLP professionals do best, according to Theresa Seagraves in her very passionate contribution. She asks the critical question, "How can WLP professionals maximize their communication about their value in a way that catches their executives' attention and consistently builds the perception of their value?" Read this article to find out how.

Holly Burkett once again brings to mind the heightened accountability workplace learning professionals must demonstrate to the bottom line and the struggles many practitioners have linking learning to tangible business outcomes. The change aspect of implementing a results-based learning focus is often overlooked and under-estimated. Given that context then, moving from an old to a new state is more successful when the fundamental shift from the "old" (activity-based measurement and evaluation) to the "new" state (results-based measurement and evaluation) is implemented with an integrated, systemic change management approach. Her transition planning process allows for the assumption that linking training to business results is still generally a new process for most managers and workplace learning staff and that the implementation of a results-based culture tends to evolve slowly. While implementing transition planning steps can be time-consuming, labor intensive, and sometimes perceived as daunting, taking the time to build organizational capacity and support for a results-based measurement culture will demonstrate many benefits.

Harold Stolovitch and Paul Flynn remind us that, if learning and performance is to be a real player and have impact on an organization, we have to show decision makers the money. Training professionals, for the most part, tend to focus on what they know best . . . training. Their emphasis is on developing and delivering appreciated and impactful courses and curricula. Their reports to management with data on dollars spent, hours of training delivered, numbers trained, and courses produced mirror this focus. All of these items represent expenditures . . . costs. They justify these with trainee satisfaction and, less frequently, knowledge test scores. When times turn tough, costs are cut, especially if there is no clear evidence of business contribution. Only the demonstrated business results derived from prudent investment count. That is where you want to be.

In the contribution titled, "We Know We Got There" by Toni Hodges DeTuncq, we are reminded that it is essential that programs be measured against the objectives for the program and that program objectives should be described in three distinct yet linked set of objectives: business objectives state those organizational problems or goals that the program must address; performance objectives that describe the intended job behaviors required to meet the business objectives; learning objectives that are the specific skills or knowledge the participants must gain in order that they perform the behaviors specified by the performance objectives. These objectives must be aligned to one another closely so that after the program is complete and the participants have had the opportunity to apply their new skills and knowledge, those business or organizational goals will be met and the program will be declared a success.

Theresa Seagraves asks, "How can WLP professionals maximize their communication about their value in a way that catches their executive's attention and consistently builds the perception of their value?" The response she prescribes is that, when communicating value, successful WLP professionals should use a four-part strategy to translate the value they bring to the table into terms that others understand and want to act on. The four segments in high-value communications are through: performance value; financial value; relevant context; and your goal for the learning. Remember: it's not only which WLP metrics are gathered or even how big they are. It's also how well the metrics are translate into incremental value, in what timeframe and how regularly and often they are communicated that matters.

Steven Rosenbaum reminds us that one of the more effective methods of evaluation is the time to proficiency. Proficiency is a measure of being able to demonstrate results at a desired level. Using proficiency as a training measure dramatically changes the way an organization approaches learning. It requires that an organization structure the entire time line from day one to proficiency, rather than just setting up a series of classes.

While measurement and evaluation is a challenge for some and intimidating for others, it is something that all learning professionals should embrace. The common theme from our leading industry experts is that you discover what is best for your learning initiatives within you organization. The goal is to demonstrate the true value and worth learning brings to achieving objectives and goals.

Beyond ROI

To Boldly Go Where No Training Evaluation Has Gone Before

Ajay M. Pangarkar, CTDP, and

Teresa Kirkwood, CTDP

Passion

What do business leaders really want?

Leaders want assurance that training produces results and is worth their investment of time and money. How do we give this to them? As we discussed in the previous article, by implementing a "balanced scorecard," and as we will discuss in this article, by developing the right performance measures in a way that is inexpensive, relevant, and moves you beyond ROI.

Recently, we had the pleasure of speaking with a senior director at a large Fortune 500 company. After an interesting conversation about evaluating training and demonstrating the possibility of measuring some form of payback, such as tangible financial results like return on investment, his response was casual but candid. He asked, "Why are you (workplace learning and performance professionals) trying to be something you are not?" and continued, "Why don't you continue to do what you do best, providing us with non-financial measures of performance? These measures help us (C-level managers) to make decisions based on leading indicators rather than on past performance (financial results) and allow us to connect our objectives with the skills and capabilities our employees need."

At first, this comment went against what the WLP community believes, namely that industry leaders want financial results, such as measuring the return on their training investment and making training and employee development initiatives accountable for their results. Our anecdotal investigation among senior managers in various organizations reveals an interesting perspective. C-level decision makers are less concerned about a hard return on investment for training, or any other intangible investment, for a few key reasons. In the context of workplace learning, the sampled managers stated that:

- Conducting a return on investment evaluation on training, even those initiatives with significant amounts vested, is expensive, demanding on organizational resources, and time-consuming;
- As objective as training and development (T&D) tries to make ROI evaluations, there is still a degree of subjectivity and bias, reducing the credibility and impact of the training initiative;
- There is too much focus on "accomplishing" training initiatives successfully, rather than on aligning expected results with organizational needs;

- Return on investment is a financial measure, a lagging indicator demonstrating past performance. What is required are leading indicative performance measures.

Many senior directors and managers are finding workplace learning professionals overly concerned and preoccupied with evaluating training delivery outcomes rather, than measuring the effectiveness or impact it has on the organization. This is not to say that return on investment is not a relevant factor in measuring significant training investments, but financial payback alone, specifically ROI, is not a convincing argument to gain management support.

Learning professionals learn early that for any type of training to be successful it must have some type of impact on the business (Kirkpatrick's Level 4). What is not evident is how too effectively measure up to Level 4 to demonstrate a learning solution delivered on the promised results. In recent years, the answer to the Level 4 evaluation question has been in financial terms (Phillips' Level 5) believing that this will instill rapid credibility, proof, and most importantly, support for workplace learning. As mentioned earlier, it appears that these criteria have not helped to build a case for workplace learning but delivered on increasing skepticism.

Moving Stakeholders Beyond ROI
Building the Business Case

In the current business reality, pleasing the financial types of the organization is not as important as developing a strong business case. Financial results are becoming irrelevant in areas defining intangible, human issues, as well as for longer-term strategic outlooks. C-level managers require performance indicators that look toward the future (strategic) and not the past (reactive). Moving beyond simply delivering an ROI figure and connecting to qualitative business indicators relevant to decision makers should be your ultimate objective. These types of indicators and metrics are useful and accurate; however, they are often difficult to define within, or convert to, a financial context. This is the dilemma for training managers and management in general.

Managers, and other stakeholders, recognize that not everything can or should be measured down to some type of financial measure; however, this still remains the primary measure of accountability. Workplace learning and performance professionals must balance this need with qualitative business-related performance measures and not focus on indicators captured solely at the course level. Kirkpatrick Level 1, participant reaction, and Level 2, participant learning, as well as other metrics such as average participant cost are relevant measures; however, training success begins when the individual returns to the job and actually applies what he or she learned (Level 3, behavior). Once we identify how the participant is applying the new knowledge we can ascertain the impact it has on the business. But how do you define and track the indicators to do this? This is quite simple as many of the indicators already exist. Tracking them over a period of time will help you to determine what areas are being applied and where improvement is required.

Metrics That Matter

Examples of metrics that help you to move beyond ROI include:

- Job productivity (items in the job that were meant to improve after training)
- Skill requirements measured against initial skills possessed
- Efficiency rates (time or methods of completing a task)
- Compliancy levels
- Proficiency standards measured against eligibility and initial base knowledge
- Learning to skills application measures

- Demand on support needs such as a reduction on calls to the help desk
- Number of employees trained in a specific skill set over time or need
- Training costs per employee
- Enrolment rates and attendance rates
- Employee retention rates
- Employee motivation and team cohesion

This is far from an exhaustive list of metrics. These types of indicators allow managers at all levels to immediately measure training results and witness behavioral change in their environments, further supporting the need for continuous learning. Many of the metrics listed above certainly exist in your organization and some, such as operational productivity, may already be used by managers to measure performance. Individually, these organizational metrics are meaningless, but combined with existing reporting and evaluation practices training effectiveness and learning acceptance will increase.

Fostering a Learning Culture to Move Beyond ROI

Organizational culture is the foundation of building a successful and strategically aligned learning environment. A supportive culture facilitates and supports the impact of learning on the business, including measuring ROI. Culture, however, is not something that is in the control of WLP professionals. Simply, organizational culture is comprised of the behaviors, attitudes, and process of the organization. Behavior and attitudes are people-related issues, and organizational process is how things are conducted. To build a learning-centered culture and foster positive behaviors and attitudes C-level managers must set an example demonstrating their involvement and commitment to learning initiatives. This is considered to be the most important point to ensuring successful adoption of any initiative. Senior management support will facilitate employee buy-in. Employees will benefit by acquiring, applying, and sharing new skills and knowledge gained from the learning culture.

The challenge for WLP professionals is to foster the behaviors and attitudes of management, ensure employee buy-in, and develop or modify internal processes to support the integration of learning as a business process.

Another way to move easily beyond measuring training ROI is to integrate a continuous monitoring process post-training to collect organizational results. Through sampling smaller groups over time, training departments can quickly gain valuable insights on the effects their learning initiative delivers. This may sound time-consuming and involved, but it is quite simple and quick. Investigation methods such as conducting surveys and forming focus groups can be used to measure specific business impacts as related to the objectives of the learning solution. So Level 3 issues (application) can be measured through productivity and efficiency metrics and Level 4 issues (business results) are witnessed through business-related metrics (e.g., customer satisfaction, goal attainment, etc.). Success with this approach is found only if you build this capacity into your training organization, reducing your dependence on ROI and allowing you to make Levels 3 and 4 as natural a part of your evaluation regimen as gathering smile sheets.

Moving Beyond ROI and Toward Strategy

With a globalizing economy, hyper-competitive markets, strong entrepreneurial initiatives, access to technological advances and continuous technological changes, and the pursuit of scarce human talent, organizations of all sizes have quickly recognized the value of their employees and how they are the drivers for innovation, growth, and achieving strategy objectives. Management is now focused on clearly communicating and connecting, in tangible and realistic terms, strategic objectives to all levels within the organization, demonstrating to employees how their roles contribute to attaining these critical success factors. This is management's challenge. On the other hand, WLP professionals know they have a critical role in helping stakeholders attain strategic expectations by linking learning solutions to organizational strategy. Their challenge is not only to provide an ROI for training, but more importantly, to show management how to leverage a learning strategy for the benefit of the organization.

For every organization, an effective and clear business strategy is essential for long-term growth and success and at the top of senior management's priority list. Management's one weakness is to tangibly communicate and connect the strategic plan to all levels within the organization and demonstrate to employees how their roles contribute to attaining critical success factors. The weakness for WLP professionals is understanding how to connect to the organizational strategy in an effective manner. Again, their first instinct is to deliver results in financial terms, specifically, delivering a return on investment value. As mentioned earlier, C-level decision makers are less concerned about hard financial returns for training and more concerned about being able to leverage learning strategy to the benefit of the organization.

The one strategic performance tool resolving this dilemma is the development of the "balanced scorecard" (BSC) that we discussed in the previous article. Also referred to as the "strategy dashboard" the BSC effectively translates the strategic plan and mission of an organization into tangible non-financial and financial performance measures within four distinct business focus categories one of which is called "learning and growth."

Like a well-oiled machine, an organization functions best when the sum of its parts (departments and divisions) works toward a common goal. Within the BSC, many of these parts (financial, internal processes, and customer) now work effectively together through very tangible objectives, measure, and initiatives.

The one component of the BSC often left unto itself is "learning and growth." There is a lack of understanding and common language between management and the traditionally functional areas of employee development (training and HR) to clearly communicate with each other. See Figure 36.1 for an illustration.

In the past, the functional areas such as training and HR were excluded, since they were perceived as not contributing directly to the overall strategic objectives. In the current business context learning is perceived as an integral part of achieving the organizational strategy in the long term.

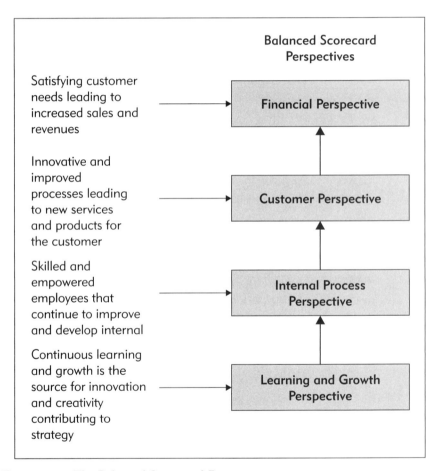

Figure 36.1. The Balanced Scorecard Perspective

Early in his study of business and strategy, Peter Drucker recognized that innovation from creative people provides the only assured source of long-term success and competitiveness, because every other activity of an organization can be duplicated by others. Having the right people with a continuous learning process should be standard, according to Drucker. It is easy to see from Figure 36.1 how learning initiates and links to the organization's other strategic focus area. This approach is strategic in nature, providing for framework allowing for proactive non-financial based leading performance measures moving away from traditional return on investment.

Conclusion

It is time to value workplace learning and performance more than simplifying it down to financial figures such as return on investment. There are many ways to measure the impact any learning initiative can have on the organization. What it comes down to is beginning with the strategic objectives of the organization and working back, linking learning objectives with immediate business concerns. By doing this you will easily determine the performance measures and metrics relevant to the need and satisfy senior management's preoccupations, such as operational performance and efficiency, compliance issues, organizational effectiveness, and workforce capacity and proficiency, as well as more intangible dimensions such as motivation, innovation, and adaptability. WLP professionals have to start thinking "outside of the course" and think in terms that connect with the business concerns and strategy objectives. This will facilitate the process of developing the right performance measures in a way that is inexpensive, relevant, and moves them beyond ROI.

Article 37

Linking Learning Strategy to the Balanced Scorecard

Ajay M. Pangarkar, CTDP, and

Teresa Kirkwood, CTDP

Passion

Can you start thinking outside the course?

How does workplace learning performance (WLP) actually gain credibility and become an integral component to business? By linking learning initiatives to organizational strategy. The opportunity for WLP has come through the "balanced scorecard." More than ever before, the most widely accepted strategic and performance management tool includes learning and performance as an integral part of achieving strategic objectives. They help WLP to gain significant credibility, contribute directly to performance, and become a catalyst and enabler of the primary operational concerns of the organization. Learn about what you need to know to link your learning strategies to the balanced scorecard.

Well it appears that implementing the balanced scorecard (BSC) as the strategic management tool of choice is a trend that is well on its way in many organizations worldwide. Initially introduced in the early 1990s as a tool to help companies translate their corporate missions to all levels of the organization, the BSC is widely acknowledged to have moved beyond this ideology. It has now become a strategic change management and performance measurement process.

According to surveys by the Institute of Management Accountants (IMA), more than 50 percent of the large companies in the United States are using some form of balanced scorecard. This is reflective of the power and simplicity of the BSC to provide direction for all levels and areas of the organization. The Balanced Scorecard, developed by Robert Kaplan and David Norton, is a management system that gives business people a comprehensive understanding of business operations. But after more than fifteen years, it is surprising that there are still many business people unconvinced about the utility and effectiveness of the balanced scorecard. And even more surprising is the number of organizations giving up on it through their own misapplication or misuse of the tool.

At its roots, the BSC is designed to give companies the information they need to effectively manage their business strategy tactically. The scorecard is similar to a dashboard in a car. As you drive you can glance at the dashboard to obtain real-time information, such as how much fuel remains, the speed you are traveling, the distance you've traveled, etc. The BSC provides similar information to all levels of the organization through performance measures connected to specific business areas. The scorecard communicates to managers in clearly defined terms how well the business is meeting its strategies and goals.

Fundamentally, the BSC is about performance measures. Coincidentally, this is also what our role as learning professionals has become as well (hence, workplace learning and performance). The BSC incorporates traditional financial performance metrics, familiar to financially oriented stakeholders and management of the organization, as they are connected to performance indicators within a financial reporting system. In the past this information would have been sufficient; however, the current reality dictates something more comprehensive.

The appeal of the BSC is its ability to include both traditional financial metrics and non-financial performance measures in its reporting capacity, thus the term "balanced." Managers can obtain information on a variety of intangible and non-financial metrics, such as customer satisfaction, cost per new hire, percent of jobs that meet schedule, percent of errors in budget predictions, etc.

The attraction of the BSC is its simplicity in its structure and function and its ability to bring together leading and lagging performance indicators. The BSC is divided into four primary business and strategic areas upon which an organization must focus in order to see a complete picture of how the enterprise is performing. As shown in Figure 37.1, they are:

- *Financial perspective:* The question here is: "How do we look to our stakeholders?" The objective of every organization is to deliver maximum value to stakeholders. For profit-oriented companies these are the shareholders and customers; for non-profit it many be government, taxpayers, or the community.
- *Customer perspective:* The question is: "How do we look to our customers?" All organizations, profit and non-profit, have customers. To survive and grow, an organization must be able to deliver quality goods and/or services providing for overall customer satisfaction.

- *Internal business processes:* The question is: "What must we excel at?" The reason for an organization's existence is what it produces or delivers. Identifying the key business processes an organization must excel at is essential if it is to meet strategic goals and customer expectations.
- *Learning and growth perspective:* The question is: "How can we continue to improve and create value?" This is the perspective management recognizes as at the root of competitive sustainability. This is also where WLP can deliver significant results, connect with strategy, and move past Kirkpatrick Level 4, business impact, and Phillips' Level 5, return on investment of training.

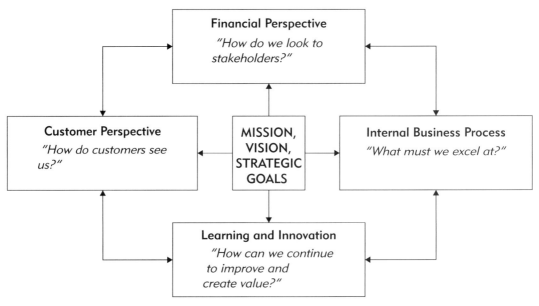

Figure 37.1. BSC Interdependency Diagram

The current business climate requires managers to have a balance between financial and non-financial measures in order to arrive at proper decisions. Financial measures provide historical results, whereas non-financial measures usually indicate the

The Trainer's Portable Mentor

positive outcomes of a particular decision. This is where our role as learning professionals comes into play. Our efforts are directly correlated to non-financial performance metrics. These metrics support, for example, why developing a specific skill set for a group of employees increases productivity, leading to strong growth, helping to build credibility for WLP and our role within the organization. Non-financial measures are essential to helping companies succeed. If used effectively, they can drive an organization—using its performance measurement system—to higher and higher levels of achievement.

The Need for the BSC and Its Connection to WLP

To truly understand the reason for the growing need for the BSC, one must understand the significance of organizational strategy. Most business professionals recognize that strategy is at the center of every business process. Successful business managers have a laser-like focus on it. Although this may be common sense for business-people, many are unable to connect their business objectives and the organization's mission, resulting in many companies not meeting their strategic goals. This is not necessarily a result of managerial incompetence (although this may be the case in some instances), but more from not knowing how to develop or connect short- and mid-term objectives in response to the proposed strategy.

Go and read your organizational mission statement in the lobby of your company and ask yourself, "How does my role or what I do fit into this objective?" In a simple framework, the BSC helps senior managers translate and effectively communicate performance objectives and measure how their roles contribute to the strategic vision of the organization.

For those responsible for talent management and employee development, strategy has never been at the forefront of their mandate or learning plans. Again, the failure may be more with senior management not effectively communicating the importance of strategic alignment with the "softer side" of the business, such as workplace learning and performance. This was the case in less turbulent economic times. As a result of increasing hyper-competitive and global markets, management's performance, specifically the C-level suite (CEO, COO, CFO, etc.), are tied directly to executing successful strategic outcomes for their organizations. Expectations are not just from the traditional "shareholders" anymore—satisfied simply with reporting of financial performance—but now include non-traditional "stakeholders," such as customers, suppliers, and employees, as well as specific business processes and innovative capability.

So why is this relevant for those responsible for employee development and workplace learning? It is relevant for a few reasons:

First, achieving strategic objectives requires organizational decision makers answer the questions "Where do we want to go?" and "What do we want to be?" In both cases this necessitates building existing organizational knowledge (human capital). In simpler terms, "What you know now got you here but will not get you to where you want or need to be." Learning professionals must acquire the strategic skills and understanding to better align employee skills and abilities with strategic objectives.

Second, contrary to what we are told by the "training ROI" movement in recent years, C-level managers are less concerned about financial outcomes of learning investments and more preoccupied with obtaining non-financial performance outcomes. In more direct terms, they want to see how T&D delivers results in relation to organizational objectives over answering the question: "Did the training solution make money over what it costs?" Again, this is because financial measures are lagging indicators of performance and, in the end, if training costs exceeded its benefits then it is too late to do anything about it. The results have already happened, and when you are concerned about what is going to happen tomorrow, you don't really want to know what occurred yesterday. Also, T&D is not perceived as a critical investment over other operational issues. Time and again many C-level directors have indicated to us the importance of having some type of forward-looking indicators.

Although anecdotal, the same decision makers also indicated that "T&D is not good at applying financial measures." They are unconvinced about the objectivity of training ROI measurement results. As learning consultants, we were told to do what we are good at; helping them obtain and connect to leading, non-financial performance indicators, something they desperately require. This may sound repetitive, but corporate leaders are concerned about strategic outcomes, and the BSC effectively facilitates this process.

Third, for many years companies preached that their employees are their greatest asset, but only in recent times have senior managers truly recognized this truth. Not to slight business leaders of the past, but it is evident that the marketplace leaders are the same ones who invest a significant percentage of their payroll in learning solutions, are able to connect employee development to strategic objectives, and effectively leverage employee knowledge to innovate in a variety of ways. C-level managers realize true competitive advantage is not through physical assets or products but through their people. Everything else is simply the result or benefit of employee skill development and creativity. One concern some clients voice is that employees leave after the company has invested in their training. We respond by saying, "What if you don't train them and they stay?"

An Opportunity to Sit at the Table: Connecting Learning to Strategy

Astrologers would say the planets are lined up for the professional learning sector. Externally, economic and market factors call for organizations to adapt instantaneously, and technological evolution is accepted now as a constant. Internally, organizations need to change and evolve quickly, resulting in the need to build employee knowledge, competencies, and skills for the future. The common thread in all of these factors is the need for continuous learning leading to improved performance. Add to the mix management's need to reconcile and integrate all these issues to achieve their strategy (the balanced scorecard) places workplace learning performance at the top of many CEOs' priority lists.

Accountability does not solely rest with senior management when it comes to incorporating workplace learning in organizational strategy. Senior managers may shoulder the responsibility for including it in their strategy development discussions (the coveted seat at the table), but learning professionals must also be held accountable as well. Until recently, those responsible for employee development did not see the relevance of connecting to organizational objectives. This is highly evident when one considers the types of performance measures used in the past, such as number of employees trained or testing scores. Add the learning profession's disdain for business, and you quickly have a learning environment very much disconnected from corporate and market reality.

Take a look at the BSC Interdependency Diagram (Figure 37.1) as developed by Kaplan and Norton. You will notice two important items. The first is that the BSC accounts for "learning and growth." Not impressed? You should be. Never before has any business trend elevated the importance of "learning" in the discussion about, let alone the development of, strategy. The second noticeable item is that it sits at the bottom of the diagram. Many business people state that the positioning clearly minimizes the importance of this perspective. Kaplan and Norton rebut this notion, stating that "It's at the bottom because it acts as the foundation for everything else above it." Dr. Kaplan once

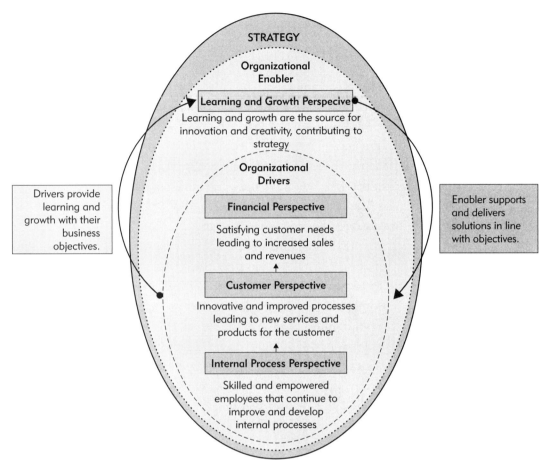

Figure 37.2. Learning and Growth Enabling Strategic Drivers

described the employee learning and growth perspective "as the roots of a powerful tree, which are the sources of support and nourishment leading to the blossoms of financial returns." Figure 37.2 above illustrates more literally the relevance and importance or learning as described by the creators of the BSC.

Making the Connections: Linking Learning to the BSC

Like a well-oiled machine, every organization functions best when the sum of its parts (departments and divisions) work toward a common goal. The driving perspectives of the BSC (financial, internal processes, and customer) work interdependently through very tangible objectives, targets, measure, and initiatives. But how does learning tangibly connect with the other business areas through the BSC? A simple example demonstrates the process more clearly.

Let's say company ABC's primary strategic objective is to increase revenue in the next three years (refer to Figure 37.3). To increase revenue, the company will have to increase production and sales by introducing and producing new products and repositioning current products. In this case, the financial perspective is the primary driver for the other three perspectives. We can derive the customer perspective by increasing customer loyalty and develop customer relationships to entice repeat purchases. This in turn requires internal processes to support new product development through R&D, ramp up production for the increasing sales, ensure adequate inventory, and ensure that purchasing processes are functioning properly. These three perspectives are the drivers for the strategy. The role for learning and growth is to enable and support the needs of the first three perspectives—similar to how internal processes support sales. By partnering with the other business areas, workplace learning is better positioned to understand their needs. For company ABC, workplace learning would collaborate with the sales and marketing department to train and coach the sales staff, work closely with customer relations through a customer service and new product training program, and even look at developing production efficiency and new equipment training courses for manufacturing. Wrapped around all of the perspectives would be specific objectives (the expected results), targets (tangible metrics), and measures (the reports to obtain the metrics), and initiatives (what you will actually do). WLP solutions are the vehicle to help other business units achieve these critical metrics.

So how do you begin? The following steps will help you to contribute to these critical business areas, become more strategic in your learning solutions, and be more tactical in your approach with your customers in the organization.

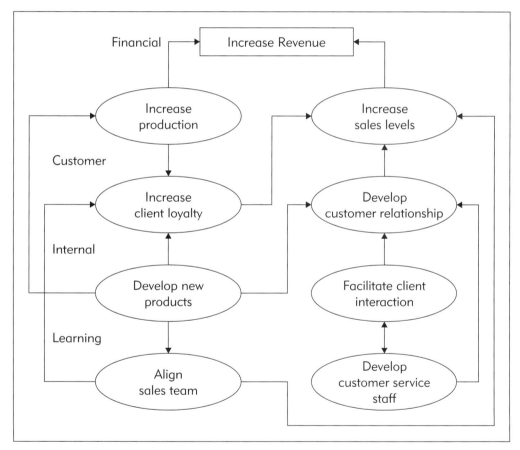

Figure 37.3. Company ABC: Example of Mapping Learning to Strategy

The first step is to clearly understand your organization's corporate strategy. Analyze the mission and vision statement, as they provide succinct insight into senior managements objectives. When done well, these statements outline the critical areas requiring support. If you are a public company, review the annual reports to gain further insight of management's message and gain an appreciation of stakeholder expectations.

Next, find the corporate balanced scorecard. If one is being developed, get involved. The BSC will provide you with the "tactical" information of what is expected from each of the business units. Review the BSC and learn about the relationships among the driving perspectives. If you are fortunate, your organization will have cascaded the scorecard through each business unit. This will allow you to work closely with every level of the organization to develop more targeted learning solutions.

Now conduct interviews with management and stakeholders. Meet with the C-level decision makers in your organization Determine their expectations from workplace learning and performance. They will provide significant amounts of information, a clear direction for the organization as a whole, and a cascading the strategy through the BSC to each business unit. Meet with business unit stakeholders and process-critical staff. Building partnerships with these groups helps to create synergy between them and your learning expertise.

Determine the measures and metrics for the objectives set forth by the BSC. When working with other business units within the BSC, be aware of their objectives and the metrics they're expected to meet.

Develop a BSC for learning and performance. Traditionally, training and development is viewed as a functional, supportive unit. In the evolved strategic context, learning and performance must interact with the other units. As a strategic business unit, WLP should develop its own scorecard. This is not solely about "training ROI." When you develop a WLP scorecard, your performance measures should be forward-looking and make a strategic contribution.

Conclusion

The role of learning in the workplace is increasingly critical and demanding. It is more than measuring business impact, more than simply measuring return on investment of training. It is about connecting to strategy. More than ever before, the most critical competitive advantage for every organization is ensuring employees not only understand strategic objectives but are able to attain them. This is where WLP must take on a strategic capacity. Your role is to value workplace learning and performance in this context, rather than simply the traditional functional role. Begin with the strategic objectives of the organization and work back, linking learning objectives with immediate business objectives. By doing this, you will easily determine the relevant performance measures and metrics and satisfy senior management.

It's time to start thinking "outside of the course" and inside the BSC to develop learning solutions that directly connect with the business concerns and strategic objectives of the organization.

Reference

Niven, P.R. (2003). *Balanced scorecard step-by-step.* San Francisco, CA: Jossey-Bass.

Taking a Strategic Approach to Evaluation

Proving and Improving the Value of Training

Timothy P. Mooney and

Robert O. Brinkerhoff, Ed.D.

Passion

We share a passion for helping organizations avoid costly short-sighted decisions. Asking the right evaluation questions will help the organization begin not just to determine what happened in the past, but learn how it can increase the results in the future.

A few years ago I witnessed a situation that many training professionals probably have experienced. A company was trying to improve sales results. They put the entire sales force from five different U.S. regions through the same training. One region used the skills, tools, and process from the training to help make several large sales (one of which was landing a new multi-million-dollar account). The sales reps and sales managers from this region stated emphatically without qualifiers that they would not have made those significant sales without the new training.

The sales reps from the other regions never really capitalized on the training. They used a few concepts and tools from the process, but never saw any significant sales come from the training and eventually stopped using the tools and concepts altogether.

It is interesting to note that the training provided to all these sales regions was identical; delivered by the same facilitator, using the same design and materials. The sales reps from the various regions were equally as experienced and successful—and were literally sitting side-by-side in the same classes. Yet, the sales reps from one region were able to turn the training into concrete business results, while for most of the participants the training never led to any worthwhile outcomes.

After the initial workshops with this training, the organization made the decision to stop providing the training, because it wasn't seeing enough tangible evidence across all the regions that the investment was paying off or that the training was being used.

This company made two fatal errors—errors we see repeated frequently by many other organizations. This situation brings out the limitations and problems that face most training evaluation and ROI methods used today by L&D departments. Most popular evaluation methods are focused on trying to prove the value of the training by:

- Trying to compute the average (arithmetic mean) results of training across all participants, and failing to dig out the truly great results the training was resulting in for some of the people.

- Assuming that the training itself delivers the results, and not measuring the other factors in the equation—factors that often have more to do with training impact than the training itself.

Looking at specific results and usage of training by individuals is valuable. Focusing on the average (i.e., in statistical terms, the central tendency) can lead to misguided conclusions and decisions. Consider this example. If we had Bill Gates (founder of Microsoft) and one thousand homeless people together in a room, the average net worth of each individual would be more than $40 million dollars. That average is an interesting statistic, but it doesn't begin to tell the real story or help us determine how to improve the financial results of the vast majority of the people in the room. By focusing on the average without digging into the specific cases, it would be easy to reach some erroneous conclusions.

In addition to the inherent limitations of relying on averages to evaluate the results of training, we also said that another mistake often made by L&D professionals is focusing almost exclusively on the training itself as the "cause" of the results.

The best result that training alone can ever accomplish is an increase in capability—the ability to perform. A good managerial skills course, for example, can increase the managers' skills and knowledge related to key supervisory tasks, such as coaching or resolving conflict. The value from this training comes when capability is transformed into improved job performance, when the newly trained supervisor effectively uses the new skills in important situations. Training that is well learned, but never used, or poorly used, produces no value for the business that invested in the training.

Getting *performance* improvements from the *capability* improvements of employees is a performance management challenge. Factors such as direction, feedback, accountability, incentives, rewards, job aids, and tools all work together to shape and drive performance. When these factors are effective, complete, and aligned, employee capability will be leveraged into superior performance. When they are not, performance will consistently remain at levels far below employee capability. Research on training impact convincingly documents the potency of these factors. Best estimates are that 80 percent or more of the eventual impact of training is determined by performance system factors, while the remaining 20 percent or so is driven by variations in the quality of the training intervention itself and the characteristics of the learner, such as inherent ability and motivational values.

It is easy to imagine what would happen to a supervisor who returns from the management skills training and encounters performance system factors that are not aligned with the training. If, for instance, the supervisor's boss doesn't put much faith in the concepts, then the boss might influence the person not to use the new approach (or simply not encourage or coach the person to use the new skills effectively). Or, for another example, it might be that using the new skills initially takes longer, and because of other work pressures on the job, this newly trained person, out of frustration, reverts to the old way of managing. In sum, any number of these and other factors, alone or in combination, are likely to impede the impact of this training despite how well the training worked to produce the desired new skills and knowledge in the trainee.

Given this reality of performance system and training interdependency, learning professionals don't need an evaluation method that keeps rediscovering this painful truth. Instead, they need a strategy and method for changing these predictable results. The overarching purpose of any training measurement strategy should be twofold:

1. To dig out and understand the many factors that keep training from being more successful

2. To use the evaluation findings to teach the key stakeholders in the organization what needs to be done to turn the training success rates from their current and miserably low rates of impact into consistently better outcomes for increasingly larger numbers of trainees

This more than anything else will continuously improve the rates of return on training investments. Training today yields about an ounce of value for every pound of resources invested. The goal is to reverse this recipe—to get a pound of value for an ounce of investment.

Returning to my opening story about the sales organization, here is how they could have avoided making their costly short-sighted decision. Instead of asking the question "On average how well is the training working?" the sales organization should have been asking a different set of questions.

- "What are the best business results the training can produce when it is used?"
- "When the training did work, why was it working?"
- "When the training didn't work, why wasn't it working?"
- "What can we as an organization do so that more people can leverage the training as well as the most successful sales reps are using it?"

The answers so these questions will help the organization begin to determine not just what happened in the past, but how it can increase the results in the future that this program—and others—can help produce.

By contrast, another organization used this strategic evaluation approach to help them get maximum return from their sales training efforts. They were investing heavily in launching new systems for the market. In addition to the substantial product development investment, they invested heavily in training to teach their sales force how to sell this new capability. By conducting an impact evaluation early in the roll-out cycle for this training and focusing their efforts on the questions above, they were able to identify numerous examples of where sales reps used the training in ways that led to improved sales results with specific accounts. They also discovered that the sales reps who achieved the greatest sales for these new systems were the same ones who worked closely with their sales managers both before and immediately after the training to focus their learning efforts and to plan sales efforts.

For HRD professionals this finding probably doesn't come as a shock. We all know that management support and coaching lead to greater use of new skills learned in training. However, armed with this information the sales training manager was able to have a different type of discussion with the sales VP, pointing to specific sales that were made because sales reps used the training AND making the link between a manager's direct support of the training and these sales increases. Based on this vital information, the sales VP mandated that, before any more reps were allowed to participate in the training, they must meet with their managers before (and after) the training to plan where they were going to apply their new skills. In short the rule became: "Don't bother getting on the plane to come to training without meeting with your manager first."

Conclusion

This approach to evaluation fundamentally changes the nature of the discussion that training leaders have with senior stakeholders. The dynamics shift from defending the results and justifying budgets to discussing examples of specific business outcomes (quantitative and qualitative) and the specific performance system factors that need to be addressed to make sure those types of results happen more often.

The real power of this evaluation strategy is not in *proving* the value of past training, but in *improving* the value of future training.

Measure and Optimize Training's Impact

W. Boyce Byerly, Ph.D.

Passion

Go after the metrics that can show training's impact! A clear analysis shows impact and lets you optimize your company by pinpointing who benefits the most.

Why does your organization train? Sometimes, training's about corporate culture: companies promote cross-cultural awareness or encourage wellness in employees. Most training, however, relates to the bottom line—you want employees to have the skills and motivation to improve performance on some business process. If business processes are improving, data should reflect it: higher sales revenue, fewer trouble tickets, and faster resolution of customer support issues. So why are you tallying questionnaires to find out whether trainees liked their lunches?

Most measurement techniques were developed in the 1960s and 1970s, when corporate data resided in file cabinets and when the computational power needed to retrieve it, visualize it, and make sense of it just didn't exist. In those days, surveys made sense. The field is well overdue for something different. Using corporate data is the most accurate and powerful way to measure training. We can show you powerful ways of visualizing data that only requires spreadsheet-level expertise.

Choosing the Right Metrics

Metrics are the cornerstone of your analysis. What metrics do you look for?

Search first for metrics that are "actual": sales revenue, number of trouble tickets solved per month, absences, product returns. Metrics can be measured in dollars, units, time, or anything else. "Indicator" metrics, like customer satisfaction ratings, can be useful, but aren't the place to start.

An ideal metric should be regularly recorded in your organization on a weekly or monthly basis. Graphing the changes in the trained and untrained groups over time makes it much easier for your audience to grasp what's happening as a result by training, and presenting it over time often provides insights into business processes. The more finely grained the data, the better: data on individuals provides a richer picture than data on a business unit.

Don't pick a metric just because it's important! In one project, the study focused on training that built better customer-relationship skills. The biggest goal of this company was to reduce expensive on-site service calls. The ROI study on the training program assumed, based entirely on wishful thinking, that customer-relationship training would reduce service calls.

No relationship was found, to the embarrassment of those who commissioned the study.

Examining multiple metrics is good. Sometimes, results show up in unexpected ways. We did one study in which the company believed training would decrease resolution time on trouble tickets. That did not happen—but more trouble tickets were solved concurrently, improving throughput and providing a handsome ROI.

Setting Values for Metrics

Studies based on financial terms have a wider audience appeal and clearer value proposition than those that merely show the impact unit-by-unit. Some values, such as sales revenue, map straightforwardly to a dollar value because they're already in dollars. In other cases, we think you need to be both *persistent* and *conservative* in your approach to finding values.

Being persistent means doing that extra step to translate to dollars. Consider a 5-point customer satisfaction rating. How much does a customer who gave you a "5" spend in a year? The "4" customers? Compute averages for each rating category, then look at the changes you get between them: you can now talk about the value of a program to increase customer satisfaction.

Sometimes the translation into dollar terms requires some creative assumptions, rather than number crunching. A mentoring program ran across an entire organization, including people in completely different jobs. We chose merit-based performance bonuses for a metric: our argument was that if someone had received an extra dollar in pay, he or she must have created at least a dollar's worth of value for the company.

Being conservative is imperative in an ROI study. The first aspect of conservatism: be financially pessimistic. If you have a range of values, take the lowest one. (For something that *costs* the company money, being conservative means taking the high estimate.) The second point of conservatism: obtain input from stakeholders early. We have seen completed studies in which an executive was surprised by overly generous assumptions, and the presenters found themselves in a defensive position with a suspicious audience. Always footnote assumptions: show your work on math, document data sources, explain reasons if you discarded data. If questions arise later, you will be very glad you did.

Finding Training Costs

Computing training costs has been covered in numerous different sources. We'll just repeat our advice to be conservative, and remain focused on *returns*, not just savings from a cheaper program.

Presenting the Results

Presenting ROI results, like any presentation, requires understanding your audience. Prepare at least two versions: one short presentation for the busy executive that details your main findings and how it should affect future investment and training operations, and a longer report for those who need details.

Focus your presentation on simple, but rich graphics. Pie charts and bar charts give a quicker visual feel for the data than a table, although they don't really provide as much data as showing performance over time. The eye is a good judge of whether a change caused by training is "significant," so use your graphs as the analysis tools.

Figure 39.1 is an example using a company with salespeople reporting their sales monthly. A new training program aimed at increasing sales revenue is given to some employees. Where we show performance over time, we condense the time line to "before" the program and "after" the program to simplify.

The graphic is a good starting point for a presentation. It's simple, but makes a point even the most coffee-deprived

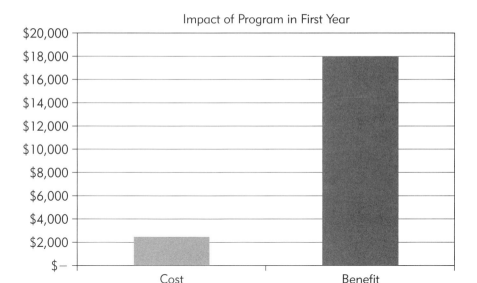

Figure 39.1. An Example of a Simple Graphic Using the Right Time Period, Clearly Labeled, Uncluttered Axes, and Consistent, Intuitive Colors

executive can't miss: benefit clearly exceeds costs in the first year. (Consider orienting graphs around whatever time period your company speaks in: monthly, quarterly, yearly.)

Let's explore a richer graph in Figure 39.2, which is slightly more complex—but answers interesting questions, and increases your credibility.

The graph in Figure 39.2 is rich in information. It shows those who participated in the training program (trained group), and those who did not (untrained group). The trained group increases their baseline performance. What else is this graph telling us?

- Both trained and untrained improve over time, but the trained group improves *more*.
- The group selected for training was *already* outperforming the group that never took training. Why? Perhaps the hardest working, most motivated people volunteered for training.

Figure 39.2. View of the Trained and Untrained Groups Over Time

Be aware how many people are in the groups you're looking at (e.g., the trainee group, after training occurred.) Because of high variability in small groups, you should take their results less seriously than groups with dozens, or hundreds, of people.

Accounting for All the Factors

We now know training produces positive results. That's a good start; but there is more to do from there. Who received the most and least from training? Potential demographics include their seniority level, job title, geographic location, and education. Baseline performance (prior to any training) is one of the best demographics. Try to group employees together into large enough "chunks" that your results are simple enough to understand. For example, seniority could be simplified down to "more than one year" and "one year or less".

In our example, let's graphically separate employees into "senior" and "junior" lines, as shown in Figure 39.3.

Notice that everyone improves over time, even the untrained group. Did anyone improve faster than the untrained people? Yes, the junior trained group shows a sharp upturn in their "before" and "after" numbers. However, the senior people improve only slightly more than the untrained. The training is working best for junior level people!

When you have such specific data, there are two possible courses of action you can offer. For fixed budgets, train the junior people first. If budgets are flexible, develop new training to address needs of senior people.

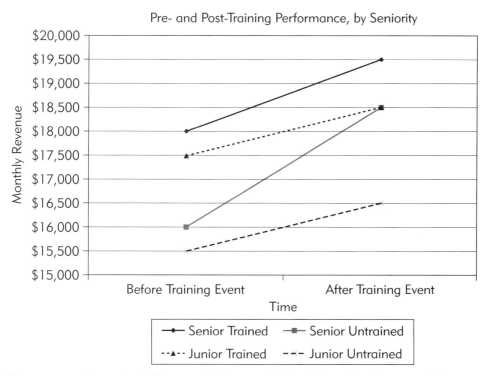

Figure 39.3. Trained and Untrained Groups, Broken Down by Junior and Senior People

Conclusion

Doing an ROI study that measures *and* optimizes your training is in your grasp. Here are a few simple points to remember:

- Pick metrics that are quantitative, collected regularly, have business importance, and have a plausible connection with training.
- Find values for your metrics whenever possible.
- Represent your results clearly; experiment with graphs. Try graphing the information over time. Try comparing trained and untrained groups. Break down the information by demographics, such as seniority, job title, or location.
- Consider your audience: What metrics do they most care about? How much financial info will they demand, and how much math can they handle? Will they agree with your assumptions?

A job aid included on the website (see Exhibit 39.1) provides a short checklist to help you consider these issues. Doing ROI studies is a great way to empower your department and to turn perceptions from "cost center" into "profit center." Your goal should not be to justify what you did *last* year; but to find ways to improve your performance *next* year.

Exhibit 39.1. Checklist for Training Analysis

 Participants

How do you identify them? (SSN, name, etc)? Does this apply to training data and metric data too? How many participants are there? (All the applicable people you have data for, not just the trainees.) Fill in the table below for the descriptors.

Descriptor	Values	Affects Performance?	Affects Training?	Number of Categories	Size of Smallest Category

Training

What is the name of the training? What dates did it occur? How were participants selected? Fill in the costs below.

Cost	Fixed	Variable
Duplication and Printing		
Books		
e-Learning Licenses		
Travel		
Other		
Other		
Other		

Metrics

Is metric data available before, during, and after training?

Metric	Units	Value/Unit	Anticipated Change from Training	Time-Sensitive?

(Continued)

Sample Summary for ROI and Optimization

Analysis/Presentation Method	Pros	Cons
Survey	Simple to do. Good way of getting at semantics, opinions, reactions.	Not good at getting at ROI. May produce errors, depending on questions, return rate. Does not scale well.
Trend Line	Does not require participant level drill down.	Requires some graphing, math expertise. Training is not separated from other changes; if things fluctuate over time, results are not clear.
Statistical Study	Detailed optimization info available. Can adjust for selection bias in who's trained. Produces highly accurate results.	Requires interpretation to understand the *why*. Requires trained people, special software.
Graphic Representations of Data	Analysis and report are pretty much the same thing. Optimization possible.	Lack of statistical certainty techniques. Requires some expertise.
Impact Study	Directly applicable.	Usually requires professionals to observe. Does not necessarily make the leap to ROI.
ProCourse ROI	Detailed optimization; statistical certainty; relatively quick and cheap compared to hiring statisticians.	Requires outside vendor; does not do interviews and surveys.
Knowledge Gain (Learning Test)	Can be administered in classroom. Directly measures learning.	Measurement ends at instructor's opinion of usefulness of materials. Few financial considerations.

From Prosource

Article 40

Formative Evaluation

Getting It Right the First Time

Donald L. Kirkey and Gary A. DePaul, Ph.D.

Passion

Our passion is for flawless and effective training delivery—the first time and every time.

Let's face it: We have all suffered through flawed training, whether inadequate, misguided, disorganized, pointless, or just plain boring. It doesn't have to be that way. Melinda Jackson (2006) has written of the poor reputation of workplace training. "Most instruction," she asserts, "whether classroom or computer-based, is bad" (p. 28). She points to poor instructional design as the culprit. The quality control of instructional design and development is formative evaluation (a process used to improve the feasibility, effectiveness, clarity, appeal, and impact of learning and performance interventions before implementation).

Through books, articles, workshops, and whole conferences, the training profession continuously addresses the importance of evaluation. Most of what you read and hear is focused on checking "after the fact," that is, verifying that the training had the desired personal and business impact. This is known as *summative* evaluation. While summative evaluation is critical, our passion is building training right the first time and implementing without major problems. By doing this, the "after-the-fact" checking is simple and straightforward. Costly post-implementation changes are minimized. One method to ensure flawless training execution is to subject it to formative evaluation.

Formative evaluation can be as simple as turning your work over to a peer for review by a fresh set of eyes or to a subject-matter expert to check your facts; it can also be a complex process that requires a detailed formative evaluation plan and detailed evaluation reports. The level of rigor will depend on a variety of elements, including the costs of design and development, the audience size, the frequency and complexity of delivery, and the criticality of the outcomes. Obviously, a half-day activity delivered once to a small team requires a different level of scrutiny than a mission-critical blended program delivered repeatedly to an audience of thousands. Regardless, it is essential that designers always subject their work to some level of formative evaluation to ensure successful delivery or implementation.

Formative evaluation is an iterative process. Occasionally, simplified instructional design process maps point to formative evaluation as a formal step after training is developed and before it is implemented. Don't be fooled! Many formative evaluation tools can and should be used as soon as something is designed or developed. Take a lesson from rapid prototyping: design, test, and adjust, develop, test, and adjust, topic by topic and module by module until you have the desired level of quality for your implementation.

Tools and Techniques

There are a wide variety of tools, techniques, and approaches for formative evaluation. This article highlights just a few. Not every one will be appropriate or necessary for every instructional design project. Go to the References section at the end of this article if you want to learn more.

1. Executive or Management Reviews

Early in the design phase, often referred to as the high-level design, we return to the executive sponsor or key stakeholders for a directional review. We want to ensure that we align training with business objectives and expectations. Typically, we present the business need we are addressing, the purpose of the instruction, the target audience description, and an overview of the planned design—especially the performance and instructional objectives. This is also a good time to review anything unfamiliar, such as new media or technology or new learner or manager expectations. Executive reviews not only include approval to proceed, but they also serve to build support and project momentum.

2. Instructional Design Reviews

As both high-level and detailed instructional designs are completed, effective designers seek a second opinion. If another instructional designer is unavailable, then an expert instructor is a good alternative. All elements of a sound instructional design should be checked. Below is a partial list of the items in a high-level design to be reviewed for logic, consistency, appropriateness, and likelihood of success. Compare it with the elements of a detailed design.

Elements of a High–Level Design

Learner description
Environment description
Task descriptions
Performance objectives
Learning objectives
Module descriptions
Media
Duration (estimates)
Delivery plans
Assessment plans
Summative evaluation plans

Elements of a Detailed Design

Detailed (supporting) objectives
Module topics
Alignment of topics with objectives
Content in topics
Instructor directions
Learner directions
Content development sources and resources
Topic duration
Exercise descriptions
Scenario or other descriptions
Final deliverables description
Assessment description

Exhibit 40.1 provides a checklist for high-level designs, which is also available on the website for this book.

Exhibit 40.1. High–Level Design Checklist

High-Level Design Checklist

Introduction

The instructional designer creates a high-level design document. This document includes:

☐ Learner analysis summary

☐ Environmental analysis summary

☐ Task and gap analysis summary

☐ Learning goals and scope of learning

☐ Description and sequence of modules for each learner group

☐ Assessment plans

☐ Evaluation plans

Instructional designers can use the following checklist to assure that the high-level design document is complete.

Design Checklist

Did the instructional designer:

☐ Adequately summarize the findings from the learner analysis?

☐ Effectively summarize the findings from the tasks and gap analysis?

☐ Design the best learning goals for the learners by answering the following

☐ Derive the learning goals from the design analysis?

☐ Identify all the learning goals?

☐ Put the learning goals at the appropriate level of abstraction (in other words, are they too specific or are they broad enough to include several behavioral descriptors)?

Identify the best selection of modules to support the learning goals by answering the following:

☐ Do the modules support the learning goals?

☐ Is the sequence of modules effective and efficient for achieving the learning goals?

☐ Have prerequisites been identified for a sequence of modules?

☐ Has the evaluation for a set of modules been carefully considered?

☐ Are the deliverables for supporting a sequence of modules appropriate?

☐ If instructors are needed, has careful consideration been given to the certification process?

Determine whether the delivery methods for the modules are appropriate by answering the following:

☐ Are the learners capable of using the specific delivery methods?

☐ Are the learners willing to use the specific delivery methods?

☐ Are the specific delivery methods feasible in terms of costs and time?

☐ Can learning and development support the delivery methods?

☐ Can learning and development expect a reasonable return on investment given the specific delivery methods?

(Continued)

References

Dick, W., Carey, L., & Carey, J.O. (2005). *The systematic design of instruction* (6th ed.). Boston, MA: Allyn & Bacon.

Gagne, R.M. (1985). *Conditions of learning* (4th ed.). New York: Holt, Rinehart & Winston.

Smith, P.L., & Ragan, T.J. (2005). *Instructional design* (3rd ed.). San Francisco, CA: Jossey-Bass.

Source: Kirkey & DePaul Formative Evaluation

3. *Subject–Matter Expert Reviews*

As training is designed and developed, instructional designers rely on subject-matter experts to provide detailed content, flesh out examples, describe typical scenarios and on-the-job experiences, and identify common challenges. In formative evaluation, fresh subject-matter experts who have not seen the training material review the content, module and topic sequence, exercises, and assessments. Subject-matter experts evaluate whether the content is accurate, complete, relevant, up-to-date, engaging, and learner-appropriate. They also review the module and topic sequencing to ensure a logical progression. Subject-matter experts subject exercises to a reality check, ensuring that exercises are analogous or applicable to on-the-job contexts? Further, they examine assessments for accuracy as well as relevance to the content. In our reviews, we often see assessments that focus on minutiae while neglecting the major training objectives.

4. *Learner Walk–Throughs*

Dick, Carey, and Carey (2005) note that "simply trying out material with a single learner and revising the materials on the basis of that data can make a significant difference in the effectiveness of materials" (p. 278). Having typical learners review instructional materials before implementation is invaluable, but a surprising number of instructional designer regrettably rely solely on their subject-matter experts.

Ideally, at least three learners should review all materials. They should represent a range of experience, or a range of attitudes if that is critical to the success of the instruction. Learners should identify what was interesting, difficult, or unclear. Instructional designers ask whether the vocabulary is understandable and the examples, illustrations, and exercises are appealing and comprehensible.

For computer-based instruction, learners "talk-through" their experience. They read the instructions, think aloud, and articulate their decisions. Learners provide feedback about navigation and interactivity. Observers can track the time to complete tasks and assessments and collect feedback on the learners' success each step of the way.

Although a learner walk-through is not a true reflection of what happens in implementation, it is still valuable to administer pre- and post-tests for comprehension and learning. An attitude survey can also be administered and the results explored in a debriefing session.

5. Instructor Walk-Throughs

For instructor-led delivery, whether in the classroom or over the web, we recommend an instructor walk-through. Typically, instructors present the materials to the design and development team, "testing" the instructor guide and talking through what they will do and say. The instructors and design team look for logical sequencing, flow, progression of topics, timing, and general feasibility of delivery. The instructors' reactions are also critical; the instructors' attitudes and motivation will profoundly affect the quality of the delivery.

6. Editing

Over time, instructional developers lose sight of their own text. For example, if you edit something too many times, it can become difficult to notice mistakes. So it is important that competent editors review all written materials. Editors can be professionals or simply colleagues with strong editing skills who will approach the materials with a keen and fresh eye. In addition to common grammar, syntax, and spelling errors, editors should look for clarity, readability, reading level, and appropriateness of vocabulary for the intended audience.

7. Pilot-Testing

Peter Drucker (1999), the famous business writer and professor, has written, "Nothing new is right the first time." He stressed the importance of pilot-testing. There is no "substitute for the test of reality. Everything improved or new needs therefore first to be tested on a small scale, that is, it needs to be PILOTED" (p. 87). In instructional design, a pilot-test is akin to a full dress rehearsal in the theatre. If you are evaluating classroom-based training, typical students—in language skills, experience, age, capability, and number—are assembled and the entire class is delivered as designed and developed. Designers, developers, and members of the client or sponsoring organization observe the pilot. They review the presentations, demonstrations, exercises, and scenarios. They also check for comprehension, timing of delivery, flow, and all other elements of the training experience. Pilots usually include careful pre- and post-testing to ensure learning. Periodically, the observers will intervene to ask the participants evaluative questions such as: Was it too easy? Too hard? What did you like? What did you dislike? What can we do to make it better? Did you learn anything new? Can you use what you learned in your job? What will keep you from doing this on the job? In an organizational context, the feedback from the pilot enables the sponsor to make a final decision about proceeding to implementation. A sample evaluation is available on the website and also as Exhibit 40.2 below.

Exhibit 40.2. Pilot Group Feedback Form

Pilot Feedback Form

Course Name

Pilot Date

Pilot Location

Module	Comments	Accept? Decline?	If accept, describe action. If decline, give rationale.	Assigned to	Priority A = High C = Low	Due Date	Status
General course							
Module 1							
Topic 1							
Topic 2							
Module 2							

(Continued)

Pilot Feedback Form

Course Name

Pilot Date

Pilot Location

Module	Comments	Accept? Decline?	If accept, describe action. If decline, give rationale.	Assigned to	Priority A = High C = Low	Due Date	Status
Module X							

Conclusion

We have presented several methods for formative evaluation. How detailed and rigorous your formative evaluations are depends on a variety of many factors. What is critical is that every instructional design and development project undergoes some level of scrutiny to ensure successful delivery. Then you will meet our goal: flawless and effective training delivery – the first time and every time.

References

Dick, W., Carey, L., & Carey, J.O. (2005). *The systematic design of instruction* (6th ed.). Boston, MA: Allyn & Bacon.

Drucker, P.F. (1999). *Management challenges for the 21st century.* New York: HarperCollins.

Jackson, M. (2006). Lies about the design of learning. In L. Israelite (Ed.), *Lies about learning* (pp. 27–41). Alexandria, VA: American Society for Training & Development.

Measuring the Impact of Leadership

Fact or Fiction?

Ajay M. Pangarkar, CTDP, and

Teresa Kirkwood, CTDP

Passion

There is a challenge in measuring soft skills, such as leadership skills, and we welcome it!

Leadership development and succession planning is at the top of the list of organizational concerns. With so much money and so many resources being devoted to leadership training, has anyone truly attempted and successfully been able to measure the return it is promised to deliver? Is it possible to evaluate your investment against current evaluation techniques? Yes it is possible, but not in the same context expected from the current measurement models.

Leadership development stands out as one of the more prevalent forms of soft-skills training within organizations. The belief is that deploying a leadership program to those directing all or parts of the organization will increase a company's bottom line. While this may be true, there is tremendous pressure on HR departments to place a value on effective leadership development programs. The questions are no longer around "What should we be doing to develop our people," but rather senior managers are asking, "What is the return on our investment?" This is a very different way to evaluate leadership development.

Measuring the value and business impact of any type learning initiative is a challenge, even for the most knowledgeable measurement and evaluation experts. Even when training proves to contribute to organizational results, many will claim bias in the measurement process, even when the training results are tangible (hard skills) in their application. Measuring the impact of soft-skills training and its application is an area that is always debated due to the nature of "soft" topics. It is to be noted, however, that the scrutiny and skepticism most soft skills face is often overlooked when it comes to the application of leadership development programs. However, with the significant investments being made in leadership development, attitudes are changing. Increasingly, management is asking the important questions such as "What is the impact of our leadership development on our organization?" "Are we reaping the benefits expected from the process?" and "Is the investment we are making worth the return we expect?"

Is it possible to actually measure leadership training impact or is too ethereal to define in any tangible way? For those responsible for training and HR, answering this question is a challenge. The traditional approach to evaluating leadership impact is to simply wait to see the outcomes and hope for the best. This type of thinking is no longer acceptable. It is possible to measure the results of any development program, including leadership, as long as your program is aligned with your organizational objectives.

Existing evaluation models do not necessarily provide an appropriate framework to measure the effectiveness of soft skills such as leadership. The impact of a leadership program is very intangible and is often dependent on the individual who receives the training. This in turn has a direct correlation on the application of the newly acquired skills and its impact on the organization. So measurement factors such as ROI (level 5) may be appropriate for financial justification in the short term but do not carry as much weight compared to more qualitative measures such as skills application (level 3) and business impact (level 4). Whether you use a Kirkpatrick, Phillips, or any other methodology to evaluate training effectiveness, the application to leadership development places different emphasis on how each level is applied. Let's look at the levels of evaluation and some ways to fit measurement of return into the design of a leadership development program.

Measuring the Satisfaction of the Participant (Level 1)

Although this is the easiest level to evaluate, it is often the most discounted because many participants tend to respond favorably to a course. Since participants in a leadership development program are also generally responsible for organizational outcomes (mid- to senior-level management), you can be sure that a level 1 measurement will receive honest and critical feedback. Measuring the satisfaction of these participants will provide an early and solid indication of whether the program is meeting the needs of the participants and whether it is headed in the right direction. The audience and nature of the topic (leadership) make the measurement at level 1 essential and important.

Measuring the Learning of the Participant (Level 2)

For traditional training programs, acquisition and retention of the content is important and, at this level, some form of "testing" is incorporated. In leadership development programs, the application of the knowledge is more relevant compared to retention. It is not that level 2 is inconsequential, but there must be more emphasis on how the knowledge is applied. The important point here is to measure the knowledge gained by the participants, compared to what they already knew. In the context of leadership development, level 2 measurement is not as critical as level 3.

Measuring the Application of the Knowledge (Level 3)

As mentioned above, the application of the new leadership knowledge and skills is critical to ensuring that it will be used for the growth of participants and the success of the organization. The application of the newly acquired leadership skills is only as effective as its connection to business strategy. Level 3 is critical, but also dependent on the business and strategy (Level 4). For "management" participants, behavioral and attitudinal change is only important in relation to its impact on the overall responsibilities and objectives of the participants. For leadership development, this is obviously critical to measure.

Measuring the Business Impact (Level 4)

Strictly defined, this level checks for direct changes in business outcomes resulting from what was learned in the training program. In a leadership development context, changes in the business are highly dependent on how the participants apply their new knowledge. These issues are not mutually exclusive. If any change is to take place in the organization, the leadership development program must be directly connected to the organizational strategy. It is essential to connect level 4 evaluation to your leadership program.

Measuring the Return on Investment (Level 5)

This is one of the most requested measures in training evaluation, especially by the individuals who are participating in the leadership development process. Essentially, measuring ROI means determining the financial benefits compared to the total program costs. Even though the financial impact is nice to know, it is not the most crucial measure to determine the effectiveness of leadership development programs. Why does it not carry the same weight in the evaluation process? In this context, ROI is a short-term measure and dependent on tangible outcomes or returns. Leadership development is very intangible and is perceived more as a longer-term process; because of this the bottom-line impact may occur months or years later. So in the short term, results are often skewed, which makes the program appear ineffectual, not providing any return compared to the significant investment.

Since leadership is primarily a non-financial performance-based skill, financial measures, such as ROI, are incompatible with the nature of the skills application. Even though it can be measured through some financial results, leadership development requires a more non-financial performance-based approach. One such approach incorporating both the financial and non-financial measures is the balanced scorecard, and chances are your organization has implemented one—or will be doing so soon. As we have discussed in other articles in this section, the balanced scorecard is most appropriate to provide very tangible and proactive results, satisfying the need for lagging financial indicators and, more importantly, the leading non-financial returns on investment.

Implementing a Measurement Strategy: Some Final Thoughts

Within each level of evaluation, you are measuring very different things, and each level of the process does not hold the same importance.

1. When making the decision to move forward with a leadership strategy, start with the organization's key strategies by conducting a "gap analysis" to determine the shortfall in talent needed to execute the strategy. Forcing management to go through the process of determining what should be measured is often an eye-opening experience. It is always worth doing. This is the first step before any other evaluation commences and will provide a benchmark to compare other results against.

2. From the analysis, create development plans for the managers and executives. Many executive development programs are still "bottom-up"—they start at the individual level and ask, "What else does the participant need to become a well-rounded and respected leader?" Instead, the process should start with the organizational needs and then determine which skills and capabilities the leaders should have. This process should drive program design, identify the leadership skills the organization requires, and help the organization to create a focused measurement and evaluation process.

Conclusion

When implementing a leadership development program, it is critical to find out what is important to your organization and build a credible process in which key members agree to the expected value of the program. When you decide to measure the effectiveness of your leadership development programs, decide on what is important to the organization and develop a leadership development strategy around these needs. When you can persuade all parties to agree on what a good investment looks like, leadership development has a much better chance of surviving the next round of budget cuts.

Article 42

Transition Planning Steps for Building and Sustaining a Results-Based Learning Focus

Holly Burkett

Passion

Our passion is to help organizations use an integrated change management approach to build and sustain a results-based learning and development focus. Proper prior transition planning on the front end improves results on the back end!

Despite heightened accountability for workplace learning professionals to show the direct contribution of L&D programs to the bottom line, many practitioners struggle with the practice of linking learning to tangible business outcomes. Implementing a results-based, value-added learning focus means more than obtaining the initial go-ahead for a measurement study on a specific program. Without a long-term "line of sight" on implementing and sustaining results-based training processes over time, there's a risk that your organization's evaluation efforts will be labeled as another passing fad or short-term phenomenon. Keep in mind that the best-designed measurement study and the most progressive evaluation tools and techniques are meaningless unless they are integrated efficiently and effectively into the strategic fabric of an organization.

The integration of a results-based measurement culture does not occur overnight and usually brings more focus, attention, steps, data, and effort to normal learning and development work. On both an individual and organizational level, this additional effort typically involves changing old habits and daily practices of conceiving, designing, developing, and delivering performance improvement solutions. This shift may also encompass reengineering of the training function, restructuring workplace learning policy, procedures, and practices, and influencing organization stakeholders around the value of the WLP function and the role that executives, managers, and employees play in achieving performance results.

Transition Planning Steps

We have worked with a number of companies that have wanted to build a results-based learning focus. Although they desire such an outcome, they often want to short-circuit the process of change that is required to link learning to measurement.

Change is the act of making something different. The change aspect of implementing a results-based learning focus is often overlooked and underestimated. Given that context then, moving from an old to a new state is more successful when the fundamental shift from the "old" (activity-based measurement and evaluation) to the "new" state (results-based measurement and evaluation) is implemented with an integrated, systemic change management approach. The following transition planning steps (Figure 42.1) will guide you in leading this process and in spelling out exactly what needs to be different with the individuals, teams, and departments responsible for achieving performance results.

Step 1. Create Readiness

Once you've decided to introduce results-based measurement processes into your existing learning or performance improvement work, it's important to first look at those people, processes, and factors in your organization that will both help and hurt your progress. *Assessing* readiness for a measurement culture can include such activities as a review of historical data (customer satisfaction reports, strategic plans, grievance records, performance management records, training feedback forms), interviews with key people in the organization, targeted surveys, and select focus groups. Sample areas to assess in this step may include:

- Gaps between where you are and where you want to be with respect to a result-based workplace learning function
- Processes or programs that may have to be changed, reconfigured, or created from scratch to support the effort
- The extent to which executives, managers, and workplace learning staff perceive current training and development efforts to be effective
- Resource constraints that may impede implementation
- Immediate opportunities for showing how learning efforts have made a difference to the business

Create readiness by initiating change management actions that will demonstrate how results-based measurement and evaluation

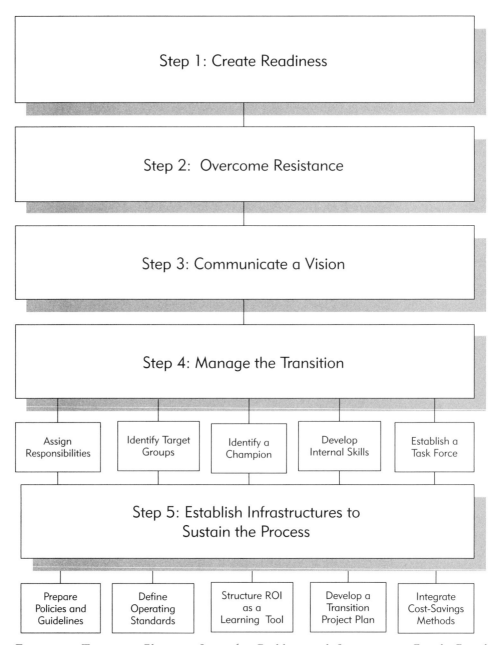

Figure 42.1. Transition Planning Steps for Building and Sustaining a Result-Based Learning Focus

strategies can help the learning function, and the business as a whole:

- Determine whether critical performance gaps were closed or narrowed
- Determine whether a learning solution is accomplishing key business or performance
- objectives
- Provide cost-benefit data for decision making about expanding or discontinuing learning programs
- Improve resource allocation for learning and development efforts

Step 2. Overcome Resistance

With the introduction of any new process or change, resistance is common. There are also many false assumptions and myths about the cost and complexity of implementing results-based learning efforts, particularly at the ROI level. Compounding these issues is the occasional misuse of measurement data as a corrective or fault-finding tool.

Communication meetings can help surface and address organizational concerns about how results will be measured, monitored, and used. Positioning results-based measurement as a compelling piece of organizational strategy and a source of continuous process improvement for the workplace learning function will help build respect, support, and commitment from internal groups, including senior executives and major program sponsors.

Step 3: Communicate a Vision

Workplace learning staff can enhance organizational readiness by actively communicating the vision, mission, and desired outcomes of a results-based evaluation strategy. Your vision, by definition, is the difference between the current reality of where you are with your measurement focus and where you want to be. Whether leading or consulting to the effort, those in charge of initial communications should assist organizational leaders in understanding:

- How a results-based learning function will align with company performance goals, vision, mission, and values
- How a results focus can add value and enhance business performance
- How evaluation data can be used to uncover barriers to successful application of critical skills or knowledge
- How measurement results data can be used to manage and correct barriers
- The role of management in ensuring performance success
- The targets for change and the resources required
- How the organization, its internal processes, and its key people will be developed to manage the change effort
- The checkpoints, process documents, and project plans that detail the scope of the effort and its impact on the business

Without a clear understanding about the purpose of a results-based learning focus, the evaluation or ROI framework being used to measure results, and its impact on the organization and its people, it's unlikely that those responsible for carrying it out will commit to action. In communicating the vision for a results-based workplace learning focus, however, it's important to emphasize that it is not a quick fix and that successful implementation requires sustained support and participation across all organizational levels over time.

Step 4: Manage the Transition

Key workplace learning tasks for managing the transition include the following:

a. *Assign Responsibilities.* Establishing a foundation of shared ownership for a results-based change effort increases the likelihood of its success. As with many change efforts, it's natural for people to underestimate the time, energy, and resources required to achieve evaluation goals. In fact, one of the most common errors made in any change effort is to inaccurately define scope, typically making it too narrow and overlooking internal dynamics of day-to-day communications and working relationships. Imagine the time and productivity loss that occurs when those tasked with supporting and participating in a new evaluation strategy are unclear about their role and the resources needed to support it.

b. *Identify Target Groups.* A major challenge in any change effort is to identify the right people, involve them, foster their commitment, and keep them well informed at all stages. For results-based learning processes to be fully integrated into your organization, appropriate target audiences must be identified and involved. Be prepared to address the most common question of any target group: "How will this effort effect my job?"

c. *Identify a Champion.* Typically, this individual is one who is most familiar with the results-based evaluation framework and/or ROI methodology, understands its value and place in the organization, and is willing to share this knowledge with others. In general, a credible champion must show the ability to translate business requirements into learning and performance outcomes; provide direction, motivation, and support; and convey a results orientation in both action and words.

d. *Develop Internal Skills.* Developing internal capacity for a results-based learning focus may start with the workplace learning staff leading the charge, but it doesn't stop there. Providing stakeholders and responsible parties with education and a thorough understanding of a results-based evaluation and ROI framework will promote a common language around how to communicate learning results and will ensure consistency in how results are measured. In making the transition from a traditional reactive evaluation focus to a more systemic and results-based effort, it is also important to dispel the myth that evaluation is an add-on process occurring at the end of a program. To that end, subject-matter experts, participants, and line managers will need education and training about their roles in defining business needs and gaps, supporting skill transfer, and identifying barriers to on-the-job application of critical skills and knowledge.

e. ***Establish an Internal Task Force.*** A results-based or ROI task force or steering committee can help establish evaluation targets, communicate a vision, lead "quick-win" pilot projects, and implement core elements of an evaluation transition plan. This type of committee typically consists of six to twelve members from functional groups across all levels of the organization. Some organizations rotate membership on a quarterly basis or establish teams that are committed to overseeing one particular project or initiative. For best results, the team must be clear about its purpose. Recommended questions to consider before convening this group include:

- What are the group's charter, purpose, and scope?
- How will roles and responsibilities be defined?
- What must be accomplished (goals, objectives, timelines, deliverables)?
- What kind of authority and resources are needed to ensure completion of assigned tasks?
- What are the established ground rules and team commitments?
- How will the group engage the whole organization and report on its activities?

Step 5: Establish InfraStructures to Sustain the Process

Webster's defines infrastructure as the underlying foundation or basic framework of a system. Information technology experts define a software infrastructure as the heart, lungs, and circulatory system that jump-start an application and keep it running. In much the same manner, workplace learning professionals need to look through an infrastructure lens to determine whether current organizational functions, goals, roles, and work processes are appropriate to jump-start a results-based focus and keep it running over time.

An infrastructure of operational structures and evaluation guidelines is needed to keep a results-based measurement strategy focused, consistent, and credible, particularly during times of organizational change or staff attrition. To establish an effective infrastructure that will stand the test of time, be sure to:

- Prepare evaluation policies and guidelines
- Define operating standards
- Structure a results-based evaluation framework, including ROI, as a learning tool
- Develop a transition project plan for tracking progress toward goals and for identifying specific individuals, timetables, milestones, and deliverables required for implementation
- Integrate cost-savings methods for providing sound, credible results in the face of real or potential resource constraints

Conclusion

Transition planning allows for the assumption that linking training to business results is still generally a new process for most managers and workplace learning staff and that the implementation of a results-based culture tends to evolve slowly. Although implementing transition planning steps can be time-consuming, labor intensive, and sometimes perceived as daunting, taking the time to build organizational capacity and support for a results-based measurement culture has several payoffs:

- It transforms the role of workplace learning in the organization.
- It increases learning and development's alignment with business needs.
- It enhances the value of learning and development in the organization.
- It improves the efficiency of solution design, development, and delivery by:
  - Reducing costs,
  - Preventing a program from being implemented after the pilot process shows that it delivers no value,
  - Expanding programs when other areas need the program, and
  - Discontinuing programs when they add no value.

Recognize your own role as an evaluation champion, coach, and change agent. Build credibility by continually developing your own evaluation skill sets and leveraging information, best practices, tools, and templates from the growing network of evaluation experts in the workplace learning field. Finally, remember this—proper prior transition planning on the front end improves results on the back end!

References

Burkett, H. (2004, August). An ROI shortcut for budget-challenged training departments. Interview by Institute of Management and Administration (IOMA). *Report on Managing Training and Development.*

Phillips, J. (2003). *Return on investment in training and performance improvement programs* (2nd ed.). Boston, MA: Butterworth Heinemann

Phillips, J., Phillips, P., Stone, R., & Burkett, H. (2006). *The ROI fieldbook: Strategies for implementing ROI in HR and training.* Burlington, MA: Elsevier-Butterworth Heinemann.

Phillips, P., & Burkett, H. (2001). Managing evaluation shortcuts. *Info-Line 0111.* Alexandria, VA: ASTD.

Article 43

Demonstrating Your Worth to Management with Credible, Business–Focused Results

Harold D. Stolovitch and Paul Flynn

Passion

To be a real player and have impact on an organization, you have to show decision makers the money. No business critical results, no respect.

You are poring over the reaction sheets for several courses. There is a big grin on your face. Session after session, the results are . . . well . . . fantastic. Scores run from 4.6 to 4.9 on your 5-point scale of learner satisfaction. Hey! If they are delighted, then so are you and so should be your management. Right? Wrong? Maybe?

There is nothing inherently improper in trainees loving their training. However, your believing that these positive reactions (aka, smile sheet scores) are strong indicators of effective learning and future on-job performance may be delusional. By far, the overwhelming evidence from research strongly suggests that high satisfaction from training translates very little into verifiable on-job application and performance improvement (e.g., Arthur, Bennett, Edens, & Bell, 2003; Clark, 1982, 1989: Ford, & Weissbein, 1997).

Our position in this article is that, if you cannot demonstrate concretely and credibly that you have made a solid contribution to the bottom line—in terms senior management and other significant stakeholders admire and value—you are in danger of being ignored for your smiley-face data. Worse, if there comes a crunch and management decision makers cast around to determine who must be retained and who can be "downsized" without organizational pain, watch out!

A number of years ago, we were in the midst of pressing a senior railway executive to increase budgets for training and performance support when he suddenly lashed back, "Show me, in dollars and cents, what the impact on our company will be if I cut *all* training for an entire year. Concretely, how will it affect my bottom line?" How would you respond to this blunt, hard-nosed question if your management posed the same query to you? Are you in a position to provide solid evidence to justify your department's activities and, perhaps more importantly, its expenditures?

By the end of this article, you will be able to answer, at least somewhat confidently, "Yes." To get there, follow us through a real-life story that will provide you with a model of how to demonstrate both impact and return on investment (ROI) in your organization. This is a true story . . . one with not only a happy ending, but also a moral and some concrete data and steps you can replicate.

The Day of Reckoning: An Automotive Tale

For years, the corporate learning and performance (L&P) group had been producing and delivering training to its dealerships across the United States. For the most part, the group and its activities had been viewed as a "normal" part of the cost of doing business. Budgets waxed and waned with sales success. Then, in one bitter moment, the world changed. Disappointingly slow sales of a new vehicle—the first ever of its kind and one for which there had been great anticipation of market success— threw the spotlight on the L&P organization. Searching to assign blame on why the model was not meeting revenue expectations, management decided that it was because "You didn't train them well enough to sell this unique vehicle." From this beginning, things deteriorated further. Soon the questions centered around: "What are we really getting for all of the money we pour into training? We know that there is an awful lot of activity going on. You tell us that people like our courses . . . but where's the beef?"

Blame

The L&P teams felt that they had been unjustly singled out as scapegoats. However, what could they offer as a defense? Accusing others of poor pricing policy, inappropriate market positioning, or ineffective ad campaigns would only sound like whining. The sad fact was that L&P had no valid evidence to demonstrate that training was *not* the culprit. With this realization came enlightenment: "We can never again allow ourselves to fall into this position. We have to show management and our dealers that what we do counts. We have to demonstrate very clearly what they are getting for their L&P dollars."

From decision to action. What follows, in very summary form, are the steps L&P undertook to transform itself from collector of activity-based data (e.g., reaction scores; numbers trained; courses run) to demonstrator of overwhelming value to the enterprise.

A Series of Fortunate Events

The L&P group began by laying the foundation for a "measurement and evaluation" culture aimed at demonstrating worth to critical stakeholders. It gained executive support and sponsorship to create a Measurement Task Force with the following mandate: Establish clear, convincing connections that link training to learning and to business goals; build a common lexicon of concepts and terms to facilitate communication within L&P teams and to stakeholders, drawing from Kirkpatrick's levels of evaluation (Kirkpatrick, 1994) and Phillips' ROI models (Phillips, 2003); identify key metrics that are meaningful to management and dealers and track these; and set concrete success criteria, accompanied by business-focused measures, for each initiative.

The next step was to set up a system, with guidelines, to ensure that each evaluation level was conducted with rigor. Level 1 (reaction) instruments were redesigned to obtain not just satisfaction data, but information on relevance and usability of learning events, materials, job aids, reference guides, performance support tools, and other elements. The purpose was not to demonstrate how happy trainees were with the training, but to gather useful feedback from the learners to help improve the training and associated materials. For every learning event, Level 2 measurement instruments were developed (with pre- and post-equivalent tests and testing-out protocols), validated, and then tracked in a learning management system (LMS) database.

The third step was to demonstrate solid, business-relevant differences between dealership personnel who were enrolled in L&P programs and those who were not. (Enrollment is voluntary.) This included sales, service, and parts personnel. The critical point to establish was that "L&P does make a difference and this has powerful business implications."

Those enrolled in L&P programs go through a certification process that includes training plus on-job performance that is tracked. Figure 43.1 shows that, in all cases, the L&P certified personnel outperformed non-certified ones. As an example, certified salespersons sold 1.7 times more vehicles than did non-certified ones. Great result! However, anticipating questions as to whether all of the difference should be attributed to L&P efforts led the group to dig more deeply.

There are strongly held beliefs in the automotive world concerning what affects bottom-line performance. With respect to sales of vehicles, a subject dear to dealers' and the corporate heart, these include: tenure (the longer you sell, the more you sell); size of dealership (the bigger, the better); exclusivity (selling only our brand results in selling more of our brand); dealership certification (certified dealers sell more). L&P decided to put these beliefs to the "meaningful data" test and included L&P salesperson certification. It ran a multiple regression analysis that

Figure 43.1. Digging into Data

included one whole year's data for all U.S. dealerships (almost four thousand) and all salespersons (almost forty thousand). Figure 43.2 reveals some astonishing results. L&P salesperson certification came out as *by far* the most powerfully correlated factor with sales success.

With respect to the particularly powerful belief that years-of-selling-experience is really the key to more sales, L&P decided to attack head on. It gathered sales results of the almost forty thousand salespersons in all dealerships and examined their sales results. Its investigation, as shown in Figure 43.3, clearly laid this belief—so dearly held by many senior managers and dealers—to rest.

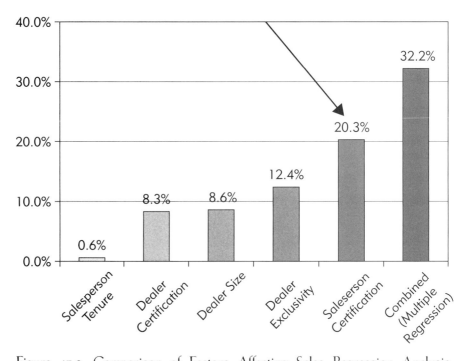

Figure 43.2. Comparison of Factors Affecting Sales Regression Analysis (% of Sales Variance Explained)

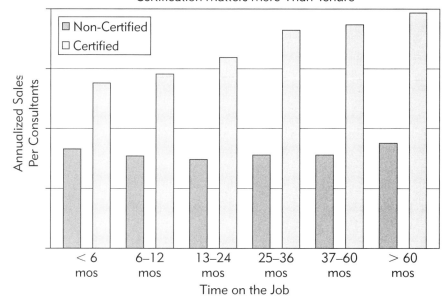

Figure 43.3. Tenure Versus L&P Certification

So What Does This Mean?

What was achieved from this effort was the establishment of an initial beachhead, demonstrating in a credible manner that the activities of L&P clearly link to bottom-line results—more so than those factors commonly believed by many stakeholders to be essential for business success. Despite this, more was necessary. On the basis of its first initiatives, L&P then moved on to a systematic analysis of what makes for exemplary (top) performance. It launched an in-depth study and analysis initiative that sent a team of its professionals into identified high-performing dealerships across the nation to interview and observe top performers and their managers. From this effort, they created performance maps that laid out specifically what exemplary performers do and what they achieve. They identified key inputs, outputs, and useful tools for every important task dealership personnel perform.

They discovered a number of major differences between these exceptional performers and their average colleagues—some to the amazement of corporate executives.

While, on the one hand, L&P began using the performance mapping information it had gathered to revise its programs, materials, tools, and support systems, it still continued to turn out data-based reports showing its contributions to business results. Figure 43.4 provides an example of how you can demonstrate the value of L&P activities.

A Continuing Saga

With its credibility at an all time high, L&P did not stop to rest on its laurels. It had begun its adventure in early 2003, and by the end of the year was able to demonstrate its impact on what counts to critical stakeholders. As Figure 43.5 illustrates, it could legitimately claim that those dealership salespersons who had enrolled and were certified by L&P, overall, outperformed non-certified salespersons by a whopping 170 percent. Maintaining L&P measurement and support efforts, it showed that improvement continued to climb. As an example, the difference between an average certified salesperson and a non-certified one in 2005

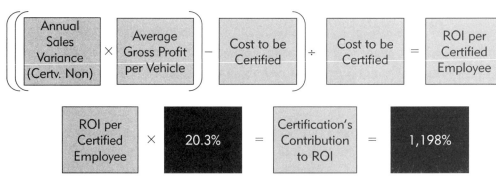

Figure 43.4. L&P Certification Return on Investment (ROI)

Figure 43.5. Annual Sales Results

jumped to 210 percent, representing a superior annual gross profit of almost $55,000.

Similar results were also reported in the Service and Parts sectors.

What is wonderful about this tale is not just the demonstration of valued contribution. The morale of the L&P organization along with its entire perspective on its mission has changed. It has gained widespread respect, which has translated into greater commitment to continuously affect business outcomes. L&P has launched similar initiatives into the internal wholesale sector—the critical interface between the corporation and dealerships—and the emerging commercial arena, a still largely uncharted territory. L&P has assumed a business leadership role with strong approval and support from both the corporation and dealers.

Once viewed as a threat, measurement and evaluation, tied intimately to the bottom line, are now embraced as vital components of L&P's strategic positioning. Design, development, and delivery activities are more frequently generated by analysis and evaluation data. The emphasis has shifted from satisfaction and bodies trained to data derived from Levels 1 to 4 of Kirkpatrick's model and Phillips' ROI Level 5. Managers' and dealers' expectations of L&P's role have altered as well. The nature of their questions and requests display a new awareness of what L&P can offer. There is a growing openness to invest and support L&P projects, but with the anticipation of business relevant results.

Conclusion: The Moral of This Tale

Training professionals, for the most part, tend to focus on what they know best . . . training. Their emphasis is on developing and delivering appreciated and impactful courses and curricula. Their reports to management with data on dollars spent, hours of training delivered, numbers trained, and courses produced mirror this focus. All of these items represent expenditures . . . costs. They justify these with trainee satisfaction and, less frequently, knowledge test scores. When times turn tough, costs are cut, especially if there is no clear evidence of business contribution. Only the demonstrated business results derived from prudent investment get to count. That is where you want to be.

Training professionals often fear measurement and evaluation, profess ignorance about how to do these credibly, or how to tell a convincing story that ties what they do to key business indicators. They often complain that they do not have the time, budgets, or support of management to do what it takes. Our automotive L&P group was there and did that, complete with suffering the consequences. It discovered, all too painfully, that this was simply a formula for long-term disaster. Forced by circumstances to take a new stance, it engaged in a series of steps that allowed it to achieve an unimagined level of success and status. So can you!

References

Arthur, W., Jr., Bennett, W., Jr., Edens, P.S., & Bell, S.T. (2003). Effectiveness of training in organizations: a meta-analysis of design and evaluation factors. *Journal of Applied Psychology, 88*(2), 234–245.

Clark, R.E. (1982). Antagonism between achievement and enjoyment in ATI studies. *Educational Psychologist, 17*(2).

Clark, R.E. (1989). When teaching kills learning. In H.N. Mandl, N. Bennett, E. de Corte, & H.F. Freidrich (Eds.), *Learning and instruction: European research in an international context, volume II.* London, UK: Pergamon Press.

Ford, J.K., & Weissbein, D.A. (1997). Transfer of training: an updated review and analysis. *Performance Improvement Quarterly, 10*(2), 22–41.

Kirkpatrick, D.L. (1994). *Evaluating training programs: The four levels.* San Francisco, CA: Berrett-Koehler.

Phillips, J.J. (2003). *Return on investment in training and performance programs* (2nd ed.). Burlington, MA: Butterworth-Heinneman.

Resources to Help You Demonstrate Your Value to Management

Seagraves, T. (2004). *Quick! Show me your value.* Alexandria, VA: ASTD Press.

Stolovitch, H.D., & Keeps, E.J. (2004). *Front-end analysis and return-on-investment toolkit.* San Francisco, CA: Pfeiffer.

Stolovitch, H.D., & Keeps, E.J. (2004). *Training ain't performance.* Alexandria, VA: ASTD Press.

Stolovitch, H.D., & Keeps, E.J. (2004). *Beyond training ain't performance fieldbook.* Alexandria, VA: ASTD Press.

Plus the books by Kirkpatrick and Phillips listed in the References above.

Article 44

We Know We Got There

Toni Hodges DeTuncq

Passion

My passion is creating careful alignment of training with business goals!

It is essential to measure learning programs against specific objectives. By closely aligning these objectives to one another and giving participants an opportunity to apply their new skills and knowledge, you help achieve business or organizational goals and your program will be declared a success.

In the "Designing Training" section of this book, Objective Mapping was introduced in Article 6, "If You Don't Know Where You Are Going, You Will Probably End Up Somewhere

Else." An example of an objective map for a sales/customer service training program was provided. The map, however, was incomplete, saving the columns outlining the methods for measuring the success of the program for this section of the book. This article will discuss how to plan for measuring programs, looking at various methods of data collection.

Measuring Against Objectives

It is essential that programs be measured against the objectives for the program. As described in Article 6, program objectives should be described in three distinct yet linked set of objectives:

- Business objectives state those organizational problems or goals that the program must address.
- Performance objectives are those that describe the intended job behaviors required to meet the business objectives.
- Learning objectives are those specific skills or knowledge the participants must gain in order that they perform the behaviors specified by the performance objectives.

These objectives must be aligned to one another closely so that, after the program is complete and the participants have had the opportunity to apply their new skills and knowledge, those business or organizational goals will be met and the program will be declared a success. Unless the objectives have been stated in measurable terminology and aligned, however, we will not be able to measure how successful the program was and never know the value of that program to the organization.

Measuring Business Objectives

Business objectives must have associated "metrics" attached to them in order that their value is determined. They are most often stated in percentages or some other index achieved in organizational terminology. For example, "sales will increase by 30 percent" or "customer satisfaction will improve 10 points on the customer satisfaction index." These are the metrics that we aim for. If no such metric exists when a business or organizational problem is uncovered, we must set one or develop a method to measure the change. For example, if the organization believes employee morale is low and that it may be impacting various areas of operation, the evaluator must work with the client to determine the existing morale as either measured from an existing employee survey or by one that is designed for this specific problem assessment. Perhaps a short questionnaire could be designed and administered to a sample group of employees that will be targeted to attend a training program to determine a "before" metric to be compared to an "after" metric. Whatever method is used to measure the extent to which the business objectives have been met, it must be recognized by the organization as the acceptable metric, one that all agree effectively portrays the problem or goal.

Measuring Performance Objectives

Performance objectives are measured by either existing or contrived methods. If the performance, for example, are those behaviors that are already measured on the job, such as a call center's customer call observations, then those observation records can and should be used. In most situations, however, accurate measures of the specific behaviors designated as necessary to meet the business objectives do not exist for individuals. In these situations, the evaluator must decide which of the many methods from the job performance measurement tool kit should be selected to use. These would include:

- *Follow-Up Surveys,* which are useful for measuring the extent to which attitudes, beliefs, and opinions have "stuck" following a program

- *Follow-Up Questionnaires,* which gather the participant, peer, or supervisor perceptions of the effectiveness of the program
- *Observations on the Job,* which are used when the performance objectives are those that can be clearly observed and can be separated from other aspects of the job
- *Follow-Up Focus Groups,* which attempt to gather constructive data, such as ways to improve a program
- *Interviews,* which can be conducted with different participants, supervisors, peers, or the program's stakeholders
- *Performance Monitoring,* which use data that exists in the organizational databases when those data are tied to individuals rather than groups
- *Action Planning,* which is a versatile method to plan for job performance and track that performance

These data collection methods can be used in combination with one another depending on the performance objectives and the purpose for the evaluation. If, for example, the evaluator is measuring a pilot program for which improvements to the program are feasible, the evaluator may choose to use both the follow-up questionnaire and focus groups. If a follow-up questionnaire is conducted that opens questions that need further investigation, the evaluator may decide to follow up the questionnaire with select or random interviews. Some of these data collection methods may also be used to gather business data as well as performance data, such as follow-up questionnaires, interviews, performance monitoring, and action planning. The evaluator, again, must know what is being measured to determine which data collection method(s) to select.

It is important to note that, whatever method is selected, the rules for data collection design and implementation MUST be adhered to. This is important for several reasons:

1. The data collection method must collect the data that is required and only the data required (instruments that are too lengthy impact their validity).

2. Data collection can be intrusive in today's workload intensive environments and that intrusiveness must be accounted for both in method selection and implementation.
3. Limited resources in data analysis and reporting may drive a realistic data collection strategy.

Sources and examples for the methods for data collection design and implementation are listed at the end of this article.

Measuring Learning Objectives

Methods to measure learning fall into two main categories:

1. *Knowledge-Based Measures,* which include tests, either online or paper-based
2. *Performance-Based Measures,* which include observations using a checklist of some sort

Learning measures for measuring programs in a workplace should be criterion-referenced rather than norm referenced. That is, they must be measured against a criteria (the learning objective) rather than against other test-takers. As with job performance measures, great care must be taken by the evaluator to make sure that the learning measures are designed and administered correctly. The designer must strive for it to be both reliable and content-valid (Shrock & Coscarelli, 2000) and administered correctly and fairly (Hodges, 2002). Tips and rules for test design and administration can be found in the resources offered at the end of this chapter.

Now that the evaluator has determined the most appropriate metric for measuring the extent to which the business objectives have been met and selected the best method to collect performance and learning data to measure the extent to which the performance and learning objectives have been met, let's take a look at how the objective map for the sales/customer service training program, which began in the previously mentioned article is completed in Table 44.1

Notice in Table 44.2 that we have selected two methods to measure the performance objectives (Column 5). The behavior being measured (Column 4) lends itself to observation because they are distinct, observable behaviors. But the evaluator has also selected to use a follow-up questionnaire in addition to the observation. The purpose of the questionnaire in this example is to determine clues to any observational scores that may come back low, that is, behaviors that are not taking place, and to determine enablers and barriers on the job. Remember that the enablers and barriers have been anticipated, and one hopes that actions have been taken to eliminate or reduce barriers, so the questionnaire will afford the evaluator the opportunity to see what has actually transpired. Note that the method to isolate the impact of the training has been noted in this column (Phillips, 1997).

Two methods have also been selected to determine the extent to which the learning objectives (Column 7) have been met. Column 8 lists both a simulated observation method as well as a paper-pencil test. Because the evaluators have planned for the data collection for this program, they will be able to design the simulator observation checklist so that it can be easily modified to become the job performance observation checklist. They have selected the paper-and-pencil test to measure the knowledge-based objectives versus the performance-based learning objectives that were measured by the observation method.

Table 44.1. Completed Example of Sales/Customer Service Training Program Objective Map

1. Business Objective	2. Metric	3. Enablers/Barriers	4. Performance Objective	5. Measurement Methodology	6. Enablers/Barriers	7. Learning Objective	8. Measurement Methodology	9. Enablers/Barriers
1. Improve customer satisfaction by 90 percent	Reduction in customer complaints	Enabler: New product line Barrier: Weak market	1a. Opens call IAW established procedures; 1b. Demonstrates interest in caller's needs; 1c. Closes call with correct understanding of actions to be taken	Observation using an observation checklist; follow-up questionnaire; isolation technique: control group versus experimental group	Enablers: Training, job performance incentives	1a1. Greets caller with standard company opening; 1a2. Introduces self; 1b1. Uses enthusiastic tone of voice(friendly, positive, non-monotone voice—happy, upbeat, cheery, pleasant); 1b2. Listens to customer without interrupting; 1c1. Conveys empathy; 1c2. Asks for customer's perspective; 1c3. Probes for agreement; 1c4. Restates agreed-on follow-up actions to be taken	Knowledge-based twenty-cuestion paper-based test; simulated observation using an observation checklist	Barrier: Lack of practice time; Enabler: realistic simulation
2. Reduce escalations by 80 percent	Cost savings due to reduction in time required of team leader and processing clerk		2a. Diagnoses customer's problem or need correctly; 2b. Gains customer agreement of follow-up actions that need to be taken	Observation using an observation checklist; follow-up questionnaire; isolation technique: control group versus experimental group	Barrier: Lack of supervisor support	2a1. Defines purpose of call; 2a2. Communicates what the initial plan will be; 2a3. Asks customer probing questions; 2a4. Uses company problem questions checklist; 2a5. Asks what has been tried before in resolving problem; 2a6. Asks about timing issues; 2b1. Checks back with the customer to make sure rep understands issue/confirms to ensure understanding; 2b2. Summarizes call; 2b3. Probes for agreement on any follow-up steps	Knowledge-based twenty-question paper-based test; simulated observation using an observation checklist	Barrier: Lack of practice time; Enabler: realistic simulation

Table 44.2. The Object Map Template

Column 1: Business Objectives	Column 2: Metric	Column 3: Enablers/ Barriers	Column 4: Performance Objectives	Column 5: Measurement Methodology	Column 6: Enablers/ Barriers	Column 7: Learning Objectives	Column 8: Measurement Methodology	Column 9: Enabler/ Barriers
1.			1a.			1a1.		
			1b.			1a2.		
			1c.			1b1.		
			etc.			1c1.		
						1c2.		
						etc.		
2.			2a.			2a1.		
			2b.			2a2.		
			etc.			2a3.		
						2b.		
						2b1.		
						2b2.		
						etc.		
3.			3a.			3a1.		
						3a2.		
						3a3.		
						3a4.		

Source: T.K. Hodges (2002). Linking Learning and Performance: A Practical Guide to Measuring Learning and On-the-Job Application. Boston, MA: Butterworth Heinemann. Used with permission from author.

The Trainer's Portable Mentor

Conclusion

This program has been carefully planned for success. Objectives are clearly stated and linked to one another; enablers and barriers have been anticipated and dealt with to whatever extent possible; and the method to measure its success have been planned for and put into place. Now we will know where we are going and the extent to which we reached our goals.

References and Resources

Hodges, T.K. (2002). *Linking learning and performance: A practical guide to measuring learning and on-the-job performance.* Boston, MA: Butterworth Heinemann.

Phillips, J.J. (1997). *Return on investment in training and performance improvement programs.* Houston, TX: Gulf.

Phillips, J.J. (1997). *Handbook of training evaluation and measurement methods.* Houston, TX: Gulf.

Phillips, J.J., & Stone, R.D. (2002). *How to measure training results: A practical guide to tracking the six key indicators.* New York: McGraw-Hill.

Seagraves, T. (2004). *Quick! Show me your value.* Alexandria, VA: ASTD Press.

Shrock, S., & Coscarelli, W. (2000). *Criterion-referenced test development.* Silver Spring, MD: ISPI.

Article 45

A Four-Part Strategy for Communicating Business Value

Theresa L. Seagraves

Passion

How you use metrics to communicate business value is just as important as having the metrics themselves.

Workplace learning and performance professionals (WLP) have been taught to speak the language of performance. After all, helping others improve their performance is what WLP professionals do best. Executives, however, have been taught to speak the language of finance. Successful executives have learned to filter out irrelevant communication and tune in to that which helps them take action and meet their most pressing goals. How can WLP professionals maximize their communication about their value in a way that catches their executive's attention and consistently builds the perception of their value?

The Four Segments

When communicating value, the successful WLP professional uses a four-part strategy to translate the value they bring to the table into terms that others understand and want to act on. The four segments in high-value communications are the:

- Performance Value Segment
- Financial Value Segment
- Relevant Context Segment
- Your Goal Segment

Figure 45.1 illustrates these four segments and gives an example of how they can be used to successfully communicate bottom line value.

Performance Value

When gathering metrics, WLP professionals often use metrics such as a "10 percent decrease in errors," a "3-point increase in customer satisfaction scores" or a "25 percent increase in leads." This type of metric describes improvements in performance or the effects of changes in employees' behavior.

Many WLP professionals make the assumption that their audience understands what an improvement in performance means to the organization's bottom line. In fact, if their audience makes a translation of value into bottom-line impact at all, it is rare that their audience makes an accurate translation.

Financial Value Segments

Performance Value Segment
  Period of Time, Intervention, Direction,
  Performance Measure, Amount of Change

Financial Value Segment
  Direction, Financial Measure(s), Amount of Change

Relevant Context Segment
  Intervention, Relevant Benefit or Impact

Your Goal Segment
  What You Want, Why, Period of Time,
  Next Step You Want Them to Take

Example:

Performance Value Segment
  In the last three months, after implementing our
  stress management program, nurses averaged a
  10% decrease in turnover and absenteeism.

Financial Value Segment
  Thereby improving our Gross Profit Margin by $750,000

Relevant Context Segment
  This means that we were able to maintain our
  profitability levels while opening our new childrens's
  ward.

Your Goal Segment
  We'd like to meet with you and your staff to show
  you how we can help create even more profitability
  in the next six months.

Figure 45.1. Four-Part Strategy to Translate Value of Training

It certainly is critical for the WLP professional to gather performance metrics because it's impossible to talk about WLP's value without them. By themselves, however, such metrics are never enough to communicate the true value that WLP is bringing to the organization.

To have more impact in communicating value, the WLP professional has to describe the performance change from a particular intervention and the period of time that it took to achieve that change. But the WLP professional cannot stop there. He or she must maintain control of how WLP's value is perceived by taking the next step and translating performance value into financial value.

Financial Value

It is absolutely imperative that WLP professionals know how to translate the value of performance metrics into bottom-line financial value in the terms that line and upper executives are measured on. This requires a working knowledge not only of the results of WLP initiatives, but also of financial terms such as free cash, debt to equity ratio, day's sales inventory, and gross profit margin.

When translating performance value into financial value, use financial terms that are relevant to the level of the audience. For example, a chief financial officer (CFO) may be very interested in the gross profit margin, while a manufacturing manager may be much more interested in improvements in the overall cost of goods sold, a component of the gross profit margin. The same performance intervention will create changes in many levels of financial metrics. The key is to find the ones that are most important to the audience and to connect WLP value to their financial measures in a logical way.

Budgets and budget variance reports are an excellent source of information about what is important financially to executives. If access to this information is not available, sitting down privately with line executives can be very enlightening regarding the financial measures they must achieve within the budget cycle. If all else fails, connecting WLP's performance to improvements in cash flow is a helpful way of communicating value.

Relevant Context

Translating performance into bottom-line value is still not enough to guarantee WLP professionals the attention of their executives. It is expected that every area of the business contributes to the bottom line in some way. Executives also need to know why paying attention to WLP is relevant to them *right now*. Giving executives a reason to pay attention to WLP's contributions is known as the relevant context. There are three types of relevant context: new product/service introductions, seasonal sales, and fiscal budgets.

New Product/Service Introductions

The example gives meaning to the performance and financial value being communicated by connecting that value to the relevant context of a new service (a children's ward). New products and services frequently draw resources and cash flow from existing products and services and require huge expenditures on marketing to be successful. The organization must rely on heavy debt or cutbacks in other areas to cover expenses. Showing how WLP's ability to improve performance is directly connected to maintaining profitability at such a critical time improves the perception of value in executives' minds.

Seasonal Sales

Seasonal sales can be a strain on cash flow. Showing how WLP's efforts have created, better managed, or conserved cash flow during different seasonal cycles is also an effective way to increase the perception of WLP's bottom-line value.

Fiscal Budgets

Finally, fiscal budgetary context refers to the four quarters of a fiscal year. For planning purposes, the third quarter is when vision setting and "what-if" conversations frequently happen. This is the most critical quarter for a WLP professional to be able to communicate strong value, because this is when the broad levels of the following year's budgets are often laid out.

The fourth quarter is more likely to be a quarter of tactical negotiations to set the broad budgets into concrete specifics. The first quarter is when new programs, initiatives, and projects are kicked off. Finally, the second quarter is when everyone looks for numbers to determine how well those programs and projects are working, because they will need them by the third quarter to communicate value and discuss future visions. To communicate budgetary relevant context, the WLP professional needs to show how WLP is helping the budget or is wisely using the planned budget resources.

Your Goal

The final, and sometimes the most critical piece of value communication, is the goal of the WLP professional in communicating value. To an executive, communication without purpose is noise. According to Dr. Robert Cialdini (1997), a leading expert on influence, one of the keys ways to influence another person is to ask for a small commitment. Once a small commitment is gained, it can be built on by asking for increasingly larger commitments over time. But the key is to know what to ask for.

What Have You Done for Me Lately?

It's important to translate performance value into financial value and make that value relevant, but every experienced WLP professional knows that the same financial numbers can still be met with either enthusiasm or yawns. That's because executives expect to hear about the *incremental* financial value, not the total financial value of an intervention.

Incremental financial value is the additional value that a program, project, or intervention has provided in the last budgetary cycle. If WLP surprises executives with an unexpected windfall in financial value, then the WLP department will be enthusiastically received during that budget period.

But in the next fiscal budget cycle, WLP's contributions will be more realistically factored into financial measures and become expected. By the following budget cycle, the financial performance for the same WLP intervention has become invisible because *incrementally* there is no additional value added. Invisible value is known as a "given."

Managing a Metric's Perception

If 50 percent or more of WLP's programs are givens, then WLP's budgets may not be justifiable in the minds of executives. It pays to consistently and clearly communicate incremental financial value. Quarterly communication keeps WLP's value relevant and visible. Gathering enough data to communicate quarterly does not have to be difficult, but if the WLP organization is not in the habit of gathering performance or financial data, the task can seem overwhelming at first.

If performance data is not readily available for the intervention that WLP wants to discuss, industry benchmarking data can provide a great way to show how well WLP is doing. Asking for some private coaching from executives who are supporters of WLP can also help when making estimates and managing value perceptions.

Conclusion

Remember: it's not only which WLP metrics are gathered or even how big they are. It's also about how well the metrics are translated into incremental value, in what timeframe, and how regularly and often they are communicated that matters.

Reference

Cialdini, R. (1997). *Influence: The psychology of persuasion.* New York: HarperCollins.

Measuring Time to Proficiency

Steven C. Rosenbaum

Passion

I have a passion for results. Proficiency is a measure of being able to demonstrate results at a desired level. Using proficiency as a training measure dramatically changes the way an organization approaches learning.

Imagine that you have just completed two years of college Spanish. In fact, you got straight A's. As a graduation present, we fly you to Mexico City. As you get off the plane, you're speaking Spanish like a native . . . right? Not really! In fact most people will say they are a long way from being fluent. This is an example of the difference between meeting learning objectives and actually being proficient.

Proficiency is a measure of being able to demonstrate results at a desired level. In business, salespeople become proficient when they are able to meet their sales goals. Factory workers become proficient when they are achieve daily production quotas while meeting standards for safety and scrap. Call center employees become proficient when they can handle a full range of calls without asking for help.

Using proficiency as a training measure dramatically changes the way an organization approaches learning. It requires that an organization structure the entire time line from day one to proficiency, rather than just setting up a series of classes. While formal training is often required to reach proficiency, it also takes a lot of coaching, practice, and experience. For example, to become proficient in Spanish, you can learn vocabulary, syntax, and grammar in the classroom. However, to become proficient you need hours, days, or months of practice with native Spanish speakers.

Proficiency is a different measure than competencies. In a typical competency model, a job or task is broken down into the require skills, knowledge, and attitudes (sometimes attributes). While these models are useful for hiring purposes or for building individual training events, they are not necessarily indicators of proficiency. To attain proficiency, a learner will often have to use several competencies at a time—often switching from one set of competencies to another quickly.

Consider a call center customer service agent who needs to use the computer, product knowledge, and empathy at the same time to respond to a customer inquiry. The agent switches quickly from listening and questioning skills to presenting skills, while at the same time documenting the call.

When looking at measuring proficiency, there are four elements to consider. The first element is the result of the job or task. This is done both in terms of the quantity and the quality of the output. For a salesperson, this might be sales volume plus profit margin. For a software engineer, it might be lines of coding and debugging required. Some jobs, such as managerial jobs, are much harder to quantify, but it is possible. You could include retention rates, productivity of subordinates, or progress on developing subordinates, as seen in Figure 46.1.

The second measure to look at is speed. One of the things that happens in any learning process is that the better a learner becomes, the faster he or she is able to perform. Over time, you can observe call center employees keyboarding, moving from screen to screen, or answering questions with greater speed. Often straight knowledge tests don't measure proficiency because they lack a speed test. Answering questions quickly shows greater proficiency than taking a long time to think about an answer before getting it right.

The third element to consider is independent action. In other words, can employees perform a job or task largely on their own? As employees become more independent, they ask fewer questions and need less help. They also work with a systematic routine or schedule that organizes their work. Often proficiency is identical to being independently productive.

The fourth element to consider is confidence. Just like speed, confidence goes up as learners become proficient. Learners

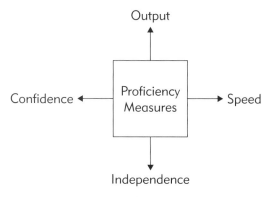

Figure 46.1. Sample of Quantifying a Job

can not only perform a task or job well, but they feel confident that they can accomplish the task or job without a lot of struggle or anxiety. This is why once learners become proficient they are less likely to give up and quit. Therefore, there is a direct link between lack of confidence and turnover.

The challenge that most organizations face when trying to measure proficiency is that they have little or no historical data about these jobs or tasks. In those cases, organizations often base the measures on business goals that may or may not be realistic. In other words, they will define proficiency by what they want it to be, rather than by what the current workforce is actually doing. It's not uncommon when business goals are used as measures that most of the current workforce won't meet that proficiency definition. Therefore, when business goals are used, they reflect a higher or new level of proficiency but not the current level.

Figure 46.2 shows how business goals or targets are often beyond what is considered proficient or independently productive.

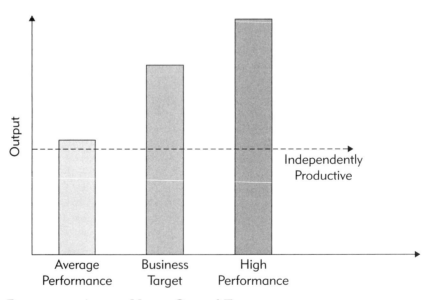

Figure 46.2. Average Versus Optimal Targets

However, those higher definitions can be the basis of ongoing improvement projects.

Proficiency seldom is the result of a single training event, even if one uses blended learning. It happens over time with considerable amounts of practice and experience. For example, in a typical five-day sales training class, learners often will practice sales calls. They might even do as many as five or six role plays. However, to actually learn how to make an effective sales presentation my take fifty, a hundred, or even more real calls with real customers. Therefore, when building training to proficiency, it's critical to consider the entire learning timeline.

When you consider the entire timeline, you have the basis for measuring time to proficiency. In other words, how long does it take to become independently productive or up-to-speed. In an organization with a lot of historical data, you can look at performance reviews and other output data to find an average time to proficiency. The first time this measure is attempted, it's rare to find this type of information. Therefore, the first time will likely be a very rough estimate or stake in the sand. Going forward, these measures can be put in place to become more and more accurate.

It is possible to do the initial estimate of time to proficiency (see Figure 46.3) through surveys or interviews. However, if you just ask when employees become proficient, you will usually get a date that is soon after formal training ends. This is more than overly optimistic; it's usually just wrong. What works better is to take the definition of proficiency and ask all key stakeholders: When do employees begin to look like this?

You will find as you begin to measure time to proficiency that you won't get a single date, but rather a time range. Some learners are either faster than others or start with more skill and experience. However, you can start improving time to proficiency with a simple average time. Again, as you go forward, you can put more measures in place to become more accurate.

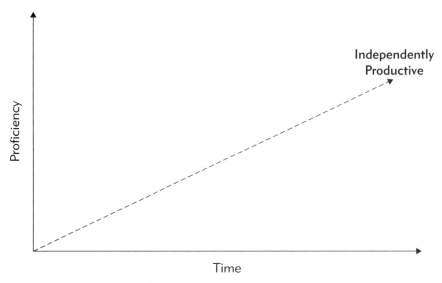

Figure 46.3. Time to Proficiency

With a proficiency definition in place and an estimate of time to proficiency, you can then tie improvements in learning to key business measures. When time to proficiency is reduced, a number of things happen. First, employees become productive sooner and often continue to higher levels because of this head start. The results can be as basic as salespeople making their first sales in month three rather than month nine. Other measures can include reduced errors, fewer accidents, lower customer complaints, and even fewer lost customers.

Another result of learning faster or becoming proficient faster is that there can be a significant drop in turnover or attrition. What happens in the learning process is that learners loose enthusiasm and confidence as they face challenges. When they think they will never get it right or can't succeed, many just give up and quit. Some quit and leave; others quit and stay. That's why in the sink-or-swim approach there are so many sinkers and so few swimmers. Working on time to proficiency has the effect of moving learners through these trouble spots sooner and with more confidence.

Conclusion

One of the key benefits of using time to proficiency as a measure is that senior executives intuitively know the benefits and will see them as significant. It often doesn't take a lot of bottom-line measurements to make an effective business case.

Finally, making the transition to measuring proficiency and time to proficiency is a significant change in the way most people have traditionally looked at training. In reality, this approach applies business processes and business process improvement to learning. What works for other parts of the business really does work for training.

Making "Cents" from Your Training ROI

How Organizations Can Make Training Accountable

Ajay M. Pangarkar, CTDP, and

Teresa Kirkwood, CTDP

Passion

Training is a significant investment for many organization and investors (shareholders and management) expect to see returns on their investments. So how do you measure the return on training investment? Methodologies exist that facilitate this process, but the process must be conducted with diligence and the results measured against comparable outcomes.

This is one article that those responsible for making training initiatives accountable to specific outcomes will recognize. We will review and address the measurement and evaluations standards set forth by both Dr. Donald Kirkpatrick (four levels of evaluations) and Dr. Jack Phillips (five levels of evaluation).

Showing the value of training begins well before the training itself—asking the right questions at the outset. These questions include: What does the organization need to develop? Who should be trained? What is the objective? Is it best done in-house or by an external provider? Is it really needed? And ultimately: What results are expected?

Once specific objectives are identified, it is time to establish "benchmarks" that will assist in building credibility for the ROI measurement. Benchmarking provides a specific measure of how much an organization improves before and after the training effort. For example, if the goal is to increase sales by 15 percent, research what the sales and marketing staff would have to do to achieve this goal, speak with the production staff to determine whether they are capable of supporting this increase, and consult the administration and customer service staff to learn what they require to be effective.

Defining and Conducting the Actual ROI Measurement

Measuring training's return on investment (ROI) is one way to tangibly show the impact of employees' acquired knowledge on the organization and on the bottom line. Used in the strictest sense, ROI answers the question, "For every dollar invested in training, how many dollars does the employer get back?" Learning professionals are taught to evaluate training using an industry standard, called the Kirkpatrick model for training evaluation. This is a simple four-level evaluation model widely used in a variety of learning environments.

Simply, the levels are defined as:

1. The reactions of the training participants, as measured through feedback surveys;
2. The evaluation of what participants learned (testing);
3. The application or transfer of the training to the participants' jobs; and
4. The measurement and impact of the training on organizational performance.

A more recent measurement practice is the Phillips' ROI methodology. This model takes Level 4 of Kirkpatrick and converts it to an ROI measure (Level 5). It also identifies non-tangible results (Level 6). The mistake many managers make is evaluating ROI based on Level 1 (evaluation of the training/trainer) and Level 2 (testing of what the employees learned). The results leave managers with a false impression that the training initiatives were successful solely based on the evaluation of the course and testing of the participants. They only realize later that having positive training evaluations and employees with more knowledge does not necessarily deliver the return expected.

Not Everything Can Be Measured

Although evaluating training is important, it is not essential to measure every training effort at the ROI level. If it is not critical to the organization's strategy or if it isn't a significant investment, then it is not wise to evaluate training at Level 4 or Level 5. The sales example mentioned earlier would meet both criteria and, hence, require a Level 5 evaluation. With an employee orientation program, however, a Level 2 or Level 3 evaluation is probably more than sufficient.

That said, most training efforts should at least be evaluated at Level 3—how participants apply what they have learned to their jobs. This is where most training evaluations fall apart. The process should be simple.

For example, before sending staff to a word processing course, an organization should first do a pre-evaluation identifying what workers know already and determining what they require to do their jobs more effectively (many learning professionals can assist with this aspect).

Once the training is complete, an organization can ensure that workers are utilizing the new skills through post-evaluation, coaching, productivity output measures, and actual tasks that require the use of the skills. This is Level 3.

Conducting training ROI analysis is not in itself a difficult process. The problem occurs when stakeholders want to see immediate results through obvious measures such as revenue or profitability. This process must take into account the benchmark process described earlier. It requires an organization to identify specifically what it wants to improve, determine the expected output, and be able to quantify the results in monetary terms. If the objective is to improve product quality, for example, the outcomes to measure would be a reduction in production defects, customer complaints, or product returns as a result of training's effectiveness.

Benchmarking such specific and tangible criteria, both before and after the training program, will build credibility for the learning strategy.

Achieving Proven Results and Returns from Training

Financial measurement is important, but should not be the only measure of training's impact on the organization. ROI data alone doesn't address other key business (Level 6) impacts, such as increased employee morale, better communication, or increased customer satisfaction. Nor will ROI data alone help improve training efforts so that they yield a higher ROI. And demonstrating a positive ROI does not necessarily mean that the organization is actually obtaining the right results or going in the right direction.

Training and employee development must be accountable to business results and strategically aligned. Simply providing training as a "solution" to a business problem will certainly result in failure. The same rules as with any other business investment apply to training. A systematic approach to researching, developing, and integrating a true learning strategy will provide measurable and proven results far beyond the standard measure of ROI.

Keep in mind that training is not appropriate for all situations. If it's decided that some type of learning initiative is the route to go, then determine who will require training and what the most effective way is to transfer this learning need. Always challenge preconceptions and groupthink. Don't be misled by what people may assume is needed, but focus on what is actually needed. Otherwise, all that effort will be useless.

Formulas for Evaluating Training

Although the Kirkpatrick model is effective in measuring the impact on business, managers regularly measure ROI based on a standard formula of business investment and expenditures similar to Phillips' Level 5. The formula is net benefits (realized monetary benefits minus total direct and indirect costs) divided by the total direct and indirect costs, expressed as a percentage.

Realized monetary benefits − Total direct/indirect costs/
Total direct and indirect costs × 100 = ROI%

There are two other formulas used in ROI measurement. One is a benefit/cost ratio (BCR), which is total training benefits divided by total training costs.

$$BCR = Total\ training\ benefits/Total\ training\ costs$$

The other formula is the payback period for training, which is the total training cost divided by total monthly benefits (the latter being total training benefits divided by 12).

$$Payback\ period = Total\ training\ cost/Total\ monthly\ benefits^{*}$$

For example, if a sales training program results in an increase of $60,000 in monetary benefit and the total cost was $10,000, the ROI would be 500 percent. In other words, for every $1 invested in training, the net benefit realized is $5 in revenue from additional sales. The BCR would be $6, and the payback period would be two months.

---

*Total monthly benefits = Total training benefits/12

Conclusion to Section Four

When it comes to the topic of measurement and evaluation, you have our full attention. This is our passion. When we speak on this topic at industry conferences, it is truly rewarding to key in on this one element that brings together the complete picture for the audience. We are more excited than they are when we are able to resolve their problems or help point them in the right direction.

For better and not for worse, measurement and evaluation of training is here to stay and will be playing an increasing role in the design, implementation, and execution for every learning initiative. It is also not just the responsibility of those specializing in this area, but it is now the responsibility of all learning professionals—from the instructional designer to the trainer—ensuring that proper results are attained and that quality feedback is provided.

We must begin treating investments in learning and performance just like every other investment made in an organization or company. Senior decision makers of organizations are fiscally responsible and must be accountable for the limited resources at their disposal. If we treat our investments in our learning initiatives with the same respect and expectations that other business leaders place on their investment decisions, we can then expect to be taken more seriously and considered as an integral part of the organization.

In Article 36, "Beyond ROI: To Boldly Go Where No Training Evaluation Has Gone Before," we said that the value of workplace learning and performance is more than simplifying it down to financial figures, such as return on investment. There are many ways to measure and evaluate the impact any learning initiative can have on the organization. What it comes down to is beginning with the strategic objectives of the organization and working back—linking learning objectives with immediate business concerns. By doing this you will easily determine the performance measures and metrics relevant to the need and satisfy senior management's preoccupation with operational performance and efficiency, compliance issues, organizational effectiveness, and workforce capacity and proficiency, as well as satisfy their need for more intangible dimensions such as motivation, innovation, and adaptability. Learning professionals must start thinking "outside of the course" and think in terms that connect with the business concerns and strategy objectives. This will facilitate the process of developing the right performance measures in a way that is inexpensive, relevant, and moves them beyond ROI.

The expectations of learning outcomes from those external to learning and performance are focused on business and strategic results. This means that learning professionals must link learning to performance. This is a theme we see growing in our profession and apparent in the contributions made by the industry experts in this field. From Tim Mooney and Robert Brinkeroff, Boyce Byerly, Holly Burkett, Toni Hodges DeTuncq,

Theresa Seagraves, Harold D. Stolovitch and Paul Flynn, the recurring theme is the need to connect our learning programs to business results.

One of the strategic tools of choice being quickly adopted by organizations of all sizes is the balanced scorecard (BSC) developed by Dr. Robert Kaplan and Dr. David Norton. This simple but effective tool helps to translates and implement corporate strategy throughout the organization. This is one of the first strategic tools to recognize the significant role learning plays within an organization. The BSC is widely acknowledged to have moved beyond its simple roots and is now seen as a strategic change management and performance measurement process. It is more than simply measuring return on investment of training; learning is now about connecting to *strategy*. More than ever, the chief competitive advantage for every organization is employees who not only understand strategic objectives but are able to attain them. This is where learning and performance must be strategic. Your role is to value workplace learning and performance in this context rather, than simply thinking of yourself in the traditional functional role.

The reality for the learning profession is that, in the eyes of those who allocate financial resources, we are simply another business investment. We must respond accordingly and, when we are asked to prove the value of what we do, we must be able to do it. Our measurement and evaluations must not stop at what participants gain from learning but show how what they learn delivers results to the organization as a whole. We must look past learners and become holistic and business savvy.

Measurement and Evaluation Resources

Forms and Worksheets on the Web

"Checklist for Training Analysis," from Article 39: Measure and
    Optimize Impact by W. Boyce Byerly

"Pilot Group Feedback Form," from Article 40: Formative Evaluation: Getting It Right the First Time by Donald L. Kirkey and Gary A. DePaul

"High-Level Design Checklist," from Article 40: Formative Evaluation: Getting It Right the First Time by Donald L. Kirkey and Gary A. DePaul

"The Object Map Template, " from Article 44: We Know We Got There by Toni Hodges DeTuncq

Further Reading on Measurement and Evaluation

We recommend several popular texts if you want to dive more deeply into formative evaluation. The Rothwell and Kazanas text below also includes additional checklists for formative evaluation on the CD-ROM that accompanies that book.

Dick, W., Carey, L., & Carey, J.O. (2005). *The systematic design of instruction* (6th ed.). Boston, MA: Allyn & Bacon.

Hodges, T.K. (2002). *Linking learning and performance: A practical guide to measuring learning and on-the-job performance.* Boston, MA: Butterworth Heinemann.

Phillips, J.J. (1997). *Return on investment in training and performance improvement programs.* Houston, TX: Gulf.

Phillips, J.J. (1997). *Handbook of training evaluation and measurement methods.* Houston, TX: Gulf.

Phillips, J.J., & Stone, R.D. (2002). *How to measure training results: A practical guide to tracking the six key indicators.* New York: McGraw-Hill.

Rothwell, W.J., & Kazanas, H.C. (2004). *Mastering the instructional design process: A systematic approach* (3rd ed.). San Francisco, CA: Pfeiffer.

Seagraves, T. (2004). *Quick! Show me your value.* Alexandria, VA: ASTD Press.

Shrock, S., Coscarelli, W. (2000). *Criterion-referenced test development.* Silver Spring, MD: ISPI.

Smith, P.L., & Ragan, T.J. (2005). *Instructional design* (3rd ed.). San Francisco, CA: Jossey-Bass.

SECTION FIVE

Professional Development

Introduction to Section Five

W e, as learning professionals, are quick to preach the value and virtue of having staff involved in continuous learning. We are also expected to maintain the skills of other professionals within our organizations and are sought after to provide the most current and innovative approaches to learning in the workplace. Many times, however, we are lax in our effort to maintain our level of knowledge and skills in being the best learning professionals for our organizations.

This section of the book focuses on the professional development of the learning professional or, in other words, your professional development. Professional development is our domain. To many, the term conjures up images of some type of obligation in a field of expertise or spending days in workshops and conferences. To others, it refers to a process in which one must work under supervision to gain or maintain professional stature and standing. In this section, professional development is viewed as an on going learning process in which learning professionals engage with experts in our profession to learn how best to develop their skills and abilities in becoming more effective learning professionals and be more equipped to meet the learning needs of their organizations and those that they are responsible for.

We know that learning is not a one-time opportunity, and neither is professional development a one-shot, one-size-fits-all event, but rather an evolving process of professional self-disclosure, reflection, and growth that yields the best results when sustained over time in communities of practice and when focused on job-embedded responsibilities. Promoting human capital development means not only developing a set of tools for evaluating potential and performance but also, above all, defining professional development paths in line with individual ambitions, motivations, and competencies. This is what the industry's leading experts in this section are passionate about.

But what is the impact of our professional development on our organizations? Like the employee development solutions that we are so passionate about, continually developing ourselves professionally delivers significant results for our employers. Moreover, the evolving nature of the workplace learning sector makes it essential that we be able to not only maintain our current abilities but strive to further advance ourselves through the innovative practices of the many new approaches we encounter in our profession, such as blended and e-learning opportunities and business and strategic acumen. We learn early that skill and knowledge development do not occur soley in a classroom, but around us all the time. This is also something that senior managers of an organization recognize. They expect us to play a major role in helping to stimulate creativity and innovation, which requires all learning professionals to be at their best and be at the forefront of the most current learning techniques while understanding organizational objectives.

Professional associations are responding to the need for continuous professional development and are striving to making the learning profession a recognized profession in the truest sense of the word. ASTD has put into place the Certified Professional in Learning and Performance (CPLP) professional development and accreditation certificate, CSTD (Canadian Society for Training and Development) has had in place for many years the Certified Training and Development Professional (CTDP). Governments are also requiring workplace learning professionals to become accredited. This is common in many European countries; however, the first and currently only jurisdiction in North America is in Canada in the province of Quebec. The Quebec ministry of employment requires that any company or any person whose primary purpose is to deliver learning solutions be accredited through the governmental certification process.

Whether it is voluntary or obligatory, the trend is clear—professional development of learning professionals is essential if we are to progress to be better than we are, meet expectations of our industry and employers, and contribute in the way we are expected to in developing innovative learning solutions relevant to our organizations.

The ten passionate articles that you will find in the workplace learning and performance chapter include:

48. What Makes a Good Trainer and Facilitator by Tom short
49. Lifelong Learning by Elaine Beich
50. Learn to Communicate in Business-Speak by Ajay M. Pangarkar and Teresa Kirkwood
51. The Trainer as a CAPABLE Leader by Dr. Vince Molinaro and Dr. David S. Weiss
52. Trusting Relationships in Learning by Dr. David S. Weiss
53. The Need for Personal Vision by K. Jayshankar
54. Ten Strategies for Building Successful Partnerships by Terrence L. Gargiulo

55. Developmental Assignments by Cynthia D. McCauley

56. Don't Fight the Future by Jane Bozarth

57. Five Ideas on How to Take Charge of Your Recharging by Terrence L. Gargiulo

Preview of Articles

Below is a brief preview of some of the interesting articles you find in this section:

One of our leading international contributors, Tom Short, asks the perennial question, "What Makes a Great Trainer and Facilitator?" Tom succinctly states that the ability to educate or develop other people is undoubtedly a highly rewarding and satisfying competency, but like many professional activities it carries special responsibilities, not least of which is an implicit duty to manage and lead the novice trainers. We all have vivid experiences of a bad schoolteacher, or can recall in great detail the key points from a really good training session, when the facilitator liberated us with a transformational learning experience. Professional trainers are passionate about their vocation and take personal development very seriously, constantly exploring new avenues and opportunities to make the learning interesting and authentic. But what makes a good trainer and how can professional facilitators maintain their effectiveness with adult learners? There are three important areas to consider: (1) Knowledge of how adults learn and adult learning principles; (2) technical knowledge appropriate to the learning program; and (3) contextual knowledge of the learners, their background, and prior learning.

Elaine Biech, one of our most recognized experts, is insistent that if you like being a trainer, don't stop there. Be a master trainer. Be a respected, knowledgeable trainer. Be a *successful* trainer. Be a *highly professional* trainer. Be all the things that you are capable of being. *Astound* yourself! She knows, and you know, that you have it in yourself to not become complacent of your abilities as a learning professional.

In our article "Getting Learning to Communicate in Business-Speak," based on our recent Pfeiffer book *Building Business Acumen for Trainers: Skills to Empower the Learning Function,* we stress the importance of learning professionals to be more involved with the business so that T&D not be an afterthought. Whatever direction an organization takes, one thing is certain, performance and accountability are the reality. As for the rest of the organization, they must leverage the role of learning to assist them in reaching their objectives. In the end, the message is simple: work together with one voice and for one goal.

Like most leaders in today's organizations, trainers and OD practitioners must attend to multiple priorities, make quick decisions, and implement initiatives at lightening speed. Dr. Molinaro and Dr. Weiss expect learning professionals to seize their role as leaders and to make a commitment to being a balanced role model in their organizations. By implementing their strategies of the CAPABLE personal leadership model, you will be able to lead in a more conscious and deliberate manner. Through the process, you will establish yourself as a strong and credible leader and better position yourself to bring value through learning to your organization.

Dr. Weiss continues to address the substantial value of building trust with a client in his article "Trusting Relationships in Learning." As he states, "The trust relationship contributes to meaningful continuous dialogue between the learning professional and the client. It allows you to communicate honestly about your issues and theirs, and to openly consider alternatives and make effective decisions. The necessary trusting relationship is then in motion that will be conducive to a long-term mutually beneficial learning relationship."

Our good friend and respected industry learning professional, K. Jayshankar, is passionate that his colleagues in the learning profession must possess a clear personal vision. He asks the essential question that we should all ask ourselves, "What is the personal vision that drives such professionals?" And do they ask themselves, "What is my personal vision?" Do they think of their position as just another job? Or is there a larger meaning they have derived from this chosen profession?. Read to see how he answers.

Terrence Gargiulo speaks to you about the ten strategies to help you to build strong and lasting internal business partnerships while maintaining and further developing key relationships. He continues to provide practical tips to help you to become re-energized with five ideas on how you need to take charge to recharging.

Cynthia McCauley points out that developing employees is more than having them participate in formal training activities. In her article, "Developmental Assignments," she points to the importance of formal programs, but explains that learning from work and life experiences is also critical and essential for effective performance.

Wise words are delivered to training professionals by Jane Bozarth in her article "Don't Fight the Future." Even though our field is filled with professionals who transfer learning to others and who are seen as "oracles," trainers tend to resist technology. She reminds us that we are not in the *classroom* business; we are in the *performance improvement* business.

What you are about to experience as you read the articles in this section is something we often take for granted and rarely give a second thought to. It is important to remember that we, as learning professionals, are learners first. It is the primary reason many of us entered and specialized in the learning sector. Although there are many important issues we need to address in our rapidly evolving learning environment, nothing is more relevant to our ability to continually learn and improve. This is what is expected from us, and it should also be what we expect from ourselves.

So read, read, and read some more! Don't stop at what is offered within these pages, but push yourself to become more than you are—continuously.

What Makes a Good Trainer and Facilitator

Tom Short

Passion

Getting off to a good start is a passion of mine! Here are some basics for the new learning professional and a refresher for you seasoned pros out there.

If you talk to any adult educator about job satisfaction, he or she will probably recall numerous examples of watching students conduct an effective training session for the very first time in front of a live peer group; in much the same way as a flying instructor observes a trainee pilot's first solo flight from the ground. For the trainee/trainer this achievement represents a *rite of passage* because it uniquely combines educational attainment, human qualities, and interpersonal communication skills—all carefully prepared for the enjoyment and benefit of the learners. Upon completion the student's renewed level of self-confidence, nervous relief and adrenalin filled excitement is infectious and most gratifying for the trainer.

The ability to educate or develop other people is undoubtedly a highly rewarding and satisfying competency, but like many professional activities it carries special responsibilities, not least of which is an implicit duty to manage and lead the novice trainers. We all have vivid experiences of a bad schoolteacher, or can recall in great detail the key points from a really good training session, when the facilitator liberated us with a transformational learning experience. Professional trainers are passionate about their vocation and take personal development very seriously, continually exploring new avenues and opportunities to make the learning interesting and authentic. But what makes a good trainer? How can professional facilitators maintain their effectiveness with adult learners? Experience indicates that this can be summed up in the simple equation:

$$EFFECTIVE\ TRAINER = (KNOWLEDGE + SKILLS + SYSTEMS) \times ATTITUDE$$

Appropriate Knowledge

Knowledge acquisition is thought to represent over two-thirds of the total learning process, and there are three important areas to consider:

1. Knowledge of how adults learn and adult learning principles
2. Technical knowledge appropriate to the learning program
3. Contextual knowledge of the learners, their background, and prior learning

1. How Adults Learn

Adult learning, often referred to as andragogy (Knowles, Holton, & Swanson, 2005), contains important but different principles to school-based learning (pedagogy) These are the building blocks of an effective training session and must be embedded into the trainer's planning and facilitation. Table 48.1 illustrates the key adult principles and associated theories on learning (Leonard, 2002). Then complete Learning Activity 48.1 to see how your training incorporates the adult learning principles.

Table 48.1. Key Principles of Adult Learning

The need to know	Adults need to know why they need to learn something before undertaking to learn it. They need to see the relevance of the learning.	COGNITIVISM
The learner's self-concept	Adults see themselves as responsible for their own decisions and lives. They like to be seen as and treated by others as being capable of self-direction. They enjoy autonomy.	HUMANISM
The role of experience	Adults bring breadth and quality of life experiences to a learning situation. These are rich resources. However, adults may have assumptions and biases that cause them to close their minds.	HUMANISM/ CONSTRUCTIVISM
Readiness to learn	Adults become ready to learn when they need to know. This helps them cope with real-life situations.	COGNITIVISM
Orientation to learning	Adults are life-centered to learning. Will the learning help them perform a task or deal with problems in real life?	CONSTRUCTIVISM/ BEHAVIORISM
Motivation	Adults are responsive to both external motivators (e.g. higher salary or promotion) are internal (e.g., desires, self-esteem, quality of life).	HUMANISM/ BEHAVIORISM

Learning Activity 48.1: Adult Learning Principles

 How could you apply adult learning principles in your training sessions? When you have finished with the chart below, compare your answers with those provided on the website.

Concept	Teaching Adults—Andragogy	Your Strategies
The need to know	Adults need to know why they need to learn something before undertaking to learn it. They need to see the relevance.	
The learner's self-concept	Adults see themselves as responsible for their own decisions and lives. They like to be seen as and treated by others as capable of self-direction.	
The role of experience	Adults bring breadth and quality of life experiences to a learning situation. These are rich resources. However, adults may have assumptions and biases that cause them to close their minds.	
Readiness to learn	Adults become ready to learn when they need to know. This is to help them cope with real-life situations (WIIFM).	
Orientation to learning	Adults are life centered to learning. Will it help them perform a task or deal with problems in life? They need learning that focuses on real-life situations.	
Motivation	Adults are responsive to both external motivators (e.g., higher wages, promotions) and the more potent motivators, which are internal (e.g., desires, self-esteem, quality of life).	

Learning Activity 48.1: Answers

Concept	Teaching Adults–Andragogy	Strategies
The need to know	Adults need to know why they need to learn something before undertaking to learn it. The need to see the relevance.	Identify a common problem or situation during the opening activity; Set the context for learning; Stress the benefits of taking part
The learner's self-concept	Adults see themselves as responsible for their own decisions and lives. They like to be seen and treated by others as being capable of self-direction.	Make the learning interactive; Recognize and acknowledge ideas; Encourage ownership for learning; Don't overstress formality/rules
The role of experience	Adults bring breadth and quality of life experiences to a learning situation. These are rich resources. However, adults may have assumptions and biases that cause them to close their minds.	Seek input from the learners; Compare and contract their ideas or experiences; Challenge the learners' assumptions; Accommodate diversity in the group
Readiness to learn	Adults become ready to learn when they need to know. This is to help them cope with real-life situations (WIIFM).	Identify learners' needs and desires; Stress what's in it for the learners; Build on pre-knowledge or experience
Orientation to learning	Adults are life cenetred to learning. Will it help them perform a task or deal with problems in life? They need learning that focused on real life situations.	Use life-centered metaphors or work-based examples; Parables and anecdotes help clarify complex points; Don't over-theorize or use too many conceptual models
Motivation	Adults are responsive to both external motivators (e.g., higher ages, promotion). The more potent motivators are internal (e.g., desires, self-esteem, quality of life).	Identify the learners motivation for attending the training session; Intrinsic motivation is often stronger than external factors; Maintain the learners self esteem and recognize achievement

2. Technical Knowledge

Effective trainers are totally familiar with the technical content of their sessions. This may seem obvious, but learners quickly detect any lack of subject knowledge, impacting adversely on the trainer's credibility. Ideally, the trainer should be a subject-matter expert (SME), but if this is not possible the following techniques help to acquiring knowledge:

- Prepare well in advance and do background research.
- Obtain comprehensive training notes from experienced tutors.
- Follow a pre-prepared session plan.
- Anticipate questions from the learners and prepare answers.
- Include group and syndicated activities to punctuate your session.
- Invite subject-matter experts or stakeholders as guest speakers.
- Sit in with an experienced trainer to learn the course.
- Use the knowledge and experience available within the learners.

3. Contextual Knowledge

Every training course will be subtlety different due to a number of variables such as the learners' prior experience, perceptions about the group, or simply the time of day. Therefore, take time to find out about the unique circumstances, or culture, of the learners and get to know their level of experience or expectations. This will enable you to facilitate the session in a proper context and to think of meaningful analogies and metaphors—adding interest and local relevance. Adult learners quickly can tell whether the trainer has taken time to learn their names, understand their unique backgrounds, and minimize irrelevant details. Contextualization should be done as part of the preparation and during the introductory stage of training sessions. The worksheet in Learning Activity 48.2 will help you with these concepts for your own training.

Learning Activity 48.2: Adding Context to Training Sessions

 Make a checklist of how you could add context to your training sessions and compare it with the example on the website for this book.

Number	Theme	Your Context
1	Big picture information	
2	Relating to previous session	
3	Relating to prior experience	
4	Recent history	
5	What will the learners gain from taking part	
6	Why the training is taking place	
7	How the training compares with other information	
8	Special conditions or consequences	
9	*Your example*	
10	*Your example*	

4. Leadership Skills

The leadership role of trainers cannot be overstated. Leadership is a complex subject, and much has been written about action-centered leadership (ACL), created by John Adair over thirty years ago. This model provides a valuable and sustainable framework for developing leadership skills in a training context (Adair, 1973; Oakland, 1999). Action-centered leadership is based on three interdependent themes; those of: (1) achieving the task, (2) building the team, and (3) developing individuals. In practical terms this means:

1. Achieving an agreed-on performance objective for the session
2. Ensuring the group learns from and support one another
3. Providing additional help for individuals with special needs.

The central challenge of ACL is to blend each theme simultaneously and not become blind to any one theme at the expense of the others. However, be aware that leadership is dynamic in nature, so a purist state of equilibrium may never be possible.

Study the leadership models below and complete the checklist on the website for this book and develop an action plan of how you can apply this to improve your leadership skills as a learner.

Learning Activity 48.3: Using Leadership Models in Training

Key Actions	Task Considerations	Team Considerations	Individual Considerations
Define the objective of the session	Identify the performance task, standard, and conditions	Hold meeting and share commitment with stakeholders	Clarify objectives; gain acceptance
Plan the session	Gather information and learning resources	Consider options; check resources	Consult; encourage ideas; develop suggestions; assess skills
	Decide on the learning content and plan the training session	Set learning priorities; establish timescales; identify standards	Allocate jobs; delegate activities; set achievement goals
Inform the learners	Clarify objectives with stakeholders and describe the session plan to learner	Explain decisions; listen to learners' feedback; anticipate and answer questions; enthuse the learners; check for understanding	
Monitor and support the learning	Formatively assess learning and check progress to plan	Coordinate activities; reconcile conflict	Advise and inform; assist/reassure; counsel learners
		Recognize effort	
Assess and evaluate the learning	Summarize progress; evaluate learning against the objectives; and recap if necessary	Recognize and gain from success and learn from mistakes	Appraise performance; assess competence; identify coaching
		Guide and train where appropriate and give praise and value contributions	

Adapted from Adair's leadership framework

5.   Communication Skills

Good interpersonal skills are vital for adult educators, and effective communication is central to the process of learning. Communication is about sending, receiving, and processing information so that training sessions should be designed to accommodate:

Learning preferences	Using a blend of visual, auditory, reading, and practical activities to accommodate different learning styles
Barriers to learning	The trainer taking personal responsibility to eliminate learning barriers, whether physical, emotional, organizational, or intellectual
Check the learning	Using a range of open questions, paraphrasing, a short quiz, a game, or group discussion to ensure that learning is taking place

How many barriers to communication can you identify? Complete the activity below and compare your answers with the answers on the website, which are also printed below.

Learning Activity 48.4: Barriers to Learning

 Consider the following twenty items and sort them into the following categories: Physical, Intellectual, Emotional, or Organizational. Each category should contain six items.

Excessive noise	Unclear explanations	Fearful	Access to restrooms
Poor visual aids	Lack of knowledge	Content too easy	Resentful
Hard seats	Lack of capability	No resources	Anger
Warm room	Note sequencing	Errors in handouts	Poor acoustics
Poorly written notes	Special diets	Bad photocopies	Insufficient demand
Frustration	Insufficient equipment	Boredom	Anxiety

Learning Activity 48.4: Solutions

Physical	Intellectual
• Excessive noise	• Lack of knowledge
• Poor acoustics	• Unclear explanations
• Hard seats	• Content too easy
• Insufficient equipment	• Poorly written notes
• Warm room	• Lack of capability
• Poor visual aids	• Insufficient demand
Emotional	**Organizational**
• Frustration	• No resources
• Anger	• Errors in handouts
• Fearful	• Note sequencing
• Resentful	• Access to restrooms
• Boredom	• Special diets
• Anxiety	• Bad photocopies

6. Facilitation Skills

Professional educators use a variety of facilitation techniques to deliver their messages, and the final choice will depend on a pre-evaluated combination of five factors. These are illustrated in the next activity.

a. Choice of learning session delivery
b. Degree of formality demanded by the circumstances
c. Level of practical participation by the learners
d. The size of the group
e. The learning paradigm

More learning sessions fail because of an inappropriate selection of the right facilitation technique, as shown in Table 48.2.

Table 48.2. Facilitation Techniques

Speech	Lecture	Instruction	Training	Coaching	Mentoring
Formal					Informal
Low Participation					High Participation
Group Learning					Individual Learning
Education-Centric		Skills-Based			Action Learning

Think about a recent training session and evaluate the style of facilitation. How did it match the chart in Table 48.2?

Learning Activity 48.5: Choice of Training Style

 Answer the following questions in relation to your choice of training delivery for each situation.

Number	Question	Your Answer
1	When would a speech format be appropriate	
2	How does a lecture format differ from a formal speech?	
3	When is an instructional training format appropriate?	
4	How does training differ from coaching?	
5	How does coaching a group differ from coaching an individual?	
6	What are the main characteristics of mentoring?	
7	What would influence the choice to adopt an informal style?	
8	What are the disadvantages of low participation among learners?	
9	When do you as a trainer consider individual training over a group session?	
10	What is the difference between an education-centric session and a skills-based training session?	

7. Defining the Learning Content

Education-based learning programs are typically structured around a curriculum, but training practitioners develop learning content. This can be directed toward a series of desired performance outcomes (behaviorism), achieving an understanding of concepts or facts (cognitivism), or building on the learners' experience through experimentation and discovery (constructivism) (Leonard, 2002). Whatever the desired outcome, a *map* or *content analysis* of the key areas should be developed well in advance of the training session. This will form the basis of a learning plan and ensure that appropriate resources are prepared and assembled.

8. Sequencing the Content

Sequencing the training content ensures that learners acquire and assimilate new knowledge in the most effective way. Arranging the content in small chunks allows learners to absorb and process information. There are several ways learning content can be sequenced:

- Simple to hard (developmental)
- Formal to informal (relational)
- Micro to macro (systematic)
- Local to global (contextual)
- Known to unknown (exploratory)
- Sequential steps (logical)

9. Scripting the Learning Content

Professional performers follow a pre-defined script and trainers are no exception. Well-prepared session plans enable facilitators to craft their learning content, take account of learning styles, punctuate the learning with activities, and especially important, repeat the session on another occasion with some level of consistency. Scripting should follow four simple segments:

- **Introduction:** To set the scene, build rapport, and explain the purpose
- **Delivery:** Passing on the knowledge and/or facilitation the acquisition of skills
- **Practice:** Assessing and testing the acquisition or practicing skills
- **Reflection:** Reviewing, summarizing, evaluating, and closing

10. Attitude

Finally we consider attitude, or more specifically the personal motivation of trainers toward their learners. This is an overarching critical factor to the whole process of learning. The best-planned learning sessions quickly fail when the trainer is not motivated and committed to the learning process. Try to avoid these pitfalls:

- **Self-fulfilling philosophy**: If you think you will have a bad experience . . . you probably will.
- **Failing to prepare:** Prepare to fail . . . your complacency will come back to haunt you.
- **Self-indulgence:** It's not about you . . . as a trainer you must give and be selfless.
- **Lack of awareness**: Reflect critically and constantly on your performance. Evaluate your training session from the learners' perspectives.

Conclusion

I hope this review has been useful for you. As seasoned professionals our roles call for us to be constantly learning and developing as individuals and as professionals. It is this imperative—and commitment on our part—that keeps excitement and challenge as a natural part of the job. Enjoy!

References

Adair, J. (1973). *Training for communications.* Aldershot, UK, Gower.

Knowles, M., Holton, E. F. & Swanson, R. A. (2005). *The adult learner* (6th ed.). Boston, MA: Butterworth Heinemann.

Leonard, D.C. (2002). *Learning theories A to Z.* Westport, CT: Greenwood Press.

Oakland, J. (1999). *Total organizational excellence: Achieving world-class performance.* Oxford, UK: Butterworth-Heinemann.

Article 49

Lifelong Learning

Elaine Biech

Passion

Thomas Edison said, "If we did all the things we are capable of, we would literally astound ourselves." To be a true model of success and professionalism, workplace learning and performance (WLP) professionals need to model the importance of lifelong learning. They need to learn continuously. Learning is paramount in order to achieve all that you are capable of—and to astound yourself.

I once read that most people achieve only one-third of their potential. Successful professionals in any position achieve much more than one-third of their potential because they continue to learn and grow. What do lifelong learners do?

- They assess where they are compared with where they want to be and determine a plan to go there.
- They improve their processes continuously. They identify new ways that are better and more efficient and implement them.
- They are on the cutting edge of their industry trends. They are aware of state-of-the-art practice as well as the fads of the day; have knowledge of the training gurus as well as their philosophies; and have knowledge of their professional organizations, journals, and newsletters that help keep them abreast of the field.
- They are "in the know" about their customers (internal and external). They keep up-to-date about all the things that are happening to their customers.

This means a lifetime of learning for anyone in the field of training and development. You have an obligation to your employer and your customers to improve your knowledge and skills continually. The rapid changes in the world today can turn today's expert into tomorrow's dolt if the person fails to keep up. How can you do it?

Take Stock and Take Action

Step back and take stock of where you are and where you want to be. Determine some measure of success, drive a stake in the ground, and head for it. You can establish measures that include both knowledge and skills. Next identify a developmental plan for continued growth. Consider several strategies.

Attend Learning Events

At a minimum, attend your professional organization's annual conference. It may be expensive, but you owe it to your clients to invest in yourself. I can think of no more enjoyable way to learn than to go to a great location, meet new people, renew past acquaintances, and attend sessions in which presenters discuss new ideas and approaches. You may very likely go home with a fistful of business cards belonging to others whom you can tap into to continue your learning.

To get the most out of your attendance, be sure to network. Don't sit on the sidelines or retreat to your room during breaks. You will not gain all the value that you can. Instead, go where the action is. Be the first to say hello. Introduce yourself to others and be interested in who is there. Identify common interests and experiences. Trade business cards. If the person has asked you for something or if you want to follow up after the conference, jot a note on the back of the business card as a reminder.

Attend Virtual Learning Events

My email box is filled with offers to "attend" webinars, teleconferences, and webcasts. Many are free, the rest have a small price tag. All will stimulate learning, produce knowledge, and encourage thinking.

Go Back to School

You may not need an M.B.A., but courses at the graduate level are critical. Take courses in finance, marketing, human performance technology, or organizational change. Take a class to bring yourself up to speed in the area of technology.

Ask Others

Ask for feedback from others on a regular basis. Ask for it from friends, colleagues, and participants. Ask your internal customers about their most pressing concerns. Although this is not related to you specifically, the learning may be fascinating, and this will enhance your relationship.

Join an Association or Group

One of the best ways to stay in touch with the field is to be an active member of your professional association. I often hear trainers say they "can't afford the dues." They have it all wrong. They "can't afford *not* to join!" Your ability to keep up with the profession is dependent on staying in touch. Affiliation with a national professional association or group is critical to maintain your professional awareness. Through the group, you will be kept informed of learning events. It is an investment in *you*. If you won't invest in you, who will?

Get Involved

Do more than just write a check for your annual association dues. In addition to attending the organization's annual conference, volunteer for a committee. You will be involved in the work of the profession, communicating with other professionals, and working with colleagues in your profession. It's an enjoyable way to continue to learn!

Network

Sometimes a professional organization will provide a networking list, designed to provide you with contacts in your geographic location. If not, form your own network. Networking is one of the best ways to continue to learn or, at the very least, to learn what you ought to learn!

Study on Your Own

Reading is one of my favorite methods of learning. Get on the mailing lists for the ASTD Press and Jossey-Bass/Pfeiffer to stay up-to-date on the most recent training and development publications. Subscribe to and read professional journals. Read general business magazines such as *Fortune, BusinessWeek,* or the *Harvard Business Review.* Read the same publications your customers read to keep yourself informed about the industry. Read the new, cutting-edge journals such as *Fast Company.* While working on another project, I learned that WLP professionals are voracious readers. Dana Robinson, for example, reads half a dozen journals each month, and Jack Phillips subscribes to almost forty publications.

Identify Resources

Visit your local technology training organization. Check out the classes they offer and other available resources they can lend you. Visit your local bookstore. Browse the shelves looking for trends in the industries you serve and business in general. Thumb through all new books about training to determine whether they should be on your bookshelf. Sign up for an online service. The World Wide Web is a dynamic source for professional development resources. Sites provide information as well as link you to other related sites. Sign up for newsletters and webzines in your particular field. *The New York Times* and your other favorite newspapers will deliver the headlines for each day to your computer if you subscribe.

Co-Train with Others

Training with a colleague is a unique way to learn from someone else in the profession. It allows you to observe someone else, elicit feedback, and learn from the experience of working together. Invite colleagues to observe you during a facilitating, consulting, or training situation. Ask them to observe specific things. Sit down afterward and listen to everything your colleagues say. Ask for suggestions.

Create Mentoring Opportunities

Meet with other professionals to discuss trends in the profession. Identify someone in the training field whom you would like as a mentor. Then ask the person if that would be possible. My mentor and I meet for breakfast four to six times each year. I pay for our meals. This has become the best $20 investment I've ever made. I'm investing in myself. Identify where the experts hang out. Then go there. Sometimes this is a related association or an informal group. More seasoned people and those with different experiences can offer you priceless advice.

Aspire to the Best You Can Be

Your participants and customers expect you to be on the leading edge. You have an obligation to them and to yourself to learn and grow. Learning is an ongoing process, even if you are at the top of your profession. Often it is what you learn *after* you know it all that counts!

Professional Delivery Standards

Establish standards for yourself that are high enough to keep you on your training toes and position a bar that encourages continual reaching. Guarantee that your training will be the highest quality your participants have ever experienced. Put quality ahead of everything else—you won't go wrong. Set your standards high and never compromise them. Quality: first, last, and everything in between.

Consider Certification

Certification or accreditation is available in many fields as a way of learning and achieving a professional standing in the profession in which you train. The accreditation could be related to your profession, such as a Certified Public Accountant (CPA) or a Certified Electrical Engineer (CEE). It could also relate to your specific training area, such as a Certified Professional in Learning and Performance (CPLP), Certified Training and Development Professional (CTDP), Certified Speaking Professional (CSP), International Coach Federation (ICF) Credential, Certified Professional Facilitator (CPF), or a Certified Management Consultant (CMC).

Check these websites for certification: go to www.nsaspeaker .org for a CSP; www.coachfederation.org for an ICF credential, www.imcusa.org for a CMC; www.iaf-world.org for a CPF; www .cstd.ca for a CTDP; or www.cplp.astd.org for a CPLP.

Improve Your Communication Skills

While last, this is certainly not least. The skill that goes awry the most often in any situation is communication. Your abilities to listen, observe, identify, summarize, and report objective information are important to be a productive trainer. Equally important are your abilities to persuade, offer empathy, solve problems, and coach others. Each of these and many other communication skills are requirements for a successful trainer. Constantly work at improving your communication skills.

Conclusion

If you like being a trainer, don't stop there. Be a master trainer. Be a respected, knowledgeable trainer. Be a *successful* trainer. Be a *highly professional* trainer. Be all the things that you are capable of being. *Astound* yourself!

Learn to Communicate in Business–Speak

Ajay M. Pangarkar, CTDP, and

Teresa Kirkwood, CTDP

Passion

We want to make sure that our business clients know that their investments pay off!

As investments in employee development increase, so to does the accountability of workplace learning professionals (WLP) to business leaders. Leaders expect to hear results in terms they understand and how learning contributed to business objectives. WLP professionals must be able to translate their knowledge of training into business terms and speak in the language of business.

Every investment in business must contribute directly to business and strategic objectives. Therefore, proposing to allocate money and resources to an activity not meeting this basic requirement would be unusual, although this appears to be the case for training in many organizations.

Despite endless promises about training becoming more accountable, a lot of work still needs to be done to link workplace learning and performance to strategic outcomes. The challenge to resolve this is two-fold.

First, learning professionals are coming to terms with their need for a better understanding of their relationships to the organizational strategy while being able to communicate learning outcomes in business terms.

Secondly, C-level managers must realign the learning function so that it is an integrated part of the strategic infrastructure. There are still too many executives resisting this change and too many learning professionals who aren't adequately equipped to deal with it.

Training and development departments must focus on two primary issues: managing internal tasks and spearheading workplace learning initiatives. These initiatives must be in line with organizational needs and help the entire organization integrate various learning activities into everyday business processes. This requires those responsible for training to have a proper understanding of business processes and their connection to other operational areas. To ensure that learning professionals become more effective and integrated in the business, three specific areas of knowledge are required: (1) an understanding of financial concepts, (2) developing lasting and result-oriented internal partnerships, and (3) communicating outcomes in business and strategic terms.

Understanding Financial Concepts

In the past, learning professionals were not called upon to be involved with or report financial requirements. They were hired, justifiably, for their training and employee development expertise.

Within your organization, these professionals are now being asked to a) report their results based on financial performance and b) to be accountable for their business needs. Even though they may not possess the skills themselves to deliver answers, it is the responsibility of senior management to ensure that their learning department acquires the necessary financial acumen to more effectively communicate with other business units while aligning with the strategic objectives. A good resource to develop your business and financial acumen is *Building Business Acumen for Trainers: Skills to Empower the Learning Function* (Gargiulo, Pangarkar, Kirkwood, & Buzel).

Developing Results–Oriented Internal Partnerships

It is important for C-level managers to step back and decide how they can take training out of the shadows. The first step is to have management and those responsible for training position T&D as a strategic asset for the organization. For example, one Fortune 500 organization (name remaining confidential) has become a leader in customer satisfaction and usability of their product. They did so by having employees become thoroughly knowledgeable of the consumer products. Employee development is constant, and regular knowledge testing is provided. The company's clients have been so satisfied for the last few years that this company is now seen as a leader not only in product innovation but in customer support and satisfaction. The results are clear from the increasing revenue growth and profitability, as well as product recognition and sales. The company continues to position its learning strategy alongside other common strategic parameters within their global plan. Training and development must develop strong relationships with its customers (other business units) to ensure that they understand their requirements and how everything fits together. Learning professionals must take on a leadership role with their customers to foster strategic discussions and innovative thoughts.

Communicating Outcomes in Business and Strategic Terms

Being understood by others is the primary objective. In business, however, communication is often more about speaking in the language that is understood by the receiver. But it is human nature to communicate in terms that we are knowledgeable about. Therefore, learning professionals tend to convey their outcomes in "learning" terms. Even though these may be impressive outcomes, the results may mean nothing to business people who receive them. These people are concerned with performance outcomes, more specifically, how their investment impacts financial, business, or strategic issues. Because of this, those responsible for learning initiatives must communicate results in performance terms the business people understand. A publication to help you develop these skills is Ulrich and Smallwood's *Why the Bottom-Line Isn't: How to Build Value Through People and Organization*.

It is also senior management's responsibility to open communication by supporting and integrating learning into the fabric of the organizational strategy. C-level managers are looking toward future performance and finding answers through non-financial performance measures. This is the strength of the learning function. Management must leverage the organizational balanced scorecard and connect the learning and innovation component to the rest of the organization and strategic direction. It is our role as training professionals to support management in doing just that.

Conclusion

If management truly believes that employees are the company's greatest asset, then it is critical that T&D not be an afterthought. In this article we have presented ideas on how learning professionals can increase management's confidence that our learning initiatives are driving performance and achieving accountability. We must see through their eyes and speak their language. In the end the message is simple: Work together with one voice and for one goal.

Reference

Gargiulo, T.L., Pangarkar, A.M., Kirkwood, T., & Buzel, T. (2007). *Building business acumen for trainers: Skills to empower the learning function.* San Francisco, CA: Pfeiffer.

Ulrich, D., & Smallwood, N. (2003). *Why the bottom-line isn't: How to build value through people and organization.* Hoboken, NJ: John Wiley & Sons.

The Trainer as a CAPABLE Leader

Dr. Vince Molinaro and Dr. David S. Weiss

Passion

Seize your role as a leader and make a commitment to being a balanced role model in your organization.

Like most leaders today, learning professionals model leadership in all that they do. They attend to multiple priorities, make quick decisions and implement initiatives at lightening speed. We believe that leaders in our field need to strengthen their "personal leadership." We define this as: How can we lead in a more deliberate and meaningful way? Taken from our CAPABLE Leader model, we practitioners can become more capable leaders by applying seven powerful strategies summarized in Figure 51.1 below."

Cultivate Credibility

Achieve Results

Practice Humility

Acquire Perspective

Build Leaders

Leverage Conversations

Exercise Balance

Figure 51.1. The CAPABLE Leader Model

The CAPABLE Leader Model

Cultivate Credibility

A leader in a large manufacturing company was known to say often, "At the end of the day, all we have is our credibility. Remember that you have to cultivate it and constantly work at it. If you ignore it or assume it is not important, then don't even bother to do your job, because you will not be effective."

The success of trainers, OD practitioners, and external consultants is largely based on personal credibility. This is something that won't just happen. It has to be made to happen and has to be cultivated with all relationships.

Training practitioners must also understand the importance personal credibility plays in their ability to influence key stakeholders inside and outside their organizations.

Credibility is cultivated when words and actions are congruent. The greater the distance between words and actions—the weaker the individual's credibility. Credibility is also cultivated when training practitioners represent the standard of strong, ethical behavior. This is particularly true for trainers and OD professionals. They need to be beyond reproach in their own ethical behavior and in the ethical guidance they provide others. While this is a tall order, it is a challenge they must take on.

Achieve Results

Truly successful training and organizational development practitioners achieve results. They understand that their key accountability is to drive results for their organizations, so they act as role models in delivering powerful business outcomes.

However, trainers and OD practitioners also help others achieve results. They do this when they help a dysfunctional team become stronger. They do it when they equip others with the skills and knowledge they need to perform better.

They also do it in the way they go about achieving results. In other words, they not only focus on getting the job done, but also on *how* to get the job done. For example, one successful OD practitioner ensured that she implemented all her projects in a way that modeled her organization's values.

Practice Humility

Another important strategy for CAPABLE leaders is to practice humility. The predominant model of leadership in organizations is often a style that is brash and brimming with arrogance and overconfidence. While confidence is critical to a leader's success, overconfidence that borders on personal arrogance can lead to ineffectiveness and potential derailment.

Humility is necessary for leadership today. It communicates that a leader does not have all the answers. This in turn fosters a culture of learning and sharing information. Learning professionals can demonstrate humility by not presenting themselves as experts to their clients. They can assume a beginner's mindset in seeking to gather all the facts before making a recommendation . . . by listening fully as their clients tell their stories.

One important way to practice humility is to be what we refer to as a "altruistic individuals." This means that individuals demonstrate an unselfish regard for the welfare of others, rather than being preoccupied with their own self-interests. It means giving credit to others for day-to-day successes. It also means leading and acting in the organization's best interests, rather than being self-absorbed with one's personal agenda.

Acquire Perspective

Too often, very successful leaders assume that they no longer need to learn and gain new ideas. CAPABLE personal leaders acquire a perspective that comes from a commitment to learning and to continually challenging themselves to see the world in new and different ways. They never are comfortable with how they have done things in the past. From this perspective, leaders and learning professionals can think more strategically and make more effective business decisions.

Build Leaders

The ability to build leaders is emerging as a new expectation of leadership. CAPABLE personal leaders work collectively throughout their organizations to build leaders—not just at the top but at all levels. CAPABLE personal leaders understand that the greatest reward a leader can provide people is to create opportunities for them to lead. Unfortunately, often domineering and over-controlling leaders minimize the opportunities for others to lead.

CAPABLE leaders try to build leaders at all levels by always searching for ways to allow their inner leadership potential to surface. For example, a trainer in a technology company made this his primary goal. Even though he led large corporate-wide training projects, he always managed to provide opportunities for others to lead and grow. He was so successful that employees competed with each other for opportunities to work with him.

Leverage Conversations

In the past, strong leaders were seen as "great communicators," able to communicate to the "masses" and motivate employees. Today, effective personal leadership is more a function of being a "great conversationalist." CAPABLE personal leaders leverage day-to-day conversations as a way to develop shared meaning with employees, peers, key stakeholders, and customers about critical business issues. Through conversation they align and engage people to their organizations' directions. The most effective conversations are mutual and interactive. There is give and take, questioning, sharing of information and ideas—and both parties are fully involved. Leaders do not dominate conversations; rather, they spend time asking good questions that encourage people to think deeply about what they are doing and to reflect on their actions. Good questions enable individuals to discover their own answers, thus developing self-responsibility and ownership for the results. CAPABLE leaders know that in today's organizations there is too much information and not enough understanding. This leads to distraction and ineffectiveness, so they consciously take the time to have meaningful conversations with others. CAPABLE learning professionals know that the quality of their conversations and relationships may be the make-it-or-break-it ingredient for their positions within an organization and in their learning initiatives.

Exercise Balance

Work/life balance is a fundamental personal leadership challenge. One senior leader described his life in the following manner: "The pressure is relentless. The pressure at work is unbelievable, and it doesn't stop when I get home. The moment

I open my front door, my kids rush out to greet me, and my second day begins. By the time I put the kids to sleep, I am usually exhausted. I watch a little TV and then go to bed, only to wake up six hours later to start all over again." CAPABLE personal leaders exercise balance because their long-term sustainable success is dependent on it.

The scenario described by the senior leader above is played out in the lives of many employees. Working in today's organizations does have its pressures. For one, everything is driven by speed and a constant sense of urgency. In one telecommunications company, the director of finance developed the habit of calling his executives at home late at night to discuss "urgent" business issues. Most people can also give personal examples of emails they have sent or received in the wee hours of the morning. Downtime and even "slack" aren't built into organizations, making it virtually impossible for leaders and employees to pause, meaningfully reflect on what they are doing, and renew their energy.

Personal balance leads to an emotional and intellectual steadiness. In other words, when leaders exercise balance, they are "steadier" as individuals—less likely to lose their composure. In essence, they demonstrate more effective personal leadership.

Make a commitment to being a balanced role model in your organization. Reflect balance in the way you design your training programs and OD interventions.

Conclusion

By implementing the strategies of our CAPABLE personal leadership model, you will be able to lead training and OD initiatives in a more conscious and deliberate manner. Through the process, you will establish yourself as a strong and credible leader and learning professional and better position yourself to bring value to your organization.

Article 52

Trusting Relationships in Learning

Dr. David S. Weiss

Passion

Trust is essential to all our relationships. I want to make sure clients feel safe to take risks and to learn.

Talented learning professionals know how to build trust. They excel at collaborating and influencing internal clients to embrace learning actively and willingly. But trust does not occur by accident. It results from delivering on assumptions and expectations through actual behavior. The behaviors are continually reinforced so that everyone's needs are met.

How do learning professionals build trust with clients? First, learning professionals need a full understanding of the characteristics of trust building and how to avoid the creation of mistrust. (See Figure 52.1.)

Trust is similar to a precious diamond that takes a long time to cut perfectly but one flaw can damage it permanently. Trust is a continuous challenge; one never arrives at full trust. As soon as one stops working at building trust, it can easily slip away. Mistrust, on the other hand, is easy to create, even unintentionally. Once mistrust is created, it is very difficult to regain trust once again.

> **Trust takes forever to build and a moment to destroy.**
> **Mistrust takes a moment to build and forever to destroy.**

Figure 52.1. Wise Saying

The Three Stages of Trust

Learning professionals who know how to foster and sustain trusting relationships intuitively utilize the three stages of trust to create deeper and more lasting relationships that can endure mishaps that may occur along the way. The three stages of trust are:

1. *Trust in your competence:* A client must have the confidence in the learning professional's competence to deliver the learning service. For example, if a training course is planned, the expectation is that the learning professional who is assigned the work has the skill to do the work or will ensure that it is done effectively.

2. *Trust in your honesty:* The trust in your "honesty" is built on the assumption that you are competent (Stage 1). Therefore, the question is not whether you are capable of

doing the work or of delivering the program. The trust stage of "honesty" reflects the expectation that you will do what you say you will do. Many times trust is broken due to unfulfilled promises to deliver commitments.

3. *Trust that if I am vulnerable you will not hurt me:* This stage of trust building is perhaps the greatest challenge for any relationship, including for learning professionals. Clients need to be able to trust that if they share information or expose their team to a learning experience that could make them vulnerable, the learning professional will be sensitive to the vulnerability and not misuse the information.

Let's consider an example to illustrate the three stages of trust in action:

A highly talented learning professional was asked by the VP of HR to lead the process of building the cross-functional leadership capabilities in an organization. The leaders in this organization were working diligently, but they focused only on their functional areas and not on what was needed for the entire organization. The leadership development program introduced all leaders to the complex challenges throughout the business and how they all needed to work together to build customer loyalty.

Initially, the learning professional wanted to influence the executives to support the cross-functional learning experience and to encourage the participation of their team leaders. He also wanted the executives to be active in the program as participants. The executives were concerned about participating in the training. They believed that they might intimidate other participants if they all attended a program at the same time, and some were concerned that they might compromise their credibility if the employees realized the executives also had problems working cross-functionally.

The executives expressed their concerns to the learning professional, who explained that the design of the program would address their concerns. No more than two executives would attend a session at one time so that the executives could blend into the program. In addition, each executive would have an executive role during the session to host the customer visits and to present the overall strategy of the business. In this way the executives could blend with the group and at the same time reinforce their leadership credibility.

The explanations and encouragement from the learning professional were effective to some extent. Two of the executives who had worked closely with him before agreed to attend the first session as participants. The other executives said they would prefer to wait and see the outcomes.

This case example is a good demonstration of the three stages of trust. All of the executives knew that the learning professional was competent as a designer and developer of leadership sessions. They did not question the content that he was proposing. They also trusted his diagnostic competence—that a session on cross-functional leadership was the right thing to do. This learning professional had the executives' trust in his competence.

The executives also trusted that the learning professional would follow through on his commitments in the leadership session. He had established his credibility with successful programs in the past. They believed that he would do what he said he would do. They trusted his honesty.

Still, not all of the executives were confident in the learning professional's ability to deliver on Stage 3 of trust—that "if the executive became vulnerable during the session, the learning professional would be there for them." The two executives who agreed to participate in the first session had a longstanding relationship with the learning professional that led them to feel secure that he would make the environment safe for them. The other executives were more concerned and had a "wait and see" attitude. They needed more time to have the confidence that they could have a Stage 3 trust relationship with the learning professional.

How to Repair a Relationship That Falls Out of Trust

When you lose the trust of a client, you must try to regain it very quickly. Mistakes with clients in high-trust relationships (Stage 3) often result in constructive and issue-based outcomes. In contrast, in lower-trust relationships, the smallest indiscretion, unfulfilled promise, break of confidence, or withheld information can result in an immediate break of trust. Mistrust that lingers builds in strength and becomes much more difficult to overcome. As soon as you see mistrust emerging, respond immediately.

You can fall out of trust due to two possible scenarios:

1. *A perception that is incorrect because of a misunderstanding:* When clients mistrust you based on a misunderstanding, your chances of persuading them to trust you are directly related to your previous trust relationship with them. If the trust relationship is strong (i.e., Stage 3), they will probably give you a chance to explain your interpretation of events and then consider rebuilding the trust. If you do not have a loyal trust relationship (i.e., Stage 1 or 2), they may see your attempts to defend yourself as a defensive reaction. That belief will only enhance the mistrust they may already have.

2. *An inappropriate action on the part of the learning professional:* Sometimes you may have acted inappropriately and deserve to fall out of trust. In these situations, the following actions are essential:

   - Admit your mistakes and take responsibility for what happened.
   - Be very honest with yourself when the skill required exceeds your competence.
   - Reestablish your agreement with the client about expectations you are confident you can fulfill, and deliver your promises competently.

Be Consistent Over the Long Run

The best way to build trust, although it takes much longer, is to consistently exceed expectations. Changing mistrust to trust by just promising to do better usually results in disbelief. Don't make promises until you have regained some credibility through changes in your behavior, and make sure you sustain the change over an extended period of time. Once your actions show that you have made a meaningful and enduring change, you can publicly commit to new expectations.

Conclusion

The return on investment of building trust with a client is substantial. The trust relationship contributes to meaningful, continuous dialogue between learning professionals and their clients. It allows them to communicate honestly about issues and to openly consider alternatives and make effective decisions. The necessary trusting relationship is then in place, and it will be conducive to a long-term, mutually beneficial learning relationship.

The Need for Personal Vision

K. Jayshankar

Passion

Life is a self-fulfilling prophecy! What personal vision have you created for yourself?

Jim Collins maintains that one of the most misunderstood concepts in management is the idea of a vision for business. Further, he believes that this is one of most important and fundamental concepts for building a great organization. Indeed, it is normal for consultants such as me to stress the need for clear vision when we begin a new assignment, as we remind managers that organizations need a clear vision to ensure that employees— and also vitally, the organization—not lose their way.

Yet, on various occasions I have found that, when I have spoken to employees and enquired what the company's vision is, I have received a variety of responses. Most of them have looked puzzled, a few had a naughty look on their face (the "Are you testing-me?" look), but barely a handful are ready with an explanation of what the company's vision is. Oh yes, most have seen the vision statement, as it is beautifully framed and displayed prominently all over the office premises, and in some cases the vision statement is printed on the rear of the individual's business card. The basic premise or ideas that underline the vision statement, however, continue to be vague and esoteric to most employees. They tend to consider "vision" to be part of the corporate PR rhetoric—not really meant to be taken seriously!

This confusion about vision is equally true when it comes to individuals, in particular, when it comes to learning and development professionals. Here knowing the organization's and their own vision is even more relevant. What is the personal vision that drives such professionals? Do they ask themselves, "What is my personal vision?" Do they think of their position as just another job? Or is there a larger meaning they have derived from this chosen profession? These are important questions.

I would strongly advocate that every professional in the learning and development arena define his or her personal vision. One's vision supplies the motivation to stay in this wonderful profession that we have chosen for ourselves—and to do the best possible job.

Let me share some personal thoughts. I have found that corporations across the globe are essentially similar in nature. Irrespective of the country of origin and the lines of business, companies are populated by people who believe that working there will enhance their lives and allow them to achieve through own and their families' goals. Most young employees start their careers very enthusiastically, with a voice inside them that urges them to boldly go forth and take on the world's challenges. As their careers progress, many begin to wonder whether they are really contributing meaningfully within their companies. Even when the company invests in their learning through multiple interventions, not all are convinced that they are progressing toward their personal goals as they would like. The lack of congruence between the organization's goals and their own goals may cause them to opt to find new avenues for themselves.

If this sounds like Frankl's (1959) thesis of "man's search for meaning," it is truly so. I believe that learning and development professionals play a significant part in helping all employees in an organization in their quest for finding "meaning" for themselves.

Having a vision helps us to overcome the daily bump and grind that often makes us want to give up. Caught in the inexorable routine of daily life, with the fast-paced demands of a changing work environment and the tussles of domesticity, it is easy to fall prey to negative vibes

So, in my chosen profession, I have shaped my professional life around a few beliefs? Let me offer you a few pointers:

- First is a basic thought. We all want to be more effective in our lives. I think our journeys as a human beings is a constant attempt to reinvent ourselves and achieve our dreams. I have found that all of us are looking for avenues for satisfying our personal quests—either through work or otherwise. We are searching constantly for the right answers to the challenges confronting us. And if we do not find the opportunities inside the company, then we are likely to seek avenues outside.

- An empowered individual can make a difference. Equipping employees with knowledge and skills and sustaining their positive outlook on life will provide multiple benefits to both employees and the organization. Therefore, I see my role as a learning and development professional as facilitating the process of creating empowered individuals.

- Facilitating learning may require going beyond the catalytic role. Personally, I have found it difficult to restrain myself when I am working with any group. There have been times when it has been necessary to be an activist and prod hard to wake people from their stupor and inertia to make them believe that they can contribute significantly to their organization. When someone is down in the dumps of resignation and believes that he or she is helpless in the face of a situation, it is necessary to be the active agent of change yourself and not just a wordsmith. Does that contradict conventional wisdom that advocates that a consultant be "objective" and dispassionate in transacting with clients? Yes, it may, but I think that personal passion compels one to step into the arena and take unconventional steps toward effective solutions.

- Your personal values will be tested. On the journey you have chosen, your values will be the only yardstick by which to judge the results of your actions. Staying close to your values will give you and inner peace of mind—the kind that we all seek. One of the most common challenges that learning and development professionals faces is the tension between long-term and short–run payoffs. However paradoxical it appears, they are inextricably aligned and linked. The question is whether you are genuinely committed to the right path, however arduous it becomes. Or will you set aside your values to suit the needs of the current situation? I have come to realize that there is no grey zone when it comes to values; it is an optical illusion!

- This is an ongoing journey. Learning and development professionals must be committed to their profession forever. This profession requires a dedication equivalent to that required in the medical profession. I must stress that yours is not a job that you complete and move on. It is more akin to a missionary's calling: you have to believe that you are contributing to developing more effective people and helping to create a better organization.

All this has convinced me that life is a self-fulfilling prophesy. My intrinsic faith in my profession fuels me with the passion to proceed with my assignments of transformation for my clients. If that seems a trifle over-stated, so be it. My faith that I can positively impact an individual and an organization enables me to seek out seemingly difficult assignments and drives me to successful completion. The vision that beckons me is to be the facilitator who empowers others through knowledge and skills and who helps them sustain their positive outlooks, enabling them to achieve their goals during their personal journeys.

Conclusion

If you too have chosen to be a learning and development professional, come and join me, sharing in this intensely exciting journey!

Reference

Frankl, V. (1959). *Man's search for meaning*. Boston, MA: Beacon Press.

Article 54

Ten Strategies for Building Successful Partnerships[*]

Terrence L. Gargiulo

Passion

Becoming adept at building partnerships is essential to your success and ongoing personal development as a professional in our field.

Here are ten ideas on how to begin building stronger partnerships today.

1. Seek to be an integral part of every functional area.
2. Be proactive.
3. Reduce administration.
4. Streamline standard offerings.
5. Get to the executive table.
6. Support partner activities.
7. Establish liaison roles.
8. Align T&D with corporate communications.
9. Celebrate successes.
10. Reinvent the partnership.

1. Seek to Be an Integral Part of Every Functional Area

Every functional area training and development (T&D) supports has its own set of business processes. We want our partners to view us as an essential resource so that we are invited to be principal contributors during strategic and tactical discussions. In other words, we want to be seen as an integral part of our partners' success. Two functional area business processes that stand out as prime candidates for our involvement are *strategic planning* and *project development*. Strategic planning varies greatly from one organization to the next; however, every functional area needs to set goals, lay out projects, and determine priorities.

We can contribute to strategic planning discussions in two main ways. First, when we have strong relationships with our partners, we can act as trusted, unbiased facilitators who lead the process and ensure that input from all the stakeholders is heard and taken into account. Second, we can articulate learning, performance, and communication activities to support the functional area's strategic plan. Why wait until a functional area comes to us for help? By that time it is frequently too late, and we may have lost the opportunity to understand the context of the challenges the area is facing. Our interventions will inevitable be more effective when we have more time, more information, and more influence.

Project planning is another opportunity for T&D. Every project in a functional area can be analyzed in terms of what role learning can play. If your organization has some sort of project management office and its project planning document template has a section dedicated to learning, don't make the mistake of assuming that section will act as a catalyst for functional areas and T&D to develop strong partnerships. It's a start and it certainly helps, but it's not enough. The goal is to have functional areas turn to T&D during the initial phases of their projects to ask for assistance with articulating a strategy for weaving learning into all areas of the project plan.

Our T&D mission of providing learning and performance solutions can be best accomplished when we are actively engaged by every functional area we support. We need their confidence. When we are perceived as an integral part of a functional area, we cease to be a "nice to have" resource and become a "must have" resource. When we are embraced as full-fledged partners, our contributions are an indispensable part of how work is done. We must do everything we possibly can to reach this position.

2. Be Proactive

One of the fastest ways to become an integral part of every functional area is to be proactive. Why wait for a request? Given your organization, how can you go out of your way to discover what people need? Simple gestures go a long way. For example, ask to be invited to some functional area meetings. Then go and listen. Absorb everything you can. This is usually not the time to offer ideas, but you will gain a wealth of insights. Use these insights to go back to key stakeholders in the functional area to ask further questions. The goal is to jump-start a dialogue and not to spout off ready-made solutions—even if you have them. Another good way to tactically execute the "be proactive" strategy is to spend more time conversing with people from the functional area. This seems such common sense, but ask yourself, when was the last time you planned and budgeted time in your schedule just to mingle with your customers, with no other goal in mind than to invest in relationships?

Being proactive takes imagination. Stop, think, and then act. Reflect on the current state of affairs of each customer. As you gather information, stay abreast of developments in each functional area so that you can anticipate what will be needed. As T&D professionals, we are like waiters in a first-class restaurant in which every need is met before customers even realize they had it. As in a restaurant, when this is done well, our customers will be unaware of our presence and the positive impact we are having on their work. Later on I'll discuss how to be sure our successes are recognized in order to win ongoing support for our work, but as we do our work it is best to be as unobtrusive as possible. There is no need to draw undue attention to ourselves. Our goal is to help our customers succeed and not seek accolades. Be sure your motivation is driven by an internal passion for excellence and supported by a strong, dedicated culture of service within the T&D department.

3. Reduce Administration

No one likes bureaucracy, but administration is necessary. Certain things must be done in order to manage and track our work; there really is no getting around it. However, how much do we really need? Can we streamline the ways our customers interface with us? And what can we do to reduce the amount of time and effort we spend on keeping our T&D shop running?

Learning management systems and other self-service systems have helped us automate some of the more routine but essential aspects of T&D. Although these are a step in the right direction, they are not enough. We need to do everything in our power to spend as little time on these things as we can. Administration shelters us from doing the real work of getting our hands messy in the unpredictable, unstable work of supporting our partners. When given the choice between uncertainty and predictability, there's no shame in admitting you favor work you've done before and know how to do. It's just not the principal way T&D adds value.

A certain percentage of our time is already occupied by organization-wide business processes that we cannot control. Therefore we should scrutinize every procedure, meeting, form, process, report, tool, and the like . . . that we institutionalize in T&D. Perform regular audits of these things, and ask each department member to offer feedback on which ones could be eliminated or simplified. Recognize that the need for these things changes over time. We all can do a much better job of purging the clutter of administrative tasks by getting rid of the ones that have outlasted their usefulness. Outsourcing certain administrative necessities might be another way of reducing them. Ask yourself this guiding question about each task: Is there any competitive business advantage to this administrative business process? If it doesn't offer any such advantage, it may be a good candidate for outsourcing. In my opinion there are very few, if any, business processes in T&D that give the organization a competitive advantage. Competitive advantage for a for-profit organization means adding to the bottom line, and for a non-profit organization it means furthering the organization's mission. T&D's ability to partner and to develop new learning and performance interventions is its competitive advantage.

4. Streamline Standard Offerings

In many organizations T&D provides a core of standard offerings. Although these courses may be necessary, they are only a small part of the value we can bring to the organization. We must evaluate what percentage of our time is spent in these routine activities. Because every organization is different, I cannot pin down the ideal percentage of time we should be spending on designing, delivering, and managing these standard courses. Each T&D department will have to take into account the size of its organization, number of its employees, industry it is in, culture of its organization, and a host of other factors. Suffice it to say, whatever percentage of time we spend on these activities, it should not get in the way of our being proactive, integral partners offering just-in-time learning and performance solutions to our customers.

Start by working with your partners to assess how many of the standard offerings are really necessary. How much does each one cost? How do your partners prioritize these offerings? Are there any trends or seasonal demands for these courses? Are there any other ways of delivering the learning and information contained in them (and I'm not talking just about turning them into e-learning courses)? Can you use outside vendors? Answer these types of questions with input from your partners. Our time is best used creating learning, performance, and communication solutions tied to our partners' organizational objectives and real-time needs. Minimize broad-stroke, cookie-cutter course offerings whenever possible. Be aggressive about it. As a general rule, our profession has been largely focused on these standard offerings. Times are different now. The future relevance of our profession is riding on our ability to transform ourselves into strategic partners.

5. Get to the Executive Table

Executive-level support of T&D facilitates our ability to effectively partner with our customers. I have highlighted the importance of building relationships at all levels, but the endorsement and commitment of executive-level management in particular makes our jobs easier. Although executive-level support is not enough in itself to build partnerships, it will open doors. New partners are far more likely to try working with us if we have strong, vocal allies in high places. Our challenge lies in getting on the bandwidth of and winning the respect of executive-level folks. If we do not already have their support, we will require a combination of tenacity, patience, and entrepreneurial spirit to acquire it. Start by identifying highly visible, large-scale projects for which training and development does not already have a role. Do your homework. Use whatever lines of communication are appropriate in your organization to offer concrete ideas about the ways T&D could help the project succeed. Work out your plan ahead of time, and involve key people in the project to be your sponsors.

Another path to the executive table is through others. Lots of little successes with our strong partners will generate goodwill and positive word of mouth throughout the organization. When influencing executive-level people, you do not need to be your own spokesperson. Often it's more effective to have others be your advocates. Remember, no matter how earnest and well-intentioned your efforts may be and no matter how brilliant your plan, there are no guarantees that you will gain executives' attention. Stay the course. Eventually, with some persistence and luck, you will earn your rightful place at the executive table.

6. Support Partner Activities

Our partners are involved in a multitude of organizational activities. We will not be directly involved in all these activities; however, many of them will provide us with opportunities to show our interest and support. It's a simple truth: people are more likely to support people who support them. Supporting others is a good way to strengthen our relationships and encourage a spirit of community. We have to be aware of our partners' activities and, without diverting too much time and energy from our major initiatives, find ways to demonstrate loyalty. If it is not always clear how to support your partners' other activities, ask them. It's likely that they will have some good ideas. Perhaps you can act as a sounding board, be a guinea pig, be an early adopter, or act as an advocate for what they are doing throughout the rest of the organization. Don't forget, however, that there may be political dimensions to supporting a partner's activities. So however we show support, it should take such dynamics into account. We wouldn't want to alienate another partner or different part of the organization. There are times to take a strong stance, but we have to be shrewd about avoiding turf wars or becoming unnecessarily involved in other people's political machinations. Besides, remember that our goal in supporting partner activities is to nurture our relationships. Here's a general rule of thumb: if our support creates more negative energy than positive energy, than we should find a different activity to support.

7. Establish Liaison Roles

Staying in sync with our partners requires a good communication strategy. Diplomacy offers us a good metaphor. Think of T&D as a diplomatic core and each functional area it supports as an embassy. We need to post an ambassador in each functional area. These ambassadors are people from our T&D team who act as trusted confidants and who are instrumental in building strong ties. They play a liaison role by shuttling information back and forth between T&D and its partners. These liaisons can also be influential in negotiating critical aspects of the partner relationship, such as priorities, strategic planning processes, project deliverables, and communication interfaces. It is their responsibility to know the pulse of T&D's partners. Treat this post as a rotating one. Select a term length that makes sense for your organization. In my experience, a year is a good length. Move people in and out of the role. You want as many of your people as possible to build relationships with your customers. Although in the short run this may appear to weaken or compromise the potential strength of these relationships, in the long run you are cultivating a greater number of relationships. This will serve to diversify the support you receive from your partners, increase the depth and diversity of your knowledge of them, and create more shared history with them. You also gain more perspectives, and you do not have to be concerned that a partnership will diminish if a key ambassador leaves the company. You want to avoid having to start again from square one.

8. Align T&D with Corporate Communications

Corporate communications has to be one of our closest allies. This functional area is an essential partner. From a philosophical point of view, communication and learning are inextricably connected. Without communication there is no learning.

Many learning and performance interventions look very much like communication strategies. The tools and processes of corporate communications are vital assets to us in T&D. Why reinvent the wheel when we can leverage the assets of corporate communications, particularly its ready-to-go infrastructure for reaching out to the organization? We have a wonderful opportunity to make sure communications are saturated with learning. In this way corporate communications benefits by having a partner who understands how to transform communication into learning.

If you do not have a strong relationship with corporate communications, make it one of your first priorities. As with any partnership, we need to learn the partner's cultural landscape. The individuals in corporate communications have a different way of viewing the world. We will benefit from a healthy dose of their perspective. They know how to grab people's attention and succinctly transmit information. People have even less time for digesting corporate communications than they do for traditional learning, so we have a lot to learn from this area. Start your efforts to make corporate communications a partner by making it a central part of T&D. Invite individuals in this area to be contributors. Seek their advice, and they will begin to do the same. Natural synergies will emerge. As each group becomes more aware of the other, there will be more and more opportunities for collaboration.

9. Celebrate Successes

Our success is our partner's success. When we celebrate our successes, we elevate our partners and generate a positive focal point for the entire organization. Because the work we do is achieved through collaboration, it is critical to exhibit public signs of appreciation and recognition of everyone's efforts. People are energized by celebrating achievements. Our partnerships will be strengthened by focusing on the positive. It also becomes easier to learn from experience and identify opportunities for improvement. Our partners are less likely to point fingers at us for aspects of a project that may not have gone as smoothly as everyone had hoped. Instead, we become better equipped to enter into a depersonalized dialogue during which accountability is not an issue because it is shared jointly. These dialogues are a wonderful way for us to grow in knowledge, increase effectiveness, and create opportunities to share lessons learned.

Celebrating successes allows us to bring visibility to T&D and reinforce our importance to the organization. If actions speak louder than words, then results speak volumes. The best way to sell T&D and encourage others to seek us as partners is to share stories that celebrate our successes. Let these stories be authentic ones. We are not in the business of advertising, and we do not need to hawk to persuade our partners to tell their stories of working with us in order to secure our role in the organization. Look for creative ways to build celebration into project methodologies. This is another good place for corporate communications to help us. Go beyond the obvious methods of sticking endorsements of courses on T&D's intranet site or in printed collaterals. As genuine as these endorsements may be, they fall into the category of advertising or "spinning." Everyone is saturated with such messages. By themselves they do not go far enough in promoting our value to the organization, and they do not enable our partners to celebrate success.

10. Reinvent the Partnership

The survival and continued relevancy of a partnership are contingent on our resolve to reinvent it. Partnerships are relationships. They are living, breathing entities that must be continually nurtured and renewed. If we are not constantly investing time, energy, and creativity into our partnerships and thinking about ways to improve them, they will become stale and irrelevant. By themselves, no processes, procedures, or even successes are going to permanently sustain a partnership. Staff changes, shifting priorities, and modifications of existing tools and processes or introductions of new ones are just a few of the sorts of things that can influence the characteristics and longevity of a partnership. Think of a partnership as possessing an almost infinite number of variations and configurations. Be guided by what is necessary and not by what is familiar. By treating partnerships as a two-way street rich in dialogue, we can discover new ways to optimize how we work with our partners. In this way the partnership will never exist as an end itself. It will always remain focused on bringing value to the organization.

Conclusion

Partnerships are not a luxury; they are a necessity in today's organizations. The complexities of contributing value-added learning and communication initiatives demand we move beyond the safe and known boundaries of our area and venture deep into the organization. These ten strategies are a starting point. Every organization has a unique set of cultural rules and norms that influence its dynamics. If you are sensitive to these and learn to pace with people in your organizations, you will be surprised at how quickly you will win a coveted seat at the strategy table.

Article 55

Developmental Assignments

Cynthia D. McCauley

Passion

Growing impatient waiting for the next great opportunity to build your leadership capacity? Look no further than your current job! With a little creativity, it can offer you plenty of ways to stretch and grow.

This is the message that human resource professionals should be delivering to the employees in their organizations. When an employee sets a developmental goal, don't just point the person toward training and development programs. Formal programs are important, but learning from work and life experiences is also critical.

Our research and experience at the Center for Creative Leadership have shown that successful leaders learn many of the skills and perspectives that contribute to their success from their job assignments. They also learn lessons from their non-work experiences—lessons that they apply back in the workplace. This is consistent with what we know about adult learning. Adults learn when their day-to-day responsibilities and challenges require it and when they have the opportunity to engage in experiences, draw lessons and insights from those experiences, and apply the new knowledge and skills to the next experience.

Ten Job Challenges

When are job assignments most developmental? When they stretch individuals, push them out of their comfort zones, and require them to think and act differently. These assignments place people in challenging situations full of problems to solve, dilemmas to resolve, obstacles to overcome, and choices to make under conditions of risk and uncertainty. Our research has identified ten key challenges—characteristics or features of assignments that stimulate learning. Encourage employees to seek these challenges:

1. *Unfamiliar Responsibilities* (handling responsibilities that are new or very different from previous ones). Taking on unfamiliar responsibilities provides an opportunity to practice new skills and expand one's knowledge base. It also helps employees learn how to operate effectively when they are early in a learning curve.
2. *New Directions* (starting something new or making strategic changes). Being responsible for new directions provides an opportunity to take initiative, explore and create, and organize people to make things happen. It also helps people learn how to operate in ambiguous situations and think strategically.

3. *Inherited Problems* (fixing problems created by someone else or that existed before the leader took the assignment). Inherited problems provides an opportunity to tackle problems, diagnose and understand root causes, and reenergize people. With this challenge, employees also can learn to make tough decisions and persevere in the face of adversity.

4. *Problems with Employees* (dealing with employees who lack adequate experience, are low-performing, or are resistant to change). Dealing with problematic employees provides an opportunity to deal with people problems, face and resolve conflict, and coach employees to higher levels of performance. It also provides an opportunity to learn to balance toughness with empathy.

5. *High Stakes* (managing work with tight deadlines, pressure from above, high visibility, and responsibility for critical decisions). High-stakes situations provide an opportunity to be decisive, work and learn at a fast pace, and have significant impact. They also help employees learn to work with those higher in the organization and to handle stress.

6. *Scope and Scale* (managing work that involves multiple functions, groups, locations, products, or services; or is large in sheer size). Managing scope and scale provides an opportunity to coordinate and integrate across groups, delegate to others, and create systems to monitor and track work. It also helps people become comfortable accomplishing tasks through others.

7. *External Pressure* (managing the interface with important groups outside the organization, such as customers, vendors, partners, unions, and regulatory agencies). Managing external pressure provides an opportunity to represent the organization, to influence and negotiate with external groups, and to build shared agendas among diverse groups. It also gives employees a chance to learn to build relationships with a wide variety of people.

8. *Influence Without Authority* (influencing peers, higher management, or other key people over whom one has no direct authority). Influencing without authority provides an opportunity to work across organizational boundaries, coordinate action across the organization, and handle internal politics. It helps employees develop a broader framework for understanding organizational issues.

9. *Work Across Cultures* (working with people from different cultures or with institutions in other countries). Working across cultures provides an opportunity to become more aware of one's own cultural biases, to adapt to different expectations, and to manage across distance. It also provides an opportunity to learn the traditions and values of people from different cultures.

10. *Work Group Diversity* (being responsible for the work of people of both genders and different racial and ethnic backgrounds). A diverse work group provides an opportunity to overcome stereotypes and biases and to persuade people from different backgrounds to work together. It also helps people learn to be compassionate and sensitive to the needs of others.

Strategies for Adding Challenge to Current Jobs

Although people may seek an entirely new job to gain new learning opportunities, job moves are infrequent, often outside the individual's control, and sometimes impractical. Adding challenge to a current job, that is, *development in place*, provides an alternative. Individuals can use the following three strategies to add challenges to their current jobs:

- *Reshape their jobs by adding new responsibilities on a more or less permanent basis.* There are a number of ways to go about doing this. Responsibilities can be moved from one person to another (e.g., from a boss to a direct report, from one colleague to another). Tasks that no one currently "owns" can become a recognized part of someone's job. For example, one employee saw the need for a liaison between her group and the finance department and worked with her boss to add this responsibility to her job. She gained new knowledge about finance and also learned from the challenge of *influencing without authority.* And finally, "new" responsibilities can be added by paying more attention to aspects of one's job that have been ignored in the past. For example, a manager had not spent much time coaching his *inexperienced subordinates,* although they were eager for him to do so. Making this a priority and devoting more time to it gave him the opportunity to hone his coaching skills.

- *Take on temporary assignments.* These are task or responsibilities that are bounded by time: projects, task forces, one-time events, and short-timeframe activities. For example, an R&D project is a great source of *new directions* challenges. Saving a client the organization is in danger of losing is an *inherited problems* challenge. Task forces are good sources for exposure to *unfamiliar responsibilities* and the challenge of *influencing without authority.* Temporarily taking on some of a colleague's work while he or she is on extended leave can be a source of *scope and scale.*

- *Seek challenge outside the workplace.* People can take on many different leadership responsibilities outside their places of employment in community, non-profit, religious, social, and professional organizations, as well as in their families. These settings often have the same challenges found in job settings. Chairing a fundraising event can expose a leader to *high stakes.* Participating in a service organization's efforts to build schools in a developing country provides the opportunity to *work across cultures.* Taking on the public relations role for a non-profit organization offers experience with *external pressure.*

Encourage employees to be creative in thinking about adding challenge to their current jobs. Ask co-workers and friends for suggestions. Seek input from the boss about what assignments might be particularly beneficial for the group.

Conclusion

When employees are creating development plans, make sure they utilize developmental assignments as one of their strategies for learning. One approach is for employees to intentionally add challenges to their current jobs that will broaden their experience bases. They should look at the ten challenges listed above and ask themselves, "Which of these challenges have I had the least exposure to? Are there some that I haven't experienced in a number of years?" A second approach is to add challenges that target the development of a particular competency (e.g., communication skills, adaptability, or strategic thinking). A key way to develop a targeted competency is to practice it in real-life settings. Perhaps the person can seek growth opportunities in a volunteer setting or as a non-profit board member. It is hard to develop new communication skills if you are never in situations that call for these skills. It's hard to become a more strategic thinker if your job calls for you to focus only on the day-to-day.

In closing, let me say that, whichever approach is taken to seek challenging assignments for development, development plans also must be built in support for learning from these assignments. How will the individual receive feedback on how well he or she is doing in the assignment? Will the individual keep a learning journal or set up structured time to talk with a colleague about what he or she is learning? Who can the individual rely on for coaching, advice, or encouragement? If you are in a management role, you can give that support or feedback. If you are an employee, make sure you ask for these essential ingredients for your success. Good luck!

References

Lombardo, M.M., & Eichinger, R.W. (1989). *Eighty-eight assignments for development in place.* Greensboro, NC: Center for Creative Leadership.

McCall, M.W., Jr., Lombardo, M.M., & Morrison, A.M. (1988). *The lessons of experience: How successful executives develop on the job.* San Francisco, CA: New Lexington Press.

McCauley, C.D. (2006). *Developmental assignments: Creating learning experiences without changing jobs.* Greensboro, NC: Center for Creative Leadership.

McCauley, C.D., Ohlott, P.O., & Ruderman, M.N. (1999). *Job challenge profile facilitator's guide: Learning from work experience.* San Francisco, CA: Jossey-Bass.

Ohlott, P.O. (2004). Job assignments. In C.D. McCauley & E. Van Velsor (Eds.), *The Center for Creative Leadership handbook of leadership development* (2nd ed., pp. 151–182). San Francisco, CA: Jossey-Bass.

Ruderman, M.N., & Ohlott, P.O. (2000). *Learning from life: Turning life's lessons into leadership experiences.* Greensboro, NC: Center for Creative Leadership.

Don't Fight the Future

Jane Bozarth, Ed.D.

Passion

Good trainers have nothing to fear from technology.

With the age of "e-learning" came the predictable nay-saying and resistance. Despite the many benefits e-learning can provide (delivery of just-in-time training, reduction in employee time away from work, consistent messaging, decreased expenses in terms of trainer time, travel, and classroom costs), it's no secret that many trainers are resisting, if not outright sabotaging, organizational efforts to adopt updated training delivery methods. Research tells us that resistance to technology on the part of trainers is grounded in their beliefs about practice as fixed, rather than evolving; their perception of their own roles as authority, expert, and "oracle," and their need for control ("*I'll* decide when it's time to go to lunch! *I'll* decide how to set up this room!").

But here's the rub: they probably aren't great trainers in the first place. They may be great *presenters*, but that's different. The resistant instructors overwhelmingly operate from a content-centered stance, believing it is their responsibility to deliver information, and the learner's responsibility to "get it." Instructors most successful in integrating new technologies? Those who see practice as evolving, who seek out professional growth activities and ideas (and then try to put them into practice), who are willing to experiment and make mistakes—and those who feel they are in partnership with their learners. Those trainers who find—or create—excitement in their work and find using new methods and technologies intellectually challenging—not problems, but opportunities. They aren't necessarily early adopters, or even pioneers, but they *are* explorers.

As an e-learning specialist, I receive two kinds of calls: the first, from trainers who want to learn more about e-learning: how to "do" it, how to make it engaging, how to get management on board, where to find good training for learning about it. The other kind of call is downright disturbing. It comes from trainers far more concerned with administrivia than with anyone learning anything: but how can we *track* it? How can we provide secure *testing*? How can we *make them finish* it? How can we get a system that will print *completion forms*? They see technology only as a way of replicating management of training tasks, not as a way of enhancing their own practice or outcomes for learners. In fact—gee, it's funny—they never even mention learners at all.

Marc Rosenberg, author of *e-Learning: Strategies for Delivering Knowledge in the Digital Age*, uses the analogy of the American railroad industry, crushed by the advent of superhighways and eighteen-wheeler trucks. The railroads, he says, failed because they defined themselves as being in the train business, not the transportation business. Likewise, the training profession may someday face a similar crisis. Trainers resisting technology would be well advised to remember that we are not in the *classroom* business. We are in the *performance improvement* business.

Training manager colleagues of mine formerly enmeshed in "change management strategies" for their training departments have finally thrown in the towel and are now simply hiring trainers who are willing to use technologies to extend their practice. So get on the technology train. Identify something that interests you, for instance, creating good visuals, or storyboarding for e-learning, or providing synchronous online training via a virtual classroom tool, and become good at it. Learn to use an authoring tool. Take an html class.

Conclusion

Trainers won't be replaced by technology. They'll be replaced by trainers who understand technology.

Article 57

Five Ideas on How to Take Charge of Your Recharging

Terrence L. Gargiulo

Passion

We are human, and we are bound to be tired and occasionally burned out. Accept these passing phases with grace. These are as real as the highs, and with some patience, care, and a little creative energy, we can bounce back to our optimum performing selves in no time at all.

I had been on the road four weeks straight. There was a queue of enthusiastic participants waiting to interact with me after a session and all I could think about was getting back to my room for a nap before dinner followed by an hour or two comatose in front of the TV. Not good. Given our charters as tireless and devoted trainers, I am sure you can empathize with my predicament. It's easy to burn out or get caught in a rut. It was time for me to take charge of recharging myself. I whipped out my yellow pad and did what every good trainer loves to do—brainstorm. Here are five of the ideas I came up with.

1. Watch Another Trainer

We all have distinct personalities and styles. It can be refreshing and insightful to watch another colleague at work. Be sure to drop your filter of comparison. The point is not to validate your techniques or affirm your worth as a trainer, but rather to bask in the energy and uniqueness of someone else. Make a point to acknowledge specific traits, characteristics, and techniques. Then resolve to try to incorporate some of what you observed in future sessions of your own.

2. Try Something New

How often do you try something new? Familiarity breeds comfort, predictability, and confidence, but a pearl would never be created without a good grain of sand. Trying new things in a session makes it exciting for us—puts us on edge. There is nothing like a little sense of the unknown to add spice to our sessions and rev up our energy. It could be as simple as explaining a concept in a new way, introducing a new workshop or exercise, or changing the order in which you present topics. Whatever you do is bound to alter the tried and true. The results are sure to surprise you.

3. Read a Book on Training

A book can vicariously transport our imaginations to new vistas. Leisurely strolling through the thoughts of an author opens our minds to new possibilities. Thought experiments lead to new behavior, and new behaviors can invigorate our sometimes-tired training routines. Recently, I have had a wonderful time making my way through, *Telling Ain't Training* by Harold Stolovitch. So call a colleague and see what he or she is reading or recommends. Retreat to the pages of a book and start recharging.

4. Tackle a New Topic

When was the last time you facilitated something totally new? In order to be effective trainers, we need to be versatile and relentless learners. Greet a new challenge head on. Even if a new topic will not be one of your core ones, it will still give you a boost. It may also give you fresh ideas or approaches to topics that you facilitate on a regular basis. I remember having to fill in for another trainer at the last minute. I was absolutely petrified. I had virtually no knowledge or experience facilitating workshops on problem solving and critical thinking. I dove right into the material; absorbing anything and everything I could get my hands on. In the process, I gained new confidence in my abilities as a facilitator, greater understanding of a new topic, and a whole new domain of knowledge that I was able to incorporate into my other workshops.

5. Rest

One of the most counter-intuitive lessons I had to learn as a competitive fencer was the importance of rest. I was driven to succeed and motivated to push myself as hard as I could.

Everything has a rhythm, and everything needs to be given the proper space to rebound and grow. In the long run, I did more harm than good if I continually pushed my muscles without building in time for rest and rejuvenation. Rest became a disciplined part of my training regimen and just as important as a workout. We are not always the makers of our schedules, nor do we always have the luxury of time, but be sure to find little ways to increase whatever little opportunity you have for rest.

Conclusion

Staying fresh is an important part of being on top of our game. If we are going to succeed in pushing others to embrace new things through learning, then we have to keep our skills sharp and vitalized.

Conclusion to Section Five

Our automatic assumption is often to ensure learning takes place in a unidirectional way, toward the participants we are involved with. By this assumption, we minimize is the importance of learning actually becoming bidirectional. To be more effective learning professionals, we must ensure that learning takes place within ourselves first—before we can go out and train others. This is the passion of the industry experts in this section.

Directly or indirectly, the contributors are asking the perennial question, "What makes a great learning professional?" The objective for those involved in learning is the ability to educate or develop other people. This is undoubtedly a highly rewarding and satisfying competency, but like many professional activities, it carries special responsibilities, not least of which is an implicit duty to manage and develop novice trainers—or rather to lead by example. We all have vivid experiences of a bad schoolteacher, or can recall in great detail the key points from a really good training session when the facilitator liberated us with a transformational learning experience. Professional trainers are passionate about their vocation and take personal development very seriously, continually exploring new avenues and opportunities to make the learning interesting and authentic. But what makes a good trainer? and How can professional facilitators maintain their effectiveness with adult learners? Three important areas must be considered: (1) a knowledge of how adults learn and adult learning principles; (2) the technical knowledge appropriate for the learning program; and (3) the contextual knowledge of the learners, their background, and their prior learning.

Your role is not to simply be a trainer, but to become a *master* trainer. Become a *successful* trainer. Become a *highly professional* trainer. Be all the things that you are capable of being and push yourself further than you believe you can reach. Strive to not become complacent about your abilities as a learning professional.

In Article 50, "Learn to Communicate in Business-Speak," based on our recently released book *Building Business Acumen for Trainers: Skills to Empower the Learning Function*, we stress the importance of learning professionals being more involved with the business so that T&D is not an afterthought. Whatever direction an organization takes, one thing is certain, performance and accountability are the reality. As for the rest of the organization, it must leverage the role of learning to assist them in reaching their objectives. In the end the message is simple: Work together with one voice and for one goal.

Like most leaders in today's organizations, trainers and OD practitioners must attend to multiple priorities, make quick decisions, and implement initiatives at lightening speed. All of the contributors expect learning professionals to take on leadership roles and make a commitment to becoming balanced role models in their organizations. By implementing the strategies of theses contributors, you will be able to lead in a more conscious and deliberate manner. Through the process, you will establish yourself as a strong and credible leader and better position yourself to bring value through learning to your organization.

As learning professionals we are encumbered with many responsibilities, one of which is that of designing and developing learning solutions. Naturally, your role to transfer learning onto others is the primary objective; however, many other skills come into play. To become truly effective, we must acquire the functional skills of business acumen, project management, organization, delegation, empowerment, and leadership. People depend on us as true enablers who will help to move them from where they are to where they need to be. Don't stop once you acquire the professional learning and developmental skills of our profession—it is even more important to maintain these skills. Just like athletes preparing for a championship event, we must continually push ourselves, developing abilities and strategies to become better than before.

The articles in this section are far from an exhaustive list of what we can offer. The responsibility lies solely in our hands. From this point, you must take the next step to create and execute your personal learning and development plan. As good as we may believe our abilities currently are, we know that we can strive to be even better. Strive to be better; strive to continually challenge yourself; strive to always be the best that you can be; and strive to assist in the development of colleagues in our profession—because you are responsible for ensuring that people receive the knowledge they require to improve and move forward.

Professional Development Resources

Forms and Worksheets on the Web

"Adult Learning Principles," from Article 48: What Makes a Good Trainer or Facilitator by Tom Short

"Adding Context to Training Sessions," from Article 48: What Makes a Good Trainer or Facilitator by Tom Short Learning Activity 48.1: Answers

"Using Leadership Models in Training," from Article 48: What Makes a Good Trainer or Facilitator by Tom Short

"Barriers to Learning," from Article 48: What Makes a Good Trainer or Facilitator by Tom Short Learning Activity 48.4: Solutions

"Choice of Training Style," from Article 48: What Makes a Good Trainer or Facilitator by Tom Short

Article's on the Web

Great Leaders Don't Aspire to Be Great Managers by Ajay M. Pangarkar, CTDP, and Teresa Kirkwood, CTDP

Further Reading on Professional Development

A guide to the project management body of knowledge. Newtown Square, PA: PMI Publishing. A basic reference for project management disciplines, with heavy emphasis on traditional PM.

Brache, A. (2002). *How organizations work.* New York: John Wiley & Sons. A roadmap for understanding organizations and how they work. Instructive for project managers who must determine how to create influence for their projects without formal authority.

Chin, G. (2004). *Agile project management: How to succeed in the face of changing project requirements.* New York: AMACOM. This book provides strategies for urgent projects that involve unique resources and elements of uncertainty. The book ties project management processes ore directly to the ever-changing requirements of business objectives.

Frame, J. (2002). *The new project management* (2nd ed.). San Francisco, CA: Jossey-Bass.

Gargiulo, T. (2006). *Building business acumen for trainers.* San Francisco, CA: Pfeiffer. Becoming a strategic partner within an organization requires a project manager to "think like the partners." This book creates a foundation in business practices and information.

Garton, C. (2004). *Fundamentals of technology project management.* Lewisville, TX: McPress Online LP.

Greer, M. (2001). *ID project management.* Englewood Cliffs, NJ: Educational Technology Publications. Tools and techniques for instructional designers and developers to help them manage projects. Heavy emphasis on traditional PM strategies.

Horine, G. (2005). *Absolute beginner's guide to project management.* Indianapolis, IN: Que Publishing. Insight, fundamentals, and techniques for managing projects successfully. Good for a beginner, or as a refresher for more experienced project managers.

Kerzner, H. (2003). *Project management: A systems approach to planning, scheduling, and controlling* (8th ed.). Hoboken, NJ: John Wiley & Sons. Coverage of the basic concepts and principles of project management, with all of the essential elements from organizational framework and structure to planning, controlling, and scheduling processes.

Knowles, M.S., Holton, E.F., & Swanson, R.A. (2005). *The adult learner: The definitive classic in adult education and human resource development.* Burlington MA, Elsevier.

Russell, L. (2000). *Project management for trainers: Stop "winging it" and get control of our training projects.* Alexandria, VA: ASTD. Practice advice and step-by-step approaches to help training and other workplace learning and performance professionals manage their training projects.

Wideman, R., & Dawson, R. (1992). *Project and program risk management: A guide to managing project risks and opportunities.* Philadelphia, PA: Project Management Inst. Publishing. A useful introduction to risk in the project or program environment, with a simplified understanding of the nature of project risk and a systematic approach to risk reduction.

Wurman, R. (2001). *Information anxiety 2.* Indianapolis, IN: Que Publishing. Rather than an information explosion, Wurman maintains that we have an explosion of data that fails to inform. Project managers need to be outstanding communicators, and this book provides insight into pitfalls and successes.

Wysocki, R. (2003). *Effective project management.* Indianapolis, IN: Que Publishing. Traditional project management theory, strategies, and applications. Expanded in the third edition to cover "adaptive" and "extreme" project management situations.

Index

A

Accountability
creating organizational training, 471–476
performance non-financial, 267–269
Action-centered leadership (ACL), 495–496
Adair, J., 495
ADDIE model, 82, 354
ALG Incorporated, 200
American Society for Training and Development (ASTD), 75, 261, 296, 485
Apathy (or amotivation), 177–178
Apple Inc., 250
Archimedes, 278, 283
Aristotle, 219
Arthur, W., Jr., 434
Articulation and reflection loops, 114–115*fig*
ASTD (American Society for Training and Development), 75, 261, 296, 485
ASTD International Conference, 201
ASTD Press, 506
Attention span
average, 146–147
emotion as extending the, 219–221*fig*
Methods Variety Scale to maintain, 147–149
Attitude of trainers, 501

Attribution theory, 18
Attributional biases, 18–19
Audience
as design consideration, 40, 41–43
identifying problem/learning objectives of, 40–41
See also Learners; Participants
Audio expert performance, 108–110
Authentic learning settings, 110–112*fig*
Autograph (game), 122–123
Automotive dealership training case
background information on, 435–436
follow-up to training in, 440–442
lessons learned from, 442
steps and process of, 436–439*fig*
systematic analysis used for ROI calculation, 439–440*fig*
Autonomy/control, 171

B

Balanced scorecard (BSC)
BSC Interdependency Diagram, 378–379*fig*
business impact measured by, 367–369, 368*fig*
described, 329, 361, 372–375, 479
four business and strategic areas of, 373–374*fig*
growing need for, 375–377

linking learning strategy to, 381*fig*–382
Balanchine, G., 120
Barbazette, J., 141
Behavior
consequences of, 172–174
reward systems for desired, 171–172
Bell Canada Enterprises, 271–273*fig*
Bell, S. T., 434
Bennett, W., Jr., 434
Biech, E., 486, 503
Blaming
attributional biases leading to, 18–19
avoiding questions of, 15
Blended learning strategies
using articulation and reflection loops, 114–115*fig*
using experts as coaching narrators, 110
mental models, "rules of thumb," and process controls, 113–114*fig*
modeling expert performance, 108–110
scaffolding, 115–117
situate learning and performance in authentic settings, 110–112*fig*
Bordonaro, F. P., 11, 97, 307
Bordonaro, S. D., 11, 97

Bozarth, J., 10, 35, 488, 555
Brinkerhoff, R. O., 254, 319, 356, 385, 478
Building Business Acumen for Trainers: Skills to Empower the Learning Function (Gargiulo, Pangarkar, Kirkwood, & Buzel), 515
Buonarroti, M., 119
Burkett, H. K., 357, 421, 478
Burn out
  problem of, 559–560
  recharging strategies to fight, 560–562
Burns, J. M., 188
Business impact
  balanced scorecard (BSC) on, 329, 361, 367–369, 368*fig*
  fostering learning culture for, 365–366
  measuring leadership training, 416–417
  metrics on, 364–365
  moving beyond ROI to, 363–364
  See also Kirkpatrick's four levels of evaluation
Business objectives
  mapping, 47–49, 451*t*–452*t*
  measuring against the, 446
  measuring of the, 446–447
  See also Learning objectives; Performance objectives
Business value. *See* Value proposition
BusinessWeek, 507
Buzel, T., 513
Byerly, W. B., 356, 391, 478

C

Camerson, J., 217
Canadian Society for Training and Development (CSTD), 485
CAPABLE Leader model, 517–522, 518*fig*
Carey, J. O., 406
Carey, L., 406
Carroll, J. M., 279
Celebrating successes, 544–545

Center for Creative Leadership, 548
Certification, 508–509
Certified Electrical Engineer (CEE), 509
Certified Management Consultant (CMC), 509
Certified Professional in Learning and Performance (CPLP), 485, 509
Certified Public Accountant (CPA), 509
Certified Training and Development Professional (CTDP), 485, 509
Champions (game), 121–122
Change. *See* Organizational change
Checklist for Training Analysis, 398*e*–399*e*
Cilliers, P., 85
Clark, R. E., 434
CLO (magazine), 337
CMC (Certified Management Consultant), 509
Co-facilitation
  benefits of, 210
  potential pitfalls of, 210–211
  proven strategies of, 212–215
  Strategies Checklist for, 215*e*–216*e*
Co-facilitation strategies
  1: prepare for your session, 212, 215*e*
  2: create synergy in the classroom, 212–214, 215*e*–216*e*
  3: debrief after the session, 214–215, 216*e*
Co-training, 507
Cognitive instructional design model, 31, 32*t*–33
Collins, J., 529
Communication
  aligning T&D with corporate, 543–544
  of business and strategic outcomes, 514
  of business value, 455–462
  CAPABLE Leader model on leveraging conversations and, 521

developing results-oriented partnerships through, 513–514
  of organizational vision, 425–426
  through stories, 229–234
  understanding financial concepts enough for, 512–513
Communication skills
  improving your, 509
  of trainers, 497–498
Competence, 170–171
Content
  available resources for, 189
  defining the learning, 500
  effectiveness and quality issues of, 98
  gathering/translating into instruction design, 193
  learning objects of e-content, 98–104
  learning strategies matching, 27*t*
  managing learning events and, 263–264
  scripting the learning, 500–501
  sequencing the, 500
Context
  adding training sessions, 495
  instructional design in, 83–85
  value of relevant, 459–460
Contextual knowledge, 494–495
Control/autonomy, 171
Coscarelli, W., 449
Cost of training, 345–346, 394
CPF (Credential, Certified Professional Facilitator), 509
CPLP (Certified Professional in Learning and Performance), 485, 509
Credential, Certified Professional Facilitator (CPF), 509
Credibility
  CAPABLE Leader model on cultivating, 518–519
  created with senior management, 319–325
  trainer establishment of, 158–160
Csikszentmihalyi, M., 83

CSTD (Canadian Society for Training and Development), 485
CTDP (Certified Training and Development Professional), 485, 509
Cultural differences
    as job challenge, 550
    leadership development sensitivity to, 291
Culture (learning), 365–366

D

De Mille, C., 8
Deci, E. L., 168, 169, 173, 177, 179
Declarative knowledge, 30, 31*t*
Delivering training resources, 206–207, 243–244, 297
DePaul, G. A., 357, 401
Design. *See* Instructional design
Designing Powerful Training (Milano & Ullius), 90
DeTuncq, T. H., 10, 45, 358, 445, 478
Dewey, J., 281
Dick, W., 406
Discovery learning approach, 281–282
Diversity issues, 550
Drucker, P., 369, 408

E

E-Learning: Strategies for Delivering Knowledge in the Digital Age (Rosenberg), 556
E-learning
    trainer resistance to, 556–557
    training through, 556
    See also Learning
Edens, P. S., 434
Edison, T., 503
Editing instructional design, 407–408
Einstein, A., 327
Emotions
    attention created through, 219–221
    entertainment as creating, 224

using stories to validate/transform, 231–232
validating people's, 237–238
Employee turnover
    "rifle shot" approach to solving problem of, 310–311
    ROI effected by, 308–309
    ten touch points to stifle, 311–317
Employee turnover touch points
    1: pre-source talent, 311–312
    2: source talent, 312
    3: refine the candidate pool (screening out), 312–313
    4: select (screen in), 313
    5: support orientation/on-boarding, 313–314
    6: manage performance, 314–315
    7: provide career development, 315
    8: provide feedback and guidance, 315–316
    9: plan for succession, 316–317
    10: outplace, 317
Employees
    cultural differences of, 291, 550
    developmental job assignments given to, 547–553
    empowering your, 261
    learning opportunities for, 258–259
    turnover of, 307–317
    See also Participants
Endicott, J., 107
Evaluation
    formative, 401–411
    measuring impact of leadership training, 413–419
    overarching purpose of, 388–390
    Phillips' ROI model for, 415, 436, 442, 472–476
    typical mistakes made in training, 386–387
    See also Kirkpatrick's four levels of evaluation; Needs assessment; Outcomes
Executive reviews, 403

Experiential training
    discovery learning approach to, 281–282
    stages of, 282–283
Experts. *See* SMEs (subject-matter experts)
Exploratory assessment questions, 15–16, 17
External motivation, 176*fig*, 177*fig*
Extrinsic motivation, 176*fig*, 177*fig*, 179–180

F

Facilitation skills, 498–499
Fast Company (journal), 507
Feedback
    lifelong learning through continuous, 505
    pilot testing, 409*e*–410*e*
    preventing employee turnover by providing, 315–316
Financial value
    overview of, 457*fig*, 458–459
    translating performance into, 460–461
    understanding concepts of, 512–513
    See also Value proposition
Flynn, P., 358, 433, 479
Ford, J. K., 434
"The Forklifts" needs assessment case
    background information on, 14–15
    exploratory judgment question, 10
    judging and blaming questions of, 15
    "mirroring" phase used in, 10
Formative evaluation
    overview of, 401–403
    tools and techniques used for, 403–410*e*
Fortune (magazine), 507
Foshay, W. R., 9–10, 29
4Ps, 83
Frankl**, 531

Front-end analysis (FEA)
    description and benefits, 73–74
    evaluation of, 75
    implementation planning for, 74
    recommendations for conducting,
        75–79
Funnel of Nurnberg image,
    279–281

G
Games
    Autograph, 122–123
    Champions, 121–122
    process of creating learning,
        120–121
    RAT Race, 124–125
    Scavenger Bingo, 123–124
Gardners, H., 303
Gardner's multiple intelligences, 303
Gargiulo, T. L., 157, 203, 227, 235,
    487, 513, 535, 559
Gates, B., 387
Geneen, H., 299
General Electric (GE), 250, 314
Gilmore, J., 84
Google, 250
Greenspan, A., 295
Group pools, 238

H
Harvard Business Review, 507
Hegg, B., 200, 201
"HELLO" game, 186
Hermman-Nehdi, A., 254, 299
High-Level Design Checklist,
    404e–405e
Hinkin, T., 308
Hodges, T. K., 47, 449
Holton**, 491
Honebein, P. C., 11, 81
Humility, 519–520

I
IBM Watson Research Center exper-
    iment, 280–281
ICF (International Coach
    Federation), 509

Influencing without authority,
    550, 551
Institute of Management
    Accountants (IMA), 372
Instructional design
    audience of, 40–43
    brief history of, 82–83
    creating effective, efficient, engag-
        ing training through, 90–94
    e-learning, 556–557
    High-Level Design Checklist for,
        404e–405e
    instructional systems design
        (ISD), 53–69
    intrinsically motivating environ-
        ment for, 174–178, 184–193
    learning experiences as factor in,
        83–87
    reviews for, 403–404e
    stories used as part of, 228–234,
        289–290
    strategies for, 29–34
    taxonomy learning, 21–28
    typical premises of, 46
    See also Learning objects;
        Teaching
Instructional strategies design
    cognitive approach to, 30–31t
    model used for, 31–33
Instructional systems design (ISD)
    cognitive processes and
        approaches to, 62–63
    conducting content analysis,
        59–61
    conducting interviews, 57–59
    debate over, 53–54
    developmental testing for, 64–65
    needs analysis process of, 54–57t
    project management for, 65–68
    software training development
        for, 61–62
    SuperFrames used for, 63–64
Instructivism, 279–281
Instructor walk-throughs, 407
Internal motivation, 176fig, 177fig
Internalized training
    benefits of, 294–295

outcomes of, 297–298
    team building aspect of, 295–296
    trainer competencies required for,
        296–297
International Coach Federation
    (ICF), 509
International Telephone and
    Telegraph, 299–300
Intrinsic motivation, 176fig, 177fig,
    180–181, 185–190
Intrinsically motivating
    environment
    design flow example of, 191–193
    moving participants toward a,
        174–178
    principles and components of,
        185–190
    tips for implementing, 190–191
    when to create a, 184–185

J
Jackson, M., 401
Jayshankar, K., 487, 529
Job challenges
    strategies for adding, 550–552
    ten types of, 548–550
Jossey-Bass/Pfeiffer mailing list, 506
Jung, C., 219

K
Kane, H., 137, 151
Kaplan, R., 372, 378, 479
KFKD factor, 179–181
Kirkey, D. L., 357, 401, 442
Kirkpatrick, D. L., 415, 436, 472
Kirkpatrick's four levels of evaluation
    achieving results and returns
        using, 474–475
    formulas for evaluating training
        using, 475–476
    Level 3 (learning), 250, 251
    Level 4 (business impact), 363
    limitations of, 473–474
    ROI measurement in, 472–473
    use of, 415, 436, 442
    See also Business impact;
        Evaluation

Kirkwood, T., 3, 257, 265, 293, 327, 333, 355, 361, 371, 413, 471, 511, 513
Knowledge
  declarative, 30, 31*t*
  learning opportunities to develop employee, 260
  measuring participant application of, 416
  procedural, 30, 31*t*
  "work product recycling" examples of, 86–87
  See also Learning
"Knowledge Base" activity, 87
Knowledge-based measures, 449
Knowles, M., 92, 281, 491
KPIs (key performance indicators), 272, 273*fig*

L
Lamott, A., 179
Leadership
  action-centered leadership (ACL) model on trainer, 495–496
  CAPABLE Leader model on trainer, 517–522, 518*fig*
  humility required for, 519–520
  measuring impact of training on, 413–419
Leadership development
  CAPABLE Leader model on, 520–521
  eight steps to implementing integrated-solution approach to, 288–292
  integrated-solution approach to, 286*fig*, 287–288
  measuring impact of training on, 413–419
  multiple-solution approach to, 286*fig*–287
  prevalence of training used for, 414–415
  single-solution approach to, 286*fig*
  three "S's" (strategic, synergistic, sustainable) of, 288

Leadership lifecycle, 291
Leadership training impact
  implementing strategy for measuring, 418
  measuring impact of training on, 413–419
  measuring levels of, 415–418
Learner walk-throughs, 406–407
Learners
  concept applications by, 144–146
  concept development by, 144
  concept sharing by, 145–146
  learning activity participation by, 142–143
  learning activity reactions, 144–146
  meaning creating memory, 223*fig*
  motivating, 168–190, 530–531
  trainer attitude toward, 501
  See also Audience; Participants
Learnertainment
  chain of events in, 219–224
  learning benefits of, 225
  the learning "searchlight," 218–219
  origins of, 217–218
Learnertainment chain
  attention creating meaning, 221–222*fig*
  emotion as creating attention, 219–221*fig*
  entertainment creating emotion, 224
  meaning creating memory, 223*fig*
Learning
  authentic settings for, 110–112*fig*
  barriers to, 497–498
  connecting strategy to, 377–379*fig*
  creating sacred space for, 90–94
  differences between training and, 328–330
  discovery learning approach to, 281–282
  experiential, 281–283
  Funnel of Nurnberg image of, 279–281

key principles of adult, 491*t*
  Learnertainment approach to, 217–226
  leveraging employee's brains for accelerated, 305–306
  lifetime, 503–509
  measuring participant, 416
  proactive, 241–242
  trusting relationships in, 523–528
  See also E-learning; Knowledge; WLP (workplace learning and performance)
Learning activities
  adult learning principles applied to, 492–493
  on barriers to learning, 497–498
  choice of training styles, 499
  "HELLO" game, 186
  learner participation in, 142–143
  learner reactions to, 144–146
  "35," 187
  what, why, and how components of, 142
  "The World's Worst," 188
Learning culture, 365–366
Learning development strategies
  adopting special education techniques, 22–23
  blended, 107–117
  elements of basic, 261–262
  managing learning as, 262–263
  managing learning events and content as, 263–264
  managing performance as, 263
  matching content to, 27*t*
  matching learning objectives to multiple, 25*fig*–26*fig*, 27*t*
  for over-stimulated work environments, 23–24
  reorienting as, 262
  stories used as part of, 228–234, 289–290
  See also Teaching
Learning environments
  created with trust and vulnerability, 237

Learning environments (*Continued*)
  managing performance to
    create, 263
  motivating, 168–169, 171–179,
    184–193
Learning events
  attending, 504–505
  attending virtual, 505
Learning experiences
  emergence technique to create,
    85–87
  instructional design in context of,
    83–85
Learning objectives
  as design factor, 40–41
  example of sales/customer service
    training, 50*t*–51*t*
  examples of business, 47*t*
  examples of enablers and barriers
    for, 49*t*, 52
  mapping, 47–49, 451*t*–452*t*
  matching learning strategies to,
    25*fig*–26*fig*, 27*t*
  measuring, 449–450
  objective mapping, 47–49
  process controls for organizing,
    113–114*fig*
  workshop, 153–154
  See also Business objectives;
    Performance objectives
Learning objects
  assess component of, 102–104
  do component of, 100–101
  review component of, 101–102
  show component of, 99–100
  structural view of, 98–99, 105
  tell component of, 99
  See also Instructional design
Learning opportunities
  developing your people's knowl-
    edge through, 260
  employee competencies/
    technology leading to,
    258–259
  holistic approach to, 259
  management focus leading to,
    260–261

Learning organizations
  advantages of, 330–331
  how to become a, 331–333
Learning styles
  adopting special education
    techniques to fit, 22–23
  assumption of unique, 22
  considerations model on,
    302–304*fig*
Leonard, D. C., 500
Lifetime learning
  actions to facilitate, 504–508
  professional standards facilitating,
    508–509
Life/work balance, 521–522
"Line of sight," 324*fig*

M

Management
  creating credibility with,
    158–160, 319–325, 518–519
  getting aligned with "line of
    sight," 324*fig*
  managing training conversations
    with, 36–38, 321–325
  misbegotten training requests
    by, 36
  partnerships between trainers and,
    513–514, 535–545
  selling worth of training and devel-
    opment (T&D) to, 336–346
  selling your worth as trainer to,
    433–442
  See also Organizations; Senior
    management
Management reviews, 403
Marquardt, M., 201
Marrapodi, J., 10, 39
McCauley, C. D., 488, 547
Meaning
  attention creating, 221–222
  memory created from, 225
Measurements/metrics
  accounting for all the factors in,
    396–397*fig*
  balanced scorecard (BSC), 329,
    361, 367–382

business impact, 364–365
business objectives, 446–447
Checklist for Training Analysis
  for, 398*e*–399*e*
choosing the right, 392–393
impact of leadership training,
  413–419
knowledge-based, 449
learning objectives, 449–450
managing perception of
  WLP, 461
non-financial performance,
  267–273
performance objectives, 447–449
performance-based, 449
presenting ROI results of,
  394–396*fig*
setting values for, 393–394
of time to proficiency, 463–469
of training's impact, 391–400
See also ROI (Return on
  Investment)
Meetings
  drawing up objectives for, 153
  eliciting/tracking input in relation
    to objectives, 153–154
  establishing the ground rules
    prior to agenda, 152
  importance of listening, 155–156
  keeping focused, 154–155
  organizing thoughts but remain-
    ing flexible, 154
  See also Training sessions
Memory
  long-term and short-term, 223
  meaning as creating, 223
  Methods Variety Scale to improve
    retention, 146–149
Mental models, 113
Mentoring opportunities, 508
Mercier, L., 217
Methods Variety Scale, 146–149
Mezirow, J., 281
Mickelson, T., 200, 201
Microsoft, 250, 387
Milano, M., 11, 89, 90
Millbower, L., 139, 217

Modeling expert performance, 108–110

Molinaro, V., 138, 209, 285, 487, 517

Mooney, T. P., 254, 256, 319, 385, 478

Motivating environments
importance of creating, 168–169
intrinsically, 174–178, 184–193
rewarding desired behavior to create, 171–172
rewards, punishment, and other factors of, 178–179

Motivation
extrinsic, 176fig, 177fig, 179–180
guilt, ego, "should," and KFKD factors, 179–181
internal and external, 176fig, 177fig
intrinsic, 176fig, 177fig, 180–181, 185–190
introduction to, 169–171
rewarding for, 172–174
value proposition to encourage, 174–178
vision as supplying, 530–531

Multiple intelligences notion, 303

Murray, R., 138, 203

Murray—co-author, 139

N

Needs assessment
exploratory questions for, 15–16, 17
five principles for conducting, 17–19
"The Forklifts" case example of, 14–15
See also Evaluation

Networking activities, 506

The New York Times (newspaper), 507

Non-financial performance measures
accountability through, 267–269
Bell Canada Enterprises use of, 271–273fig
limitations of, 270–273

Norton, D., 372, 378, 479

The Nurnberg Funnel (Carroll), 279

O

Objective mapping
example of training, 451t–452t
overview of, 47–49

Objectives
business, 47–49, 446–447, 451t–452t
performance, 447–449
See also Learning objectives

Once Upon a Time: Using Story-Based Activities to Develop Breakthrough Communication Skills (Gargiulo), 139, 234

Organizational change
breakdown of training for, 279
"discovery learning" approach to, 281–282
experiential learning application to, 282–283
importance of, 278–279
instructivism and the Nurnberg funnel, 279–281
transitional planning for, 421–431

Organizations
capturing learning opportunities within, 257–264
creating training accountability of, 471–476
driving forces behind achieving change in, 277–283
fostering learning culture in, 365–366
leadership development by, 286fig–292
learning, 330–333
leveraging employee's brains for learning/performance, 305–306
See also Management

Outcomes
celebrating successful, 544–545
communicating business and strategic, 514

internalized training, 297–298
presenting ROI metric, 394–396fig
See also Evaluation; Results

P

Palmer, P. J., 89

Pamela syndrome, 71–72

Pangarkar, A. M., 3, 257, 265, 293, 327, 333, 355, 371, 413, 471, 511, 513

Participants
attention span of, 146–149, 219–221fig
"call on the next speaker" format for, 164
Checklist for Training Analysis on, 398e–399e
establishing numbers of, 165
measuring learning of, 416
measuring satisfaction of, 415
motivation of, 168–190, 530–531
obtaining commitment by, 163
toward training value proposition, 174–178
validating emotions of, 237–238
See also Audience; Employees; Learners; Training sessions

Participation
enlarging training session pool, 161–165
learning activity, 144–146

Partnerships. See Trainer-management partnerships

Performance
drivers of, 273–274
financial based measures of, 266
keeping it simple to keep it real, 274
KPIs (key performance indicators), 272, 273fig
learning environment by managing, 263
leveraging employee's brains for performance, 305–306
limitations to non-financial measures of, 270–273

Performance (*Continued*)
  need for non-financial account-
    ability of, 267–269
  preventing employee turnover by
    managing, 314–315
  understanding your definition of,
    300–301
  See also ROI (Return on
    Intelligence); WLP (workplace
    learning and performance)
Performance improvement
  capability improvements leading
    to, 387–388
  financial based measures of, 266
  need for non-financial account-
    ability of, 267–269
Performance objectives
  data collection on, 448–449
  measuring, 447–449
  See also Business objectives;
    Learning objectives
Performance value
  overview of, 456–457*fig*, 458
  translated into financial value,
    460–461
Performance-based measures, 449
Phillips, J. J., 415, 436, 442,
  450, 472
Phillips' ROI model
  achieving proven results/returns
    using, 474–475
  formulas for evaluating training
    using, 475–476
  ROI measurement using,
    472–473
  used for evaluating training, 415,
    436, 442
Pilot-testing, 408–410*e*
Pine, J., 84
Planning
  implementing front-end analysis
    (FEA), 74
  for succession, 316–317
  transitional, 421–431
Plato, 219
Porter, M., 260
Proactive learning, 241–242

Problems
  awareness of attributional biases
    regarding, 18–19
  identifying the, 40–41
  training needs assessments for,
    13–19
Procedural knowledge, 30, 31*t*
Professional associations
  attending learning events of,
    504–505
  joining and involvement in, 506
Professional resources, 507
Professional standards
  certification, 508–509
  establishing your own, 508
Proficiency
  average versus optimal targets for,
    466*fig*–467
  definition of, 463–464, 468
  measurement components,
    464–466
  measuring time to, 467–468*fig*
Project ISD management, 65–68

Q
Questions
  allowing for the unexpected, 19
  answering seven essential training,
    343–346
  needs assessment exploratory,
    15–16, 17
  using stories to answer, 228–229

R
RAT Race (game), 124–125
RAT ("Remote Association Test"), 124
Reactive teaching, 242–243
Recharging strategies
  1: watch another trainer, 560
  2: try something new, 560
  3: read a book on training, 561
  4: tackle a new topic, 561
  5: rest, 561–562
Relatedness, 171
Results
  CAPABLE Leader model on
    achieving, 519

celebrating successful, 544–545
developing trainer-manager internal partnerships for, 513–514
Kirkpatrick's four levels of evaluation on achieving, 474–475
measurements presenting ROI,
  394–396*fig*
Phillips' ROI model for achieving, 474–475
See also Outcomes
Retention
  memory and, 223
  Methods Variety Scale to
    improve, 147–149
Return demonstration, 147
Reward systems
  consequences of, 172–174
  for desired behavior, 171–172
  intrinsic motivation and,
    178–179
  needs assessment by examining
    the, 17–18
Rezak, C. J., 253, 277
Richter, M. S., 138, 167, 183
Robert's Rules of Order, 152
Robinson, D., 507
ROI (Return on Intelligence)
  four different components of,
    301–302
  whole brain learning consider-
    ations model on, 302–304*fig*
  See also Performance
ROI (Return on Investment)
  defining and conducting actual,
    472–473
  employee turnover and cost to,
    308–309
  measuring leadership training,
    417–418
  sample summary for optimization
    of, 400
  turnover reduction and, 309
  See also Measurements/metrics
Role plays, 108–110
Rosenbaum, S. C., 359, 403
Rosenberg, M., 556
Rosile, G. A., 9, 13

Rothwell, W. J., 249
Ryan, R. M., 169, 177, 179

S

Sacred space for learning, 90–94
Sales/customer service objective map, 451t, 452t
Sanders, E. S., 249
S.C. Johnson, 314
Scaffolding, 115–117
Scavenger Bingo (game), 123–124
Seagraves, T., 357, 358, 455, 479
Self-determination theory, 175
Senior management
  creating credibility with, 158–160, 319–325, 518–519
  getting aligned with "line of sight," 324fig
  importance of tangible training benefits to, 336
  selling worth of training and development (T&D) to, 336–346
  See also Management
Short, T., 486, 489
Shrock, S., 449
Silber, K. H., 9–10, 29
Silberman, M., 137–138, 161
Silverman, L., 234
Simulations (Methods Variety Scale), 147
Sink, D. L., 10–11, 53
Smallwood, N., 514
SMART (Specific, Measurable, Attainable, Realistic, and Time-bound), 202
Smeaton, G., 138, 197, 201
SMEs (subject-matter experts)
  as coaching "narrators," 110
  instructional design reviews by, 406
  modeling performance of, 108–110
  trainer as ideally being a, 494
Soper, J. G., 249
Soule, C. O., 281

Special education techniques, 22–23
Standards. *See* Professional standards
Stolovitch, H. D., 11, 71, 253, 358, 433, 479
Stone, D., 12, 107
Stories
  answering people's questions with, 228–229
  changing group's energy by telling, 230–231
  changing group's perspective through, 232–233
  elicited from the group, 229
  using joke or tangent using, 233–234
  as leadership development strategy, 289–290
  using metaphor or analogy in, 229–230
  validating/transforming emotions with, 231–232
Stories Trainers Tell (Wacker & Silverman), 234
Strategic Value of Learning study (ASTD/IBM, 2006), 305
Strategy dashboard, 367–369
Structured experience (simulation), 147
Sugar, S., 12, 119, 122, 123, 125
SuperFrames, 63–64
Swanson**, 491
SWOT analysis, 329

T

Takacs, G., 125
Taxonomy learning design
  customer focus training example of, 26–28
  implementing change example of, 24–26fig
  train the trainer for designers example of, 28
Taxonomy learning design process
  adopting special education techniques for, 22–23

description of, 21
  two key components of, 22
Teaching
  adopting techniques of special education, 22–23
  reactive, 242–243
  stories used in, 228–234, 289–290
  See also Instructional design; Learning development strategies
Technical knowledge, 494
Technology
  e-learning used for training, 555–557
  learning opportunities by managing, 261
  learning opportunities using employee competencies and, 258–259
"35" activity, 187
Titanic (film), 217–218
TM (talent management), 250
  See also WLP (workplace learning and performance)
Tough, A., 281
Toyota, 250
Tracy, J. B., 308
Trainer knowledge/competencies
  1: how adults learn, 491–493
  2: technical knowledge, 494
  3: contextual knowledge, 494–495
  4: leadership skills, 495–496
  5: communication skills, 497–498, 509
  6: facilitation skills, 498–499t
  7: defining the learning content, 500
  8: sequencing the content, 500
  9: scripting the learning content, 500–501
  10: attitude, 501
Trainer-management partnerships
  developing internal results-oriented, 513–514
  strategies for, 535–545

Trainer-management partnerships strategies
 1: seek to be integral part T&D areas, 536–537
 2: be proactive, 537–538
 3: reduce administration, 538–539
 4: streamline standard offerings, 539–540
 5: get to the executive table, 540–541
 6: support partner activities, 541–542
 7: establish liaison roles, 542–543
 8: align T&D with corporate communications, 543–544
 9: celebrate successes, 544–545
 10: reinvent the partnership, 545
Trainers
 comments on misbegotten training requests, 36
 creating motivating environments, 168–181
 credibility of, 158–160, 319–325, 518–519
 internalized, 294–298
 partnerships between management and, 513–514, 535–545
 professional beliefs shaping professional lives of, 531–533
 recharging to avoid burn out, 559–562
 resistance to e-learning approach by, 556–557
 selling your worth as, 433–442
 tips on managing training conversations, 36–38, 323–325
 understanding financial concepts, 512–513
Training and Development (T&D)
 aligning corporate communications with, 543–544
 automotive dealership training case of, 435–442
 business approach to selling worth of, 336–340
 business objectives alignment with, 445–453
 costs of, 345–346, 394
 delivery as key to, 206–207, 243–244, 297
 designing sacred space for, 90–94
 differences between learning and, 328–330
 using e-learning for, 555–557
 experiential approach to, 281–283
 internalized, 294–298
 managing conversations about, 36–38
 preparing workshops/meetings, 152–156
 professional beliefs shaping, 531–533
 self-determination applied to, 183–194
 value proposition of, 174–178, 455–462
Training and Development (T&D) sales pitch
 1: proving T&D's worth, 337–338
 2: knowing your audience: gaining buy-in, 339–345
 3: answering seven essential questions, 343–346
Training guiding principles
 1: make no assumptions, 236
 2: creating environment of trust/vulnerability, 237
 3: validating emotions, 237–238
 4: poll the group., 238
 5: be flexible with timeline, 238
 6: be opinion-less, 238–239
Training pre-discussions, 163
Training publications, 506–507
Training sessions
 adding context to, 495
 drawing up objectives for, 153
 eliciting/tracking input in relation to objectives, 153–154
 establishing the ground rules prior to agenda, 152
 examples for creating more effective, 198–202
 flexible timelines for, 238
 guiding principles for, 235–239
 importance of listening, 155–156
 keeping focused, 154–155
 Learnertainment approach to, 217–226
 organizing thoughts but remaining flexible, 154
 paced to maintain attention/retention, 146–149
 participation in, 144–146, 161–165
 See also Meetings; Participants
Training styles, 499
Training tips
 1: give up control, 204
 2: use questions, 204–205
 3: think fast on your feet, 205
 4: visualize the group, 205
 5: make people work, 205–206
Transitional planning steps
 1: create readiness, 423, 425
 2: overcome resistance, 425
 3: communicate a vision, 425–426
 4: managing the transition, 426–428
 5: establish infrastructures to sustain the process, 429
 illustrated diagram on, 424*fig*
Trust
 consistency required for building, 528
 creating open environment of, 237
 learning relationships built on, 523–528
 repairing relationships with broken, 527–528
 three stages of, 524–527
 Wise Saying on building and destroying, 524*fig*

U

Ullius, D., 90
Ulrich, D., 514

V

Value proposition
  four segments of, 456–460
  managing metric's
    perception, 461
  motivating by creating,
    174–178
  performance, 456–457fig, 458,
    460–461
  relevant context of, 459–460
  self-determination theory on,
    175–176
  training intention element
    of, 175
  translated performance into
    financial, 460–461
  See also Financial value
Verbal reinforcement, 206
Video expert performance,
    108–110
Villachica, S., 107

Vision
  as misunderstood management
    concept, 529
  motivation supplied by,
    530–531

W

Wacker, M., 234
Wal-mart, 250
Webber, P. G., 281
Weiss, D. S., 9, 21, 285, 487,
    517, 523
Weissbein, D. A., 434
Whole brain learning considerations
    model, 302–304fig
*Why the Bottom-Line Isn't: How to
    Build Value Through People
    and Organization* (Ulrich &
    Smallwood), 514
Why We Do What We Do (Deci),
    168, 173

Willett, C., 122, 123
WLP (workplace learning and
    performance)
  beyond the classroom, 327–333
  definition of, 249
  discovery learning approach to,
    281–282
  increasing importance of, 251
  learning development strategy for,
    262–264
  linking balanced scorecard (BSC)
    to, 371–385
  See also Learning; Performance;
    TM (talent management)
"Work product recycling," 86–87
Work/life balance, 521–522
Workshops. *See* Training sessions
"The World's Worst" game, 188

Z

Zeinstra, R., 337

Who's Who in Training and Development

The Editors

Terrence L. Gargiulo, MMHS, is a learning and communication architect who has an uncanny ability to design and deliver solutions that put people in the driver's seat of their professional and personal growth. He holds a master's of management in human services from the Florence Heller School at Brandeis University and is a recipient of *Inc* magazine's Marketing Master Award and the HR Leadership Award from the Asia Pacific HRM Congress.

Terrence is a frequent speaker at international and national conferences, including the American Society for Training and Development, International Society for Performance Improvement, Academy of Management, Conference Board, and Association of Business Communications. He is a Field Editor for ASTD. His articles have appeared in *American Executive* magazine, *Journal of Quality and Participation, ISPI Journal, International Association of Business Communicators*, and *ASTD Links*.

Books

Making Stories: A Practical Guide for Organizational Leaders and Human Resource Specialists (translated into Chinese)

The Strategic Use of Stories in Organizational Communication and Learning

On Cloud Nine: Weathering Many Generations in the Workplace (translated into Korean and Spanish)

Stories at Work: Using Stories to Improve Communications and Build Relationships

Building Business Acumen for Trainers: Skills to Empower the Training Function

Once Upon a Time: Using Story-based Activities to Develop Breakthrough Communication Skills

In the Land of Difficult People: 24 Timeless Tales Reveal How to Tame Beasts at Work

Contributor

From Analysis to Evaluation: Tools, Tips, and Techniques for Trainers, Jane Bozarth

Handbook of Experiential Learning, Mel Silberman *2005 ASTD Source Book*

Clients

GM, HP, DTE Energy, MicroStrategy, Fidelity, Federal Reserve Bank, Ceridian, National Geographic, Countrywide Financial, Washington Mutual, Dreyer's Ice Cream, UNUM, U.S. Coast Guard, Boston University, Raytheon, City of Lowell, Arthur D. Little, KANA Communications, Merck-Medco, Coca-Cola, Harvard Business School, and Cambridge Savings Bank.

Personal Mission Statement

I have a passion for inciting insights in others.

Specialities

- Design group processes that elicit people's narratives/stories. Help people connect with themselves and each other in order to rapidly form new networks of ideas, insights, and learning

- Train-the-trainer initiatives
- Advance facilitation skills
- Breakthrough communication skills
- Innovation
- Business acumen
- Instructional design

Fun Facts

Member of three U.S. Junior World Championship Teams in Fencing
Wrote an opera titled, "Tryillias" with father that was accepted for the 2004 Pulitzer Prize in music
Avid SCUBA diver
Lyrical baritone—cantor for religious services
Passionate chef and foodie

Contact

Email: terrence@makingstories.net
Web: www.makingstories.net
Phone: 781-894-4381

Ajay M. Pangarkar, CTDP, is president and senior learning strategist of CentralKnowledge Inc., leaders in developing measurable strategic learning solutions and delivering innovative on-demand e-learning and assessment systems (LearningSourceonline.com) dedicated to on-demand learning and examination systems. He is one of the leading learning strategists in the world, a foremost authority on integrating learning strategies into the balanced scorecard, business acumen for trainers, and is an industry-recognized speaker on strategic employee development, blended learning, learning measurement, evaluation, and ROI methodologies. Ajay's passion is to align learning infrastructure and deliverables with an organization's strategic objectives.

Ajay regularly writes for many prominent publications, including *Chief Learning Officer, Talent Management* magazine, *HR Reporter, HR Professional,* and *CMA Management.*

Ajay helped initiate the Quebec chapter of the Canadian Society for Training Development (CSTD), is the past chapter chair, and serves as vice chair of CSTD's National Board of Directors. Most recently, CSTD awarded Ajay, as senior practitioner, CSTD's industry-recognized Certified Training and Development Professional designation. He is currently involved with some of the most innovative e-learning and online assessment management solutions available.

Ajay is a frequent speaker at international and national conferences, including the American Society for Training and Development, International Society for Performance Improvement, Canadian Society for Training and Development, and Training.

Books

Building Business Acumen for Trainers: Skills to Empower the Training Function
The Portable Training Mentor
Linking Learning Strategies to the Balanced Scorecard

Contributor

Pfeiffer's Training *Annuals*
Chief Learning Officer
Talent Management magazine
CMA Management Magazine

Clients

Business Development Bank of Canada, Scotia Bank, Apple Inc., City of Reno, Nevada, City of Tampa, Florida, IATA, SkyService, Canadian Management Centre, RBC Investments, Order of Chartered Management Accountants of Canada (CMA), IMS Health, Pfizer Canada, DHL, Nordia, Atomic Energy of Canada,

Public Works Canada (Government of Canada), Academy for Educational Development, CancerCare Manitoba, and Cereal Food Processors.

Personal Mission Statement

It is never too late to become what you might have been.

Specialities

- Developing learning strategies and initiatives
- Aligning learning strategies to strategic objectives
- Developing the balanced scorecard with a focus on learning and growth
- Building business acumen skills for learning professionals
- e-Learning solutions and tutorials
- Assessment and examination management systems
- Training for trainer initiatives and programs
- Advanced facilitation skills
- Course design, development, and deployment
- Instructional design

Fun Facts

Hosted and co-produced a business TV show for four years. Enjoys watching the Stanley Cup playoffs, especially if the Montreal Canadiens or another Canadian team is involved. Enjoys cigars so much that it has become a hobby. I enjoy having a single malt scotch and an aged Cuban cigar with friends. Been involved with a community organization for the past eleven years helping entrepreneurs start businesses

Contact

Email: ajayp@centralknowledge.com
Web: www.centralknowledge.com
Phone: 450-689-3895

Teresa Kirkwood, CTDP, is a founding partner and vice president of CentralKnowledge Inc., a company dedicated to developing measurable strategic learning solutions and delivering innovative on-demand e-learning and assessment systems (LearningSourceonline. com). She brings over eighteen years of industry and workplace learning experience and is recognized for helping companies to align their learning strategies to organizational objectives. Her learning knowledge extends to developing assessments, course design and deployment, training of new trainers and subject experts, and supporting those with responsibilities for managing the training function. She is a widely published author writing for several major HR and workplace learning publications and books. Teresa is government accredited and delivers learning programs educational and business institutions.

Teresa is exceptionally involved in community activities, including mentoring business start-ups for youth and regularly speaks for women entrepreneurial groups. She was nominated for the Ernst & Young/Canadian Business of the Year award and is regularly interviewed by business and news media appearing in newspaper articles and radio broadcasts. Teresa is a founding member and vice chair of the Canadian Society for Training and Development (CSTD), Quebec chapter, helped to establish the Quebec Training ROI Network, and is a member of many CSTD development committees.

Teresa is also invited to speak at learning industry and business conferences on the topics related to learning strategies and entrepreneurship including *Chief Learning Officer, Talent Management* magazine, *HR Reporter, HR Professional*, and *CMA Management*.

Books

Building Business Acumen for Trainers: Skills to Empower the Training Function

The Portable Training Mentor
Linking Learning Strategies to the Balanced Scorecard

Contributor

Pfeiffer's Training *Annuals*
Chief Learning Officer
Talent Management
CMA Management

Clients

Business Development Bank of Canada, Scotia Bank, Apple Inc., City of Reno, Nevada, City of Tampa, Florida, IATA, SkyService, Canadian Management Centre, RBC Investments, Order of Chartered Management Accountants of Canada (CMA), IMS Health, Pfizer Canada, DHL, Nordia, Atomic Energy of Canada, Public Works Canada (Government of Canada), Academy for Educational Development, CancerCare Manitoba, Cereal Food Processors.

Personal Mission Statement

Don't take no for an answer, never submit to failure and no matter what people tell you being hardheaded isn't a bad strait.

Specialities

- Developing learning strategies and initiatives
- Aligning learning strategies to strategic objectives
- Developing the balanced scorecard with a focus on learning and growth
- Building business acumen skills for learning professionals
- e-Learning solutions and tutorials
- Assessment and examination management systems
- Training for trainer initiatives and programs
- Advanced facilitation skills

- Course design, development, and deployment
- Instructional design

Fun Facts

Hosted and co-produced a business TV show for four years. If I don't know something I become obsessive about it until I find the answers. I love to travel; a favorite place is Venice, Italy.

I taught my dog Dakota to count and answer yes or no questions. I treat my four pets like children and they run my life and I love it.

Contact

Email: teresak@centralknowledge.com
Web: www.centralknowledge.com
Phone: 450-689-3895

The Contributors

Jean Barbazette is the president of The Training Clinic, Seal Beach, California, a training consulting firm she founded in 1977. The Training Clinic is the leading "Train-the-Trainer" company in the United States. Jean and a field staff of twenty present hundreds of workshops nationally and internationally on the techniques of train-the-trainer each year. The Training Clinic presents some of its workshops in the Netherlands, Hungry, and Latin America through licensees. Jean recently presented train-the-trainer and management workshops in Malaysia, Singapore, Hong Kong, Thailand, Indonesia, the Philippines and Vietnam. She is an active national and local member of ISPI, SHRM, and ASTD.

Jean has been in training and development for over forty years. Former employers include Blue Cross of Southern California and the City of Long Beach. Jean has a BA in social science from Notre Dame de Namur University and an MA in education from Stanford University. She has taught at the University of California at Los Angeles (UCLA) and Coastline Community College. She is on the faculty for *Training* magazine's "Live and Online" training programs.

Books

> *Successful New Employee Orientation*
> *The Trainer's Support Handbook*
> *Instant Case Studies*
> *The Trainer's Journey to Competence*
> *Training Needs Assessment*
> *The Art of Great Training Delivery*
> *Managing the Training Function for Bottom-Line Results*

Contributor

A chapter on new employee orientation to the *Intervention Resource Guide: 50 Performance Improvement Tools*
Inventory exercises in the McGraw-Hill *Training and Performance Sourcebooks* in 1999, 2000 and 2001, 2002, and the Pfeiffer *Annuals* in 1993, 2004, 2005
A chapter on "Self-Directed New Employee Orientation" in *What Smart Trainers Know*
A chapter on "What's Your Priority" in *90 World-Class Activities by 90 World-Class Trainers*
A chapter to the ASTD *Training & Development Sourcebooks*, 2002 and 2003

Clients

Chevron, UNOCAL, Nestle', U.S. Navy, Internal Revenue Service, U.S. Department of Justice, Immigration and Naturalization Service, Orange County Transportation Authority, Hilton Hotels Corporation, the Automobile Club of Southern California, Price Waterhouse Coopers, John Hancock Insurance Company, American Express, Toyota Motor Sales, Federal Emergency Management Agency, Telmex, Matsushita Electronic Components, Singapore Airlines, Ameritech, Bechtel International, Baxter Healthcare, The Nature Conservancy, Raytheon.

Personal Mission Statement

I model and use learning by doing, not just by listening. All of our workshops require a high level of participation by the learner. Learners work on the organization's real issues and develop action plans and materials to use on the job the very next day.

The course content is, above all, realistic and practical. Although each workshop is based on solid adult learning theory and enough theory is discussed to provide participants with a foundation, these are not "theoretical" or "academic" programs.

Specialities

- Training trainers
- New employee orientation
- Needs assessments
- Designing training programs
- Administrative assistant effectiveness

Fun Facts

Precious Life Shelter nominated Jean as 1996 Catholic Woman of the Year for Orange County. Jean is a volunteer at the Precious Life Shelter in Los Alamitos. PLS serves homeless pregnant women in crisis. She received an award for her dedication and commitment to the shelter since 1994. She is the 2008 president of St. Anne's Women's Guild.

Jean received three awards from Orange County Chapter of ASTD: The President's Award in 1998 for twenty years of continuous and outstanding service to the chapter and The Distinguished Service Award in 1999, Award of Merit in 2003.

Jean is an avid golfer and has visited more that forty-five countries in her travels.

Contact

Email: jean@thetrainingclinic.com
Web: www.thetrainingclinic.com
Phone: 562-430-2484

Elaine Biech is president and managing principal of ebb associates inc, an organizational development firm that helps organizations work through large-scale change. She has been in the training and consulting field for thirty years, and works with business, government, and non-profit organizations.

Elaine specializes in helping people work as teams to maximize their effectiveness. Customizing all of her work for individual clients, she conducts strategic planning sessions and implements corporate-wide systems such as quality improvement, reengineering of business processes, and mentoring programs. She facilitates topics such as coaching today's employee, fostering creativity, customer service, time management, stress management, speaking skills, training competence, conducting productive meetings, managing change, handling the difficult employee, organizational communication, conflict resolution and effective listening.

She has developed media presentations and training materials and has presented at dozens of national and international conferences. Known as the trainer's trainer, she custom designs training programs for managers, leaders, trainers, and consultants. Elaine has been featured in dozens of publications including *The Wall Street Journal, Harvard Management Update, The Washington Post,* and *Fortune* magazine.

Elaine has her BS from the University of Wisconsin-Superior in business and education consulting, and her MS in human resource development. She is active at the National level of ASTD, serving on the 1990 National Conference Design Committee, a member of the National ASTD board of directors and the Society's Secretary from 1991–1994, initiating and chairing Consultant's Day for the seven years, and as the International Conference Design Chair in 2000. In addition to her work with ASTD, she has served on the Independent Consultants Association's (ICA) Advisory Committee and on the Instructional Systems Association (ISA) board of directors.

Elaine is the recipient of the 1992 National ASTD Torch Award, the 2004 ASTD Volunteer-Staff Partnership Award, and the 2006 ASTD Gordon M. Bliss Memorial Award. She was selected for the 1995 Wisconsin Women Entrepreneur's Mentor Award. In 2001 she received ISA's highest award, The ISA Spirit Award. She has been the consulting editor for the prestigious Training and Consulting Annuals published by Jossey-Bass/Pfeiffer for the past ten years.

Clients

As a management and executive consultant, trainer and designer she has provided services to FAA, Land O' Lakes, McDonald's, Lands' End, General Casualty Insurance, Chrysler, Johnson Wax, PricewaterhouseCoopers, American Family Insurance, Marathon Oil, Hershey Chocolate, Federal Reserve Bank, U.S. Navy, NASA, Newport News Shipbuilding, Kohler Company, ASTD, American Red Cross, Association of Independent Certified Public Accountants, the University of Wisconsin, The College of William and Mary, ODU, and hundreds of other public and private sector organizations to help them prepare for the challenges of the new millennium.

Books

The Business of Consulting
Thriving Through Change: A Leader's Practical Guide to Change Mastery
90 World-Class Activities by 90 World-Class Trainers
Nine volume set of ASTD's Certification Study Guides
12 Habits of Successful Trainers, *ASTD Info-line*
The ASTD Info-line Dictionary of Basic Trainer Terms
Training for Dummies
Marketing Your Consulting Services
The Consultant's Quick Start Guide
Successful Team-Building Tools
The Consultant's Legal Guide
Interpersonal Skills: Understanding Your Impact on Others
Building High Performance
The Pfeiffer Annual for Consultants and *The Pfeiffer Annual for Trainers*
The ASTD Sourcebook: Creativity and Innovation—Widen Your Spectrum

The HR Handbook
Ten Mistakes CEOs Make About Training
TQM for Training
Diagnostic Tools for Total Quality, Info-line
Managing Teamwork
Process Improvement: Achieving Quality Together
Business Communications
Delegating For Results
Increased Productivity Through Effective Meetings
Stress Management, Building Healthy Families

Interesting Facts

Elaine likes to collect waterfront properties and shoes!

Contact

Email: ebbiech@aol.com
Web: www.ebbweb.com
Phone: 757-588-3939

Frank P. Bordonaro, Ph.D., helps companies to become "learning organizations" that achieve higher performance through people. As an entrepreneur, consultant, speaker, **and author,** Frank works with business leaders, HR executives, and talent management and learning executives. He has worked in five continents and several industries, helping executive teams shape learning strategies and carry them out successfully. Bordonaro's work has appeared in the case literature of the Harvard Business School, the University of Michigan's executive program, *The Economist* and *Information Week*. His architectural projects have been featured in *Design* magazine. He is co-founder of CareerDNA, LLC, a provider of digital products and consulting in talent development (www.careerdna.biz).

A Vanderbilt University Ph.D., he was on the business administration faculty at Indiana University in Bloomington, Indiana, prior to his career in business.

Books/Articles

Corporate Learning: Proven and Practical Guidelines for Building a Sustainable Learning Strategy
"The New Learning"
"The Artist's Walk: A Message for Leaders from the World of Art"

Contributor

"Put Your Stock in Learning: The Prudential Financial Story," in *Learning Architectures*
"Budgets are Tight: Time to Invest in Learning," in HRM
Frank's leadership in the design and construction of the Boeing Learning Center will appear in a 2008 book by renowned architect Gyo Obata of HOK

Corporate Experience

Director, Johnson Management Institute, learning center of S.C. Johnson, a Family Company (1989–1995)
Chief Learning Officer, McDonnell Douglas Corp,/ Accountable executive, creation of the Boeing Learning Center (1995–97)
Chief Learning Officer, Prudential Financial (1997–2002)
Manager, Frank P. Bordonaro, LLC management consulting (2002–2004)
Co-founder, Head of Corporate Solutions, CareerDNA, Inc. (2004–present)

Personal Mission Statement

Produce highly original solutions that increase the capacities of people—to learn, work together and lead.

Specialities

- Design of Next Generation Talent Development Tools
- Corporate Learning Strategy
- Creation/Leadership of Corporate Universities/Learning Centers
- Executive Coaching
- Organizational Change

Fun Facts

Still learning: Frank is currently under tutelage at the Giuliani School of Music for piano and at the Silvermine Art Guild for painting. With his wife, Sally, he has redesigned and renovated five homes. He has illustrated three children's books produced by his grandchildren. He keeps a somewhat cluttered office/studio/design shop in Wilton, Connecticut.

Contact

Email: frankpb@optonline.net
Web: www.careerDNA.biz
Phone: 203-762-3838

Steve D. Bordonaro, M.Ed., is all about delivery consulting. As a learning designer of new media, he melds IT esoterica into practical terms. He is a graduate of Ohio University and holds degrees in visual communication (E.W. Scripps School of Journalism) and microcomputer applications for education.

Steve is a producer of photo-graphics and web-based learning content, serving hundreds of thousands of people world wide. He is a thought leader for the next generation of learning technologies in primary and secondary education and a conference speaker for the National Council for Online Learning (NACOL).

Clients

Amgen, Communication Arts, DeVry Learning, Education Management Corporation, Kaplan University, k12 Inc., Laureate/Sylvan Learning, *National Geographic* contributors, NCAR, NOAA, Tenet Health Systems, University of Pennsylvania, University of Colorado, USGS, and several of the nation's leading statewide, public K-12 virtual schools

Personal Mission Statement

I will define education for the 21st Century

Specialities

- Building multi-generational teams and innovating online publishing processes
- Mentoring subject matter experts (SMEs) to author online content
- **Constructing measurable objectives and related assessments**
- Designing self-paced, instructor-led, and blended learning environments

Fun Facts

The dimensions of my digital photography are measured in feet, instead of inches. I introduced poetry to fourth graders using the principles of Dada (the anti-art); created a mobile, video feed-back booth used as a library resource; brought cell phones to rural areas (many years ago) for an interactive TV series on PBS; and am a snowboarder extraordinaire—catch me if you can.

Contact

Email: steve@bordonaro.com
Web: www.bordonaro.com

Jane Bozarth, M.Ed., oversees North Carolina state government's award-winning e-learning program. A popular conference presenter, recent speaking engagements have taken her to Ireland, Canada, Australia, and Montana. Jane has an M.Ed. in training and development/technology in training and is finishing her dissertation for her Ed.D. in training and development.

Books

e-Learning Solutions on a Shoestring: Help for the Chronically Under-Funded Trainer
Better Than Bullet Points: Creating Engaging e-Learning with PowerPoint
From Analysis to Evaluation: Tools, Tips, and Techniques for Trainers

Contributor

The e-Learning Handbook: Past Promises, Present Challenges
The 2008 Pfeiffer Annual: Training
The Accidental Trainer
ASTD Handbook for Workplace Learning Professionals

Personal Mission Statement

I want to stamp out bad training, help trainers solve problems, and help position training as a profession. Words to live by: If you aren't making waves, you aren't kicking hard enough.

Specialities

• When others say, "We can't do that, we don't have any money," I say, "How can we do that without any money?" Good training is about design, not software.
• Constructivist learning theory

- Trainer fears of e-learning,
- Rapid instructional design
- Train-the-trainer undertakings
- Communities of practice

Fun Facts

I can play the fire out of a five-string banjo and find golf a good metaphor for life: if you don't play by any rules, then you can't cheat. I also drive too fast.

Contact

Email: jane@bozarthzone.com
Web: www.bozarthzone.com
Phone: 919-452-8712

Robert O. Brinkerhoff, Ed.D., an internationally recognized expert in evaluation and training effectiveness, has provided consultation to dozens of major companies and organizations in the United States, South Africa, Russia, Europe, Australia, New Zealand, Singapore, and Saudi Arabia.

Brinkerhoff is an author of numerous books on evaluation and training, and has been a keynote speaker and presenter at hundreds of conferences and institutes worldwide. Scores of leading corporations and agencies ranging from Dell Computer and Ford Motor Company to the World Bank and Central Intelligence Agency have adopted his methods and tools for training effectiveness and evaluation.

He earned a doctorate at the University of Virginia in program evaluation, where he also coordinated a "street academy" for disadvantaged youth for four years. He is currently a principal consultant and alliance partner with Advantage Performance Group and professor emeritus at Western Michigan University.

Brinkerhoff's work experience includes a five-year stint as an officer in the U.S. Navy during the Vietnam era, a carpenter, charter-boat mate in the West Indies, grocery salesman in Puerto Rico, and factory laborer in Birmingham, England, where he saw the original Beatles. He has four children, thankfully mostly chronologically grown, and lives with his wife and several unruly dogs in Richland, Michigan.

Books

Courageous Training
Telling Training's Story
Success Case Method
High-Impact Learning (ISPI national award 2004)

Clients

Scores of agencies and companies around the globe, including Dell Computers, Hewlett-Packard, Ingersoll Rand, Ford Motor Company, Steelcase, and Pfizer.

Personal Mission Statement

I want to be known as a kind and helpful person.

Specialities

- Design of leadership development
- Evaluation of training
- Training organization strategy

Fun Facts

Guitar and folk signing (unrecovered hippie)

Contact

Email: robert.brinkerhoff@wmich.edu
Phone: 269-629-4161

Holly Burkett, MA, SPHR, CPT, principal of Evaluation Works, has more than twenty years' experience assisting public- and private-sector organizations design and implement a wide range of measurement systems, tools, and processes for showing the business value of workplace learning and performance efforts. Certified as an ROI professional (CRP) since 1997, she is a frequent conference presenter, workshop leader, and author on performance measurement topics.

Holly is editor-in-chief of ISPI's *Performance Improvement* journal, a select item writer for the Human Resource Certification Institute's SPHR/PHR credentialing exams, and also serves as an ROI field editor for ASTD. Holly earned her master's in human resources and organization development from the University of San Francisco and is currently pursuing doctoral studies in human capital development.

Books

The ROI Fieldbook, Strategies for Implementing ROI in HR and Training (co-authored with Jack and Patti Phillips, and Ron Stone)

Contributor

"Evaluating a Career Development Initiative" in *Evaluating Training Programs: The Four Levels*
"ROI on A Shoestring: Measuring More with Less" in *Industrial & Commercial Training*
"Getting and Keeping Your Seat at the Table: HR Trends, Issues, and Opportunities" in *Human Resources Journal*
"Case Study: Measuring the ROI of a Career Development Initiative" in Human Resources Journal
"Building and Sustaining Management Buy-In for ROI Implementation: Tips for the Evaluation Leader" in *ROI in Practice: ASTD Links*

"Using Action Plans to Measure Job Performance, Business Impact, and ROI" in *ROI In Practice: ASTD Links*
"ROI as an Emerging Practice: A Compilation of Lessons Learned from the Field" in *ROI In Practice: ASTD Links*
"Take Me to Your Leader: The Value of Sponsorship in Managing Evaluation Projects" in *ROI In Practice: ASTD Links*
"ROI on a Shoestring" in *ROI In Practice: ASTD Links*
"An ROI Shortcut for Budget Challenged Training Departments," Institute of Management and Administration
"Evaluation: Was Your HPI Project Worth the Effort" in *HPI Essentials*
"Leveraging Employee Know-How with Structured How-to Training" in *In Action: Implementing On the Job Learning*
"Program Process Improvement Team" in *In Action: Return on Investment.* "Managing Evaluation Shortcuts,"*Info-line 0111*
"Measuring a Train-the-Trainer Approach to Support Build to Order Capabilities" in *In Action: Measuring Learning and Performance*

Clients

Apple Computer, Chevron, Intel, National Security Agency (NSA), the State of California, the California Department of Transportation (CALTRANS), Roche Biomedical Laboratories, Premera Blue Cross, Raleys, Los Rios Community College, the California State Teachers' Retirement System (CALSTRS), the County of Sacramento, University of California Davis (UCD), USCS International, Community Healthcare Association of the Dakotas (CHAD), and California State University Sacramento (CSUS).

Personal Mission Statement

I have a passion for empowering individuals and organizations to use evaluation as a tool for showing how their work matters.

Specialities

- Evaluation and ROI, especially performance contracting, action planning, and Level 3 measurement processes
- Transfer of learning strategies
- Measurement or ROI "on a shoestring," cost-effective measurement practices
- Change management
- Group facilitation
- Employee certification or qualification processes
- Community development and capacity building, including grant-review and technical assistance around outcome-based measures
- Instructional design, especially train-the-trainer
- Continuous process improvement, quality initiatives

Fun Facts

Worked as horseback trail guide in Zion National Park
Helped Katrina rebuilding efforts by volunteering with Bayou Area Habitat for Humanity
Resides in the town named "Bicycle Capital of the USA" by *Outdoor* magazine
Avid traveler, hiker, bicyclist, and outdoor enthusiast
Ran in the California International Marathon for Leukemia Society's Team-in-Training
Very familiar with the Napa Valley!
Former ASTD chapter president and national advisor to chapters (NAC) representative
Former live-in counselor for residential facility serving runaway youth
Strong supporter of Women for Women International, Mercy Corps, and SEVA foundation

Contact

Email: burketth@earthlink.net
Phone: 530-400-8875

W. Boyce Byerly, Ph.D., is chief scientist and chief technical officer at Capital Analytics, where he leads the consulting and software engineering teams. He holds a master's in computer science and a Ph.D. in cognitive psychology from Duke University. His research passions include human learning and cognition, and he has published on measurement and evaluation, computer-supported collaborative work, and spatial cognition.

He is a frequent speaker at conferences on measuring and evaluating human capital investments, with an emphasis on turning operational data into ROI. His most recent appearances were at Corporate University week, the Society for Applied Learning Technologies conference, ASTD International, and the CLO symposium.

Clients

My current active client list includes Sun Microsystems, Daimler-Chrysler, Farmers Insurance, Bellevue University, Knowlagent, Sprint, Skillsoft, McKesson, and US Bank.

Personal Mission Statement

To change the way corporations invest in human capital.

Specialities

- Lead stakeholder discussions in corporate human capital investments.
- Identify, valorize, and organize key performance indicators.
- Execute vigorous statistical analyses of investments and operational data,
- Translate statistical reports into clear, action-oriented business English.
- Develop complete strategies for the measurement of human capital investments.

Fun Facts

- Worked as an expert systems knowledge engineer in areas as diverse as diamond mining and AIDS/HIV treatment.
- A committed Scoutmaster with my own troop.
- Wrote the mathematical core of the software product that we use for client data analysis.

Contact

Email: boyce@alumni.duke.edu
Web: www.procourse.com, www.boycebyerly.com
Phone: 919-403-3770 ext 13

Gary A. DePaul, Ph.D., is senior manager for performance excellence at Ceridian Benefits Services, Inc. At Ceridian, Gary manages the Knowledge Management department, Training department, and Quality Assurance department. Prior to Ceridian, Gary worked at Fidelity National Information Services (FIS) as the performance improvement director and at Johnson Controls and Arthur Andersen as an instructional designer and performance technologist. Gary completed his Ph.D. and Ed.M. from the University of Illinois at Urbana-Champaign. Gary has a BA in philosophy and history from the University of Alabama at Birmingham. Gary is a Certified Performance Technologist (CPT).

Gary is the 2008 president of the Tampa Bay ISPI and has presented locally and at the ISPI annual conference.

Book

Alternative Types of Learning in Clinical Specialty-Interest Areas of Family-Practice Medicine

Contributor

"Probative, Dialectic, and Moral Reasoning in Program Evaluation," in *Qualitative Inquiry*
"The Evolving Syntheses of Program Value," in *Evaluation Practice*

"Review of the Literature of Adult Education: Implications for Academic Advisors," in *NACADA Journal*

Personal Mission Statement

Lead people to success by helping them innovate and grow in their work and life performance.

Specialities

- Project management and design techniques for improving instructional systems design
- Formative evaluation
- Performance consulting and coaching
- Corporate knowledge management

Fun Facts

Assist Tami McNally, his spouse, with her wildlife photographic expeditions in Florida wetlands, uplands, and coastal areas. Tami is a professional photographer specializing in wildlife photography and business-related photography; Gary's photograph is an example of her work. Volunteer for the local Audubon Society by hunting Caesar Weed. Retired motorcyclist (too many injuries to count).

Contact

Email: gary.depaul@ceridian.com
Web: www.ceridian.com
Phone: 727-395-8434

Toni Hodges DeTuncq (previously published under Toni Hodges) is a measurement and evaluation specialist who provides state-of-the-art expertise to private and non-profit organizations trying to prove the value of their performance improvement programs. She designs tools that organizations are currently using to assist them in what could be a daunting task, but ends up being practical as well as effective. Her flexibility allows her to apply solid evaluation principles to the various circumstances and challenges each of her clients face.

Toni provides workshops designed to train her clients as well as the American Society for Training and Development (ASTD) Certificate attendees. These include *Measuring and Evaluating Learning, Return on Investment (ROI), Test Construction and Validation* and other custom-designed workshops. Over the past twenty-five years, Toni has been selected as one of nine "Training's New Guard" by Training and Development magazine; awarded ROI Practitioner of the Year by the ROI Network, Inc.; selected best practice among over two hundred companies by the American Productivity and Quality Center; served as chairperson for the American Society for Training and Development (ASTD) Publishing Review Committee; and been president of ROI Network, Inc.

Books

> *Linking Learning and Performance: A Practical Guide to Measuring Learning and On-the-Job Application*
> *In Action: Measuring Learning and Performance*

Contributor

> *Make Training Evaluation Work*
> *ROI at Work: Best Practice Case Studies from the Real World*
> *In Action: Implementing Evaluation Systems and Processes*
> *In Action: Measuring Return on Investment, Volume 2*

Clients

TD Bank, Canada, BMW Manufacturing, NASA Goddard Space Flight Center, Boston Scientific, National Security Agency (NSA), BAE Systems, U.S. Army, Countrywide University, BMW North America, Charter Communications, Nextel

Communications, Chubb Insurance, Franklin Covey, Eli Lilly Pharmaceuticals, Bank of America, World Bank, American Society for Training and Development (ASTD), Charles Town Raceway and Slots, Servco Pacific Inc., and HMSA: Blue Cross Blue Shield of Hawaii.

Personal Mission Statement

To demonstrate how valuable each person is to their organization, no matter what position.

Specialities

- Author and HRD strategic planning
- Develop evaluation processes and measurement tools
- Conduct ROI analyses
- Conduct measurement and evaluation skill enhancement workshops and seminars
- Conduct benchmarking studies

Fun Facts

Enjoy making good friends of my colleagues and clients; ride a bright yellow *Oliver City* Scooter throughout the neighborhood; love old movies and historical novels; worked at the White House during the last two years of the Nixon administration and first three months of the Ford administration; balance work, family, friends, fun and hobbies and love every minute of it; designed the weather alert user-interface system used in all U.S. aircraft and Air Traffic Control Centers; designed the physical and user-interface consoles used by ARINC traffic controllers in New York, Hawaii, Scotland, and Nova Scotia (labeled the "Hodges Console")

Contact

Email: toni@thdandco.com
Web: thdandco.com
Phone: 410-956-0475

John Endicott is a senior instructional designer at DLS, where he specializes in computer-based and systems documentation, online help systems, web-based evaluation systems, interface design, and electronic performance support. He has written and coded training and online support in a wide range of disciplines, including telecommunications, securities, and customer sales and service. John earned his master's degree in technical and scientific communication from Miami University in Oxford, Ohio, with an emphasis in computer science. He is the 2008–9 president of the Society for Technical Communication, Rocky Mountain Chapter and a member of the Front Range Chapter of ISPI. In his spare time, John enjoys cycling and reading and is the proud father of two dogs named Austin and Lobo.

Contributor

"KICS: Best Practices Caught in the Web," in *Case Studies in Performance Improvement*
"Performance Support Systems," in *Handbook of Human Performance Technology: Improving Individual and Organizational Performance Worldwide* (3rd ed.)
"Prototyping for e-Learning That Works!" *SPBT Focus, 13*(2), 63–67.

Client

DLS Group, Inc.

Personal Mission Statement

He who is not busy being born is busy dying.

Specialities

- Writing
- Researching

- Process improvement
- Bleeding-edge technologies

Fun Facts

Volunteer usher at the Denver Performing Arts Center; grew up in a double-wide trailer in northern British Columbia; and fledgling keyboardist and music enthusiast with a library nearing 10,000 LPs and CDs

Contact

Email: jendicott@dls.com
Web: www.dls.com
Phone: 303-333-4513

 **Wellesley R. (Rob) Foshay, Ph.D., CPT,** is director, research for the Education Technology division of Texas Instruments, Inc. Rob's experience includes over thirty-five years in education and training, including twenty-five years leading research and design efforts in private sector educational technology companies, most recently for the PLATO system. Prior to joining TI, his company, The Foshay Group, consulted with Fortune 500 companies on training and assessment of high-value expertise in high-level problem solving. He was appointed to the faculty of the University of Illinois–Champaign. He has served on the editorial boards and as a consulting editor for six refereed journals in educational technology, learning sciences and instructional design. The International Society for Performance Improvement has recognized him as Member for Life, and as a Certified Performance Technologist. He has been cited as a distinguished alumnus by the College of Education of Indiana University. His doctorate is in instructional systems technology from Indiana University.

Books

Writing Training That Works: How to Train Anyone to do Anything: A Practical Guide for Trainers Based on Current Cognitive Psychology and Instructional Design Theory and Research

Contributor

Rob has published over seventy major peer-reviewed articles and book chapters on a wide range of topics in education and training, Among his most recent contributions are:

"Can We Really Halve Development Time? Reaction to Scandura's Commentary," *Technology, Instruction, Cognition and Learning*

"Building the Wrong Simulation: Matching Instructional Intent in Teaching Problem Solving to Simulation Architecture," *Technology, Instruction, Cognition and Learning*

"Designing Instructional Strategies: A Cognitive Perspective," in *Handbook of Human Performance Technology*

"Design Science Issues in Evaluation of Technology in Education and Training," in *Innovations to Instructional Technology: Essays in Honor of M. David Merrill*

"Can Instructional Design Deliver on the Promise of the Web?" in *Issues in Instructional Technology*

"Do We Need Authoring Systems? A Commercial Perspective," *Technology, Instruction and Cognitive Learning*

Clients

Johnson Controls, A.C. Nielsen, Ingite! Learning, Software and Information Industry Association

Personal Mission Statement

Training should concentrate on the highest-value performance needs of the enterprise: high-level expertise in solving ill-defined and ill-structured problems. Current cognitive science gives us many new tools to meet these needs. Yet all too often, we don't even recognize them, and instead we focus on trivial skills.

Specialities

- Training and assessment of expertise in high-level problem solving
- Instructional simulation/game design
- Evaluation of training impact
- Human performance technology

Fun Facts

Amateur radio operator since 1960, and certified severe weather spotter; built his first computer in 1963

Contact

Email: rfoshay@foshay.org
Web: www.foshay.org
Phone: 630-215-4120

Ann Hermann-Nehdi is CEO of Herrmann International, a global training and consulting company and publisher of the **Herrmann Brain Dominance Instrument (HBDI).** The work of the North Carolina company is based on thirty years of research on thinking and the brain. Key applications of the company's *whole brain thinking model* include innovation, strategic thinking, problem solving, management, leadership, sales teaching and learning, self-understanding, communication and team/staff development. Herrmann International works worldwide with offices throughout Europe, the Pacific Rim, and Latin America.

The work of the North Carolina company has been featured in *O Magazine, BusinessWeek, USA Today, Discover, Scientific*

American, and *The Harvard Business Review* and was recently featured on the Australian Today Show. Ann is an ISA board member, an advisor to the American Creativity Association, a founder of the Hickory Nut Gorge Community Foundation, and serves on other non-profit and for-profit boards.

Her personal goal is to promote better understanding of how individuals and organizations think and become more effective, as well as enhance creativity, learning and communication technologies worldwide through the application and development of the whole brain concept.

Books

> *Return on Intelligence: Getting to People Head First* (in press)

Contributor

> *Training for Dummies*
> *The ASTD Handbook for Workplace Performance*

Clients

Direct clients include AIG, Allstate, AXA, Air France, Bank of America, Barclay's, Boeing, BMW, Cirque du Soleil, Cintas, Cisco, Coca-Cola, GE, Hallmark, IBM, Limited Brands, Milliken, Microsoft, MTV, Nortel Networks, Shell Oil, JP Morgan, P&G, Purdue Pharmaceuticals, Rogers Communications, State Street Bank, Target, the U.S. Forest Service, Novartis, the NSA, MIT, PWC, The Wharton School, Queens University, Miami University, and partner distributors around the globe.

Personal Mission Statement

Applying the principles of flexible, whole brain thinking to help individuals and organizations around the world achieve better results through better thinking.

Specialities

- Creative thinking
- Innovation
- Team process
- Strategic thinking

Fun Facts

Ann grew up being "tested" by her father after school using an EEG and is an avid Francophile, having lived in France for fifteen years. Roller-coasters are a favorite activity. Frequent domestic and international travel takes Ann away from the tranquil lake home she shares with her husband of twenty-nine years in the mountains of North Carolina.

Contact

Email: info@hbdi.com
Web: www.hbdi.com
Phone: 828-625-9153

Dr. Peter C. Honebein blends the disciplines of marketing, instructional design, psychology, management, and technology to craft solutions for launching innovations and improving performance of customers and employees. His range of work includes developing the system that tracked the cleanup of the Exxon Valdez oil spill to crafting strategies that will change the energy usage behaviors of millions of Californians. Peter splits his time between consulting and academic endeavors. He is a principal of Honebein Associates, Inc., and Customer Performance Group LLC, and a research scientist with The Academic Edge, Inc. He serves on the faculty at Indiana University and the University of Nevada, Reno, where he teaches courses in instructional design, performance technology, marketing, and customer experience design. He is the author of two books, *Creating Do-It-Yourself Customers* and *Strategies for Effective Customer Education*, and is a frequent speaker at various industry conferences. Peter received a BA from Pepperdine University and a Ph.D. in instructional systems design from Indiana University. He lives in Reno, Nevada

Books

Creating Do-It-Yourself Customers: How Great Customer Experiences Build Great Companies
Strategies for Effective Customer Education

Contributor

"Jackson Diehl," *HPT Casebook*
"Do It Yourself," *The Deluxe Knowledge Quarterly*
"Customers at Work," *Marketing Management*
"Improving Performance: Sometimes Sales Training Isn't Enough," *Marketing News*
"Seven Goals for the Design of Constructivist Learning Environments," *Constructivist Learning Environments: Case Studies in Instructional Design*

Clients

Applied Biosystems, AutoClerk, Citibank, Fluidigm Corporation, Guava Technologies, Hewlett Packard, Learning Tree International, Perkin-Elmer Instruments, Premiere Technologies, Quantum Dots Corporation, San Diego Gas and Electric.

Personal Mission Statement

To facilitate the adoption of ideas and technologies that have a positive impact on our world.

Specialities

- Marketing and management strategy
- Customer experience design

- Human performance improvement
- World class instructional design

Fun Facts

- Two-time winner of ISPI's Award of Excellence
- Expelled from Pepperdine University
- Certified Dillon Beach giant clam digger
- Avid backpacker

Contact

Email: heyhoner@yahoo.com
Web: www.honebein.com
Phone: 775-849-0371

K. Jayshankar (Jay) has a passion to inflame minds to push towards the unconventional and to achieve more! With over twenty-five years' experience in industry, he specializes in strategic planning, change management, and empowering learning throughout organizations. He is the managing director of **Empowered Learning Systems and** has contributed to a large number of organizations and individuals across India, the Middle East ((Saudi Arabia, UAE, Oman, Qatar), and Southeast Asia.

Besides this, he has been a faculty member at various management schools in Mumbai and Pune and at the Tata Management Training Centre and at the Maharashtra government's Academy of Development Administration (YASHADA). Jay has also been a member of different professional bodies, including the American Management Association and the American Society of Training and Development. Further, he has been a speaker at a number of international conferences in Japan, the United States, Panama, the Netherlands, and South Africa.

His education included graduation from the Madras Christian College (majoring in economics with mathematics and statistics as additional subjects), a post-graduation from the reputed Tata Institute of Social Sciences, Mumbai (specializing in personnel management and industrial relations), and a law degree. In 1999, he was one of the chosen few to be selected for the prestigious Cheveningg Gurukul scholarship to the London School of Economics on Global Leadership and Excellence.

After a stint in the corporate world with Tatas, he moved on to fully engage in wider organizational consultancy, setting up Empowered Learning Systems in 1992. His assignments have been for a wide range of companies, both nationally and internationally. Participants for his workshops have been drawn from all levels of employees—front-line managers, supervisors, middle, and senior managers.

Clients

Quintiles Transnational, Motorola, Kotak Mahindra Bank, Avantha Group, Club Mahindra, Unilever, Aditya Birla Group, GE, Dun & Bradstreet, Bausch & Lomb, F.L. Smidth, YASHADA, Mumbai and Thane police departments, Avesthagen, Danfoss, HSBC, and Blue Star

Personal Mission Statement

Inspire, aspire, empower, achieve!

Specialities

- Strategic planning
- Organization development
- Leadership development
- Creating and managing strategic change
- Learning in the outdoors

Fun Facts

Enjoys the outdoors; skydiver and bungee jumper; facilitated India's first Corporate Leadership Expedition and scaled Mount Kilimanjaro; loves music

Contact

Email: jay@empoweredindia.com
Web: www.empoweredindia.com
Phone: +91-20-3291 3895
Telefax: +91-20-2683 3814

Hal Kane, Ph.D., specializes in putting together teams of technical professionals who operate under severe time and budgetary constraints. The process involves developing clear roles and responsibilities, strong lines of communication, and the means to measure progress, individually and collectively

Clients

Ford, Hewlett-Packard, General Motors, General Electric, Boeing, DoD, Department of Labor, State Department, Sears, Goldman-Sachs, Bear Stearns, Merck, American Re-Insurance, Mattel, and other Fortune 500 companies and industries across the country.

Personal Mission Statement

To design and deliver the kinds of training and OD interventions that meet or exceed the customer's expectations for skills transfer and behavioral change.

Specialities

- Project management
- Team building

- Effective communications
- Negotiations
- Facilitation
- Organization design and development
- Requirements capture and documentation

Fun Facts

Hiking in beautiful places, cooking great meals, using my telescope to see farther into the heavens, herding cats (n = 2), reading everything about most subjects, discovering new ways to restate eternal truths.

Contact

Email: halkane@comcast.net
Phone: 707-980-4035

Donald L. Kirkey has worked for over twenty years leading technical field service, customer relations, employee and customer training and development, and performance consulting. Don studied history at Concordia University, Montréal, and McMaster University, Hamilton, Ontario; adult education at St. Francis Xavier University, Antigonish, NS; management at McGill University, Montréal; and is just completing a doctorate in organization leadership at Nova Southeastern University, Fort Lauderdale. Don currently leads a team responsible for performance consulting, analysis, curriculum design and development, instruction, and evaluation for a major business unit in Johnson Controls, Inc., Milwaukee. Johnson Controls' Learning and Development team is a repeat winner of *Training* Magazine's Top 100 / 125 and ASTD's BEST Awards.

Don is a regular presenter at the International Society for Performance Improvement (ISPI) and help build and continues in the governance of the society's prestigious Certified Performance Technologist (CPT) designation. He is the vice president of the Milwaukee Community Service Corps, which takes inner-city youth from corrections, foster care, and school referrals, prepares them for a GED and driver's license, teaches them life skills, trains them in environmental remediation and construction, and puts them to work cleaning up and rebuilding Milwaukee's shattered city core.

Personal Mission Statement

Developing the leader in everyone.

Specialities

- Research and analysis
- Evaluation
- The practical business of training
- Linking learning activities to business impact

Fun Facts

Loves cooking but not baking. Is the proud father of four grown children. Lives with his wife of twenty-nine years, seven cats, and one old and grumpy Shi Tzu named Murphy. Loves New Orleans: the music, the people, the food. Likes every musical style except country and western, but is particularly fond of the blues. All other things being equal, he would rather be canoeing and fishing at his cottage in western Québec.

Contact

Email: Donald.L.Kirkey@jci.com
Phone: 414-365-4894

Jean Marrapodi, Ph.D., CPLP, has been in the learning and development world for the last twenty years, working in corporate America in training departments in retail, banking, healthcare, and the dot-com arenas. She readily shares her talents in the non-profit sector, serving the inner city in the world of church ministry development and literacy.

A frequent workshop leader at conferences, Jean has presented at both the local and international levels for organizations including ASTD, ISPI, the eLearning Guild, and ProLiteracy. Jean's award-winning innovative learning designs for participatory training programs have transformed operational training in her sphere of influence and been the model for subsequent training in these organizations. She has designed, developed, and presented materials for all venues including classroom, webinar, and online synchronous and asynchronous platforms. Her Ph.D. is in adult education with a specialization in adult literacy learners.

Books

PowerPoint 2002 for Visual Learners
The Visibooks Guide to PowerPoint 2003
PowerPoint 2003 in Pictures
Metacognition in Native English-Speaking New Readers: A Phenomenological Study

Contributor

The eLearning Journal (now *Learning Solutions*), First Project: An eLearning Odyssey
IMAGINE: Thinking Online with Mind Manager
Jean blogs on the world of learning and her personal discoveries at Learning About Learning (www.bloglines.com/blog/PHCSJean) and is a frequent contributor in ongoing blog discussions on e-learning and adult literacy around the Internet

Positions

Jean has been a senior training and education specialist in the training departments at:

Mimeo.com
MultiPlan/PHCS
Staples
BankBoston/Fleet
CompUSA

Personal Mission Statement

In whatever sphere, learning must intentionally be full of discovery and lots of fun if it's ever going to stick.

Specialities

- Instructional design
- Operational training
- Technology training
- Adult literacy
- Learning styles
- MBTI and learning
- e-Learning

Fun Facts

Every Sunday morning, Jean teaches a group of Liberian senior citizens how to read. Prior to arriving in the United States, they had never held a pencil or touched a book. It's been as much discovery for her as it has been for them. Jean is the director of training for Literacy Volunteers of RI, sharing her skills with those who seek to help others learn to read.

Jean is a Bible teacher, frequently teaching at women's retreats and conferences around New England. She serves as the director of Christian education at her inner-city church, where she oversees the ministry, runs the literacy center, and often teaches children's church time classes.

Contact

Email: rejoicer@aol.com
Web: www.applestar.org
Phone: 401-453-5972

 **Cynthia D. McCauley** is a senior fellow at the Center for Creative Leadership (CCL). During her more than twenty years at CCL, she has held various positions in research and management. She co-developed two of CCL's assessment instruments, *Benchmarks* and the *Job Challenge Profile*. Her research has focused on how developmental experiences (360-degree feedback, job assignments, developmental relationships, and formal development programs) contribute to leader development and effectiveness. Cindy has written numerous articles and book chapters on these topics for scholars, HR professionals, and managers. She received her Ph.D. in Industrial and Organizational Psychology from the University of Georgia and is a Fellow in the American Psychological Association.

Books

The Center for Creative Leadership Handbook of Leadership Development
Developmental Assignments: Creating Learning Experiences Without Changing Jobs

Contributor

The Handbook of Mentoring at Work
The Nature of Leadership
Handbook of Industrial, Work, and Organizational Psychology

Personal Mission Statement

I don't organize my life around anything as specific and inspirational as a personal mission. I like to add value, create things people find useful, explore complex challenges, and follow my nose.

Specialities

- Strategies and tactics for leader development
- Qualitative research
- Development of assessment instruments

Fun Facts

I've never worn nail polish or owned a cell phone.
I have forty-eight first cousins.
My husband knows pi to 50 places.

Contact

Email: mccauley@ccl.org
Web: www.ccl.org
Phone: 336-286-4420

Michael Milano has been designing learning events since he was in his early twenties—a time when space travel was still a fantasy on "Flash Gordon"! Early on he realized that he loved being involved in the art and dance of creating and facilitating adult learning. Most engaging has always been the great challenge of how to fully engage past learner experience/wisdom and integrate it into the new learning—it has always felt like being on holy ground. This fascination has been the foundation of his work in adult learning as well as organization development. As president of Murphy & Milano, Inc., Arlington, Virginia, he had the great fortune to do the work he loves with a rich variety of clients.

Michael is currently the director of the Bon Secours Health System Institute, which provides leadership learning for a 19,000 employee Catholic healthcare system. The roots of Bon Secours are compassion, healing, and liberation and Michael is grateful to work in a system where those three words define the leadership brand.

Book

Designing Powerful Training: The Sequential-Iterative Model

Clients

Bon Secours Health Systems, Capital One, Gates Foundation, Gay Men's Chorus of Washington, D.C., Georgetown University Hospital, International AIDS Society, INOVA Health Systems: HIV Services, Library of Congress, MCI Telecommunications, National Academy of Sciences, National Association of Secondary School Principals, National Institutes of Health: Office of Research on Women's Health, Nextel, The United Nations, The World Bank, United Way of America, W.R. Grace.

Personal Mission Statement

My mission is to create sacred space: the space where people tell and listen to their own stories and the stories of others so that they might hear their own inner teachers.

Specialities

- Adult learning
- Learning design

- Leadership development
- Process design (large-system dialogue, analysis, and decision-making processes)
- Trying to figure out what I want to be when I grow up!

Fun Facts

Love music: listening and singing

After twenty-two years of running my own consulting business and loving it, I just took a full-time position with a client . . . amazing where our lives can lead us if we find ways to stay open to possibilities! Amazing also what can happen when we fall in love, and I found that that is exactly what happened with this client. For the past four years they have asked me to help their leaders have serious conversations about the places where spirituality and leadership intersect, and how could I help falling in love? I get to do the work that makes my soul sing!

Contact

Email: MikeyM1125@mac.com
Phone: 703-892-8000

Lenn Millbower, BM, MA, the Learnertainment® trainer, delivers Oscar caliber, show-biz-based Learnertainment® seminars and workshops for trainers, educators, and speakers seeking enhanced learning effectiveness; provides instructional design consulting to businesses, turning dry, boring, ineffective training programs, presentations and communications into engaging, memorable, successful events; and creates products that help non-entertainers deliver dazzling results through Learnertainment®.

He is an in-demand speaker, with successful presentations at international conferences including ASTD, ASCD, SHRM, ISPI and IAL; a creative and dynamic instructional designer and facilitator formerly with Walt Disney Entertainment; an accomplished arranger-composer skilled in the psychological application of music to enhance learning; a popular entertainer with vast performance experience having performed extensively as a comedian, magician and musician; and the president of Offbeat Training®, where he teaches learning professionals to keep 'em awake so the learning will take.

Lenn Millbower received his BM in composition from Berklee College of Music and his MA in human resource development from Webster University. He is a member of the International Alliance for Learning, the National Speaker's Association and ASTD.

Books

The CLOUT Creator Inventory: The Trainer's Route to Organizational Effectiveness

Using Music as a Training Tool

Show Biz Training: Fun and Effective Business Training Techniques from the Worlds of Stage, Screen and Song

Cartoons for Trainers: Seventy Five Cartoons to Use or Adapt for Transitions, Activities, Discussion Points, Ice Breakers and More with CD-ROM

Game Show Themes for Trainers: Introductions, Discussions, Quizzes, Team Building, Reviews

Training with a Beat: The Teaching Power of Music

Contributor

"What's in the Box?" in *90 World-Class Activities by 90 World-Class Trainers*

"Foreword" in *Creative Learning: Activities and Games That REALLY Engage People*

"Lyrical Look: Finding Insight in Song," in *The 2006 Pfeiffer Annual: Training*

"Seven Tips for Maintaining Professionalism," in *The ASTD 2006 Training & Performance Sourcebook*

"Tune Up the Music: Rev Up Participants' Emotions Through Song," *T&D* journal

Personal Mission Statement

To help trainers, speakers, and educators keep their learners awake so the learning will take.

Specialities

- Presentation skills
- Applications of music, comedy, magic, and props to learning
- Instructional design
- Creativity

Fun Facts

Lenn performed as a magician-musician on a cruise ship for almost two years. He still loves cruising. The combination of fine food, exotic locals, and readily available entertainment make for an unbeatable combination. When not cruising, Lenn is an avid political junkie who has correctly predicted the winner in every U.S. presidential election since 1968.

Contact

Email: lennmillbower@offbeattraining.com
Web: www.OffbeatTraining.com
Phone: 877-SAY-LENN

Vince Molinaro, Ph.D., is principal and national practice lead–organizational solutions with Knightsbridge Human Capital Solutions. He is responsible for leading the organizational consulting arm of Knightsbridge, which specializes in providing strategic facilitation, team effectiveness, leadership capacity, and talent management solutions to clients.

Vince has dedicated his career to helping leaders and their organizations build strong leadership capacity required for driving sustained business success. An insightful practitioner, Vince is uniquely able to turn innovative ideas into practical solutions—he is known for taking the complex and making it simple and actionable. He has designed and implemented award winning programs that have transformed leadership cultures for his clients.

Through his extensive consulting engagements and leadership experience, pioneering research, and writing, Vince has established himself a leading thinker and practitioner in the field of leadership. He is called upon by the media for his innovative opinions on leadership and creating high-performance organizations. An engaging speaker, Vince conducts keynote presentations within corporations, international conferences, and business schools.

He received his doctorate from the University of Toronto and has degrees from Brock University and McMaster University.

Publications

Vince has published over one-hundred articles in journals, business magazines, and newspapers. He is the co-author of two books: *Leadership Solutions* and *The Leadership Gap*

Personal Mission

On the work front, it is my passion for creating strong and vibrant leadership cultures that help companies achieve sustained business success. I also strive to be a good leader and create a compelling place for people to work and be their best. On the personal front, my passion comes from my family—my spouse and three children, who ground me and remind me what is truly important in life.

Specialities

- Designing and facilitating "leadership forum" events with the top leaders of companies that drive greater alignment and engagement, and build strong leadership cultures
- Facilitating executive team interventions leading to enhance levels of performance
- Designing and facilitating integrated leadership development initiatives that help leaders gain new skills and insights to lead their companies in the future
- Advanced facilitation skills

Fun Facts

Avid hiker, amateur chef, traveling with my family, wannabe musician, love to write

Contact

Email: vmolinaro@knightsbridge.ca
Web: www.knightsbridge.ca
Phone: 905-338-9701 x227

Timothy P. Mooney is a vice president and practice leader with the Advantage Performance Group, a wholly owned subsidary of BTS Group AB. A seasoned performance consulting expert who specializes in assessment, organizational change, and sales effectiveness, Tim has delivered projects in Great Britain, France, Germany, South Africa, and North America. With more than twenty-five years of corporate sales management and consulting experience, Tim is a frequent speaker and writer on the topic of achieving measurable business impact from training.

Prior to joining Advantage in 2000, he served in a senior management capacity for Development Dimensions

International (DDI), where his roles included vice president of sales and marketing for assessment and regional vice president. Tim earned a B.A. degree in psychology from Butler University in Indianapolis and an M.A. degree in industrial/organizational psychology from the University of Akron.

Books

Courageous Training: Bold Actins for Business Results

Contributor

2008 ASTD Handbook—Level III Evaluation

Clients

General Motors, Nortel, Sun Chemical, Nokia, Sony, Toyota, Blue Cross Blue Shield, and Medrad

Personal Mission Statement

Ensuring that organizations turn learning into measurable business results through Courageous Training principles.

Specialities

- Organizational change
- Assessment
- Implementing processes that ensure measurable business results from training
- Sales effectiveness
- Training evaluation

Fun Facts

Live in Glen Ellyn, Illinois, with my wife Beverly, our daughter Anne, and our German shepherd Greta (who rules the house); addicted golfer; practicing oenophile

Contact

Email: tmooney@advantageperformance.com
Web: www.advantageway.net
Phone: +1 630-469-6080

 **Robb Murray, MA,** is a software and technology educator and training contractor. His watchwords in instruction are "to be clear, interesting and practical." He has a broad background in the promotion of information and people resources, having started as a reference librarian. Robb's company provides contract training and courseware development services in the areas of end-user software and web literacy and it utilizes over ten subcontractors.

Robb also takes side jobs as a commercial voiceover talent and as a creative panelist for generating new product ideas. He edits books, as well, and, to date, has edited eight full-length works. He is an enthusiastic contributor to Wikipedia and also leads the Chicago Science Field Trips Club. Robb is an avid networker and has a growing Web 2.0 presence. You can see his interests and creative projects at www.explain.com/robbmurray. htm. Your call is always welcome.

Book

The Reading Notebooks of Literary Authors: A Comparison of Some Published Notebooks

Articles

Interactive Web Demos from Chicago Museums
The 5-Minute Phobia Cure
The Power of Goals Clubs
Harvesting Group Brain Power: the "Delphi Technique",
Power on the Web Requires Caution, Too
How to Stimulate Classroom Follow Ons

A Walk in Their Moccasins,
The ATARI Musical Tutor
A First Audition for Orchestra-80

Recognition

Who's Who Among Emerging Leaders in America
Who's Who in Advertising and Entertainment
Who's Who in America
Who's Who in Education
Who's Who in the Midwest
Who's Who in the World

Clients

A.C. Nielsen; Abbott Laboratories; America's Best AMOCO AO Smith; Archdiocese of Chicago; Bessemer Trust; Bronner Consulting Group; CBS Cable; Chicago Board of Education; Chicago Law Bulletin; Chicago Mayor's Office for Workforce Development; Chicago Tribune; City of Detroit; Commonwealth Edison; Dunn and Bradstreet Business Education; Eli Lilly and Company; Field Museum of Natural History; Gardner; Carton and Douglas Attorneys-At-Law; Kendall College; Learning Tree International; McDonald's Corporate Headquarters; Motorola University; Northern Trust Bank; Northwestern Memorial Hospital; Oppenheimer Family Trust; R.R. Donnelley; Ringling Brothers; Rotary International Headquarters; Skillpath; Tech Resource Group; The University of Chicago Medical Center; Time/Warner Cable; Upjohn Pharmaceuticals; UNUM Insurance; USDA; VA Hospital System; Wm. Wrigley Jr. Company

Personal Mission Statement

I stand for the practical application of the best knowledge available.

Specialities

- Fresh training content involving tools that are newly on-stream.
- Creative, tested approaches to clear objectives, direct delivery, learner involvement, and skills retention.
- Keeping the energy, fun, and common sense in training.

Fun Facts

Robb made a solo study trip entirely around the world in 1990, stopping at thirty-two destinations in only forty days. He produced the world's first commercial record album of music that was composed and performed solely on a microcomputer (*Classical Mosquito!*) in 1984. He competed on the Grammy ballot that year in eight categories. Robb was the composer and lyricist for a short musical comedy called "Macho Motors" that was performed in Chicago in 2006. It can be seen on YouTube.

Robb has been the announcer on national TV commercials for O'Boisies Potato Chips (Keebler), for a game called "Brain Bash" (Tiger Toys) and for Nissan. His narration loops have run nationally in True Value Hardware Stores and also in Chicago's Museum of Science & Industry. Robb taught voiceovers for eight years.

Robb won the General Knowledge Contest in 1977 at the University of Chicago. Robb was high school valedictorian in a class of 600 and voted "Most Likely to Succeed." Robb won the commencement essay contest in college for an assigned piece on the topic of "Spring Fever."

Robb has run for exercise nearly every day since 1971 and has completed the Chicago Marathon three times.

Robb has led over sixty partnerships in weekly goal setting in an arrangement he calls the "Goals Club."

Robb has an autobiography on the web called *Scenes from Half a Century.*

Robb was trained by Al Gore in Nashville in 2007 as part of The Climate Project.

Contact

Email: ctoncall@aol.com
Web: www.explain.com
Phone: 773-975-8020
Office: 444 West St. James Place, #1203, Chicago, Illinois 60614

Catherine J. Rezak, with partner Raymond Green, founded Paradigm Learning in 1994. Paradigm Learning is an employee training and communications organization, specializing in the use of innovative "discovery learning" techniques to design business games, simulations, and Discovery Maps® programs to educate learners around critical business issues.

As chairman, she is involved in a variety of projects, most notably in the areas of new product development, marketing, and client relations. Over the years, Cathy has led the development of Paradigm's innovative employee learning programs: Zodiak®: The Game of Business Finance and Strategy; Mosaic: The Art of Talent Leadership™, Neon Buzz®: Lighting Up Organizational Performance; Countdown®: A Strategy Game for Project Teams; Impact5®: The Business of Leadership Game; Right Turns: Change in Action®; and FastMaps™.

Cathy has more than twenty-five years of experience in the human resource consulting and training field, having worked with Fortune 500 clients around such issues as employee selection, leader assessment, management training, employee development, project management, customer service, financial literacy, team effectiveness, and change management. She has accepted numerous awards, including a New Venture Award from Success Magazine, the President's Leadership Award from the Florida

Council on Economic Education, and the 2001 Business of the Year Award from ISA. In 2003, she was elected president of ISA—The Association of Learning Providers—and served for three years. The organization focuses exclusively on the issues and needs of executives in the training industry.

Cathy is a graduate of the University of Cincinnati's School of Education.

Clients

Boeing, Sony, International Paper, Raymond James, Sabre Holdings, Sears, Mercedes Benz, Toyota, Hyundai, Honda, Pitney Bowes, Verizon, Halliburton, Merck, Pfizer, Nationwide, Bank of America, Honeywell, AT&T, Expedia, Caterpillar, Dell, Kimberly-Clark, Anheuser Busch, Lockheed Martin, Marriott, Regence Health Care, Pepsi, Coors/Molson, Macy's, USAF, US Bank, La-Z-Boy, Sara Lee, and FedEx.

Passion Statement

I have a passion for educating others and making a difference in corporate training.

Specialities

- Developing business games and simulations using discovery learning methodology
- Frequent speaker at corporate learning events, including the American Society of Training and Development's annual conferences

Fun Facts

Enjoys writing, traveling, kayaking, and scuba diving. Involved in community efforts to save coastal waterfronts.

Matthew S. Richter is the president of The Thiagi Group. He is a facilitator, game designer, instructional designer, and management consultant. He is an expert in the areas of management, leadership, and performance technology. He specializes in employee motivation. Matthew mixes corporate, not-for-profit, academic, and independent experience, enabling him to adapt and best serve his clients.

Matthew is the co-creator of MAPS (Motivation, Assessment, and Performance System), an innovative performance management system that breaks all of the traditional paradoxes of management. He also co-created MESA, the Motivation an Employee Satisfaction Assessment.

He is a sought-after public speaker and has delivered keynotes and conference presentations internationally. He was the 2006 International Society for Performance Improvement National Conference Chair and has been an encore presenter for the last five years for his presentation Creating a Motivating Environment.

Contributor

2001, 2002, and 2003 Training and Performance and/or *Team and Organization Development Sourcebook*

Clients

Cadence Design Systems, Redwood Trust, CenturyTel, Electronic Arts, State Farm, Exelon, SONY, Xerox, Guidant, and others

Personal Mission Statement

To be the best at anything I do.

Specialities

- Employee motivation
- Performance management

- Training design
- Game design
- Business consulting

Fun Facts

I love U.S. history—particularly presidential history. I am a classical music geek. I attend concerts in every city I travel to and I am addicted to Shostakovich. My favorite U.S. orchestra is Cleveland. In Europe, Berlin under Sir Simon Rattle. I also collect super-hero comic books.

Contact

Email: matthew@thiagi.com
Web: thiagi.com
Phone: 415-385-7248

Steven C. Rosenbaum is president of Learning Paths International. Steve has over twenty-five years of experience in training and development working with major corporations in six different countries. His major focus involves working with organizations on dramatically reducing the time it takes to get new employees up-to-speed. To date he has installed Learning Path initiatives that involve over 20,000 employees and four hundred different functions. Steve also has extensive experience designing and developing training for call centers, sales forces, customer service agents, managers, and internal consultants. He has worked in almost every industry from banking to high-tech to health care to manufacturing. Steve has developed training and led training projects in a wide range of delivery methods.

Books

Learning Paths: Increase Profits by Reducing the Time It Takes to Get Employees Up-to-Speed

Managing and Measuring Productivity
Fair Employment Interviewing
Breakthrough Selling Skills

Clients

GE, Disney, Carlson Wagonlit Travel, Ceridian, Caremark, AutoZone, GE Capital, United Health Care

Specialities

- Dramatically reducing time to proficiency
- Instructional design
- Training consulting

Contact

Email: Learningpaths@gmail.com
Web: www.learningpathsinternational.com
Blog: http://learning
Phone: 952-368-9329

Grace Ann Rosile, Ph.D., teaches management at New Mexico State University and is an organizational change and management development consultant. Her focus is on how organizations and individuals can learn to recognize the ways they story themselves so they can "restory" for growth. She specializes in story embodiment and in-the-moment story mindfulness. She received the national Champion of Integrity award in 2005 from Duke University's Center for Academic Integrity for her work on ethics in education. Her dozens of articles include topics such as "restorying" for organizational change, empowerment and disempowerment, and ethics. She is on the boards of the Journal of Management Education, the Standing Conference on Management and Organization Inquiry (www.scmio.com), and the Storytelling

Organization Institute (http:/storyemergency.org). She is the creator of "Horse Sense at Work," the management development program for humans using structured experiences with horses. This approach, which integrates mind-body-spirit in management training, together with her work in narrative and storytelling, led to her unique perspective on embodied story.

Book Chapters

"Critical Business Pedagogy and Ethics: An Epic 4-Quadrant Model" in *Critical Perspectives on Business*

"Managing with Ahimsa and Horse Sense: A Convergence of Body, Mind, and Spirit" in *At Work: Spirituality Matters*

"Death, Terror, and Addiction in Motivation Theory" in *The Passion of Organizing*

"Restorying and Postmodern Organizational Theater: Consultation to the Storytelling Organization" in *Changing the Way We Manage Change*

"The Implications of the Postmodern Turn in Ethnography for Service Learning" in *The Disciplines: Management*

Selected Articles

"Cheating: Making it a Teachable Moment" in the *Journal of Management Education*

"Enron Spectacle Theatrics: A Critical Dramaturgical Analysis" in *Organization Studies*

"Life Imitates Art: Enron's Epic and Tragic Narration" in *Management Communication Quarterly*

"Enron Whodunit? Storytelling and Plots" in *Ephemera* electronic journal

"Managing with Horse Sense" in the *Journal of Management Inquiry*

"Power and Co-Power: Discourse, Identity, and Network Aspects of Organizations" in *Business Research Yearbook*

"Where's the Power in Empowerment?: Answers from Follett and Clegg" in *The Journal of Applied Behavioral Science*

"Of Stallions and Mares and Gendered Management Discourse" in *Business Research Yearbook*

Clients

Hospitals, universities, small businesses, a local government, a military organization, a church, and a volunteer organization.

Personal Mission Statement

I love to facilitate connections, with self and others, using stories and horses.

Specialities

- Restorying for personal and organizational change
- Co-creating multi-voiced story
- Horse Sense at Work: Human development through working with horses (leadership, teamwork, communication, and conflict handling)

Fun Facts

I acquired my first horse (a completely untrained young Arabian stallion Nahdion) after finishing my Ph.D. in business management. I owned and operated a full-service stable, where for ten years I bred, raised, and trained my own Arabians for the Olympic sport of Dressage. Nahdion will be twenty-eight years old in June 2008. He is the horse in the mirror on my website and business cards.

Contact

Email: garosile@zianet.com
Web: www.horsesenseatwork.com
Phone: 575-532-1693

Theresa L. Seagraves: With more than twenty-two years of experience working in workforce development, career development, total quality management, service and support, information systems and high technology, Theresa became a recognized leader at Hewlett-Packard for creating innovative, world-class data and people development systems. An inside sales group that Theresa helped developed was named the best in the world by leading industry analysts after only two years in existence.

Theresa has helped several organizations with large-scale skills assessments, ROI evaluations, coaching on aligning and communicating financial value. Theresa has written newsletters on personal success, articles on ROI measurement and two "In Action" series case studies on ROI measurement and training scorecards for ASTD. She has been an invited encore presenter at the annual International Society for Performance Improvement conference.

Theresa is a past chair of the ASTD ROI Advisory committee, served on the 2007 ASTD International Conference and Exposition Program Advisory Committee and was a 2007 ASTD ROI Awards reviewer.

Books

> *Quick! Show Me Your Value!: A Trainer's Guide to Communicating Value and Connecting Training and Performance to the Bottom Line.*

Contributor

> *In Action: Measuring Return on Investment, Volume 3, Mission Possible: Selling Complex Services Over the Phone*
> *In Action: Implementing Training Scorecards, The Competitive Weapon: Using ROI Measurement to Drive Results*

Clients

Hewlett-Packard Company, LexusNexus and DexMedia; Best Buy, Covidien, Respironics, and Philips

Personal Mission Statement

I love to help develop great talents in each unique person and to help others find and communicate the value of what they do every day.

Specialities

- Business acumen
- Communicating value of training and development
- Evaluation return on investment measurement
- Competency assessments
- Sales tools
- Conjoint analysis

Fun Facts

One of my best bosses never let me say the word "can't" in his presence. It made a lasting impression on how I approach life. Married the boy next door and my high school sweetheart. Watercolor artist. Grew up as the fourth child in a family of eight children. Had a mental block about math until I reached college. If you were to have told me then that I would be helping people work with numbers, I'd have never believed it!

Contact

Email: theresa@growsr.com
Web: www.growsr.com
Phone: 720-746-1900, ext 4

Tom Short, MA, FCIPD, MCMI, is passionate about adult learning, and since the early 1970s has helped hundreds of people in Europe, North America, and Oceania to transform their careers through vocational training and professional development. He is committed to lifelong learning and how this influences the modern workplace, and society.

Tom currently leads an Auckland-based private training organization and was formerly director of the Performance Improvement Centre at the University of Auckland, Faculty of Education, in New Zealand. He has held roles in management consulting, human resource management and general management in the UK manufacturing sector. He holds a master's degree in human resource management and is a Chartered Fellow of the Chartered Institute of Personnel and Development and a member of the UK Chartered Management Institute.

Over a period of twenty years, Tom has spoken at numerous international conferences, taken part in expert panel steering groups, judging panels, chaired training and development forums, and led consulting-based research assignments in the private and public sector. He has written for professional magazines about contemporary human resource development issues; and is currently an active doctoral researcher with the Centre for Research in Education, Equity and Work (CREEW) at the University of South Australia.

Recent Clients

Air New Zealand, Auckland City Council, Aviation Security Services, BP Oil, Department of Corrections, Department of Internal Affairs, Eka Chemicals (NZ), Fletcher Aluminum, IAG Insurance, Land Transport Safety Authority, Meridian Energy, Ministry of Agriculture and Fisheries, National Bank of New Zealand, Telecom NZ, Tongan Telecommunications

Corporation, University of Auckland Business School, Vodafone NZ, Veolia Transport NZ, Work and Income NZ

Personal Mission Statement

I have a passion for liberating talent by "putting knowledge to work."

Specialities

- Aligning human resource development strategies with business success
- Expertise on train-the-trainer and coaching adult learners
- Learning-centered leadership
- Assessment and evaluation of learning
- Competence-based learning/qualification pathways

Fun Facts

Over three decades of volunteer work with the UK cadet forces and marching band movement; granted the esteemed status of "Honorary Nobel" in the Kingdom of Tonga for one day; failed golfer, windsurfer, and amateur photographer; long-time aviation enthusiast; discerning consumer of fine New Zealand wines; semi-retirement goal to write a well-respected text on "people development"

Contact

Email: tom@piclearning.co.nz or www.trainingimpact.com
Phone: +64 (0)9 623 7111

Mel Silberman, Ph.D., is known internationally as a pioneer in the areas of active learning, interpersonal intelligence, and team development. As professor of adult and organizational development at Temple University, Mel has won two awards for his distinguished teaching. He is also president of Active Training, Princeton, N.J., a provider of products, seminars and publications in his areas of expertise.

Mel shares his original and practical ideas throughout his books, and through active training programs and customized seminars for corporate, educational, human services, and governmental organizations. His training skills, psychological insights, and engaging personality make him a popular speaker at conferences of the American Society for Training and Development, the International Society for Performance Improvement, *Training* magazine, and the North American Simulation and Gaming Association.

A graduate of Brandeis University, Mel received his Ph.D. in educational psychology from the University of Chicago. He is also a licensed psychologist in the State of New Jersey. His book *101 Ways to Make Training Active* was voted one of the five best training and development books of all time by *Training* magazine. Recently, Mel was honored with a Lifetime Achievement Award at the annual conference of the North American Simulation and Gaming Association.

Books

Active Training: A Handbook of Techniques, Designs, Case Examples, and Tips (3rd ed.)
101 Ways to Make Training Active
101 Ways to Make Meetings Active
PeopleSmart: Developing Your Interpersonal Intelligence
The Best of Active Training I & II
The Handbook of Experiential Learning
Training the Active Training Way
Working PeopleSmart: Six Strategies for Success

Clients

American Management Association, BMW, U.S. Senate Office of Education and Training, Consolidated Edison, Nationwide Insurance, the Federal Reserve Bank, the Stockholm School of Economics.

Personal Mission Statement

To inspire people to be people smart, learn faster, and collaborate effectively.

Fun Facts

Has six "active" grandchildren, ten-year cancer survivor

Contact

Email: Mel@activetraining.com
Web: www.activetraining.com
Phone: 609-987-8157

Darryl L. Sink is president of Darryl L. Sink & Associates, Inc., (DSA). DSA has 26 years of experience designing and developing great learning experiences. His firm specializes in learning and performance consulting and custom training design and development.

Darryl's graduate work was at Indiana University, Bloomington, Indiana where he specialized in the Instructional Systems Design and Educational Psychology. He is the author of six comprehensive guides to instructional design and development that are used with DSA's workshops to provide fundamental instructional design training and processes. These processes have been adopted and are being used by many Fortune 500 companies, public institutions and non-profit organizations.

He is a contributing author to the *International Society of Performance Improvement's (ISPI) Handbooks of Human Performance Technology.* He is the recipient of ISPI's Professional Service Award, and was three times awarded the Outstanding Instructional Product Of The Year Award by ISPI.

Contributor

Success Strategies for the Human Performance Technologist. Handbook of Human Performance Technology. The International Society for Performance Improvement

The Business of Human Performance Technology. 2nd ed. Handbook of Human Performance Technology. The International Society for Performance Improvement

ISD Faster Better Easier. Performance Improvement Volume 41 number 7. International Society for Performance Improvement

Instructional Design Models and Theories. The ASTD Workplace Learning Professional's Handbook

90 World–Class Activities by 90 World-Class Trainers, Elaine Biech, Editor

The 2000 and 2001 Training and Performance Sourcebooks, Mel Silberman, Editor

Clients

Learning Tree International, Caterpillar, Inc., Johnson Controls, Inc., HP, Kohl's, Target. Inc., GE Health Care, Microsoft, Inc., Citigroup, Inc. The Charles Schwab Company, Inc. Bechtel Corporation, Sandia National Labs

Personal Mission Statement

I'm happiest when I am teaching, managing, designing, and developing great learning experiences.

Specialities

- Instructional design & development consulting services
- Teaching instructional design and development
- Media production
- Project management
- Managing large design/development teams

Fun Facts

DSA started business with Apple Computer when they were just five years old. Has worked with his wife, Jane Sink, for over 16 years. Worked in community colleges for nine years prior to starting DSA as a full time consultant to faculty. Enjoys cooking and entertaining

Contact

Email: darryl@dsink.com
Web: www.dsink.com
Phone: 831-649-8384

Glenn Smeaton is owner/consultant for Learning and Performance Support, LLC. Smeaton has over thirty years of experience. He has worked as science teacher, adult technical trainer, field consultant, senior training specialist, and training manager. In his capacity as a training manager, his experimentation with facilitated learning, led to his concepts about learning and performance support. He named his process, "Learn While You Work."

Smeaton graduated from the University of Wisconsin with a master's degree in water resource management, specializing in information and education. He started working for the Wisconsin Department of Natural Resources to develop a training and certification program to assure qualified operations of the many newly built water and wastewater treatment facilities in Wisconsin. This was his start in the world of adult learning and performance support.

The heart of Smeaton's approach to working with operators of water and wastewater treatment facilities is to treat them as full partners in the learning process. This was consistent with the approach of consultant Thomas Mickelson's "Facilitated Implementation Training." It was in combination with working with Mickelson and attending ASTD conferences that helped Smeaton pull together his approach to adult learning and performance support or "Learn While You Work."

Glenn has written articles for technical and training publications he has also made presentations to local ASTD conference meetings on learning and performance support.

Personal Mission Statement

To help others identify and achieve their personal learning goals and implement their own learning and professional development programs.

Specialities

- Facilitated implementation training: "Learn While You Work"
- Knowledge capture and sharing
- Succession planning
- Workflow management
- Communications and conflict resolution
- Development and delivery of customized technical training programs

Fun Facts

It could be easy to make light of the fact that Glenn Smeaton's working experience started out on his family's farm raising pigs and, after seven years of college and twenty years of experience, he made his way up to working in a wastewater treatment plant as a training manager. The job of being a skilled wastewater operator, however, is a very difficult job, requiring knowledge in chemistry, biology, engineering, mechanical and electrical maintenance, first aid and safety training. Developing learning programs for water and wastewater treatment plant operators is very demanding because of the wide range of subjects covered. It was in response to the need for training in all these areas at once that led Smeaton to develop his style of facilitated implementation training. Work in this field also provided many opportunities for testing various approaches to learning and performance support in some very rugged applications!

On a different note, Glenn Smeaton plays a French horn. His personal learning and performance support includes taking private lessons. He currently performs in small ensembles and with the Madison Municipal Band in Madison, Wisconsin.

Contact Information

Email: smeatongrs@aol.com
Phone: Home: (608) 223-9953/Cell: (608) 219-2992

Harold D. Stolovitch, Ph.D., CPT, is Emeritus Professor, Université de Montréal, and a principal of HSA Learning & Performance Solutions LLC, an international consulting firm. He completed a Ph.D. and post-doctoral studies in instructional systems technology at Indiana University. Harold is an experienced workshop leader and a keynote speaker at major conferences and organizations throughout the world. His many research and consulting activities have included projects with major corporations.

Harold is the regular, featured "human performance" columnist for *Talent Management* magazine. He has won numerous awards for his contributions to the fields of instructional and performance technology, including the 2001 ISPI Distinguished Professional Achievement award and ISPI's highest award, Member for Life. He is a past president of ISPI. Harold received the 2003 President's Award for Lifetime Achievements from the Canadian Society for Training and Development, their highest honor. In 2004, he and his team won the ASTD Outstanding Research Award for their work on incentives, motivation, and workplace performance.

Books

Telling Ain't Training
Training Ain't Performance
Beyond Telling Ain't Training Fieldbook
Beyond Training Ain't Performance Fieldbook
Engineering Effective Learning Toolkit
Front-End Analysis and Return on Investment Toolkit
Handbook of Human Performance Technology: Improving Individual and Organizational Performance Worldwide (editor)
Handbook of Human Performance Technology: A Comprehensive Guide for Analyzing and Solving Performance Problems in Organizations (editor)
Introduction à la technologie de l'instruction
Frame Games
Audiovisual Training Modules
Instructional Simulation Games
Games with the Pocket Calculator

Contributor

Thirteen book chapters, sixty-one published articles, and fifty-five published technical reports

Clients

Alcan, ArborMaster, Bank of Montreal, BBDO, Bell Canada, Cisco, DaimlerChrysler Academy, General Motors, Hewlett-Packard, International Association of Fire Fighters, Merck, Pfizer,

Prudential, Qwest, Sun Microsystems, Telecom Asia, The Coffee Bean & Tea Leaf, as well as many others.

Personal Mission Statement

I help clients and their organizations to achieve performance they, their customers, and all other stakeholders value.

Specialities

- Workplace learning and performance
- Games and simulations for learning and performance
- Workplace learning and performance audits

Fun Facts

Have run numerous marathons; have taught and worked in every inhabited continent on the globe; avid roller-blader

Contact

Email: hstolovitch@hsa-lps.com
Web: www.hsa-lps.com
Phone: 310-286-2722

Deborah H. Stone has been the CEO of DLS Group, Inc., headquartered in Denver with offices in Washington, D.C., since 1982. She has co-received over twenty professional awards, including Microsoft's Award of Excellence for the Outstanding Performance Support System and ISPI's for the Outstanding Human Performance System, Instructional Intervention, and Systematic Approach. A certified Human Performance Technologist, Deborah served on ISPI's Board of Directors as well as ASTD's Program Advisory Board for ICE. Deborah's recent consulting projects have focused on cognitive task analysis, cognitive apprenticeships and blended learning strategies to capture and support the decision-making processes of knowledge workers. Renowned for her talent in sparking elegant paradigm shifts, Deborah has an uncanny knack for pinpointing organizational performance issues—accurately— the first time. Deborah was awarded a full fellowship to Brown University, and completed her graduate work in instructional technology at San Francisco State.

Contributor

"KICS: Best Practices Caught in the Web," in *Case Studies in Performance Improvement*

"Performance Support Systems," in *Handbook of Human Performance Technology: Improving Individual and Organizational Performance Worldwide* (3rd ed.)

"Rapid Application Development for Performance Technology: Five Strategies to Deliver Better Interventions in Less Time," in *Performance Improvement Interventions: Performance Technologies in the Workplace*

"CORNERSTONE: A Case Study of a Large-Scale Performance Support System, in *Performance Improvement Interventions: Performance Technologies in the Workplace*

Clients

Amgen Pharmaceuticals, Corporate Management Systems, AT&T/AT&T Broadband, Avaya, Datalaw, Dayton-Hudson Corporation, Target Stores, Bank of America, Department of Justice, Bell Atlantic, En Pointe Technologies, Biosound, Farm Credit Bank of Baltimore, Canadian National Railway (CNR), Flight Safety, Chrysler Corporation, Gambro BCT, Citicorp Diners Club, Gerry Baby Products, CliniCom, Inc., Hewlett-Packard, COBE Laboratories/Aastrom Biomedical, Hughes Aircraft, Colorado Department of Education, Integrated Medical Systems, Conoco Oil, International Business Machines (IBM)/SRA, Continuing Education Program for the Securities

Brokers/Registered Representatives, Kaman Instrumental Corporation, Litton Data Systems, Omega Performance Corporation, Lockheed Martin, Oracle, Lucent Technologies, PacerCats, Manville Corporation, PASAR, Marriott Corporation, Public Service Company of Colorado

Raycom, McDonnell Douglas Astronautics Corporation, Raynet, MediaOne, Rockwell International (Rocky Flats), Mincom USA, Australia, Sandia Labs, National Association of Securities Dealers, Regulation, Storage Technology, National Geospatial-Intelligence Agency (NGA), National Geospatial College, Texas Instruments, National Institute of Corrections, United Banks Service Company (Norwest), New York Life Insurance Corporation, United States Army Air Defense School, New York Stock Exchange, United States Army Corps of Engineers, Northern Telecom, Inc., United States Army Intelligence School, Octel Communications Corporation, United States Army Security Agency, United States Army Transportation Schools, Wilson Learning Corporation, United Technologies, Williams-Labadie/Fujisawa Healthcare, Inc./Astellas Pharma US, Inc., US West Communications, Zimmer Arthroscopy Systems, Wells Fargo Bank

Personal Mission Statement

Talk less, listen more and wear natural fiber clothing.

Specialities

- Informal learning/performance support systems
- e-Learning
- Cognitive task analysis to capture expert decision-making processes and mental models
- Blended learning
- Cognitive apprenticeship-based performance systems
- Enterprise-wide architectural blueprints/roadmaps for multi-year initiatives, prototyping

Fun Facts

Around the office, Deborah can often been seen roaming the hallways munching on a red bell pepper. Deborah can professionally score a baseball game. She owns a rare 1984 factory wide-body/tail, turbo clutch, Porsche Carerra Cabriolet with 28K original miles—and has the speeding tickets to prove it. She is one of the original Robibos. Deborah enjoys skiing and international travel with her teenage son, Sam.

Contact

Email: dstone@dls.com
Web: www.dls.com
Phone: 303-333-4513

Steve Sugar. Despite, or perhaps because of, suffering under the "lecture-and-learn" mantra, Sugar began to "see games" in inanimate objects, such as plates, musical bells, and classroom lectures. His games career began with doodling during lectures, first in high school and continuing during his undergraduate economics (zzzzz) degree at Bucknell University. An invitation from a kindly Uncle (Sam) led to two tours in Vietnamese waters, after which he earned my MBA at George Washington University.

His first stint as a college professor at San Diego State University provided the opportunity to create an operational classroom game, *RAT Race*. Later, teaching assignments in federal government and University of Maryland classrooms inspired him to develop over three hundred learning games—available in assorted books, articles, and stand-alone game systems. Sugar currently teach in the UMBC business curriculum, where he brings a mix of lecture and games to every class.

Books

Games That Teach
Games That Teach Teams
More Great Games
Primary Games
Games That Boost Performance
Training Games

Contributor

"Customizing a Board Game with Your Classroom Material" in *The ASTD Handbook of Instructional Material*
"The Game of Academic Ethics" in *To Improve The Academy*
The 1999 and 2000 Training and Performance Sourcebooks
"Using Games to Energize Dry Material" in *The ASTD Handbook of Training Design and Delivery*
The 2000 and 2001 Pfeiffer Annuals
"Customizable Orientation Bingo: Old Wine, New Bottle" in *Creative New Employee Orientation Programs*

Personal Mission Statement

For the "slow learner" in all of us, I believe in develop/using activities and games that are "fun with a purpose"—specifically: parlor-game quality activities that increase retention while being fun-to-play.

Specialities

- Board games
- Wall games
- Floor games
- Prop games (props, such as bells, egg cartons, plates, balloons)

Fun Facts

An avid TV viewer since 1947, I enjoy watching sportscasts ranging from the traditional mix of football, baseball, and basketball, to the less-traditional viewings of college wrestling and pro boxing.

I had the honor of being at two ground-breaking sports events—the 1958 classic Colts-Giants football playoff and the ground-breaking 1966 NCAA basketball final between Texas Western and Kentucky.

Contact Information

Email: stevesugar@verizon.net
Website: www.thegamegroup.com
Phone: 410-418-4930

Steve Villachica, Ed.D., is an associate professor of instructional and performance technology at Boise State University. He also sits on DLS Group's Strategic Advisory Board. A frequent presenter at international conferences and member of ASTD, Steve also co-authored the chapter on PSS appearing in the second edition of the *Handbook of Human Performance Technology*. A two-time winner of ISPI's Outstanding Systematic Approach award and Certified Performance Technologist, he completed his doctorate in educational technology at the University of Northern Colorado.

Contributor

"KICS: Best Practices Caught in the Web," in *Case Studies in Performance Improvement*
"Performance Support Systems," in *Handbook of Human Performance Technology: Improving Individual and Organizational Performance Worldwide* (3rd ed.)

"Rapid Application Development for Performance Technology: Five Strategies to Deliver Better Interventions in Less Time," in *Performance Improvement Interventions: Performance Technologies in the Workplace*
"CORNERSTONE: A Case Study of a Large Scale Performance Support System," in *Performance Improvement Interventions: Performance Technologies in the Workplace*

Clients

Amgen Pharmaceuticals, Corporate Management Systems, AT&T/AT&T Broadband, Avaya, Datalaw, Dayton-Hudson Corporation, Target Stores, Bank of America, Department of Justice, Bell Atlantic, En Pointe Technologies, Biosound, Farm Credit Bank of Baltimore, Canadian National Railway (CNR), Flight Safety, Chrysler Corporation, Gambro BCT, Citicorp Diners Club, Gerry Baby Products, CliniCom, Inc., Hewlett-Packard, COBE Laboratories/Aastrom Biomedical, Hughes Aircraft, Colorado Department of Education, Integrated Medical Systems, Conoco Oil, International Business Machines (IBM)/ SRA, Continuing Education Program for the Securities Brokers/ Registered Representatives, Kaman Instrumental Corporation, Litton Data Systems, Omega Performance Corporation, Lockheed Martin, Oracle, Lucent Technologies, PacerCats, Manville Corporation, PASAR, Marriott Corporation, Public Service Company of Colorado, Martin Marietta, Raycom, McDonnell Douglas Astronautics Corporation, Raynet, MediaOne, Rockwell International (Rocky Flats), Mincom USA, Australia, Sandia Labs, Mountain Bell, Southwestern Bell, National Association of Securities Dealers, Inc., Storage Technology, National Geospatial-Intelligence Agency (NGA), Texas Instruments, National Institute of Corrections, United Banks Service Company (Norwest), New York Life Insurance Corporation, United States Army Air Defense School, New York Stock Exchange, United States Army Corps of Engineers, Northern Telecom, Inc., United States Army Intelligence School, Octel Communications Corporation,

United States Army Security Agency, United States Army Transportation Schools, Wilson Learning Corporation, United Technologies, Williams-Labadie/Fujisawa Healthcare, Inc./ Astellas Pharma US, Inc., US West Communications, Zimmer Arthroscopy Systems, and Wells Fargo Bank.

Specialities

- Cognitive task analysis
- Strategic planning
- Assessment and evaluation
- Performance interventions for knowledge workers
- Application of software engineering methodologies to the discipline of instructional systems design

Fun Facts

Likes fishing in his belly boat and is rated as an A-level player at his local pool hall.

Contact

Email: dstone@dls.com
Web: www.dls.com
Phone: 303-333-4513

David S. Weiss, Ph.D., CHSPC, CTDP, FCHRP, is president and CEO of Weiss International Ltd. David and his team of organizational consultants lead innovative consulting projects that generate effective strategy, leadership, and HR solutions for boards, executives, and senior leaders throughout North America and Europe. David also is an affiliate professor of the Rotman School of Management of the University of Toronto, a "Senior Research Fellow" of Queen's University, and a faculty member of the Technion Institute of Management.

David's doctorate in applied psychology is from the University of Toronto. He also has three master's degrees in psychology, education, and philosophy. He also was honored in 2008 with the "HR Leadership Award" from the Asia-Pacific Human Resources Association in India, and was honored in 2007 with the "HR Distinction Award" from the Israel HR Management Association in Tel Aviv. He also is a Lifetime Honored Member of the Global Directory of Who's Who," one of four professionals honored as a lifetime "Fellow Canadian Human Resources Professional (FCHRP)," a past president of the Organizational Psychology Section of the Ontario Psychological Association, and an editorial board member of the *Canadian Learning Journal.*

Books

Leadership Solutions: The Pathway to Build Leadership Capacity
The Leadership Gap: Building Leadership Capacity for Competitive Advantage
High Performance HR: Leveraging Human Resources For Competitive Advantage
Beyond the Walls of Conflict: Mutual Gains Negotiating for Unions and Management

Articles

"Leadership Capacity: The New Organizational Capability," *The Canadian Learning Journal*
"Integrated Leadership Development," *Journal of Industrial and Commercial Training (UK)*
"Driving Employee Engagement," Banff Centre for Leadership
"Obituary: David Bakan (1921–2004)," *History of Psychology Journal*
"Closing the Leadership Gap," *Management* magazine
"Filling Your Leadership Gap," *Ottawa Business Journal*

"HR Metrics That Count: Aligning HR Metrics to Business Results," *Human Resource Planning*

"High Potential Leadership Development," *Leadership Compass*

Clients

Healthcare (pharmaceutical companies and hospitals), finance (banks, insurance), communications (telecom, hi tech) and government (local and federal). Clients are mostly national and multinational and are located throughout the United States, Canada, and Europe.

Personal Mission Statement

Finding innovative ways to help companies and leaders discover their pathways to success—and then knowing the right moment when to pull back so the client can take ownership of the process. Facilitating learning and development sessions that are research-based, meaningful, and results oriented, and at the same time dynamic, reflective, and fun.

Specialities

- Strategic and business planning
- Executive leadership development and coaching
- Innovative learning and development,
- Organizational and HR consulting
- Designing and facilitating innovative, meaningful, and fun leadership development learning sessions
- Facilitating senior executive team development and strategic planning
- Coaching executives and facilitating their individual and group development
- Identifying organizational designs to enable strategic alignment to occur
- Designing web-based culture surveys and 360-degree multi-rater feedback processes

Fun Facts

Sings in a chamber choir that competed in the World Choir Game Olympics in 2006; Also, a lyric baritone and guitar player who sings at community and religious events. Baseball enthusiast who helped launch the Toronto Parks Senior Baseball League as its executive, a team coach and a third baseman. Founder and president of the volunteer organization "National Havurah Community of Canada" and chaired fifteen of its annual retreats.

Contact

Email: david.weiss@weissinternational.ca
Web: www.weissinternational.ca
Phone: 416-944-9080, ext 222